W9-CHA-402

Dam Nation

DAM NATION

How Water Shaped the West and Will Determine Its Future

STEPHEN GRACE

Guilford, Connecticut

To buy books in quantity for corporate use
or incentives, call **(800) 962-0973**
or e-mail **premiums@GlobePequot.com.**

Layout artist: Kirsten Livingston
Project manager: Ellen Urban
Map by Design Maps, Inc.

Library of Congress Cataloging-in-Publication Data

Grace, Stephen.
  Dam nation : how water shaped the west and will determine its future / Stephen Grace. — 1st ed.
    p. cm.
  Includes index.
  Includes bibliographical references and index.
  ISBN 978-0-7627-7065-6
  1. Water-supply—West (U.S.) 2. Water-supply—West (U.S.)—History. 3. Hydrology—West
(U.S.) 4. Dams—West (U.S.) 5. Water resources development—West (U.S.)—History. 6. West
(U.S.)—History. I. Title.
  TD223.6.G73 2012
  333.9100958—dc23

                                                                        2012003167

CONTENTS

Author's Note

I am a citizen of the West curious about its past and concerned about its future. Like many others in this droughty place where people fight over streams so small they can walk across them without getting their ankles wet, I spend a lot of time thinking and reading about water.

Most books about water are, unfortunately, quite dry. The stuff upon which empires are founded and works of art are built, water should never be dull; to make it so by letting legalese and technical jargon deaden water's capacity to stimulate avarice and awe, to make poets write verse and politicians wage war, is to drain a teeming river to a dusty bed. Water moves through our bodies, through the world we inhabit, through the societies we construct. When you explore water, you explore everything.

The story of water in the western United States begins with confronting a hostile wilderness, crescendos in epic political battles and heroic feats of technology, and turns into an increasingly tense tale of survival as scientists chart the future of a diminishing substance essential for life. My hope for this book is that it will ignite the curiosity and concern of readers, leading them to more deeply examine the West's history with water and to further explore the future of this crucial resource surrounded by controversy.

Water in the American West wends its way through a multitude of disciplines: geography, geology, hydrology, meteorology, climatology, biology, ecology, agronomy, engineering, economics, history, law, political science, urban planning, and public policy, to name some that spring to mind. The drawback to a book that covers as much ground as this one is that it can be a bit like looking at paintings while galloping on horseback through a gallery. By no means is this book meant to be comprehensive; it is intended to whet the appetite of readers for a vast and sprawling subject that is endlessly fascinating, and for which there exist scores of scholarly studies and literary treatments. Should you choose to delve deeper into the subject of water in the West, in the Sources section I have noted the works that gripped my attention and proved the most useful in my research.

Learning the logic and terminology of water law is like studying a foreign language. It consumes time and effort and can be a bit tedious; but becoming conversant with basic vocabulary and principles is essential to understanding the issues surrounding water. A student of the West must learn to speak and understand the strange language of western water law with a reasonable degree of fluency.

As a reader, when I am faced with a chapter titled "Fundamentals of Western Water Law," or some such thing, I glaze over. Forced continually to consult a glossary, I become comatose. In this book I have spread information about water law throughout, allowing for what I hope will be pleasurable interludes between tackling concepts such as "prior appropriation" and the "public trust doctrine"—which when studied exhaustively and without interruption can be about as exciting as watching cement set.

To the portions of this book that contain historical narratives, I have added details based on my own observations of the natural world. I have done so in an attempt to convey the fundamental aridity of the West, in its harshness and its elegance, and to depict the land's overarching indifference to the people who inhabit it.

S.G.

South Boulder Creek watershed, Colorado

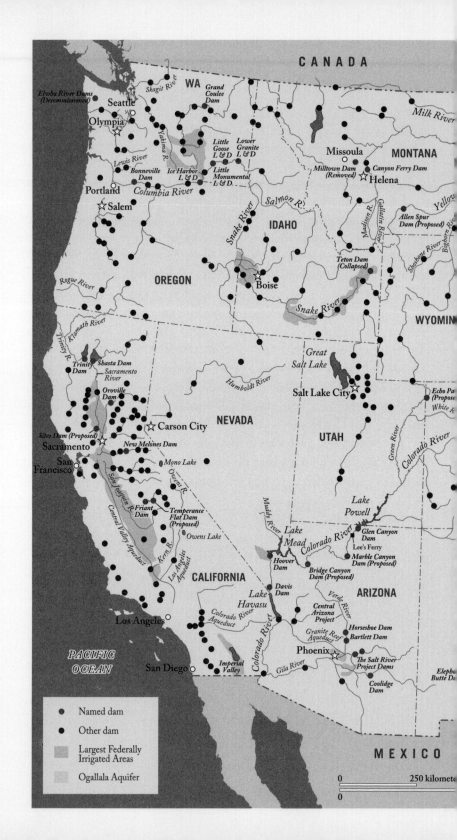

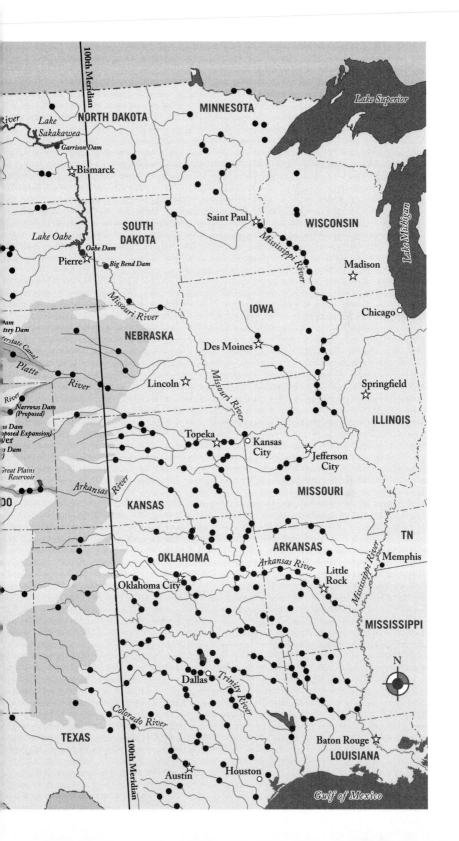

For I will pour water on the thirsty land, and streams on the dry ground.

—Isaiah 44:3–4

There is no lack of water here, unless you try to establish a city where no city should be.

—Edward Abbey, *Desert Solitaire*

I bought instant water. Now I don't know what to add.

—Steven Wright

Introduction: Trouble

Whenever you put a lot of people in an area with little water, there is going to be trouble. The trouble might be as focused as the engineering challenge of moving a river from one side of a mountain to another; it might be as all-consuming as the collapse of a civilization. Though the United States as a whole has a wealth of freshwater, the resource most vital to life is not distributed evenly throughout the nation. The 100th meridian—which cuts the Dakotas roughly in half and runs through Nebraska and Kansas, cleaves Oklahoma's panhandle, and forms the eastern edge of the Texas panhandle—provides a dividing line for rainfall. East of this line, at least twenty inches of precipitation spills from the sky each year, enough to sustain agriculture. Land west of the line, with the exception of a strip of temperate rainforest along the Pacific Northwest coast and scattered patches of lushness on mountain slopes, receives less than twenty inches of precipitation—not enough for crops to flourish without irrigation. Simply put, the West begins where moisture tapers off and dryness takes over.

Early explorers of western lands labeled the frontier that stretched beyond the 100th meridian the Great American Desert. Into these parched wastes adventurers trekked and then returned to the rich gardens of the East with tales of the West's burning plains stretching dry and treeless in all directions and its mountains wrapped in shrouds of snow beneath a sky so wide it seemed of a world that could not be. The West was as alien as Mars to Anglo-Americans. That they chose to settle there, and still to this day do so in droves, demonstrates the region's pull on the imagination. From these arid lands grow dreams of wealth and fresh beginnings in a world of bright sun and boundless possibility.

Recent arrivals to Phoenix or Las Vegas, surrounded by splashy water parks and golf courses of vivid green, have been known to mutter, "I heard somewhere this was a desert." A real estate developer in Denver recently said to me, "The only thing I know about water is that it comes out of my faucet." Water managers across the West have done such a superb job of making sure cities have adequate supplies they have created an illusion of profusion, which can make people take water for granted. But mention water to a Westerner whose great-grandparents homesteaded a patch of land as dry as a legal brief and listen to the stories flow. Water might not seem like a big deal to someone from a state that sloshes with rain, but people whose ancestors settled this water-shy region know that the West was won not by men on horseback with six-shooters hanging from their holsters, not by sheriffs with stars of tin pinned upon their chests and guns blazing in high noon shootouts. It was won by farmers and ranchers with irrigation shovels in hand—and by politicians and lawyers divvying up water rights in a dry land.

If the talk in the West is not of drought, it is of flood. For days on end rain buckets down and then for weeks or months there is none at all. The West is a place of extremes (temperatures can swing more than seventy degrees from midday to midnight), and water is no exception. Dearth or surfeit, feast or famine: The rivers swell with surplus beyond their banks and then dry to useless trickles. Today's headline in the local newspaper: Bridge Destroyed by Surging Creek. Record-breaking temperatures have melted snowfields in the mountains and turned the stream that usually slips gently through town to a deadly gush. Ripping trees from the ground, stretching and twisting bridges until they crack apart, the melee of mud and debris now threatens people and property across the floodplain. Mountain snows have disappeared too quickly in this sudden blast of heat. There won't be enough water left to feed the summer flows. The creek will run dry, and soon the headlines will shout of drought.

—◆—

Across the West's deserts and plains, precipitation often evaporates before it touches the earth. Dangling in dark tendrils known as *virga*, it hangs teasingly above the ground. Some of the rain that does reach the soil is lost to evaporation powered by the sun's energy; some is absorbed by the roots of plants and transpires from their leaves, returning to the air as vapor. Pulled by gravity, some drops of water dribble down into aquifers beneath the ground, and some liquid moves across less porous surfaces as runoff, spilling toward low-lying areas to gather in lakes and streams. Precipitation in frozen elevations of the West's mountains falls, of course, as snow. Peaks reach skyward toward clouds born in Pacific storms. Sodden billows snag on summits and dump their loads of wetness before wringing themselves dry and then moving on, eastward. Each blizzard builds the snowpack, and the white blanket thickens throughout the winter. Some of the frozen water sublimates, turning directly from ice to vapor that blows away on dry winds. When mountain snows thaw in spring, runoff pours toward the valleys and plains, swelling the rivulets, streams, and rivers that nourish civilization in the West. High in the mountains we ski in snow that stores the water we drink below.

Outside my home in Colorado, where the Great Plains hinge upward toward the Rocky Mountains, the sun is shining and it is raining. Each drop sparkles as it falls, and a breeze blows waves of damp coolness through windows framed by furling curtains. The air is rich with the odor of wet pavement and plants, sharp with the smell of ozone. Plump drops turn to hailstones that ping against the roof and scuttle through the yard. The sidewalk is a foot deep in water, and the creek behind my home, which earlier in the morning was nothing more than a few moss-slimed puddles boiling with tadpoles, is suddenly deep enough to float a kayak. An hour later the sun is burning down. Rocks steam in the heat along the banks of the creek, and a great blue heron stands still as a stick, waiting to spear a fish or a frog with the dagger of its beak.

"When I lived on some ranchland outside of town," a friend tells me later in the day, "the people there tacked notes to fenceposts to let each other know when they wanted to use water from the local stream for their fields. No computers, e-mail, or anything like that—just putting up handwritten notes on the fences, the way it had been done forever." This same day, another person says to me, "I remember hearing that on the frontier, in a lot of the homicide cases there was an irrigation shovel found at the murder scene."

Westerners have mostly stopped hitting each other with shovels, but water is still on our minds, and for many of us it is an obsession. To stave off dehydration in this dry climate, we drink water as if it's our second job. The weather report means more than a wardrobe choice or what time we will water the lawn. When clouds bunch up and block the blue sky, we may curse the rain that falls because it stalls our bike ride or our ballgame, but we watch drops patting the dust and know we need the moisture. We understand that downpours and blizzards replenish the rivers and fill the reservoirs, and in the West, storms are less a nuisance than a sign of salvation. We read about the snowpack in the newspaper, scanning daily updates of its depth to know the quality of the skiing, but also to understand the amount of liquid that will flow toward our cities when the mountains release their meltwater in spring torrents and summer trickles. A thin snowpack means lean rivers, emaciated reservoirs. It means water-starved cities and water rationing and more talk of projects to bring more water to places that have run short of supply.

Scientists have verified what old-timers already know: Annual snowpack across the West is dwindling as the world warms. But the cities that sprawl across the deserts and plains beneath the West's snowcapped peaks are filling with people, burgeoning with thirsty hordes. The Hohokam once lived here, as did the Ancestral Puebloans. Their civilizations rose around their skill at manipulating water. For centuries they made this dry land bloom, and then their great waterworks fell to ruin and their canals filled with dust. They abandoned their cities and roamed in haggard bands across a burning land, beneath a pitiless sun.

The Continental Divide runs along thin, serrated mountaintops of the western United States, forming a knife-edge of hydrology. Water that shears to one side flows to the Atlantic; water that slices down the other side runs to the Pacific. In the cloud-shrouded heights of castellated peaks, the Colorado River, the central character in so many narratives of the

West, begins its story on the Continental Divide before it ventures from its mountain home and journeys toward the sea. But our story now is of a smaller stream, one that also begins on the divide, but one that holds nowhere near the power or prestige of the Colorado—a modest trickle in comparison. From the spine that splits the continent in two, this stream spills not west to merge with the Colorado River, but east, toward the dry prairie that holds the metropolis of Denver. The city is desperate for the stream's liquid bounty, and engineers have devised structures of concrete and steel to store its flow and send it where the city needs it to go.

As scarcity has increased the stream's economic value, so the rarity of water in this land of cracked brown earth and dusty sky has sent its scenic value soaring. Between boulders big as houses and through slopes of scrambled talus, the little stream meanders down the mountains. It glides over beds of polished rocks and slips past pads of moss. In huddles of wind-twisted trees, it floods the gaps between roots. From other streams it gathers volume until it is too wide for a person to leap across. Each riffle creates a small violence of water, and in curved and hollow places the stilled flow deepens. Mayflies ride across its rippled skin. Among the forests that crowd its shores, owls open the soft fans of their wings and dippers dive from the trees. Ponderosa pines armored in bark that smells like vanilla reach their stiff limbs across the water. Children gather to swing from ropes above pools that darken to jade. Anglers cast flies into eddies, droplets of water flinging from the arcs of their lines in a bright scatter. Retirees with binoculars in hand scan the banks for birds. Adventurers craving jolts of adrenaline pilot tipsy boats through whitewater that lifts in leaping peaks and gnashes in scissoring waves. Denverites on the plains below drink from it and grow their grass with it and flush their toilets with it, and they head to the mountains seeking solace and adventure in its flow. This stream is in their bodies and homes and souls. It is everything, it is life itself. And it is not enough. Water managers warn that the city will need more, much more. As Denver sprawls its way across the plains and toward timbered folds of hill, it will drain this stream and many more, and one wonders will there ever be enough.

Denver represents the leading edge of America's next great urban explosion. As Denver goes, so goes the rest of the West, and so goes the nation. David Brooks of the *New York Times*, in a column titled "I Dream of Denver," cites a 2009 Pew Research Center survey that identifies Denver as the most desirable place to live in the country. Denver and other western cities, Brooks writes, "offer the dream, so characteristic on this continent, of having it all: the machine and the garden. The wide-open space and the casual wardrobes."

In order for dreams to grow in Denver, water must be piped through tunnels punched into the crest of the continent. Most of the state's water is on the western slope of the mountains, where the green land is veined with rivers; the majority of the state's population lives on the eastern slope, where tan grasses hiss in the wind. Diversion projects already crisscross and plunge through the Rockies, creating a plumbing system of staggering scale and complexity, and new pipelines are being proposed to slake the thirst of cities on the eastern plains. Colorado, along with many other western states, is predicting a population boom in coming decades.

Between 2000 and 2010 growth in the West was atomic in its explosiveness, accelerating at a rate nearly twice the national average. Many of the fastest-growing cities and states in the nation are in the western United States, and their supplies of freshwater, paltry compared to those of places that are depopulating, are under increasing strain. Moreover, Mexico's northern states are booming, putting additional demands on water that flows through the broiled borderlands of the Southwest.

Cities from Boise, Idaho, to Bend, Oregon, beckon transplants from the East and Midwest with employment opportunities and active outdoor lifestyles. Job creation in the western Sunbelt has outpaced the nation as a whole, and advances in technology have created opportunities to telecommute. One can sip cappuccino at a cafe in Denver's Larimer Square and trade stocks in New York, or check in with headquarters in Indianapolis, while basking in the three hundred days of sunshine that wash across Colorado's Front Range each year. Why live amid the dreary winter skies of Chicago when you can conduct business from a smartphone while riding a ski lift at Vail? Why hustle through the rat race of Boston when you can be based in Bozeman working from a virtual office and fly fish on your lunch hour?

In 2008 *Forbes* ranked Boulder, Colorado, as the "most educated city in America," and in 2010 *Business Week* named this western town without a rodeo the best city in the United States for startups. The Rocky Mountain foothills are full of venture capitalists and tech entrepreneurs hiking on their lunch breaks. University professors cram the coffee shops, and professional athletes race their bikes along the trails. But without "ditch riders," none of the money and talent that has made this region thrive would matter.

Ditch riding is the second oldest profession in the West, and the duty of a ditch rider is to keep water flowing through the thousands of vital arteries that distribute the lifeblood of a community. The job entails everything from scooping mud and pulling weeds from ditches to making sure all users receive, according to schedule, the exact amount of water to which they are legally entitled, no more. When miners realized water was worth more than gold because every enterprise in the West depended on it (without water even the bordellos would close their doors), they put down their pickaxes and pans and started ditch companies.

If water stops running through the ditches, there are no more lush lawns in Denver, no more bike rides on lunch breaks in Boulder, no more information-based economy. Everything in the arid West, from its universities to its aerospace industry, depends on carefully tended ditches.

⌁

America's Jeffersonian vision of a nation stretching from the Atlantic coast to the Pacific shores almost vanished in the Great American Desert, that expanse of semi-arid plains between the 100th meridian and the Rocky Mountains. But the nation was determined to fill the brown void with verdant life, to turn it into a garden and make it yield riches. With a bit of slick marketing, the Great American Desert was repackaged as a region where prosperity could take root in fertile soil. The Homestead Act of 1862 sent a flood of settlers west into lands of brittle grass rattled by wind, places of murderous heat and killing cold. These pioneers were promised free land and assured that the water-poor region would, almost miraculously, be transformed into an agrarian paradise. As they made their way across terrain bare of rivers, their tongues swelled with thirst and they put pebbles in their mouths to make saliva flow. The pioneers understood that water is life, and when they failed to secure adequate supplies of water they were lowered into prairie graves.

The pioneers who managed to make lives for themselves in the West fought over water with fists and shovels and guns, providing much of the region's delicious lore. Mercenaries guarded canals with pistols strapped to their hips and rifles clutched in their hands, bloodless knuckles bright in the sun. The region's arid environment wasn't simply a setting where events took place; the viciously parched land was an active participant— and arguably the most important agent—in the history of the West.

Legendary explorer and esteemed scientist John Wesley Powell warned that without a water plan crafted to suit the arid landscape, the region would remain mired in conflict. But Congress ignored Powell's recommendation to create small-scale communities based around watersheds. Instead it began a building frenzy. Soon an audacious system of federal projects siphoned off streams, transporting their flow far from their sources and diverting the elixir of the West to thirsty deserts and droughty plains. This was not an effort that aimed to help people survive in a hard land; it was a program of conquest, the goal of which was to transform the desert and build an empire. Water went from being something rare and cherished, a blessing delivered in bags draped across the backs of burros and hauled by the bucketful in wagons, to a commodity that surged through steel siphons and was transported in aqueducts guarded by fences. Water brawlers traded pistols for pinstripes as lawyers and lobbyists fought over the precious resource, and rivers were turned to concrete trenches empty of willows, fish, and birds.

The story of the West is above all the story of dams. Promethean dams allowed the region to be replumbed on a scale unprecedented in world history, providing the water and power that allowed a new nation hungry for growth to surge westward and develop its economy into a juggernaut. Farms blossomed scores of miles from the nearest stream. Cities fed by sluiceways grew from sagebrush and sand. Almost every major river in the West was dammed many times over, and engineers managed to squeeze abundance from lands where life had always been sparse. Confident that technology would deliver water in unlimited quantities, people poured into the western United States, packing themselves into artificial oases. Today, as farmers and cities clash over rivers and aquifers, and as water infrastructure across the region is stretched close to collapse, Powell's skepticism that the West's limited water supplies could support unrestrained growth is not as easy to dismiss as it had been back in the days of Manifest Destiny. And his warnings about the problems that would ensue seem prescient and precise.

If we run out of oil, we can make use of other energy sources. There are no alternatives to water. A dehydrated child cries without tears, and a person who doesn't drink water develops dry and sunken eyes, a rapidly beating heart, and bluish-gray skin that is cold to the touch. And then that person dies. Because water is rare in the western landscape and the region is so vulnerable to drought, lack of fluid essential for life lies at the heart of the West's culture, and this absence of water is intimately connected with things that have been and things that will be. The scarcity of water in the western United States has caused conflict in the past and will lead to trouble in the future.

"When the well's dry, we know the worth of water," remarked Benjamin Franklin.

—⁓—

Scientists have determined that during the decades the frontier filled with people, the weather in the western United States was abnormally wet. By studying tree rings, which form patterns that reflect the amount of moisture available in the environment, researchers can reconstruct rainfall and riverflows before historical records were compiled by measurements made with instruments. Tree ring data has shown the twentieth century to be one of the wettest centuries in the last five hundred years. Put simply, the development of the urbanized West was based on a fluke. The worst droughts Westerners have endured were short-lived and lush by comparison to the megadroughts of the past. And those episodes of deadly dryness will almost certainly visit the region again.

The United States Global Change Research Program (USGCRP), which coordinates and integrates federal research on climate change, warns that the West is heating up, and as temperatures rise, snowpack across the region will shrink, creating "a serious water supply challenge." Even if precipitation amounts in the West remain the same, the moisture will fall increasingly not as snow but as rain. Liquid from a rainstorm is quickly spent; water banked as snow in the frozen vaults of mountaintops is distributed downhill throughout the spring and summer. The timing of water supplies in the West is as important as their quantity. Warmer weather turns mountain snowpack to running water sooner in spring, lifting the level of flood danger; streamflows peak early and are diminished throughout the hot months when they are needed most by cities and farms. Higher temperatures in the sunburned lands of the West increase transpiration, meaning more water sweats from the pores of leaves. And the rising heat drives evaporation, turning more water in snow, soil, rivers, and reservoirs into vapor wafted by weather currents to other regions of the globe, where it precipitates and is lost to the West. A hotter climate also means thirstier people and crops, creating a spike in demand for dwindling supplies of water.

Richard Seager, lead author of a paper in the journal *Science* that made headline news across the West in 2007, has concluded that the American Southwest is entering a period of "permanent drought" similar to the 1930s Dust Bowl. And the Southwest is by no means the only area of the West heating up and drying out. The Sierra Nevada snowpack, which along with the Colorado River supplies water to California, is thinner than it was a few decades ago and is melting two to three weeks sooner each spring. Springtime snowpack in the Cascade Range has decreased in some places by more than 50 percent since 1950. A study published in the *Bulletin of the American Meteorological Society* bluntly states, "The West's snow resources are already declining as the climate warms." Soon we will no longer be able to say that the West is in drought, because drought conditions will be the new norm, and when combined with rising population demands, will lead to "increasingly costly, controversial and unavoidable trade-off choices," in the words of the National Research Council. This is polite speak for "water wars."

Water wars are nothing new in the West. As the old western saying attributed to Mark Twain goes, "Whiskey's for drinking, water's for fighting over." Rarely are there win-win scenarios in the world of western water. Whenever one party lays claim to a limited supply, another party, be it Las Vegas or a lettuce farm, a thirsty suburb or the desert pupfish, suffers. To manage water is to manage conflict. Occasionally peace breaks out in the West's water wars, but usually the struggle for the lifeblood of the region produces winners and losers. As the scarcity of water intensifies, competition for the resource will accelerate, pitting farmers against cities, states against each other, putting the United States and Mexico at odds, and perhaps even causing the United States and Canada to clash over the great rivers of the north that still run uncurbed to the sea. The West's increasingly stressed water supplies have already been causing trouble.

Thanks to irrigation, eastern Colorado began growing a thick carpet of crops in the late 1800s. Some farmers diverted the flow of the South Platte River to their fields; others pumped water from beneath the ground. This worked fine for everyone until a drought in 2002 dried up the plains.[1] By drawing water from an aquifer that feeds the South Platte, pumpers shrank the river, killing the crops of farmers who relied on the river's flow. The pumpers pumped their way to a bountiful harvest while the diverters watched the river shrivel and their fields go to rot. The diverters demanded action. The state intervened in 2006, forcing the pumpers to stop drawing water from underground—and then the pumpers watched their crops toast in the sun as the decision of state water officials bankrupted them. After hearing rumors of some pumps still operating secretly, farmers and communities that relied on the river's flow launched a spy campaign, hiring private investigators to snoop around pump-fed fields. These water sleuths looked for puddles and for healthy crops of corn, telltale signs of clandestine pumping. "I wish I could have caught them on my property," said a local farmer with wells on his land. "We shoot every

---

1 The definitions of drought are many and vague; I use the term to mean a lack of precipitation over an extended period of time (generally a season or more) that leads to a shortage of water for agriculture, cities, or environmental needs.

other trespasser and he'd be the second one." Diverters versus pumpers on the High Plains: a modern-day water war.

In Oregon's Klamath Basin, when irrigation water was shut off by the federal government to boost river levels so endangered fish would be protected during a drought, farmers stormed the headgates. With blowtorches and power saws they forced one open, briefly restoring the flow. Federal marshals arrived to establish order, death threats were issued, and three men who hailed from the town of Bonanza drove a pickup truck to a town that held the offices of the Klamath Tribes, who have lived along the river for some ten thousand years. The Bonanzans, while shouting "sucker lovers"—a reference to fish that the Klamath consider sacred and would be harmed if water was diverted to irrigate crops—blasted shotgun pellets at street signs and a portable outhouse.

Water wars are more commonly fought not with spies and shotguns but with politics. At the annual meeting of the Western Governors' Association in 2010, Montana governor Brian Schweitzer suggested to reporters that they ask Wyoming governor Dave Freudenthal a question: "I'd ask that fella why he won't stop stealing our water," Schweitzer said. "That'd be a good question."

In addition to the mountain snowpack that makes surface water when it melts, groundwater is the other main source of the region's freshwater. Moisture percolates into the soil and trickles downward, saturating layers of gravel and sand, flooding the cracks and fissures of fractured rock, and pooling in porous stone. Rainfall and snowmelt recharge these aquifers when their moisture infiltrates the ground, and seepage from lakes and streams helps to fill them too. But farms and municipalities across the western United States are sucking aquifers dry. Cities such as Phoenix have watched the earth beneath them buckle and fold as it droops downward toward hollows in the ground emptied of water.

Water seems like the ultimate renewable resource; it does, after all, fall from the sky. But the period it takes for nature to fill an aquifer such as the Ogallala, which underlies the High Plains and has allowed land seared by sun and raked by dry winds to become the nation's breadbasket, is on a geologic timescale, not a human one. Groundwater pumping in most parts of the West is not much better than a free-for-all. Water is being pulled out of aquifers far faster than it is being replenished, and in many areas no one is sure how many people are pumping or how much water they are guzzling. In an unregulated world of extraction, the tragedy of the commons unfolds.

The tragedy of the commons, a dilemma first described by Garrett Hardin in a 1968 issue of the journal *Science*, has become a central concept in ecology and natural resources management. Hardin based his idea on the overgrazing of nineteenth-century community pastures—these are the "commons." Imagine a pasture shared by herders. A herder, in order to maximize his own gain, increases his number of cows. This allows him to enjoy the profits of grazing more animals on the pasture; but the costs of the damage caused by his additional cows are spread among everyone. The herder fears that if he doesn't add more cows, others will expand their own herds and rob him of his share of grass. Rationally acting to further his self-interest, he continues to add cows; others do the same, until eventually the pasture is overgrazed to the point of collapse.

When allowed unlimited access to a finite resource, people go after short-term profits at the expense of the resource's long-term ruin. The path toward destruction is predictable—it is rooted in human nature. This is the tragedy.

Some water officials in the West are scrambling to find solutions to the problem of diminishing rivers and aquifers by promoting conservation and pioneering more efficient methods of use. Others are developing grandiose schemes to rework the plumbing that distributes water across the region. The projects of which they dream, megadams and mammoth pipelines, are reminiscent of an earlier era, when greening the brown expanse west of the 100th meridian was a cause undertaken by the nation at any cost, and with an intensity approaching religious fervor. That era provided the great waterworks the West relies on today—dams such as

Hoover and Grand Coulee, diversion systems such as the Colorado River Aqueduct and the Central Arizona Project. Understanding the dam-everything-that-flows mentality of that crucial time in the development of the West's water resources goes a long way toward explaining where we are now. But before we delve into that era to witness the tense political dramas that played out on the West's arid stage, we will begin at the beginning. We will follow the first white explorers into the parched frontier.

CHAPTER 1

Into the Parched Frontier

IN 1540, THE SPANISH CONQUISTADOR FRANCISCO VÁZQUEZ DE CORONADO led an army of men bristling with spears and sheathed in armor deep into the unmapped wilderness north of Mexico. Coronado was searching for the mythical golden cities of Cíbola; instead he found adobe villages and people living in squalor on barren terrain. In what are today Arizona and New Mexico, his army wandered through roasting deserts with floors cracked open into countless canyons, and the rivers they encountered seemed meager threads of water swallowed up by stony dryness. A scouting party stood on a rim of the Grand Canyon and guessed that the river in the shadows below was eight feet wide or so.

Stories of great wealth in a place called Quivira spurred Coronado to push his ironclad army deeper into uncharted wilds. In what are now Texas, Oklahoma, and Kansas, his men crossed shadeless plains beneath the fierce orb of the sun. Mad with thirst, they staggered in circles, searching for water in a land as flat as a sea. From the level smoothness of the baking plains rose mirages that tormented their dehydrated brains. Sweat pooled behind their chestplates and dripped from their helmets, and metal clanged and leather creaked as they stumbled through the heat. Upon finally reaching Quivira in present-day Kansas, Coronado saw an oasis "very well watered by the rivulets and springs and rivers," but he didn't find golden cups hanging from the trees, as he'd been promised he would. After concluding his ordeal and returning to the Rio Grande, he reported back to Spain that the wilderness he had traversed was too far from the oceans and too desolate to sustain civilization.

1

An exploratory party led by two priests, Silvestre Vélez de Escalante and Francisco Domínguez, set out in 1776 to find an overland route from the Spanish settlement of Santa Fe through the deserts and badlands of the Great Basin to reach the missions of California's coast. In what is now western Colorado, the group lost its way in a land of howling wastes, where dry lakebeds shimmered with heat and naked mesas rippled in the broiling air. By day the travelers crouched in thin sanctuaries of shade offered by boulders in this inferno. When the sun sat low on the horizon and shadows spread like spilled ink, they saddled their horses and rode. As their journey stretched on through present-day Utah, Arizona, and New Mexico, they were almost killed by thirst. Their bodies turned spindly from starvation and they devoured their horses and mules. In wind-blasted mountains a blizzard nearly buried them alive. The party never came close to reaching its goal of California, making it back to Santa Fe after traversing more than seventeen hundred miles of the Southwest's most sere and sterile terrain.

In 1803, a young American republic acquired from the French a vast parcel of land in the Louisiana Purchase. The following year President Thomas Jefferson sent Meriwether Lewis and William Clark to discover what lay within this sprawling wilderness and to find a navigable water route across the continent. They followed the Missouri River over the Great Plains to its headwaters on the Continental Divide; then in canoes they descended the Clearwater, Snake, and Columbia Rivers, finally reaching the Pacific Ocean. West of the volcanic cones of the Cascades, they found themselves in forests hung with draperies of moss. But between St. Louis and the fern-strewn greenery of the Pacific Northwest stretched heaving mountain barriers and horizontal lands covered with bunchgrass and herds of ten thousand buffalo. The bewildered party traveled among sculpted palisades and along bare bluffs and gullies that rattled with dust-covered stones. This was a strange new world of prairie wolves and pronghorn antelope and vistas that swept toward an infinity of sky—a realm of creatures and landscapes so different from those of the East, where the vine-tangled forests were crawling with squirrels and rivers rolled fatly down every ravine.

In 1806, as Lewis and Clark were heading homeward, an expedition led by Lieutenant Zebulon Pike set off into the southern part of the Louisiana Purchase, traveling through what are now Kansas and Colorado. The expedition aimed to cross the arid flatlands and then explore and map the unknown region at the headwaters of the Arkansas River. In his reports, Pike noted the dry monotony of the landscape and wrote, "These vast plains of the western hemisphere may become in time equally celebrated as the sandy deserts of Africa."

An expedition led by Major Stephen Long, sent by President Monroe to explore the southwestern boundary of the Louisiana Purchase in 1820, produced a map that labeled the parched sprawl of the plains the Great American Desert. In the report submitted with the map, Edwin James, the expedition's geographer, described the region as "almost wholly unfit for cultivation, and of course uninhabitable by a people depending upon agriculture for their subsistence." The report warned that the grim wilderness with no wood and little water was best left as a buffer against nations that were vying with the Americans for control of the continent's land and resources. If trees couldn't find enough to drink, then crops didn't stand a chance. No trees, no farming. No farming, no people. The Great American Desert: This idea held sway for nearly fifty years.[2]

Following the lead of explorers such as Pike and Long, legendary mountain men such as Jedediah Smith probed unknown reaches of wilderness seeking streams rich with beaver. To feed a European fashion craze for hats crafted from the animals' soft pelts, Smith and his colleagues captured the critters in traps jagged with metal fangs. Smith was easy to pick out of a crowd—his face was marred by scars from a grizzly that had crunched his skull between its muscled jaws. Fellow mountain men had sewn Smith's scalp and ear back onto his head and bound his broken ribs, and then he was back trekking through the wilds with his Bible and rifle,

---

2 The term *desert* had a different meaning in the nineteenth century. Instead of the sand dunes bunched up like ocean billows that the word now conjures, it referred to an area that couldn't be settled and farmed, and thus had no commercial value. The Great American Desert was home to grasslands and buffalo, not sand and sidewinders—those deserts farther west were home to Jedediah Smith.

blazing trails the Mormons would use when they embarked on a quest to build a civilization in the desert, and pathfinding routes that treasure seekers would follow when they pushed into the mountains searching for bright veins of ore.

Seeking a mythical river named Buenaventura that was said to flow to the sea, Smith led a group west of the Great Salt Lake. They passed into lands more barren than the prairies of the Great American Desert, sun-blasted bowls where chunks of stone lay cleaved on sandy floors and stood shelved in towering piles. The terrain was colored brown and red and rust and there was nothing green. Rattlesnakes coiled in the dust, black tongues testing the air. The sun bulged against the horizons and burned wickedly overhead, cooking the world with shimmering heat. The poisoned waters of saline lakes glimmered like pools of mercury. What plants there were had hooks and spines and vicious nests of thorns. A few scraps of cloud formed and then scudded through the emptiness above. Smith's party pressed on, their skin tightening in the dryness, their eyes stinging in the clarified light. Distant vistas wavered in the heat, and the vastness that surrounded the men seemed without end. From this white and waterless hell they turned away and headed north into the high desert of eastern Oregon. They crossed a sea of pale-green sage before reaching the relief of the Snake River, a wide watercourse in an empty land.

No sooner had Smith made his way back to the shelter of the Green River and joined the first trappers' rendezvous, a gathering centered on trade and bacchanalian revelry, than he was setting out again in search of beaver in the uncharted West. Smith led a party into southern Utah through cratered voids and great gashes of canyon. Forests gave way to scattered clumps of sagebrush and the land turned to reddish sand. The group forded the brown flood of the Colorado River and climbed through the Black Mountains of northwestern Arizona. They crossed baking tablelands bare of trees and sometimes naked of plants, a snarl of flies the only living thing. Stones that had cooked beneath the glare of the sun leaked some warmth into the chilly dusk, but with so little moisture in the soil and air to hold the day's heat, temperatures plunged and the men lay shivering between drifts of sand as stars fluoresced above. The group's horses, bony from hunger and crazed with thirst, died in droves, and the men staggered forward on foot after drinking the animals' blood. In a valley green with willow and mesquite, Smith's party met Mojave Indians, who took pity on the tattered brigade and nourished them with food and drink. When the men had recovered some of their strength, they crossed the Mojave Desert. The sun was a white scream, and they were forced to carry all their water. Delirious with thirst, they followed a river that taunted them by popping out of holes and then slithering back beneath the ground. Finally they climbed across a mountain pass and arrived in a coastal paradise of mild temperatures and gentle breezes, home to the San Gabriel Mission near present-day Los Angeles.

There Smith and his men fled the Mexican authorities, who didn't welcome this illegal incursion into their country. They traveled northward into the Sierra Nevada, following mountain creeks. Water tumbled through meadows that combusted with flowers beneath glittering peaks of snow. Along the ponded flow of streams, Smith saw the white points of branches whittled by the teeth of beaver and the wickerwork of their dams. His men set their traps and then piled their horses with a fortune in pelts.

After trying to lead his group eastward across the High Sierra and being turned back by snow that buried the horses to their bellies, Smith took two of his toughest men and some horses and mules and managed to cross the snowbound slopes. From the east side of the mountains, he led his party down into a desert pale with dust. They crossed the basins of what is now central Nevada, passing through terrain wild and dry, where cracked clay floors stretched to each horizon. The skin and clothes and hair of the travelers were all painted white with alkali as they trudged through the immensity of the land. In crossing six hundred miles, they saw but three small streams. Stones trembled in the glaring light. The lips of Smith and his crew split apart in stinging cracks, sand between their teeth. They dropped to their knees and clawed at the ground in search of moisture while lizards crouched under rocks in puddles of shade and vultures squatted on greasewood wrapped in the dark robes of their wings.

Amid the blinding whiteness of sand dunes and hallucinatory heat, the men probed canyons for hidden seeps. What water they found was brackish and foul. Gnats covered their faces, drawn to the liquid of their eyeballs. They walked on, passing through boundless reaches of blazing sand where crystal citadels rose in cityscapes from the shimmering flatness and a fantasia of blue waves lapped at the edges of lakes that dissolved in dust as the men tottered toward their shores. The Indians Smith's party encountered stumbled in rags through this feverland gnawing on beetles and roots. Blasts of dry lightning showed mountain ranges trembling in the distance, and spouts of dust rose in wobbly columns that twisted and bounced along the desert floor. The men marched at night across salt flats silvered with moonlight, and when they collapsed with thirst burning their throats they dreamed of brooks running sweet and cool through mountain meadows. In the mornings, when rays of sun began to strobe across the blistered ground, they dug holes and buried themselves in the sand. One day Smith followed turtledoves hoping the birds would lead his people to water, but in all directions the earth was leached of color and there was no wetness. The land was rimmed by stones that had been seared and blasted in the sun and the air breathed with heat.

Eventually the bedraggled group stumbled out of the desert. Smith rendezvoused briefly with other trappers and mountain men at Bear Lake in what is today Utah; then he led a party back toward California to relieve the men he'd left there. After enduring another series of desert ordeals and narrow escapes that took him all the way to the Columbia River, Smith went to St. Louis and tried to make a settled life for himself within its stuffy confines. But shortly after returning to civilization, he was drawn again to the wild spaces of the West. He finally met his end while guiding a group of traders along the Santa Fe Trail. Passing through a stretch of Cimarron River country with no water, the wagons got stuck in sand and the party grew desperate with thirst. Smith left to seek out a spring. After scooping handfuls of moisture to his lips, he saddled his horse and turned to head back to his group so he could bring them to the life-giving waterhole, but bullets fired by Comanche warriors pierced his flesh and their lances ripped his skin.

Though Smith opened the trails that led masses of Americans westward, the dangers he and his fellow mountain men endured gave would-be pioneers pause as tales filtered east of a land of hardship and misery beneath an endless canopy of sky. Desolate precincts of treeless prairie and great scourged wastes of desert, all of it cooked beneath a merciless sun and frozen in the dead of winter—this was no place for farming, no place for families. But it was a place of dreams, a place where men could get rich. Following the discovery of a soft yellow rock at Sutter's Mill on the American River above Sacramento, treasure seekers filled the frontier with their makeshift camps as they hustled westward in search of gold.

Water was essential to gold mining. Snowmelt from the Sierras was swirled in pans and run through sluices—tilted troughs paved with riffles—to separate gravel from heavy flakes and nuggets of gold. After all the good claims along streams were taken, gold miners worked dry diggings, to which they sent streamflow by hacking diversion channels in the hard ground. When hydraulic mining was developed in the late 1850s, water was shot in copious quantities through narrow canvas hoses. These pressured sprays packed enough power to kill a person. They blasted whole hillsides apart, and then water was used to wash the debris and sift out precious metal.

The first miner to put a stream's water to use, regardless of how far his mining claim was from the riverbank, owned the rights to continue using that same amount of water—the doctrine of "prior appropriation." This was markedly different from "riparian water rights," which American colonists had borrowed from English common law and established in the East. The riparian system allowed people who owned land abutting rivers (*riparian* refers to the banks of a river) to take as much water as they needed, as long as they returned it to the watercourse and didn't harm downstream users. This system served well in the humid East, where there were plentiful streams, and water was used in small quantities in homes and was diverted by businesses to rotate mill wheels and then returned to the rivers. Eastern farmers didn't need to irrigate because of the region's abundant rainfall. Westerners visiting the East commented that they couldn't see the rivers because they were so full of water. But west of the 100th meridian, where rain was stingy and lonely trickles of streams wandered down vacant beds, farmers weren't so fortunate. Mark Twain quipped that he fell into a California river and "came out all dusty."

The arid West forced farmers to divert water from skinny rivers to their fields, sometimes over great distances. Little irrigation water found its way back to streams after evaporating from the ground and transpiring from plants—the water was permanently removed from the already meager streamflows; it was, in the language of water law, "consumed."

Another peculiarity of western water law was the separation of water rights from land. The miners who first developed the prior appropriation system worked claims on federal property that they didn't own. As a consequence, water in the West was not married to the land as it was in the East. Under western water law, the right to use a specific amount of water was divorced from land and could be clearly defined and defended in court—vested water rights in the West were treated as private property. They could be bought and sold, traded and leased.

The West's water laws developed into a system about as strange to the eastern states as, say, the four tones of Mandarin would be to a farmer in Idaho. Prior appropriation is often summarized as "first in time, first in right." The first person to divert water from a river and put it to use has "senior rights" to the resource. Those who later use water from the river hold "junior rights." This means that someone downstream who lives miles from the river, but who was the first to use the water, can prevent someone who later arrived upstream, and who owns land bordering the river, from using water that flows by his front door.

Prior appropriation, by rewarding entrepreneurs with secure water rights, protected their investments of effort and capital to divert streams, thereby encouraging economic development in the West. It also, in historian Donald Worster's words, created "a fevered, competitive race to exploit." The doctrine left no room for society to allocate water to uses it deems the most important (for instance, alfalfa farmers have rights prior to those of semiconductor manufacturers). Nor did it allow for curtailing uses that society decides are harmful to the public interest (a city with priority water rights can drink a river dry, killing fish and ruining the river's aesthetic appeal and recreational value, for example). Users simply raced to form a line, with those who held senior rights at the front. There is now a long queue for water rights in the West. And there is not enough water for everyone waiting. When the argonauts who'd made their way across the continent arrived in the mountains of California to scratch at cliffs with pickaxes and to pan the gravel bars of streambeds in search of gold, they didn't imagine metropolises filling the western night with galaxies of light, nor did they see that the water they ran through sluice boxes to wash their ore would give rise to an empire in the desert.

After being driven from their homes in Illinois by angry mobs, the Mormons were led by Brigham Young on an epic trek that spanned more than thirteen hundred miles. In the wilderness of the Salt Lake Valley, beneath the furnace of the sun and beyond the boundaries of the United States, he proclaimed, "This is the place." The settlers called it Deseret, a name that in the Book of Mormon means "honeybee."

At the edge of a dying sea, the Mormons set about the business of irrigating arid land. Though they hailed from wet regions, they had dispatched emissaries to Santa Fe to study the irrigation techniques of Hispanic communities along the Rio Grande. On the morning of their first day in the Salt Lake Valley, they hunched to their task beneath the exploding sun. Their sweat vanished in the hot wind; their skin was streaked with salt. Using only shovels, no machinery, they piled up a small dam of dirt and stone, and they carved ditches in the ash-colored earth to divert a stream spilling from the Wasatch Mountains, the uppermost reaches of the peaks painted white with snow.

By noon on the day of their arrival, they were plowing. By the end of the following day, they were planting potatoes and spreading water across furrowed fields. Honeybees indeed.

After agriculture was established in the Salt Lake Valley, Brigham Young sent parties across the Colorado Plateau to settle some of the driest, most inhospitable terrain on the continent. A realm of perpetual drought punctuated by occasional rain, the place had been called by Jedediah Smith a "country of starvation." The Mormon pioneers thrust their shovels into hard earth and busied themselves with building waterworks to make barren wastes of desert bloom. A ruinous wind scoured the land and stung their eyes with dust. All around in this new Zion, rock towers stood in varied states of decay like the remains of cities built upon cities, and turrets of stone slumped and crumbled in the western sky as if ruins older yet lay buried beneath those red and drifting sands where the sun is put to rest each day in a holocaust of color.

When the US government got into the business of irrigation at the beginning of the twentieth century, it based its program largely on the Mormons' technical achievements turning dry earth to flourishing fields. But the key to the Mormons' success in a hostile desert was their social organization, which focused the group toward a common purpose. The hierarchy that had evolved from their religion lent itself well to the task of irrigating a desert. Everyone knew his or her place, and leaders were empowered to make decisions for the group, which faithfully followed the directives they were given. The Mormon Church controlled water, making crucial decisions about how this society in a dry land would use its most important resource. Water was a common good shared by all members of the faith, so there were no disputes over water rights. Any conflicts regarding water use were resolved by the Church, which was the final word in how water was captured and distributed.

John Wesley Powell, one of the most perceptive observers of geography and hydrology in the West, admired the Mormons' industry and their ability to share and conserve water while working toward a common goal. Their irrigation practices based on a communitarian approach inspired his vision of how water resources in the West should be developed and managed.

— ◂◂

Relentlessly curious and largely self-educated, John Wesley Powell ran his family's farm in Wisconsin as a young man, worked as a schoolteacher to earn a living, and fought as a major in the Civil War. During the Battle of Shiloh, one of his arms was blasted apart by a bullet, and its infected remains were sawed off by a surgeon. The pain this caused him throughout the remainder of his life didn't stop this polymath from compiling an astounding list of pursuits. He pioneered the systematic study of Native American cultures and languages, made major contributions to the science of geology, oversaw one of the nation's most important cartographic surveys, worked tirelessly as a public servant, and published accounts of his adventures and his studies of geography and settlement in the West. Throughout the course of a frenetically busy life, he was defined above all by a probing need to know what things filled the world and how these things worked.

On trips west in 1867 and 1868 to the Rocky Mountains, Powell heard rumors and legends about the Colorado River country. Known as the Plateau Province, it was one of the last unexplored regions of America. As large as any European country and encompassing parts of what are now Colorado, Utah, New Mexico, Nevada, and Arizona, it was cut through the middle by a great river sketched in with guesses—that was the extent of information supplied on maps. From the borders of this shadowy region, explorers had peered into a disturbing wonderland of sheer cliffs and tangled canyon mazes. They had glimpsed towering mesas and snowcapped peaks that hovered like phantoms in the distant sky. This fantastic and forbidding realm was shunned by westward travelers and avoided by adventurers. Its topography was considered too severe, its resources too scant. The one big river that drained the desert lands was rumored to hold vast whirlpools that swallowed and smashed anything that came near them, and the river was said to crash over falls taller than

Niagara and to disappear in places, dragging all who tried to ride it into a watery underworld beneath the ground. Lieutenant Joseph C. Ives, who in 1857 and 1858 explored the river below the Grand Canyon by traveling upstream by steamboat from its mouth at the Sea of Cortez, wrote that the region looked "like the Gates of Hell. . . . It seems intended by nature that the Colorado River along the greater part of its lonely and majestic way, shall be forever unvisited and undisturbed." Powell could not resist the call of this wild place, for its uncharted interior surely held a trove of scientific treasures—undiscovered fossils and minerals, unknown plants and animals. And the allure of journeying through the heart of this last blank place on the maps of a continent with its spaces swiftly filling in pulled relentlessly at Powell.

On May 24, 1869, traveling by way of four wooden dories custom built in Chicago and shipped on the newly completed transcontinental railroad, John Wesley Powell launched the Colorado River Exploring Expedition from the town of Green River, Wyoming. The expedition was not funded by the government, and Powell's purpose wasn't to expand the American empire or secure new sources of wealth. He led a motley crew of nine other men—mountain men, frontier drifters, shell-shocked Civil War veterans—into the last unexplored wilderness in America not in search of power or treasure, but of knowledge. Bewhiskered and bearing the stump of an arm that sent jagged bolts of pain along the phantom limb, Powell went because he had to know what was there, in what he called the "Great Unknown." To turn away from the journey would have been harder for Powell than to embark on it—even though the uncharted canyons held danger in such profusion the journey seemed to some less an adventure and more a suicide mission. Powell knew that the river dropped a vertical mile over the course of the journey, but he had no clue whether the river fell gradually like a ramp, or plummeted straight down in places. The crew could paddle around a corner and find itself on the lip of a waterfall that made Niagara seem a harmless splash.

The expedition began by floating down the Green River, a tributary of the Colorado that builds from trickles of glacial meltwater in the Wind River Mountains. After gathering the flows of smaller streams on the high steppes of Wyoming, the river runs thick with mud and oozes brown in its bed. Powell's band of misfits had no experience with river running. They had to learn as they went along, and their classroom was some of the continent's most violent whitewater. The only life jacket on the trip belonged to Powell. No polypropylene paddling clothes or neoprene booties for this bunch—they rowed in woolen long johns, and leather boots rotted on their feet. Some rapids the group avoided by lining their boats as they stumbled along the banks, taut ropes creaking under the strain, the friction of the hemp burning their hands. Some snarls of rock and spume the men portaged. They crept tediously around the rapids as they hauled their boats and several tons of gear along loose and slippery shores. Some rapids the group ran. Powell stood upright in his boat, his one arm wrapped around a strap for balance as he surveyed the roiled path ahead and shouted orders, his wild whiskers dripping with spray from the river.

Early in the trip, a dory careened over a waterfall on the Green River and then slammed into a boulder and cracked in half. The men in the boat survived, but critical food, clothing, and scientific instruments were lost. At the end of the first month, a member of the group, claiming he had "seen danger enough," abandoned the odyssey and wandered overland back to civilization.

Some of the men's adventures were more comic than tragic. A campfire that set brush ablaze left the crew wearing wigs of fire as they leapt into their boats to flee the inferno, smacking at the flames that singed their beards and charred their clothes. In another episode, Powell got himself stranded while scaling a cliff. His climbing partner had to take off his long underwear bottoms and dangle them down to the major in lieu of a rope.

The men killed and ate the scant game they found amid the canyon walls and tablelands through which they traveled. Though desolate, the terrain offered a trove of geologic wonders. Powell, who in his written account of the expedition never felt the need to mention he was missing an arm, climbed crags so he could take in panoramic views of the surreal landscape, where the earth's chronicles were written in water and stone.

Great mesas towered up from the beds of prehistoric seas, and beneath the vacant sky lay an upheaval of domes and spires eroded into strange shapes and streaked with brilliant color.

The Green River joins the Colorado River, heaving with snowmelt from the Rockies, in what is now Canyonlands National Park in southern Utah.[3] Powell's team followed the chaotic flow of the merged streams downward through canyons that squeezed the river to speeding froth. Whirlpools sucked at the boats, and waves crashed across the gunwales. In Cataract Canyon a fury of water forced the men to portage almost every rapid. Where the rock walls closed so tightly together that passage around the edges of the river was impossible, they ran their boats through whitewater, bucking and spinning, tossing and tilting through a madness of excited currents before being dumped into calm stretches where they could stop to catch their breath before entering the liquid chaos of another rapid. They used pitch from pine trees to patch their battered boats. Oars lost in rapids were replaced with new ones carved from logs.

The river grew as it received tributaries draining the Southwest, and on August 13, the team neared its greatest challenge, a series of deep gorges Powell named Grand Canyon. He wrote, "We are now ready to start on our way down the Great Unknown. . . . We have an unknown distance yet to run, an unknown river to explore. What falls there are, we know not; what rocks beset the channel, we know not; what walls rise over the river, we know not."

In a canyon formed of sheer walls five thousand feet tall, the earth's history for hundreds of millions of years revealed itself in bare stratigraphy. The cones of dead volcanoes stood perched on canyon rims, and

---

3 At the time, the Colorado River from its headwaters to its confluence with the Green River was known as the Grand River. Against the protests of Wyoming and Utah, in 1921 a politician from Colorado convinced Congress that the Grand River should be renamed the Colorado River. Hydrologists pointed out that the Green River was drained by a basin far larger than the area that drained the Grand River and should, in accordance with sound hydrological principles, be considered the main stem of the Colorado River. But the boost to tourism in the state of Colorado that was provided by claiming the Colorado River as its own trumped science, and politicians relabeled the map of the West's most important river system.

beneath these cindered ruins, in a place where fire and water had met in an ancient cataclysm as violent as the death of a star, Powell's team faced the most daunting rapids yet. Great chunks of basalt turned the river to waves that lifted and collapsed with enough force to crack bones, and the swirling currents formed holes big enough to swallow boxcars. Whitewater bashed the wooden boats with such fury their seams had to be recaulked each day.

The men threw out their rancid bacon and survived on leathery scraps of unleavened bread. Endless cups of coffee sloshed in the empty sacks of their stomachs. By day they baked in temperatures that rose to 115 degrees; at night they shivered on the cold ground through rains that dumped down from cloud-covered gloom. Thunder reverberated like battlefield artillery and lightning lashed the sky. Powell stopped effusing in his diary about stones colored buff and vermillion, and he ceased to wax poetic about fossils and ferns—he began referring to the interminable Grand Canyon as "prison." His party avoided the worst of the whitewater by portaging, but finally the group was faced with a rapid it was forced to run. Bottlenecked between cliffs, it presented such a sickening spectacle that some members of the team simply said no. Powell was certain they were nearing the end of the canyon and tried to convince the rattled members of his crew to continue. But with the end of the journey just two days away, three men abandoned the river and hiked out of the canyon. They never made their way back to civilization.[4]

Powell and the five men who remained with him pressed on, rowing toward billowing rapids that filled the sky with froth. Whirlpools pulled the boats into churning waters and surging waves spat them back out. The group rested below what became known as Separation Rapid. Then they headed toward whitewater more furious yet, reaching a rapid named Lava Cliffs, its mad white foam now smothered beneath the waters of Lake Mead. The boats bucked and bashed their way through the tumult, and no one was lost in the violence of rock-strewn water.

---

4 Powell, after revisiting the area where the three men disappeared with an interpreter and interviewing local Shivwits Indians, concluded they had been killed by the Indians in a case of mistaken identity. Another theory claims Mormons murdered them.

On August 30, 1869, three months and six days after launching boats on the Green River, and after descending some nine hundred miles, Powell and the five remaining members of his crew concluded the last great exploration of the continental United States—and what was arguably the boldest feat of river exploration in history—by rowing toward the placid mouth of the Virgin River, where three Mormons and an Indian stared at the boatmen in stupefied surprise. They were there waiting for the wreckage of the expedition to float past. Powell and his party had been presumed dead.

Chapter 2

Settling the Great American Desert

HAVING SURVIVED THE UNCHARTED WATERS OF THE COLORADO RIVER, Powell was a national hero, the most lauded American adventurer since Lewis and Clark. He parlayed his fame into funds for more expeditions. As Powell headed west in the late 1870s to further explore and survey the frontier, pioneers pushed past the 100th meridian into terrain where sudden hailstorms pummeled the dry earth and blizzards buried houses to their eaves. Settlements sprawled across lands where the wind held dominion, and each shelter stood small against the empty plains, the spreading sky, the upended slabs of stone raised by a great violence below.

While Powell watched with concern the relentless march of civilization into the harsh frontier, Nathan Meeker, the agriculture editor of the *New York Tribune*, followed the advice of his editor, Horace Greeley, who famously declared, "Go West, young man." West young Meeker went, and on the plains of the Colorado Territory he founded Union Colony, a utopian community nestled near the confluence of the Cache la Poudre and South Platte Rivers. The settlement was based on temperance and religion—and most important, on cooperative irrigation. A system of canals was dug by Meeker's pious, teetotaling colonists (nearby towns overflowed with saloons for settlers fed up with sobriety, and later for college students when the colony became the city of Greeley and home to a university). The extensive canals allowed the agricultural outpost to survive on the High Plains, a region higher and drier than the Central Great Plains.

Other pioneers didn't fare as well as the citizens of Greeley. On the High Plains, a vast sweep of land made of eroded debris slopes gently down from the base of the Rockies. Peaks pull the moisture from storms and cast a dry shadow far to the east. The soil of the plains is rich with nutrients, but streams are few and rain is rare. When clouds failed to spill moisture on settlers' fields, hot winds fried their crops. The boards of buildings split apart in the dry heat and dust sifted in through cracks. Pioneers' lips turned black and peeled as they praised each pittance of rain. They lived in terror of the sun's fierce glare and longed for the leafy shade of sycamores, the wet breath of maples. There was nothing to catch the eye on the pancake-flat prairie, no relief, just endless grass and the blank sky. Across the emptiness the wind crashed like waves of storm-rolled ocean, and the ever-present howl held within it sounded like a million gibbering voices. Bands of crimson and sulfur colored the horizons as the autumn sun poured the last of its molten light across the plains. Winter was a white nightmare, and cases of insanity among the pioneers were as common as head colds.

—◆—

"It is our manifest destiny to overspread the continent allotted by Providence for the free development of our yearly multiplying millions," declared John L. O'Sullivan in an 1839 article modestly titled "The Great Nation of Futurity." The West loomed large in the American imagination, serving both as a source of desire and a repository for fears: It was a fierce wilderness populated with blood-slaked assassins; it was a land of plenty providing the raw material to build a glorious empire.

The West provided the pioneers who settled it with endless acres of timber on mountain slopes and fertile lands as vast as seas. What it did not offer them in abundance was water. The scarcity of this crucial resource formed a natural limit to expansion and settlement, but the pioneers, pushed by politicians dizzy with the idea of an American empire spanning coast to coast, pressed on, struggling to build civilization in the West. Wind-flung particles of dry grit peppered their bodies like buckshot when they toiled in their fields, and at night their frozen breath gave them beards of frost as they huddled in their beds wrapped in cozy dreams of empire.

William Gilpin, a former soldier who fancied himself a scientist and philosopher, and who wrote articles and gave speeches that were often impassioned and sometimes downright loony, gave voice to the rumblings of the nation's soul: "The American realizes that 'Progress is God.' The destiny of the American people is to subdue the continent—to rush over this vast field to the Pacific Ocean . . . to change darkness into light and confirm the destiny of the human race. . . . Divine task! Immortal mission! The pioneer army perpetually strikes to the front. Empire plants itself upon the trails."

As white settlers coursed westward in covered wagons, buffalo that had blackened the plains in their multitudes were exterminated in a frenzy of slaughter. Farmers, to make some extra cash and to ready the land for plowing, cleared the buffalo bones from their fields, loading them onto trains in great clattering piles that were shipped east to be ground by smoking machines into fertilizer and then sent back west in sacks. As the once thunderous herds disappeared, imperiling the way of life of the Native Americans who depended on the animal to provide them with food, clothing, and shelter, tension between the settlers and the tribes of the plains ratcheted up, resulting in a war in which the Indians were trounced. Those who didn't die from introduced diseases, starvation, and warfare were herded onto reservations, which usually consisted of barren land for which the federal government could find no other use. These original inhabitants of the West had understood that dryness precluded widespread settlement. Instead of trying to farm the plains, they had trekked across vast expanses of terrain, moving with the seasons in search of water and food.

As the creaking wheels of wagons cut ruts in prairie sod, the frontier was transformed in the American imagination from a forbidding waste-land into a paradise of wealth. Cattle drives shook the earth and spread veils of dust that glowed with gauzy light. While the nation pushed past the Mississippi and toward the Pacific Coast, prominent Americans pro-claimed, "Rain follows the plow." This phrase, born of junk science and wishful thinking, was repeated so often it became a mantra for those leaving the fecund fields of the East and heading into the poorly watered wilderness beyond the 100th meridian, where the pioneers plowed under the panicgrass and prayed for rain.

The Great American Desert did seem to recede as settlers moved westward in the 1870s. In the sizzling heat of summer, kind shields of cloud covered the sun. Rain showers brought cool refreshment to the air and softened the cementlike hardness of the ground, and for several years a generous amount of moisture allowed crops to take root in saturated soil. Respected climatologist Cyrus Thomas and eminent geologist and geographer Ferdinand Hayden were among the vocal proponents of the theory that rain would increase as the frontier was settled. The foundations for this new meteorology ranged from freshly plowed land releasing its store of moisture into the sky to rainstorms being caused by the smoke from trains chugging by. One school of thought claimed that all the commotion created by people settling in a new area made vibrations that formed clouds. Believers detonated dynamite to rattle rain from the air.

Restless Americans in search of new opportunities left their lives in the East to see what all the fuss was about, and for a few years the treeless plains turned green as the Irish countryside. Seeps and rills were rich with water, and the settlers' dryland farms (farms that rely only on rainfall, not irrigation) thrived. But what was driving the increased moisture that allowed the Great American Desert to turn resplendent with greenery was not regional weather patterns altered by plowed soil or smoke or vibrations. Some unusually wet years happened to coincide with America's westward migration. The pioneers were not blessed by a god that smiled upon their dreams of growing a mighty nation all the way to the Pacific. Their dreams were watered by luck. And eventually their luck ran out.

Railroads, more than anything else, banished the Great American Desert from the maps and minds of Americans. When the Union Pacific and the Central Pacific coupled at Promontory, Utah, in 1869 to complete the first transcontinental line, a new era of westward expansion began. Railroads grew at breakneck speed, wrapping the peaks and plains of the West in a web of steel rails. And in the process, the railroad companies buried themselves beneath a mountain of debt.

The federal government, which viewed a rail line stretching across the wilderness of the western United States as critical national infrastructure, helped finance the enterprise. But after the last tracks of the transcontinental line were laid, the government continued to help the railroads fund their frantic growth. When the railroads were faced with crushing debt, Congress awarded them land grants, transferring massive amounts of property from the public domain to private ownership so the railroads could develop the land to help repay their loans. The Southern Pacific Railroad, for example, was given one-tenth the state of California in federal land grants. Flush from government largesse, the railroad companies opened real estate offices to parcel out their grants as farmland. The new spreads they sold needed freight and passenger transportation, which, conveniently, was provided by the railroads—and they could set whatever fees they felt like charging. But to sell the farmland, they had to lure settlers westward. In the minds of many Americans, the frontier was still a worthless place of cactus and cold, a wasteland with random sprigs of snakeweed and weathered humps of stone, where an occasional coyote would chase a prairie dog into its hole, or a stray sage-grouse would cluck and mutter as it wandered through the dust.

The rain-follows-the-plow pseudoscience of the day provided just the material that clever railroad marketers and salesmen required to flog their product. Ruthless promoters published phony testimonials, paid off journalists to file false reports, and made outrageous claims, all of which convinced gullible dreamers that if they wanted an easier life than the one they were scratching out now, if they wanted to get rich quickly and with minimal effort, then they better head west and buy a farm near a railroad line. When the hucksters ran out of nonsense to say about corn in Kansas growing taller than a man and rain falling benevolently at exactly the time crops needed moisture most to thrive, they advertised the health benefits

21

of the West, making it seem some magical place where illness evaporated in all the hot air. Tuberculosis, more than gold or silver, sent people stampeding westward as they chased the cure across the dry frontier. Merchants set up shops to supply settlers, sufferers with raspy lungs flooded in, and towns popped up across the plains and perched themselves in mountain valleys. Newspaper editors touted their hamlets as future metropolises. Eager politicians claimed their territories were at the forefront of a rising tide of American prosperity and power. Elevation, extreme weather—and most important, lack of water—were all conveniently ignored by boosters. Soon the transformation was complete: The American West was viewed not as a desert destined to halt the spread of civilization but as a promised land, above which stretched a sky of pure and lucid light as crystalline as creation's first dawn.

All one had to do to partake of this cornucopia was to claim the 160 acres to which he was entitled. The Homestead Act of 1862 identified the figure of 160 acres—a half mile square, commonly known as a "quarter section"—as the ideal amount of land for fulfilling the Jeffersonian dream of an agrarian paradise. This utopia of small farms would be built by slicing quarter sections out of the public domain and selling them for a nominal filing fee to farmers who were willing to work hard. And as these little farms flourished, so would the nation's strength and character.

Congress eventually took into account the unique topographical features of the West, modifying the Homestead Act into versions it thought would suit the region's landscape. But the Homestead Act's variations—the Desert Land Act, the Timber Culture Act, and the Timber and Stone Act—were all based on the premise that plots of land of fixed size could, with hard work, be made to bear food, regardless of where they lay in a watershed. (A *watershed* is an area of land that drains water downhill into a lake or river or sea; its boundaries are formed by ridges that divide it from neighboring basins.) This approach was reasonable in the East, where rain fell often enough to grow crops throughout each watershed. A person could throw seeds on the ground virtually anywhere in the East and they would grow into plants that burst with food. But the land west of the 100th meridian was scorched by frequent droughts, and large portions of watersheds didn't have enough rainfall even in the wettest times to grow corn or wheat or potatoes. A western farmer could work his land until his hands were chapped and bleeding, and for a few years when rain dumped down his crops might briefly flourish. But without irrigation the stressed plants died during times of inevitable drought. Cows stood gaunt and ribby against vacant horizons, and the skeletons of the dead lay bleaching on the thirsty ground. Settlers recalled the railroad company advertorials that had drawn them westward and scratched their sunburned heads.

If dryness didn't chase the pioneers back East, flash floods often crushed their towns and swept the remnants away. Wild weather roiled above the mountains and poured across the plains, pounding the ground with hail and rain. Gouts of runoff raced across bare stone and hard earth that funneled toward rivers, turning them to muddy slurry. When a nine-inch rainstorm fattened the Republican River, which drains the eastern plains of Colorado and western Kansas and Nebraska, a bloated flow swelled through the basin. People clung to trees that bobbed like matchsticks, and the floodwaters entrained snarls of barbed wire that writhed with rattlesnakes, these tumbling balls of wires and serpents like hideous medusas rising from the froth.

Along with drought and deluge, the pioneers were faced with alkaline soils in which nothing could grow, plagues of grasshoppers, hard frosts in spring and fall, days of burning sun followed by blizzards, tornadoes that ripped across the countryside and reduced barns to piles of splintered boards, hailstones the size of baseballs that thrashed crops dead—a whole host of Old Testament troubles that farmers in the East didn't have to contend with.

The mountain men, those indefatigable adventurers who blazed trails across the frontier and knew the land intimately, viewed the West in terms of topography, not political boundaries. Natural barriers to settlement such as jagged mountain ranges and sterile salt flats were obvious to pathfinders like Jedediah Smith and explorers like Powell. But the bureaucrats who ran the General Land Office, most of whom had never ventured beyond the Mississippi into lands cauterized by sun and scarred by dry gulches, looked at maps of the West and saw a simple grid. Their task was to fill the grid with farms. They created rules such as requiring people to plant trees on their homesteads to increase the amount of rain—but trees planted in western lands that rammed their roots against hard layers of clay and failed to sip enough moisture from the soil turned to dead husks that were blown over by wind. Irrigation was required as part of the Desert Land Act, but irrigation projects were all but impossible for homesteaders to build on most of the waterless terrain covered by the legislation. Even the spacious 640-acre parcels offered to a married couple under the Desert Land Act were too small for sustainable grazing. Homesteaders overgrazed their plots until weeds and mesquite took over, and speculators acquired the properties from banks that took possession of them when the pioneers failed. Ruthless operators gained control of streams, monopolizing their waters and forcing neighboring homesteads to dry up and fail—and then they snatched up those spreads for themselves.

Wallace Stegner, one of the West's most celebrated writers, wrote that the Desert Land Act and the Timber and Stone Act "could hardly have been better devised to help speculators and land-grabbers if they had been written for that specific purpose." There was so little oversight and control on the western frontier, federal land giveaways formed a crazed gold rush of graft. Entire townships were built on legal frameworks as flimsy as a Nigerian e-mail scam. Enormous spreads, some hundreds of thousands of acres, were taken from the public domain when tycoons filed bogus paperwork and used false names to build empires. Cattle companies paid claimants to transfer their land titles, and cattle kings soon controlled estates large enough to make European royalty writhe with envy. From people placing birdhouses on tracts of property to fulfill an "erected domicile" requirement, to schemers pouring buckets of water on land and then having a witness swear the property had been irrigated, there was no end to the trickery that moved parcels from the public domain into the hands of private citizens. Legendary land shark Henry Miller used a wagon to drag his boat across California's Central Valley and claim part of a million-acre empire under a law that allowed a person to acquire flooded terrain that could be traversed in a boat.

All of this was a long way from the Jeffersonian ideal of self-reliant farmers working modest plots to bolster the moral character of the nation. And it proceeded as if the resources of the West had no limits.

—————

Unlike the bureaucrats at the General Land Office who sat indoors fingering the waxed curls of their mustaches and shuffling papers, John Wesley Powell had felt his lips split open in the heat and dryness of the West. He had tasted the dust the wind carried, and he found dreams of unlimited growth dubious. Strip away the ambition of boosters promoting the region, look beyond the willingness of the pioneers crossing the prairies to suffer now and work toward an opulent future, and what was revealed was one basic, inescapable fact of nature: West of the 100th meridian, rainfall averaged less than twenty inches per year—not enough moisture to grow crops without the help of irrigation. Powell looked at the West and saw possibility, but he also saw limits imposed by a bony land sprigged with sun-cooked grass that crunched loudly underfoot.

In 1878, nine years after the Colorado River Exploring Expedition concluded, Powell published *A Report on the Lands of the Arid Region of the United States.* The main message of Powell's report was that the settlement of the West was limited by the region's aridity. Finding no scientific merit in the claim that human settlement increases precipitation, Powell explained that droughts and heavy rainfall tend to move in cycles. The West was experiencing a wetter-than-usual spell, but dryness would surely follow. Powell concluded that due to the region's scarce surface water, no more than 3 percent of the West could ever be successfully irrigated. Following this principle, he argued for the reform of the nation's land laws. Standard 160-acre plots worked fine in muggy environs where gray skies were lumpy with moisture; they made no sense in the sun-drenched West with its flood of glaring light. One hundred and sixty acres was far too small for an unirrigated farm, where struggling crops would be stunted by drought. But given good soil and irrigation, a farm in the West would flourish, and 160 acres was much too large. One hundred and sixty acres was an arbitrary number that meant nothing when faced with the fundamental reality of the West—its aridity.

Beyond the 100th meridian, the ideal pace of development, as Powell imagined it, would be slow and methodical, and the scale would be modest. With thoughtful planning, patches of the West could grow food and support small communities, but the land could not sustain development at anywhere near the level that was taking place as the result of the reckless settlement spurred by horribly misguided government policies—the result not of sensible planning but of a fever dream of growth, wracked by spasms of greed and graft. Powell called the General Land Office, which oversaw this mess, "a gigantic illustration of the evils of badly directed scientific work." He offered an alternative vision of how the West should be developed that was rational and fair—which all but guaranteed that politicians would regard it as madness.

Powell, whose ideas about watershed communities had been influenced by Mormon and Hispanic irrigation societies in the Southwest, proposed a system of small farms organized into irrigation districts, and ranches joined into grazing districts. Everyone who owned land within these districts would share equally in the ownership of the water. Powell's recommendations to restrict growth and treat water as community property did not mesh with prevailing American values of individualism and empire building, and thus were largely dismissed. Treating water as private property encouraged entrepreneurship, and settlement of the continent was based on an assumption of unlimited resources.

While watching the economic changes rippling across America in the wake of the Civil War, Powell worried about a rapacious few monopolizing resources. An underlying premise of westward expansion was that the more resources that could be developed, the more people could participate in the wealth generated, and the more democracy would thrive. That the resource of water could be controlled by an elite of bureaucrats or capitalists, harming democracy rather than expanding it, was not a concern that gave western irrigation boosters pause. But it nagged at Powell. To safeguard the resource for the public, he proposed attaching water rights to small parcels of land farmed by families so that water could not be treated like a commodity and bought up like herds of cattle or cords of wood. Powell was convinced that allowing water to be controlled by a manipulative few would threaten the very basis of democracy.

The map of western states looks normal to us because we have been staring at it since we sat in tiny chairs in social studies classes when we were children. But it is actually quite odd.

Streams meander and merge. They braid and twist across terrain in sinuous ways that bear no relation to the arrow-straightness of surveyors' lines. Instead of stuffing local and regional units into artificial boundaries, Powell would have the natural world dictate the size and shape of districts of governance. These districts would follow the contours of watercourses and the land around them that drains into their flow. Each watershed district would be, in Powell's words, "a commonwealth within itself." Citizens would collectively make decisions about how best to use the watershed for the benefit of their farms, ranches, homes, and communities. In short, the people in each watershed commonwealth would control the resource indispensable to their survival. Citizens living within a watershed, not some corporation or government agency based in a faraway place, would be responsible for the management—and the consequences of mismanagement—of their water. Wallace Stegner described Powell's approach to settlement in the West as "revolutionary" and "as bold as [his] plunge down the canyoned river."

The West comprises landscapes of remarkable diversity. One side of a mountain range can be a rainforest, the other side a desert. To treat the region as one homogenous whole and carve it up into tidy rectangles as if resources such as water were equally distributed would lead to conflict and disaster, Powell believed. He implored the government to map and divide the West watershed by watershed (instead of acre by acre) and to require each community to develop a plan for the management of its resources. Water throughout the entire watershed, even where it flowed through private farms, would be the property of the community, every member of which would have an interest in conserving it and using it carefully.

"Congress, dominated by boosters and local patriots," wrote Wallace Stegner, "ignored [Powell's] proposals, and settlement went ahead by tradition, habit, mythology and greed instead of by observation and forethought." Though Powell's ideas about new systems of governance in the West were as welcome as water in a leaking ship, his surveys of the region's land and resources were widely embraced by the scientific community. As he shifted his focus from running rivers to measuring them, he pushed the science of hydrology forward. He created a river gauge station along the Rio Grande, the first of its kind in the United States, and he is credited with coining key terms such as *runoff*. Powell was appointed director of the US Geological Survey, which at the time was the preeminent organization for scientific research sponsored by the government. Under his leadership the agency sent cartographers to survey the West and make accurate and beautiful maps of its topography, including the branching, twisting rivers that drain from mountains toward the valleys and plains, cutting canyons and moistening thin margins of bottomland before they spill into the sea. Maps published by the US Geological Survey while Powell presided depicted a West of water—of the land's division into natural systems of rivers, streams, and lakes—rather than a place linearly divided along state boundaries contrived by the pens of politicians. To look at one of Powell's maps was to see that although the vast expanse of America that lay west of the 100th meridian was made up mostly of dry land, it did offer some places where civilization could survive, clustered within the winding sanctuary of watersheds, if carefully planned.

But speculators and robber barons, who were focused on profiting from the region's resources, were not moved by Powell's maps and plans. Nineteenth-century Americans spoke the language of quick cash, not hydrology. They wanted as little government involvement in the West as possible. And states and territories hungry to gain control of the public domain and dole it out in parcels based on ways best suited to enhance their power and wealth were not worried about the conservation of watersheds. Many politicians were suspicious of Powell because his ideas about settling the West were based on science. They insisted that their constituents could more easily understand a simple grid system of dividing up the land rather than one based on complicated concepts such as watersheds.

In 1890, addressing a gathering of the House Select Committee on the Irrigation of Arid Lands, Powell displayed his maps, and he patiently explained that the West is a mosaic of forests and fields, mountains and plains, all of them interconnected and threaded together by rivers and streams. What happens to one part of a watershed affects everyone who lives within the basin. Chop down trees on a mountain slope upstream and farmers downstream will suffer when the river clogs with silt. The West, Powell argued, should be managed as a series of natural systems containing shared resources. To let states with arbitrarily drawn boundaries that bisect watersheds squabble over the West's most precious resource based on what best served them within their borders would surely lead to mayhem. Trouble was already brewing, Powell pointed out. People in the Rio Grande Valley were petitioning the secretary of war for troops to protect old water rights from new users. Powell urged Congress to carefully plan the West's development before turning over control of the public domain to the states so that further fights could be avoided.

In the spring of 1892, vigilantes bankrolled by wealthy landowners and on the hunt for cattle rustlers rode into Johnson County, Wyoming. A posse of locals battled the hired gunfighters, and the bloodshed that ensued became the stuff of western legend. Whether told as a story of cattlemen punishing renegade rustlers, or as a tale of besieged homesteaders defending their way of life against ruthless cattle barons, the Johnson County War had at its heart a drought and disputed water rights. The iconic range wars of the West, which provided fodder for works from Owen Wister's novel *The Virginian* to the movie *Shane* to the Broadway musical *Oklahoma!*, were about scarce water as much as contested range. Grazing rights were the stuff of wealth in the West, but without water land was worth nothing, and across the frontier people were murdered over access to rivers and springs.

To a group of irrigation boosters gathered in Los Angeles in 1893, Powell offered this warning: "When all the rivers are used, when all the creeks in the ravines, when all the brooks, when all the springs are used, when all the reservoirs along the streams are used, when all the canyon waters are taken up, when all the artesian waters are taken up, when all the wells are sunk or dug that can be dug in all this arid region, there is still not sufficient water to irrigate all this arid region." Booed by those who refused to believe that the West's lack of water should limit growth, Powell replied, "I tell you, gentlemen, you are piling up a heritage of conflict and litigation over water rights, for there is not sufficient water to supply these lands."

Silenced by the irrigation faithful who couldn't tolerate his heretical viewpoint, Powell made no more public statements about settlement in the arid West. He disappeared from the spotlight and faded into obscurity as settlers poured westward. But his parting words echo loudly to this day: "you are piling up a heritage of conflict and litigation over water rights . . ."

Powell's unique form of grassroots democracy, termed "watershed democracy" by Donald Worster, did not fit neatly into the diametrically opposed philosophies of laissez-faire capitalism and centralized planning. He aimed to prevent corporations from monopolizing the West's most critical resource; yet he didn't see the solution to the region's water challenges as stifling control by a centralized bureaucracy. His approach to governance was something of a middle way: The proper role of the federal government, to Powell's way of thinking, was to supply scientific information and to create a framework of regional planning that allowed communities to govern themselves. "I say to the Government: Hands off!" he declared. "Furnish the people with institutions of justice, and let them do the work for themselves."

Powell's sweeping plans often failed to address important details. For example, how would conflicts between his watershed commonwealths be resolved if they battled over shared resources? Each watershed nests inside another watershed, which forms part of a larger river basin, which fits into an even larger basin, and so on. A watershed forms a more logical unit of governance than a straight state border, but the boundaries that part waters in different directions don't prevent birds and animals and airborne pollution from moving between basins. And, more to the point, what if the commonwealths lacked the sense even to conserve the resources within their own boundaries? Each one would be a commons, after all, and the fate of a commons is often tragedy.

But the American spirit of optimism was strong in Powell. He believed that people, when given factual information upon which they can base their decisions, will make good ones. Science reveals that the health of a watershed is paramount to the health and prosperity of the people who inhabit it. Those people, when allowed control of the resources upon which their lives and livelihoods depend, will probably conserve them, Powell believed. He believed in science, in democracy, and in the intelligence of the American people. Above all, he believed in the willingness of Americans to work toward the common good of their communities. He was, in this regard, perhaps slightly nuts.

But Powell's ideas were not brushed aside for their instances of naïve optimism. They were dismissed because Powell refused to be afflicted by the delirium of the day: national expansion toward the mists of the Pacific without regard to the limits of nature. Powell's insistence that the majority of land in the West could not be settled because of its lack of water, though borne out by the facts of geography, did not sit well with a nation intoxicated by Manifest Destiny, a republic drunk on dreams of peopling every last space as it crashed westward toward the coast. Where Powell saw deserts where no farms or towns should be, others saw land that could form the foundation of an empire such as the world had never known. The water would come—it had to. By the grace of God it would fall from the sky, or by the effort of man it would be brought to the barren lands to make them bloom: Such was the thinking that prevailed.

The federal government ignored Powell's approach of dividing the region into watershed commonwealths that would raise their own capital to finance irrigation projects. Instead it raided the national coffers to build dams and aqueducts larger by several orders of magnitude than any Powell had imagined—gargantuan structures that rerouted rivers over great spans of terrain, profoundly altering the hydrology of the West. Powell's dream of irrigation systems nurturing clusters of small farms and common pastures at the heart of communities morphed into a phantasmagoria of concrete edifices tall as skyscrapers and reservoirs vast as inland seas. Pipelines pierced mountains, redistributing the West's meager water in a scheme of wildly ambitious complexity and cost. Fruit trees and lettuce grew cupped in lush profusion among brown bowls of desert, and certain men and businesses grew rich beyond imagining.

～～

The first settlers in the West had been forced to take on the task of diverting water themselves. With their own capital and labor, and without government assistance, they carved ditches in the dry plains and along stony mountain slopes. A few farmers and ranchers eked out a living, and a scattering of communities based around water diversions established a toehold of civilization in arid lands.

While farmers and ranchers were constructing modest irrigation works in the Great American Desert, the federal government was establishing control of western resources. The first national forest reserves were created by Congress in 1891; they would eventually swell into a system that blanketed the West. One of the main purposes of setting aside forested land was to protect watersheds by slowing runoff and preventing erosion. President Theodore Roosevelt, a passionate supporter of creating federal parks, forests, and wildlife refuges, is viewed as an early champion of American conservation. But his views, which were part of the politics of the Progressive Movement and were also held by his chief forester, Gifford Pinchot—considered another founding father of the conservation movement—were in one important regard very much at odds with those Powell professed.

Roosevelt, determined to mold America into a mighty empire more powerful than leading global giants such as England, Germany, and Russia, believed that wisely using America's storehouse of natural resources, the lion's share of which lay in the West, was key to ensuring its dominance. In Roosevelt's first annual message to Congress, he called forest preservation "an imperative business necessity," and he stated, "The western half of the United States would sustain a population greater than that of our whole country today if the waters that now run to waste were saved and used for irrigation." Roosevelt was not an environmentalist in today's sense of the term. He believed in carefully using America's natural resources to create wealth and expand the nation's power. A reckless approach to growth that allowed capitalists to monopolize resources, that allowed unchecked greed and unregulated markets to shave mountain slopes of timber and sully water—this was, in Roosevelt's estimation, no way to sustain the country's long-term economic development.

Powell is often claimed by the modern environmental movement as a sort of patron saint. But he was no Thoreau or Muir. Powell wrote eloquently about the abrupt beauty of canyonlands and the giddiness of confronting deep time amid the earth's layer cakes of stone; but he didn't celebrate the power of the wilderness to fill human souls with freedom and healing, nor did he argue for the protection of wild places. Like Roosevelt, Powell believed in using every drop of water for human benefit. Powell advocated building dams to create reservoirs that act as giant sponges, soaking up water during wet weather, squeezing it out during drought. Without dams, farmers in the West would be at the mercy of nature; they would fail whenever the skies were stingy with rain, and the parched frontier would never be settled. Powell thought the watersheds of the West should be plumbed with diversion works and the desert's dry vacancy filled with green fields. "All the waters of all the arid lands will eventually be taken from their natural channels," he wrote. Powell would no sooner have protested damming wild rivers than a person today would call for an end to the Internet.

But while Powell believed that western communities should be able to utilize the resources within their watersheds for their own economic well-being and under their own governance, Roosevelt exercised federal control to efficiently develop western resources for the good of the nation. Though both men were ahead of their time in their visions to conserve rather than allow the wholesale exploitation and destruction of wildlands and watersheds, neither would recognize today's environmental movement that aims to preserve the natural world not for the sake of advancing human society, but as an end in itself. Roosevelt's vision for America as a great global power, fueled by the federal government's conservation and careful development of the West's forests, rangelands, and rivers, crushed Powell's quaint notion of watershed democracy benefiting local farmers.

———

A few small settlements in the Southwest managed to grow around the egalitarian use and governance of irrigation systems. These communities, which helped inspire Powell's ideas about watershed democracy, may seem unimportant in the grand scheme of how the rivers of the West were developed. But they offer counterpoints to the water empire that evolved: They illustrate how the West might have looked had politicians paid attention to maps made by the man who knew more about western lands than any other. And they provide an example relevant today to people and organizations throughout the western United States searching for new models of managing water. It turns out that "modern" ideas such as educating community members about their water sources, and organizing watershed groups that are less interested in political boundaries and private property rights than in conserving the river systems that sustain them, are very old indeed.

The oldest water right in the state of Colorado is attributed to the San Luis People's Ditch. An earthwork irrigation channel in the San Luis Valley, where mountains rise in shining pleats above a dusty plain, the People's Ditch was based on the *acequia* system of Spanish origin that was introduced to the desert Southwest by Franciscan friars. Spanish and Mexican water law emphasized a fair division of water—the law was geared more toward promoting the common good of the community than to protecting individual water rights.

Acequias are gravity-fed ditches designed to carry water from streams to fields. Everyone who planned to use the irrigation system participated in its construction and was responsible for its maintenance. The community created rules to govern its acequia and elected a *mayordomo* (boss) to enforce the rules. Long, narrow parcels of property were laid out to connect to the edges of a ditch, ensuring that many farmers had land with equal access to water.

In 1851 almost every member of the Hispanic community of San Luis, including women and children, helped to build the People's Ditch. Using wooden shovels to pry apart the sun-baked earth of the alpine valley, the citizens of San Luis constructed a channel running from the Culebra River toward fields of fertile bottomland, where beds of alluvium that had been deposited by the river layer upon layer, year after year, had formed a rich floodplain. After completing the *acequia madre* (mother ditch), more ditches followed. Cooperation and careful management maintained these vital conduits, ensuring productive harvests and the survival of the town in a burnt land battered by dry winds. The acequia formed the coursing heart of the community. To commemorate its opening each year, children would crowd its banks to collect toys and presents set afloat by adults. And the waters rolled on, spilling through tended ditches toward the fields that fed all the families in town.

The People's Ditch to this day remains at the center of community life in San Luis. Every June 24 the opening of the canal is commemorated by the town with prayers and blessings. Local farmers still prefer the traditional acequia approach to contemporary large-scale irrigation systems, and the Colorado Historical Society has called Costilla County's sixty-six active acequias "a thriving example of environmentally wise self-government."

Stanley Crawford, in his book *Mayordomo*, an elegantly rendered account of his experience as a ditch boss, writes, "There are few other civic institutions left in this country in which members have as much control over an important aspect of their lives; relatively autonomous, in theory democratic, the thousand *acequias* of New Mexico form a cultural web of almost microscopic strands and filaments that have held a culture and landscape together for hundreds of years." In times of drought, everyone, beginning with the first irrigator along the ditch, uses less water so that the last users along the ditch still have a share. This communitarian approach is decidedly at odds with the way water came to be managed in the West.

❧

As the frontier populated with settlers, states codified their practices governing water into voluminous systems of law. Colorado and Montana even set up "water courts": entire court systems devoted to water rights—an absurd notion to Easterners. Why not have a court system to sort out arguments over parking places?, they ask with a smirk. Maybe courts to regulate lawn mowers?

"Perhaps to get into the mood of the waterways one needs to have seen old Amos Judson asquat on the headgate with his gun, guarding his water-right toward the end of a dry summer," wrote Mary Austin in *Land of Little Rain*, published in 1903. The doctrine of prior appropriation (first in time, first in right) that became the guiding rule in mining camps was first enforced by pointing the boreholes of a shotgun, like the blank eyes of justice, at a miscreant who took water out of turn. Later, prior appropriation was affirmed by western states in landmark court cases. In 1855 a decision that came out of a water rights' conflict in California's gold country used the doctrine to settle the dispute, turning frontier justice into law in California. In 1882, the *Coffin v. Left Hand Ditch* decision in Colorado applied the doctrine to a fight between irrigators, forming the foundation of the state's water law and officially establishing prior appropriation in the Rocky Mountain region. Throughout the West, the substance of life came to be managed by courts, through lawsuits.

Along with prior appropriation, "beneficial use" became an important component of the arcane legal framework that emerged to govern water in the western United States. In order to secure water rights, people had to put water to beneficial use—applying it to agricultural, industrial, or domestic purposes. And they had to use the water continuously. Failure to put it to use for a certain amount of time caused them to forfeit their rights: the "use it or lose it" principle.

Because people were only given rights to the water they could use, the system discouraged hoarding and speculation. It also discouraged conservation. If miners or farmers made an effort to use water more efficiently, they gave up the rights to the water they saved, which was appropriated by the next person in line. The legal system rewarded water users for drying up a stream; it punished them for leaving water in its natural bed for the benefit of trout and herons and bears.

Elwood Mead, something of a legend in western water law, wrote Wyoming's water code while serving as its territorial engineer. Mead noted that until sound institutions for settling water rights disputes were created, "there was either murder or suicide in the heart of every member" of western irrigation communities. Mead set up a regulatory system that in theory protected water for the good of the public—echoing John Wesley Powell's insistence that water should be treated as a community resource, not private property. In practice, however, Mead's system of administering water rights in Wyoming, along with similar systems that were adopted by other western states, perpetuated the laissez-faire frontier ethic of allowing individuals to appropriate streamflow for private gain. State governments simply rubber-stamped appropriations, and the public interest in water was seldom defined and rarely enforced. Essentially states gave their water away to anyone who wanted to use it to make a profit.

You want to flood a field of alfalfa, allowing most of the water to evaporate in the dry air? No problem—just file the paperwork and the right to do so will be yours. You want water to remain in a stream so children can catch minnows in mason jars and study the work of a river wearing its way through stone? Don't be ridiculous—there's no money in that.

Water rights had at first been traded freely on the frontier like any other form of private property. But many western states, heeding Mead's warnings that unfettered markets would lead to speculation and monopoly control of the most important public resource, enacted laws to either ban or regulate the transfer of water rights. Water in the West attained complicated legal status: You could own the right to use a quantity of water, but you were restricted by state laws in how you used the water and whether or not you could transfer the right to another party. Owning water rights was similar to owning land yet completely different.

To further confuse things, states such as Colorado adopted a pure form of prior appropriation law, while others, most notably California, adopted a hybrid approach that blended elements of riparian rights with prior appropriation, creating legal mazes of bewildering complexity. Anyone who claims to really understand western water law is either lying, delusional, or an attorney whose bookshelves sag beneath the weight of legal tomes. Lest I be accused of overstating the case, I should point out that Colorado has a legal category of water called "Not Non-Tributary Groundwater." If you want to understand how "Not Non-Tributary Groundwater" differs from "Tributary Groundwater," first you must figure out how to finance $100,000 worth of law school education.

State water laws in the West, while sharing common core principles of prior appropriation and beneficial use, diverged into various state constitutions, statutes, and case law. This legacy is apparent today in, among other aspects, the stream access laws that vary wildly among western states. Wade in a stream in Montana, and as long as you stay within the high water mark, no one should bother you because it is your right according to the Montana Supreme Court. But cross the border into Wyoming and set foot—or even drop anchor from a boat—on the bottom of a river, and you could find yourself being prosecuted for trespassing under Wyoming state law. Paddle down a river in Colorado and you might get wrapped around barbed wire strung tightly across the current: a common practice of landowners in the state to keep the public from floating streams commercialized for private ranching and fishing.

No system of interstate laws emerged to govern water in the West, and one donnybrook after another ensued as people within states and between them fought over control of the region's priceless resource. Adjudication—the process of legally sorting out who owns water rights, which rights are senior, how much water has been put to beneficial use, and so on—can drag on in courts for many years, leading to some of the lengthiest and most complicated civil proceedings in US history. State and federal court systems are crammed full of water rights cases, and lawyers devote entire careers to hacking their way through the tangled thickets of western water law that grew from simple origins, on the banks of western streams, when the first miners devised rules to protect the water they used to work their claims and aimed guns at people who disagreed with them.

Under the riparian water rights system in the East, in times of scarcity the pain of water shortages is shared equally by everyone: The amount of water in a stream that can be used is relative to how it affects other users. But under the system of prior appropriation that governs most water rights in the West, the amount of water that can be used is exclusive and absolute. Those who first put the water to beneficial use hold senior rights and receive priority—they get their water no matter what. Those with junior rights get whatever water is leftover, if any, and they bear the brunt of a drought. In short, the water rights system of the East ensures that during a water crisis each member of a community suffers equally; in the West, the damage caused by the region's frequent droughts is distributed disproportionately.

Conflict over water certainly isn't confined to the western United States. The word *rival* is derived from the Latin *rivalis*, meaning "one using the same stream as another." Water rivalries date back to the dawn of human civilization, and many international affairs specialists are predicting that as population pressures mount and claims on limited water supplies continue to pile up, water conflicts will escalate into wars that will define the coming decades.

One doesn't have to be a particularly astute observer of human nature to see that the West's water laws are especially prone to creating scenarios ripe with conflict. There is no end to the trouble caused by a system that made sense for a handful of miners scrambling to make fortunes in the hardscrabble West, and for the first farmers who followed them into the frontier. But the frontier has long since filled with cities, and the laws that govern the liquid that sustains them have stayed essentially the same. The great veins of gold played out long ago, but the legacy remains: grab it first; use it and it will be yours. Get as much as you can and never let it go. Myths die hard, if at all. The West is wrapped in freeways, and satellites each night move between the stars, but the ethics that evolved in this once wild place are with us still.

The myth of rugged individualism survives despite the integral role the federal government played in the settlement of the frontier. From laying the rails for the transcontinental railroad to crisscrossing the West with interstate highways, the US government has shaped the landscape and the culture of the region enormously—likewise with water, the massive manipulation of which allowed civilization to boom in the dry and empty spaces of the American West. The original intent of subsidized federal waterworks programs was to help foster small family farms; the reality was that large corporations used shady strategies to make fortunes while benefiting from the public dole. The small-scale cooperative irrigation projects at the heart of communities such as the San Luis People's Ditch are but minor curiosities in a land where water is controlled by big government and big business, ruled over by legions of bureaucrats, and litigated by armies of lawyers—this has come to be the prevailing viewpoint. Spurred by revisionist histories of reclamation such as Marc Reisner's *Cadillac Desert*, widely accepted as the most important book ever written on water in the American West, popular opinion in the nation has tilted away from lionizing reclamation toward demonizing it.

CHAPTER 3

Reclamation

RECLAMATION, THE PROCESS OF RECLAIMING LAND FROM A LESS USEFUL
condition, restoring or recovering it so that it can be put to productive
use, came to be defined in the western United States as building dams.
Formed of sculpted concrete and designed to last a thousand years, dams
rise like monuments in the deserts of the West. They are America's cathedrals, its castles, its pyramids. The immensity and gorgeous symmetry of
these monoliths will stun future worlds looking back on ours. We were
worshippers of wetness in a dry land, penitents before the meager flow of
water in a world of sun-blasted stone and drifting dunes of sand.

Before the great dams came the settlers. Waves of them migrated
westward, driven by a biblical belief in their destiny and by the certainty
that rain would follow the plow, which indeed it seemed to for a few years.
The plains greened beneath the feet of the pioneers who settled them, and
crops reached skyward toward drenching rains, as if prophecy had been
fulfilled.

But then in the late 1880s, following a winter in which blizzards
pounded the plains without reprieve, the West reverted to its dry ways.
Mud in the beds of dried-up rivers cracked and peeled like paper, and
the tongues of livestock turned black with thirst. Crops sagged beneath
a merciless sky, and cattle grazed dying grasses down to nubbly nothing.
Clouds gathered and then vanished in the scorched air, and the world
around turned crisp and brown. There was little to drink and less to eat.
Dust coated the tongue and teeth. Pioneers turned back east in droves,

abandoning their homesteads to grasshoppers and sand. Winds raised puffs of worthless soil that boiled black as thunderclouds in the prairie sky.

While land in the West cooked to desiccated powder, soil in the East grew soggy beneath a burden of rain. A privately built dam in Pennsylvania collapsed, releasing a roaring torrent that twirled trees and houses as it rampaged through a town downstream, killing more than twenty-two hundred people—one of the worst disasters in American history.

The federal irrigation movement, rising from dryness in the West and deluge in the East, gained momentum. Safe, government-built dams were needed to prevent hellacious floods and to irrigate crops during times of devastating drought—this was the only way the western United States could be developed, many believed. All the sites in the West with easy access to streams had already been settled, but private irrigation schemes hadn't created the infrastructure necessary for farms and ranches to thrive on a scale that would fulfill the nation's dreams of Manifest Destiny. The Mormons, bound together by a common faith, had worked collectively to construct and maintain irrigation networks, and they had an effective system of self-government that could oversee their projects. But they were an exception: Very few other private irrigation projects achieved any long-term success. Some entrepreneurs had shared the costs of water infrastructure and the benefits of irrigation by forming private "mutual irrigation companies," and states had authorized the formation of public "irrigation districts" with the authority to tax the lands within their boundaries to raise money for water projects. But efforts to create large-scale irrigation had foundered and failed. The great rivers still spent themselves in the sea. It was up to the federal government to build the waterworks needed to settle the western lands, President Theodore Roosevelt and other politicians believed. Aridity was the scourge of the West. A federal reclamation program would be its salvation.

Western senators and congressmen resisted the idea, insisting that the private enterprise of their rugged individualist constituents would solve the problem. Regardless of their protests, in 1902 the Reclamation Act was passed. In his book *Rivers of Empire*, Donald Worster writes that the

Reclamation Act "has been the most important single piece of legislation in the history of the West. . . . The West, more than any other American region, was built by state power, state expertise, state technology, and state bureaucracy." To many Americans, the act looked an awful lot like socialism. But the prevailing wisdom was that the only way the nation would be able to expand beyond the 100th meridian was with a federal irrigation program, and the United States still very much wanted to spread its civilization from shore to shore. A dry wilderness that covered two-fifths of the country lay sandwiched between the settled East and a few outposts along the Pacific Coast. Some Mormon enclaves on the Colorado Plateau, scattered acequias in the Rio Grande Valley, a smattering of irrigation colonies on the High Plains, small ditch-watered farms in California dotted with orange groves and wrapped with grapevines—this was not the stuff of empire. Manifest Destiny trumped concerns over federal control and creeping socialism. And fear of Japan, which was rising as an imperial power in the Pacific and was hungry for resources, added more motivation to fill the empty spaces of the American West so that the nation would be less vulnerable to attack.

The Reclamation Service immediately attracted some of the brightest engineering minds of the day. Excited to be part of building modern marvels that would lift rivers out of their ancient beds and move them over mountains, ambitious engineers joined in droves. Attracting talent was easy; financing the enormous undertakings was another matter. The Reclamation Act established a fund to pay for water projects. Revenue from selling federal land in the West would be used to fill the fund; then water sold to farmers would keep it afloat. Interest on the farmers' repayment obligations would be paid not by the farmers who profited from the water projects, but by taxpayers.

The first director of the new reclamation program, Frederick Newell, was quick to get started, figuring that the sooner he could spread projects around the western states, the sooner their hostility toward a federal irrigation program would wane.

One of the Reclamation Service's first efforts, Pathfinder Dam, was constructed on the North Platte River in Wyoming to supply water for irrigation downstream in Nebraska. Settlers in Wyoming initially supported the project because they assumed they would receive some benefits from the giant structure built on the sagebrush flats of their state. But they were outraged when the federal government placed a moratorium on development upstream in Wyoming so that all the water could be used for irrigation projects downstream in Nebraska. Years of angry protest ensued, proving true Powell's warnings about the conflicts that would occur when political boundaries bisected rivers, when watersheds were not managed according to plans that took into account the needs of all upstream and downstream users, and when settlers were not allowed to create the rules to develop and govern the resources that sustained them.

A dam sited on Arizona's Salt River was another of the Reclamation Service's early efforts. Settlers had already irrigated fields adjacent to the river; the dam, instead of opening up public land for small farms, put an end to floods and provided the existing farmers with more water, increasing the value of their properties to a point at which poor migrants couldn't afford to purchase them. By providing water to farms substantially larger than the 160-acre limit that Congress had created to discourage speculation and to prevent land monopolies, the project clearly violated the Reclamation Act. Theodore Roosevelt Dam combined the craftsmanship of stonecutters and masons with the bold blueprints of engineers to store runoff that spilled down the spiny flanks of the Superstition Mountains, creating what was for a time the world's largest artificial reservoir. The dam was an elegant achievement, an engineering triumph. But in terms of supporting the principles of the federal reclamation program, it was an abject failure. And it set an example for future water projects.

Soon the Reclamation Service was building dams all over the West with little regard for the Reclamation Act that Congress had passed. In his book *Water Law in a Nutshell*, David H. Getches writes, "Acreage limitations [of the 1902 Reclamation Act] were successfully evaded by use of leases . . . as well as by various multiple ownership subterfuges that allowed a single operator to control thousands of acres."

As great structures rose to block the flow of rivers, the ideals under-pinning western reclamation eroded. Michael Robinson, in *Water for the West*, a semiofficial history of the Bureau of Reclamation, points out that projects were built in a pell-mell fashion with little regard for the realities of local climate and soil conditions. In many cases, water was dumped onto fields with poor drainage, turning crusty dirt to quagmire. Low-value crops that could never generate enough revenue to pay for the projects were grown, and fields went to rot because the irrigation works were located too far from the transportation needed to move the crops to markets. In short, reclamation engineers were very good at building dams and very bad at creating comprehensive irrigation plans. Powell would not have been pleased. The Reclamation Service's haphazard planning efforts were a long way from his dream of enlightened watershed management centered on carefully thought out irrigation systems based on facts of geography and hydrology. Reclamation engineers worshipped at the altar of technology, not science. They were usually clever but rarely wise.

Western politicians, after their first taste of irrigation water, couldn't get enough. While continuing to condemn the idea of a federal recla-mation program as anathema to their libertarian ideals, they shouted for more projects in their districts and states. Principles were fine, but water was better, and farming and ranching constituencies expected their representatives to deliver projects that could irrigate their land and increase its value. Once the cheap water and hydropower started flow-ing, few western citizens or politicians sat on the sidelines. They wanted in on the game. They wanted their own projects and were willing to do whatever it took to outmaneuver other districts and states to get the feds to raise dams. The Reclamation Service continued its mad rush to build as many projects as possible to make the seventeen western states comfortable with the idea of a national program of reclamation. And utilizing these ill-conceived waterworks were hapless farmers. Many of them had no experience with the most fundamental aspects of irrigated agriculture, such as clearing their ditches of silt. Nor did they understand the importance of cooperation. Instead of banding together to maintain their tenuous irrigation systems in lands where the sun dazzled cruelly above earth cracked with heat, they bickered and battled among themselves, and they failed en masse—even with the bounty of water that was being delivered to them by the generosity of the US government at the expense of the American taxpayer.

The Reclamation Service, made up of engineers better at building magnificent dams than at managing the minutiae of finance and guiding the social mandate of the program, rarely turned off the water when farmers didn't settle their bills. Many in Congress could see what a mess this was becoming. Some of them insisted on reforming the fiscal mischief, but their efforts amounted to trying to hold back a flood with a cork. Most politicians longed for more projects, regardless of whether the dams made financial sense or were really needed. Water projects got them votes, votes got them reelected, reelection gave them the chance to get more water projects. Farmers defaulted on their interest-free repayment obligations, and the government bailed them out.

With the Reclamation program in a perpetual state of economic crisis because of the foolishly planned projects it was building, Congress enacted measures to fix the fiasco. It extended the repayment period for farmers from ten years to twenty. When that didn't work and farmers continued to default in droves, the repayment period was raised from twenty years to forty. Then fifty.

Crop surpluses made things even worse. As a national glut drove down the value of crops grown on land watered by Reclamation projects, more farmers couldn't afford their repayment obligations. Many of them had begun to feel entitled to the water they were receiving. Believing they were contributing to the national good by fructifying barren lands, regardless of the fact that the nation was buried in more food than it could eat, they simply refused to pay for the water they used. A new policy set water prices according to farmers' "ability to pay." But still the farmers couldn't, or wouldn't, pay. More dams were built, more water flowed to irrigated fields. More farmers didn't pay for water but continued using it. More projects lost money. This pretty much became policy—business as usual at the Reclamation Service, which in 1923 became the Bureau of Reclamation.

A report issued by the Committee of Special Advisors on Reclamation in the 1920s concluded that "in almost every project undertaken by the Reclamation Service the ultimate cost greatly exceeds the estimates." A commission chaired by Herbert Hoover reported in 1955 that the ninety projects the Bureau of Reclamation had under construction at the time would cost twice their original estimates. The Bureau's Missouri Basin Project and Colorado–Big Thompson Project ran *four times* their initial cost projections. You could pilot a 747 through the Bureau's budgets and not bump into a piece of truthful math. Artificially low cost estimates enticed Congress to bring to life projects it might otherwise have left alone. And once a government water project had begun, it was rarely halted, regardless of spiraling costs.

A private irrigation enterprise that operated with such an absurdly poor financial record would, of course, be crushed by the brutal realities of the market and quickly vanish. But the Bureau of Reclamation had taxpayers to supply it with an endless stream of money, and it had a nation's faith in its mission to sustain it. Bringing water to the desert had powerful moral overtones that could be traced back to the Old Testament: "I will make rivers flow on barren heights, and springs within the valleys. I will turn the desert into pools of water, and the parched ground into springs." And from the New Testament: "To the thirsty I will give water without cost from the spring of the water of life." These passages could have been mottos for the Bureau of Reclamation. God had supplied the West with good soil and with plenty of sunshine to help crops thrive. The land was fertile. It just needed water, and to true believers in the Bureau, it was America's duty to deliver the water, to rearrange nature so that a garden could grow. Turning the desert green and filling it with people was a goal pursued by many with what amounted to religious zeal. Because it was the nation's divine mandate to make barren lands bountiful, dollars didn't much matter. From the desert would spill forth fruit and grain—at any cost.

John Widtsoe, an irrigation expert and a member of the Mormons' Quorum of the Twelve Apostles of the Church of Jesus Christ of Latter-Day Saints, helped build the Bureau of Reclamation into a powerful bureaucracy. He proclaimed, "The destiny of man is to possess the whole earth; and the destiny of the earth is to be subject to man. There can be no full conquest of the earth, and no real satisfaction to humanity, if large portions of the earth remain beyond his highest control." Franklin Lane, the secretary of the interior under Woodrow Wilson, put it bluntly: "The mountains are our enemies. We must pierce them and make them serve. The sinful rivers we must curb."

Rather than ending the Reclamation program when it bankrupted itself in the 1920s, Congress decided to give it more funding. Oil and mining revenues were routed to the Reclamation Fund under the premise that because profits were being pulled out of the West by drilling oil and extracting minerals, some of that money could be used to give the West water. But still Reclamation bled money. And while its water projects were failing financially, they were increasing the value of property. Water subsidies provided by the federal government were often worth more than the cost of the land they irrigated. Many cash-strapped farmers sold their spreads to speculators who swooped in and snatched them up. Though this was technically illegal and certainly violated the intent of the Reclamation Act, which had been expressly designed to guard against capitalists monopolizing land and water in the West, it did allow agriculture to gain a foothold in dry lands. And the speculators were often better at repaying their interest-free loans than were the small farmers, who were defaulting at a phenomenally high rate and draining the Reclamation Fund. And so, as had happened with the Homestead Act, a piece of well-intentioned legislation succumbed to graft, corruption, and greed, and lawlessness prevailed across the arid West.

The winners in all this were the Reclamation Service bureaucrats, who had steady work; the engineers, who got to build state-of-the-art dams; and the land speculators, who amassed irrigated kingdoms. Water meant for independent farmers flowed toward money and power, toward agribusiness empires that profited at taxpayers' expense. Within a couple of decades of its inception, a program of federal water projects had led to socialism for the rich. Frederick Newell, the first commissioner of the Reclamation Service, decried the program he had once run, claiming that it had raised total crop production in the United States less than 1 percent while consuming a vast amount of the government's money and effort. And reclamation, in Newell's words, had led to "a disastrous loss in the higher ideals of citizenship, and that the invaluable qualities of self-reliance have been undermined by the insidious forms of paternalism, more than offsetting the crop gains." The Reclamation Service, with its water projects that made no financial sense and a social mandate that had transmogrified from helping small, independent farmers gain a foothold in the desert to putting big business on the public dole, had become surreal. And it only got stranger.

The reputation of the Bureau of Reclamation was in tatters. Damming rivers to create irrigation projects in the American West was financially hopeless. But the Bureau had a brainstorm: Dams designed to generate electricity could pay for irrigation dams. And a really big hydropower dam, by generating a lot of electricity, could pay for several money-losing irrigation dams on that same river. This financial legerdemain, known as "river-basin accounting," allowed the Bureau of Reclamation to build projects from the headwaters of a river to its delta, erecting dam after dam in the hopes that hydroelectricity would balance the books. In short, the solution to dams that lost money was to build more dams, bigger dams. And upon this logical foundation, and against the backdrop of national calamity as the economy tanked in the Great Depression, was built the biggest dam of all—one that ushered in an age of engineering marvels that transformed the West, allowing swimming pools in Beverly Hills to be filled by snowstorms in Wyoming, and a city with rainfall on a par with Egypt to blast misting fountains into a neon sky.

Had the cleverest minds in the world collaborated to design a system of water management as illogical, wasteful, and unsustainable as possible, it would have looked a lot like what the Bureau of Reclamation came up with.

Diane Raines Ward, in her book *Water Wars*, offers an interesting twist by profiling farmers in Powell, Wyoming, who conscientiously paid back every penny of the cost of the Buffalo Bill Dam the Bureau built them (though the loan was interest free), and who have worked hard on small family-owned spreads to use water efficiently and make crops grow in an environment inherently hostile to agriculture. People such as the family farmers in Powell don't appear in anti-Bureau jeremiads because they don't fit the prevailing narrative—that of total and profound failure on the part of the Bureau to help family farms and to use federal tax dollars for projects that contribute substantively to society. The public loaned the money for the Buffalo Bill Dam to be built, and it absorbed the interest payment on the loan—which is a significant subsidy, to be sure. In return, however, the farmers in Powell generated sizable amounts of revenue for federal and state tax coffers with the sales of their crops and livestock. They provided the people of the West with grain, vegetables, and meat; they helped ensure the taxpayers of America a secure food supply; and they contributed to creating a surplus of crops that could be sold overseas to help balance the nation's trade deficit.

Water projects in the western United States, however precarious their financial underpinnings or moral mandate, provided jobs for construction workers and engineers and allowed ranching and farming communities to coalesce in rural places. They led to the development of western cities with their museums and universities and performing arts centers, their restaurants and skyscrapers and sports stadiums. The Bureau of Reclamation may have made a mess of its mission, but to say that only a handful of special interests benefited from its waterworks is not entirely true. The library where I did much of the research for this book, uncovering myriad shortcomings of the West's water projects, would not exist, and neither would the home to which I returned each day after finishing my research, were it not for those water projects that flume liquid from one side of the mountains to the other.

Of course, if it weren't for those water projects, the library and home might still exist—but on the other side of the mountains, where nature placed the rivers.

Arthur Powell Davis, nephew of John Wesley Powell and an engineer in the US Geological Survey, used his influence to push through a proposal in Congress that would profoundly alter the waterscape of the West. Davis envisioned the rowdy flow of the Colorado River, with all its fluctuations and relentless push toward the sea, stalled, diverted, and drained through a series of dams and reservoirs along the river's length. The most important of these structures would be an immense dam, the likes of which America, and the rest of the world, had never seen—and which served as an especially astounding sight during the Great Depression.

Davis was an engineer, and engineers like to build things. Building very big things makes them very happy. And these big projects make the nations that sponsor them very proud. But Davis was driven by more than the basic human urge to build bigger and higher. Like his famous uncle, he worried about monopolizing powers snatching up all the land and water in the West and controlling the population. He also worried about the corrupting influence of urbanization, and he decried the crime and poverty of America's sprawling industrial centers. Davis yearned for a simpler time, an agrarian past with a more pure morality. This nostalgia and pining for a return to the Jeffersonian ideal of the yeoman farmer (honest, hardworking cultivators of small, independent farms who would form the foundation of democracy in a mainly agrarian nation) was part of the zeitgeist at the turn of the century as America left its rural roots behind and raced headlong toward an industrialized future.

Davis's solution to preserving the values of a fading past was to use modern technology to create monumental structures. By building the world's largest dams, the dry West would be transformed through irrigation into productive farms and pastures, allowing scores of self-reliant people to return to the land and revive the rural values that had shaped America. Completing such a project would demand prodigious amounts of capital and planning. Only the federal government, Davis believed, could undertake such a task.

The Reclamation Service was receptive to Davis's ideas, but he couldn't find the funding and support he needed to begin developing the Colorado River Basin. For nearly two decades his plan stalled—until politicians in California caught on to how much they stood to gain from such an undertaking.

The Colorado Desert, located in the south of California and so named because the Colorado River forms its eastern border, is a land of sandhills and black lava rocks sprigged with creosote and saltbush. From the desert's western edge rise pine-clad mountains prowled by bobcat and harboring bighorn sheep, where clear, cold streams tumble down canyons to disappear in a desert floor of hissing sand imprinted with the tracks of tortoises and scarab beetles. Beneath the scanty shade offered by occasional palo verde trees, temperatures reach 115 degrees. Less than three inches of rain a year moistens the chapped earth. Establishing farms in this place seemed to most Americans about as likely as building a furniture factory on the moon. But some bold developers envisioned luxuriant groves of fruit trees and endless acres of crops growing in the rich earth and bathed by abundant sunshine. To make this happen they needed water. Lots of water.

"Whoever shall control the right to divert these turbid waters will be the master of this empire": so wrote William Smythe. A man on a mission to reclaim the desert and stop water from flowing wastefully to the sea, he was referring to the Colorado River. Irrigation proponents such as Smythe, who published a book timidly titled *The Conquest of Arid America*, were enthralled with the idea of using water from the Colorado to transform prairie and desert into productive farmland, to tame nature and turn it into wealth. Smythe and other irrigation evangelists understood that water in the West, despite its scarcity, could be more dependable than rainfall in the East. Irrigation flows could be applied by farmers scientifically to crops when they benefited most from the moisture, leading to a more sophisticated, productive—and profitable—form of agriculture than that which was practiced in the rainy East. The Colorado was touted as an "American Nile," the potential lifeblood of a great civilization in the deserts of the Southwest.

In 1849 a man named Oliver Wozencraft set out with a band of fortune seekers across the Colorado Plateau to the California gold fields. The group moved in the cool of night, and by day they hid beneath blankets to escape the roar of the sun. At the edge of the Alamo Barranca, Wozencraft squinted through scrims of blowing dust into a vast basin. What he saw was not one of the continent's great parched wastes, not a landscape of seared earth boundless and bare, but a brilliant hallucination of burbling irrigation canals and lush greenery. He spent the next twenty-eight years trying to make this vision real. But before his death, a congressional committee dismissed his dream as the "fantastic folly of an old man."

A decade later an ambitious land speculator named Charles Rockwood made the dream of turning the Colorado Desert into an agriculture paradise a reality. He hired George Chaffey, an engineer who had developed successful irrigation projects in Southern California and a less successful project in the Australian outback. Using scrapers drawn by mules, Chaffey gouged a notch in the Colorado's riverbank, and he carved a canal in the dry earth that directed water into a channel abandoned long ago by the river. The freed Colorado filled its old bed, and after wandering south of the border, it continued flowing downhill as it headed back north, snaking into California by bypassing sand dunes that barricaded the valley's eastern edge. The water spilled into a broiled trough that lay 275 feet below sea level. Though it was known as the "Valley of Death" for its lethal heat and crackling dryness, Chaffey cleverly rebranded it "Imperial Valley." Farmers swarmed in, digging irrigation canals to send water to fields thick with good soil. The tracks of sidewinders disappeared beneath tended furrows, and rows of green alfalfa replaced scraggly greasewood. The desert was reclaimed and turned into a garden; the dry nightmare was transformed into a dreamscape of abundance. Crops flourished and towns sprang up to service the pioneers as the population of the valley boomed.

But then the canal opening that diverted water from the river began to fill with silt, clogging faster than it could be scooped clean. Bypasses were dug, but these too filled with silt that the river snared in its scouring flow. As the inlet plugged up, the irrigation canal ran dry, and crops in waterless fields of the Imperial Valley wilted. The government of Mexico allowed Rockwood's company to dig a new notch in the riverbank within its borders, and the flow of water to the Imperial Valley was restored, providing a reprieve for dying plants and desperate farmers. But there was a problem. Rockwood's company had failed to install an adequate headgate on the new opening in Mexico. The river, swollen with floodwater, throbbed through the narrow gap in its bank, chewing it wider and wider. A makeshift levee of brush and burlap sacks was built, but the river tore it to pieces. Soon the notch had grown to a gaping hole large enough to let the whole river through. The entire flow of the Colorado surged toward the Imperial Valley, drowning fields and carrying in its turbid currents enough silt to reengineer its own plumbing and rework the landscape to its own design. The Salton Sea formed almost instantly—California's largest lake. The growling river snatched and ripped at whatever lay in its path, and from its muddy maw it blew blasts of dust and wind. Boulders clacked together as they tumbled over one another and rolled downstream. Buildings collapsed as if made of balsa. Entire farms vanished beneath floodwaters that filled the desert depression. At the place where the river poured into the newly formed Salton Sea, a waterfall surged upstream at the rate of more than half a mile a day, eating through soft earth and spitting muddy slop into the sky. A gorge a hundred feet deep and a thousand feet wide was excavated by the rampaging waters as the townspeople looked on. The landscape was transformed not in eons of geologic time but before their terrified eyes. From godforsaken wasteland to agricultural paradise to biblical cataclysm—all in a matter of months.

In the breach where the river had exited its bed, gravel and stone were dumped in mountainous piles, but each load was washed away like a handful of sand. For two years trainloads of debris crashed into the seething river, until finally the gap was filled and the Colorado turned back into the channel from which it had been freed. A few years later, however, the river reengineered its course with its own dams and channels built of mud. It broke free from its bed and once again headed toward the Imperial Valley, drowning the desert beneath its restive flow. When the river finally settled back down, farms and fields began to flourish and the valley's agricultural industry thrived.

But the Imperial pioneers weren't satisfied. For their grand designs in the desert to grow, they needed a secure supply of plentiful water. Local leaders proposed an "All-American Canal" that would replace Rockwood's shoddy canal and free the Imperial Valley from its dependence on Mexico. Mexico was entitled to take a portion of the water for its own use—as much as half the flow—as payment for having allowed Rockwood's company to build the canal in its territory. Initially this hadn't posed a problem because northern Mexico was sparsely settled, but as cotton growers started irrigating land south of the border, the flow from the canal into the United States diminished, leading to water rationing in the Imperial Valley. When political instability in Mexico pushed the country toward revolution, Mexican soldiers with machine guns crossed the border, striking fear in valley settlers that Mexico was scheming to take control of their water. California's governor dispatched a battalion of state troops to the Imperial Valley, and locals formed their own militia that prepared to invade Mexico and secure the valley's water supply.

The crisis cooled and no shots were fired, but still the Imperial Valley residents clamored for a canal built on American soil to liberate their water from Mexico. The Mexican canal that carried their supply, in addition to being threatened by political problems, seeped large quantities of liquid through its porous banks that bordered sloughs and swamps, and its flow was fouled by the carcasses of livestock that were dumped in it daily, and by the rotting bodies of murder victims. Also, Mexico refused to cooperate with the United States in making engineering improvements to the canal to prevent floods like the one that had swamped the valley when the notch in the riverbank had burst open.

But what really rankled Imperial Valley residents was that the land in Mexico that benefited from their canal was owned by a group of Americans, including Harry Chandler, the publisher of the *Los Angeles Times*, and was leased to Chinese and Japanese farmers. Racist cries of "yellow peril" fueled hysteria among Imperial Valley residents. They directed tirades toward Asian immigrants in the United States and toward Chandler, whom they accused of stealing water from "red-blooded, free Americans."

The Imperial Irrigation District, which controlled the valley's water, urgently wanted to end its dependence on the Mexican canal, but it couldn't afford to finance a new irrigation system. It turned to Washington for funding. A bill was introduced in Congress to authorize the construction of the All-American Canal. Aptly named, the canal required the use of tax dollars from all Americans—a project constructed on a monumental scale to benefit a handful of large farms in one remote desert valley doused by river water carried from more than eighty miles away.

Arthur Powell Davis, the engineer determined to subdue the Colorado, harnessed the momentum behind the All-American Canal bill to propel forward his plan for a high dam on the lower river. He argued that without a dam to control the mercurial flow of the Colorado and store water, the new canal would be useless. Davis believed that to leave the Imperial Valley at the mercy of such devastating forces of flood and drought would be folly. Diverting a little bit of the unregulated river to irrigate fields was like trying to sip from a fire hose. Something had to be done about the tempestuous river. That something had to be a dam: the bigger, the better. One hulking enough to hold back twice the annual flow of the river would protect the Imperial Valley and other agricultural lands from punishing deluges and would store enough water to ensure a steady supply, no matter the amount of snowmelt that spilled down from the mountains each year.

Davis's proposal gathered support from government engineers who yearned to build big projects, from groups advocating a return to the land to revive agrarian lifestyles and values, and from Imperial Valley leaders, who after being initially reluctant to link their canal to larger plans to reengineer the river, finally saw the wisdom of joining forces with Davis. Another key supporter of Davis's plan was Los Angeles.

No history of water in the West would be complete without telling how the Owens River was snatched from its bed and made to flow to a town stoked on stucco, money, and ambition, a dusty pueblo tucked between mountains and sea that dreamed itself into a bright metropolis.

The epic water drama was fictionalized in Roman Polanski's 1974 film noir classic *Chinatown*, which tells through a plot as complicated as a western water rights court case a tale of power and greed, contains grisly nostril slitting, and climaxes in a bizarre slapping scene when Jack Nicholson forces the truth from Faye Dunaway. The film is fine entertainment, but the Academy Award–winning script by screenwriter Robert Towne takes liberties with the truth. To view *Chinatown* as a factual account of water development in California makes as much sense as watching John Wayne movies to understand the history of the West.

William Mulholland, born in Belfast, Ireland, in 1855 and raised amid the lush greenery of Dublin, signed on as a sailor aboard a merchant ship at age fifteen. After arriving in New York City in the early 1870s, he worked odd jobs in places ranging from lumber camps in Michigan to mines in Arizona. He walked across Panama to save train fare, fought the Apache for pay, and ended up in Los Angeles working as a ditch-tender cleaning conduits clogged with debris. He read Shakespeare by the light of a coal-oil lamp late into the night, and though he hadn't graduated from grade school, Mulholland kept maps and details of the city's entire water system in his head. His keen mind and sharp work ethic earned him the attention of Fred Eaton.

Eaton, a native son of Los Angeles and precociously smart, taught himself hydraulic engineering, and by age twenty he was superintendent of the privately owned Los Angeles City Water Company. He groomed Mulholland to take his place and left the company to pursue his political ambitions. Charming and urbane, Eaton was elected mayor of Los Angeles in 1898. He ended private control of the city's water supply by creating what eventually became the nation's largest municipal utility, the Los Angeles Department of Water and Power. Mulholland was retained to head the department, largely because he had kept no written records of the city's water system—the critical information was stored solely in his memory.

California's southern half is bathed almost continuously in sun beneath a zone of high pressure that diverts storms northward. Los Angeles, with no timber or minerals, no port or navigable river, and with really no reason other than a pleasant climate to evolve beyond a little desert town with wooden water pipes and rickety waterwheels rattled by earthquakes, was spurred to grow by the arrival of a train line and an aggressive chamber of commerce. William H. Kahrl, in *Water and Power*, writes, "By the end of the nineteenth century [Los Angeles's business leaders] had succeeded, through puffery, advertising, and sheer force of will, in laying the foundation for a modern city in a spot where God clearly never intended large numbers of people to live."

Mulholland warned that the city would either need to stop expanding or find more water as it swelled. It was building its future on groundwater from a shrinking aquifer that would eventually be sucked dry. The Los Angeles River, which overran its banks a few weeks every year and then shallowed to a thin trickle, offered no relief. Hemmed in by deserts and ocean, the sun-blessed city could tap no nearby sources of freshwater, and its wells started bringing up sand.

For more than a decade, Fred Eaton had been scheming to divert water from the Owens Valley, located between the high peaks of the Sierra Nevada and the broiled wastes of Death Valley. He was convinced that moving the water to Los Angeles from the Owens River, nearly 250 miles away, would make him rich.

After collecting snowmelt from the steep walls of the Sierra Nevada's eastern slope, the Owens River swelled with runoff as it spilled toward the valley floor. Before spending itself in the glistening salt basin of Owens Lake, the river nourished the farms and ranches of settlers who had dug irrigation canals to water their crops. One resident remembered the bucolic valley this way: "The orchards were loaded with luscious peaches, pears, plums, and apples, and the arbors hung heavy with ripening grapes." Another resident spoke of skies crowded with ducks, which when shot down "would burst open from fatness which was butter yellow." Before these white settlers arrived with their fences and water laws to displace the native people who had lived in the valley for centuries, Paiutes had built little dams and dug ditches, diverting water to grow food.

The Owens Valley sits at an elevation of four thousand feet; its water could flow through a gravity-fed aqueduct to Los Angeles, located near sea level. No power would be needed to pump the water, and there was a lot of it—enough to allow Los Angeles to expand into the metropolis Eaton and other boosters envisioned. Mulholland had promoted water conservation and had tried to persuade Los Angeles to live within the limits of its natural supply, but his efforts had been stymied by a city determined to grow. Mulholland finally agreed to take the river from the Owens Valley, knowing it would involve more than a little skullduggery.

The newly formed Reclamation Service was planning a project in the Owens Valley to increase irrigation, which would provide local residents with an agricultural windfall. For Los Angeles to get the water it wanted, the city would have to put a stop to this project. What followed may not have been theft, technically. But to say it was a little shady is like saying an atomic bomb blast makes a bit of light and noise.

The Reclamation Service had one of its agents stationed in the Owens Valley, a man who, unbeknownst to Reclamation Service leaders, was in cahoots with Eaton. Eaton put him on the city's payroll to help secure the water of the Owens Valley. This double agent of the coming water war passed surveys compiled by the Reclamation Service along to Eaton. And Eaton himself went to the valley to study crucial deeds and records under the pretense of doing work for the Reclamation Service; then he began buying up water rights and land, telling everyone in town he wanted to get into the ranching business and not bothering to disabuse them of the notion that he was acting on behalf of the federal government to move forward its irrigation project for the good of the valley.

Los Angeles, through a combination of regular purchases and bribery, soon owned the land and water rights necessary to subvert the Reclamation Service's irrigation plan in the valley and build its own aqueduct. A headline in the *Los Angeles Times* trumpeted TITANIC PROJECT TO GIVE CITY A RIVER. A headline in an Owens Valley newspaper wailed LOS ANGELES PLOTS DESTRUCTION, WOULD TAKE OWENS RIVER, LAY LANDS WASTE, RUIN PEOPLE, HOMES, AND COMMUNITIES.

Not only had the residents of the Owens Valley been swindled, people in Los Angeles were made to believe by Eaton and Mulholland that if Los Angeles didn't get control of the Owens River, the city would shrivel and fade. The truth, however, was that most of the water from the Owens Valley was slated to be used for irrigating the San Fernando Valley, located north of Los Angeles, and at the time not part of the city. A syndicate of private investors, made up of tycoons and power brokers whom Eaton had tipped off that water would soon transform the valley, had been buying up parcels of worthless San Fernando land. They stood to make fortunes once the water flowed. And when a bond issue to finance the aqueduct came up for debate in 1905, this group of Los Angeles oligarchs used all manner of malfeasance to make sure it passed. One of the members of the syndicate, Eaton's close friend Harrison Gray Otis, was the publisher of the *Los Angeles Times*. The paper ran sensationalistic scare stories about drought and manipulated water shortage statistics to build support for the bond. Mulholland's enemies accused him of secretly dumping water from reservoirs at night to make it seem as if the city's water supplies were in peril, but the bond measure was approved by voters in a landslide.

When a bill to grant Los Angeles the rights of way across federal lands for its aqueduct ran into trouble in Congress, California senator Frank Flint went to the White House. He convinced President Roosevelt and his advisor, Gifford Pinchot, head of the Forest Service, that the water in the Owens River would be put to better use in the vibrant city of Los Angeles than in the dull orchards of the Owens Valley. Roosevelt, claiming his decision was "the greatest good for the greatest number," cancelled the irrigation project planned by the Reclamation Service. Then he went even further and added most of the Owens Valley, conspicuously empty of trees, to Inyo National Forest. The forest preserve locked up land that wasn't already owned by Los Angeles, preventing Owens Valley residents from developing farmland and claiming water rights. This ensured that Los Angeles could do as it wished with the Owens River. By executive decision of the famous trustbuster Theodore Roosevelt, water would flow away from the small farms and ranches of a rural community, toward the money and power of a budding megalopolis on California's coast.

With the city bond in place and with the blessing of the federal government, Mulholland launched in 1908 a project of incredible scope. One of the great engineering feats of the day, the undertaking required an army of thousands to create a manmade river through waterless mountains. Itinerant laborers walked to the worksite in the Mojave Desert with their bedding strapped to their backs. Blasting tunnels through walls of rock with record-breaking speed, they endured triple-digit heat during the day, bone-chilling cold at night. The vast waterworks system required its own roads be built, along with networks of power lines and railroad tracks. The steel pipe of the aqueduct was big enough to hold locomotives and had to be dragged by teams of mules because the most powerful motorized tractors of the day weren't up to the task. The workers and the livestock were always thirsty; supplying them with enough drinking water to survive the desert heat and dryness was a constant struggle.

The 233-mile-long Los Angeles Aqueduct was completed in 1913. At the opening ceremony, as water from the Owens River cascaded down the stone steps of a sluiceway in the San Fernando Valley, the people of Los Angeles crowded around the aqueduct to dip tin cups into the flow and taste the precious water.

With its new supply, Los Angeles was assured a place as one of the West's most dominant cities. Its dusty landscape burst with imported palm trees and glowed with green gardens and citrus groves. A building boom fueled by the water seizure allowed Los Angeles to swell beyond its boundaries and annex surrounding communities that wanted to drink from its aqueduct. At night the lights of the bloated metropolis blotted all but the brightest stars.

Though Los Angeles had doubled in population from the time construction of the aqueduct began, the city only needed to draw a small portion of the flow from the Owens River. Eaton's cabal, however, needed the water to flow to the San Fernando Valley so they could realize a fat return on their investment. Mulholland used the water rights Los Angeles had acquired and the giant aqueduct it had constructed, financed by the taxpayers of Los Angeles, to divert the river into the bank accounts of some of the city's richest and most powerful citizens. Croplands in the Owens Valley turned to desert while the San Fernando Valley, annexed by Los Angeles, grew bright with peaches and lemons. Then the orchards were plowed under with tract homes as the real estate values skyrocketed. Acquaintances of Eaton who had purchased land in the San Fernando Valley grew fabulously wealthy; farmers in the Owens Valley fell to ruin as their river ran dry.

The people of Owens Valley make sympathetic victims, but in reality they had done a fine job of drying up the river themselves before Mulholland got to it. Inefficient irrigation practices by local farmers had turned many of the valley's fields to salty swamps and had emptied the river during the driest days of summer. But citizens of the Owens Valley did not take kindly to Los Angeles removing water from their river. What really riled them was that the city was draining their irrigation ditches not for its drinking water but for its own irrigation scheme in the San Fernando Valley.

After the aqueduct was completed, Mulholland at first managed to leave enough flow in the Owens River for locals to continue farming and ranching. But drought and explosive population growth in Los Angeles spurred Mulholland to begin ruthlessly buying up more land and water rights in the valley. His agents divided ranchers and played them against each other, turning the Owens Valley into "a hotbed of suspicions, prejudices, and hatreds" as Los Angeles prepared to drain what remained of the Owens River. Some valley residents decided they'd had enough and dynamited a spillway gate of the aqueduct. Mulholland, when asked about dissatisfaction with his practices in the valley, quipped that he "half-regretted the demise of so many of the valley's orchard trees, because now there were no longer enough trees to hang all the troublemakers who live there."

When defiant ranchers illegally irrigated their fields, Mulholland ordered their waterworks demolished. A posse of armed locals held the Los Angeles crew at gunpoint and dumped its equipment into the river. But then the majority of these rebels responded to the higher prices Mulholland offered and sold their water rights to Los Angeles. It is tempting to turn the Owens Valley conflict into a simple tale of virtuous rural people defending their water against a corrupt and bullying city. But violent resistance in the valley had less to do with preserving the river than it did with extracting the highest possible price for water rights from Los Angeles.

In November 1924, seventy Owens Valley men seized control of aqueduct gates and sealed them shut, preventing water from leaving the valley, directing the river back into its age-old bed. A local sheriff confronted two carloads of armed city police sent by Los Angeles and talked them out of trying to wrest control of the aqueduct gates from the renegades, who were joined by seven hundred of their friends. They picnicked beneath a haze of barbecue smoke. A movie star who was in the area shooting a film sent over an orchestra to play for the merrymaking mob. The governor of California refused to use the state militia to restore order. The water war made national and international news as reporters traveled from places as far away as Paris to report on the ruckus. Newspapers took the side of the valley ranchers and painted Los Angeles as a water vampire and a villain. Even the *Los Angeles Times* expressed sympathy for them in an editorial.

Having made their point to a wide audience, the valley residents relinquished control of the aqueduct gates, and no shots were fired. But a few years later, after a state assembly committee hearing held in Sacramento to investigate disagreements between valley residents and Los Angeles erupted in a fistfight on the assembly chamber floor, the conflict escalated. In an act Los Angeles labeled as sabotage but almost everyone in the Owens Valley saw as self-defense, valley ranchers blew a section of the Los Angeles Aqueduct to shards and smoke. The following months saw more attacks on the waterworks as masked bandits rode at night. Mulholland sent private detectives with Winchesters and tommy guns to the valley and issued orders to shoot to kill anyone hanging around the aqueduct. Yet siphons and gates continued to explode in the dark stillness beneath the stars. Mulholland dispatched a trainload of guards carrying sawed-off shotguns, and searchlights swept back and forth across the aqueduct at night. By day bandits hid in the hills with caches of dynamite, their deeds heroic in the folklore of the valley.

The Owens Valley War came to an abrupt and uneventful end when the Owens Valley Bank collapsed. The men in charge of the bank, prominent citizens of the valley and leaders of the resistance to Mulholland's water grab, were convicted of embezzlement and fraud. Organized opposition in the Owens Valley unraveled as the men were sent to prison. Los Angeles city workcrews bulldozed farmhouses and filled in irrigation ditches, and the valley's orchards were replaced by sagebrush and sand. The war was over. Mulholland had won. He had snatched water from settlers who had plundered it from the Paiutes. Los Angeles drained the river, and Owens Lake dried up.

～⌣

Mulholland wanted more. He watched the political maneuvering over the All-American Canal and Arthur Powell Davis's dam proposal with the intensity of a desert nomad who has spied a glint of wetness in distant sands. Sticking a pipeline in the dammed Colorado would provide additional water for a city that had grown by almost 600 percent in two decades.

The aqueduct to supply Los Angeles with Colorado River water would be longer even than the one that drained the Owens Valley, and diversion dams and pumping stations to lift the flow over mountains would be needed. Gravity pulls water down mountain slopes, but in the West, it has often been said, water flows uphill toward money. "The value of our homes, businesses, and the security of our jobs all depend upon an ample water supply," yelled a 1928 film intended to stir up support for the aqueduct. "If we are to survive and to grow, we must have the water that will enable us to maintain our mastery of the desert!"

But even with all its new wealth, Los Angeles couldn't afford to build such massive infrastructure. The city joined forces with nearby communities to create the Metropolitan Water District of Southern California to supply more water to the state's southern coastal plain. Now Los Angeles, twenty-six other agencies in Southern California, and the Imperial Valley were pushing with Davis to dam and redistribute through a maze of aqueducts the flow of the Colorado. The momentum was at this point unstoppable as California's cash and political power shoved Davis's dream forward.

The mighty dam Davis had envisioned was built, but his yeoman farmer was nowhere to be found. What replaced the Jeffersonian ideal of independent men working the land with the sweat of their brows, sustained by simple values born from the modest patches of frontier they farmed, were the behemoths of big government and big business. Davis's uncle, that prophet in a parched land, had warned a nation dead set on building a boundless civilization in the desert that these things would be its doom.

CHAPTER 4

The Law of the River

TASTE A GLASS OF TAP WATER IN DENVER; STAND BENEATH A SHOWER-head in Salt Lake City; watch a fountain spit into the sky in Las Vegas; splash in a pool in Phoenix; listen to a toilet flush in Los Angeles; dig into a meal in Mexicali. All this is made possible by the Colorado River. From its headwaters cradled in mountain snows atop the Continental Divide, the river stretches some 1,450 miles and drops some fourteen thousand feet before it reaches the sea—or rather, it would reach the sea if anything were left of it. Taxed by human use, the ruddy giant swells in the desert reservoirs of the Southwest and is sucked to a salty trickle that dribbles across a scabbed delta in Mexico. Though it is much shorter than the Mississippi and carries far less volume than the Columbia, the Colorado distributes more water to users—thirty million of them in the United States and Mexico—than any other river system in North America. Cities and farming areas outside its basin have built enormous canals and conduits to siphon its fluid, in the process laying claim to a percentage of its flow. The Colorado River is relied upon by western agribusinesses and metropolises with few other options to find water. Every drop has been promised to someone, and more drops have been promised than the river holds. This scarcity has brewed trouble, turning the Colorado into the world's most heavily litigated river—ensuring a surplus of work for lawyers.

The voluminous body of compacts, treaties, legislation, regulations, and court decisions generated by controversy surrounding this overused watercourse is termed the "Law of the River." In the West, it is the Ten

Commandments and the US Constitution rolled into one—only far more serious. The story of how the Law of the River came into being is told by straight-faced Westerners with steady voices as something like Moses coming down the mountain bearing the tablets, or the signing of the Declaration of Independence.

In the American West, a place where the stories in the pages of blood-and-thunder pulp and on the silver screen have created a world of images and ideas separate from the mountains and plains and the people who populate them, the Colorado River often takes on larger-than-life status. Its physical reality becomes layered with lore. And so too the Law of the River, laden with historical complexity and overflowing with high drama, can seem less a series of legalities that control the flow of water and more the product of a playwright trying to capture in dozens of frenzied acts the workings of human power, hubris, and greed.

In a speech before Congress, one of Arizona's first senators declared, "To become a paradise we need only two things. . . . We need water, and we need lots of good people." A senator from New England retorted, "If the distinguished gentleman will pardon me for saying so, that's all they need in hell."

The Law of the River begins with the Imperial Valley's rise and the rapid growth of Los Angeles, a city dubbed by historian Norris Hundley Jr. "the West's most notorious water hustler." Political leaders throughout the Colorado River Basin watched the goings-on in Southern California as the Imperial Valley and Los Angeles scrambled to secure water supplies, and Arthur Powell Davis's plan to develop the river, with great concern. States in the upper Colorado River Basin were particularly worried—they were poised for growth and didn't want states in the lower basin establishing priority rights to use the river, leaving their own cities dry in the coming decades. Denver, the little cow town east of the Continental Divide in Colorado, a dusty outpost busy with brothels, saloons, and gambling halls, had emerged as the "Queen City of the Plains," doubling its population in two decades. Like Los Angeles, Denver lay outside the drainage basin of the Colorado River but wanted a share of its water.

In 1922 the US Interior Department issued a report recommending construction of an All-American Canal that would divert nearly one-fifth of the water in the Colorado River to the Imperial Valley, a dam to corral the river's flow at Boulder Canyon or some nearby site, and the development of hydroelectric power to help finance the gargantuan project.

The Colorado runs through land that leans steeply downward—the river's gradient is ten times as steep as that of the Mississippi. This sheer drop, which had carved some of the most stunning canyons on the planet and rendered the river worthless for transportation, made engineers swoon. Water could back up to lofty elevations behind skyscraping dams, providing magnificent amounts of what engineers call "hydraulic head": The tremendous pressure could spin turbines faster than any other river in America. The narrow clefts of the Colorado's canyons would store deep bodies of water with small surface areas that would lose relatively little moisture to evaporation. The solid rock of sites such as Boulder Canyon, its walls chiseled and sheared by the violence of time, would support the abutments of bulky dams and provide sealed basins for reservoirs. There were no towns in the rugged terrain that would have to be relocated when the area was inundated. Perhaps most important, bringing the willful Colorado under control would be the ultimate expression of America's ability to rearrange the natural world to meet the needs of people. A Boulder Canyon bill (also known as the Swing-Johnson Bill) was quickly introduced in Congress to make the Interior Department's recommendations a reality. But states in the upper reaches of the river basin fought it like cornered wolverines.

In 1922 the US Supreme Court, in *Wyoming v. Colorado*, determined that prior appropriation was not affected by state boundaries. Thus a fast-growing state like California could put Colorado River water to beneficial use and claim priority rights to continue using it, depriving slower-growing states, such as Colorado and Wyoming, the right to access its flow—even though most of the water originates in the Rockies. Determined to put a stop to California's water grab, states upriver implored Congress to stall reclamation projects on the lower Colorado until they could secure water for the cities they hoped would fill with people and pavement and light.

Delph Carpenter, a Colorado lawyer experienced in water litigation, called for an interstate compact: a negotiated agreement between states that must be made with the consent of Congress—according to the Interstate Compact Clause of the US Constitution. A compact to apportion water had never been tried. To some it seemed a radical idea. Carpenter thought a compact necessary because litigation, in his estimation, was too time-consuming and costly, and it rarely resolved water disputes satisfactorily. Along with his practical concerns was an ideological one. He worried that if the states failed to sort out their water conflicts themselves, the federal government would intervene and control the region's water supply. Carpenter wanted the states to work out a Colorado River compact to lessen the likelihood of the federal government infringing on their water rights. This kind of concern over the government meddling in the affairs of the West, this keep-your-hands-off-our-stuff attitude, evolved long before Carpenter came onto the scene and is still prevalent in the region today. The issue of states' rights has always been a hot one in the West, along with another stance toward Washington: demanding that it build projects with federal tax dollars. This ambivalence toward the federal government's relationship with the West's resources and economy is one of the defining features of the region's political landscape. Western politicians are expected by their constituents to berate meddlesome Washington bureaucrats while at the same time bringing home the federal bacon.

The legislatures of all the Colorado River Basin states heeded Carpenter's call, and Congress agreed to help negotiate a compact. Herbert Hoover, an engineer by training and the secretary of commerce at the time, chaired the sessions that forged the details of the compact controlling the Colorado's flow. The states spent most of 1922 squabbling, each trying to maximize the amount of water it would be allowed to use. Eventually the delegates, unable to negotiate specific volumes of water for each state, settled on dividing the Colorado's flow between upper and lower sections of the Colorado River Basin. This wasn't ideal, as it left a lot of room for future conflict between individual states within the two basins. Arizona's delegate complained that the approach "doesn't arrive at any conclusion, and . . . it leaves the two divisions to work out their own salvation."

But the delegates were eager to reach accord: California wanted an agreement that would satisfy Congress so the federal government would start building projects that would deliver water to its sprawling cities and farms; Colorado and the other states upstream wanted an agreement that would protect a share of the water for their own use. The delegates decided that dividing the river into two basins would go a long way toward resolving major disputes.

A line was drawn through the river at Lee's Ferry, an old river-crossing site in northern Arizona near the border with Utah. The only area of the Colorado River easily accessible between a labyrinth of canyons and lofty plateaus, and located roughly halfway between the river's origin and its terminus, Lee's Ferry was chosen as a political boundary to split the river in half. Above Lee's Ferry was designated the "Upper Basin"; below it was labeled the "Lower Basin." Though some states had small pieces sliced by the line, the majority of Colorado, Wyoming, New Mexico, and Utah were in the Upper Basin; the Lower Basin contained the bulk of Arizona, Nevada, and California.

All parties agreed to apportion the river into 7.5 million acre-feet (maf) per year for each basin.[5] Basically, California and the other Lower Basin states were agreeing to reserve almost half of the Colorado's flow for the Upper Basin states. There was a catch, however. During long stretches of wet years when the river ran full, the Upper Basin states could meet their obligation to deliver water to the Lower Basin states without a problem; but during a long dry spell when the river ran low

---

5 An acre-foot is the amount of water that will cover one acre, roughly the size of a football field, to the depth of one foot. An acre-foot is equal to about 326,000 gallons and is generally considered enough to meet the annual needs of two families of four.

for several years, the Upper Basin states would still have to fulfill their delivery obligation—even if doing so meant there wasn't enough water left for them to satisfy their own needs. As pointed out by law professor Robert Adler, if the Upper Basin states had been required to deliver half of all *available* water in the river, instead of some fixed amount, the effects of a protracted drought would have been distributed *equally* between the two basins. But the system devised in the compact placed the burden of drought *disproportionately* on the Upper Basin. At the time this seemed a trivial technicality; several decades later it would loom as a problem so large it would lead to the construction of one of the biggest and most controversial water projects in the West: The problem would be fixed not by crafting a new regulatory framework but by building a wall of solid concrete across the river.

During compact negotiations, no one wasted time worrying that the Colorado River would one day not carry enough water to satisfy all the demands placed upon it. The volume of water apportioned by the compact was based on a Reclamation Service estimate that pegged the average annual flow of the Colorado at Lee's Ferry at 16.4 maf. This figure was derived from records that spanned 1899 to 1920, a mere blip in hydrologic time, and a period that scientists now know was a moist anomaly—one of the wettest periods of the past 450 years. The state delegates, all eager to complete a compact, didn't question the methodology used to determine the figure, which after the apportionments for the basins had been divvied out, still left a hefty surplus. But the figure was based on a twenty-one-year sample of a river that had been flowing for more than five million years. This was like taking a snapshot of an escarpment from a foot away and assuming the image represents canyonlands that stretch for hundreds of miles in all directions. The inaccuracy of the figure would later cause conflict when the river, in the second half of the twentieth century and the beginning of the twenty-first century, reverted to a lower flow more consistent with its average across the ages, and the states realized that the Colorado was not as large as their water needs.

Herbert Hoover succinctly summed up the feeling of the states and federal government regarding the water rights of Mexicans: "We do not believe they ever had any rights." Likewise, the water rights of Native Americans who lived in the Colorado River Basin were labeled "negligible" and a provision stated, "Nothing in this compact shall be construed as affecting the obligations of the United States of America to Indian tribes." Allocations of water for Mexico and Native Americans, ignored during compact negotiations, would later pose critical challenges to the Law of the River.

Nevertheless, on November 24, 1922, the delegates signed the compact at Santa Fe's plush Palace of the Governors. And thus was created the first and most important piece of the interlocking water puzzle that is the Law of the River.

A congratulatory spirit was in the air at the signing in Santa Fe, but it dissipated soon after the delegates returned home. Within five months the compact was ratified by all the states save one. Arizona's reluctance to sign threatened the entire compact, which required unanimous approval. Arizona governor George Hunt's flamboyant refusal to compromise with other states over use of the Colorado earned him reelection to a fourth term, prompting Arizonans to quip, "Jesus may have walked on water, but Arizona has a governor who ran on the Colorado River." Hoover referred to him as that "blunderbuss of a governor in Arizona, who knew nothing of engineering." Governor Hunt argued that because the Colorado River ran along or through Arizona for nearly half its length, his state was entitled to most of its water, and he lambasted the failure of the compact to divide water between individual states.

The compact suspended prior appropriation between the Upper Basin and Lower Basin but did nothing to alleviate the conflict between states within basins, which worried Arizona. And Arizona's pugnacious governor didn't see anything for his state in the bill allowing Davis's Boulder Canyon Dam—while California stood to gain a great deal. The dam would allow the Metropolitan Water District of Southern California to tap the controlled flow of the Colorado so Los Angeles could build itself into a behemoth. Arizona, too, had big plans for development. It saw the compact and the Boulder Canyon bill authorizing construction of the canal and dam as benefiting the Upper Basin and California while choking off the flow it would need to water its own dreams. Arizona also worried that the dam-regulated Colorado would allow Mexico to expand its agriculture, and then a future treaty could acknowledge the nation's prior appropriation and divert from Arizona more of the river. The Upper Basin, California, Mexico: Arizona saw threats to its water supply on all sides, and the cantankerous state was about as happy with the compact and the Boulder Canyon bill as it would be years later with daylight saving time and Martin Luther King Jr. Day.

The other six basin states, anxious to ratify the compact, revisited their requirement of unanimity. Moving forward to ratify the compact without Arizona's support, while not ideal, seemed preferable to doing nothing. All the states save California approved the six-party agreement. Californians wanted assurance that the Boulder Canyon project would move forward. Once Congress authorized the construction of the dam and the All-American Canal, California would agree to the six-state compact.

In 1925 the Boulder Canyon bill was reintroduced in Congress with the compact attached to it. While many in the East groused about financing costly water projects in the West, and private power companies wailed about the cheap power the dam would provide, putting them out of business, the bill stalled.

Arizona and California were given more time to work out a solution between themselves—as easy as nailing water to a wall. Water politics may seem complicated, but just about everything you need to know about how water in the West came to be divided among squabbling factions can be learned on a school playground, by watching children maneuvering for power. After two years of negotiations, Arizona and California failed to come up with a solution. The exasperated Upper Basin states finally agreed to support the bill—under the condition that California promise to limit its use of water from the Colorado River. The Upper Basin clique worried that in the absence of such a limit, California would take as much Lower Basin water as it wanted, leaving Arizona dry. And then Arizona, in desperation, might try to snatch water away from the Upper Basin by building projects of its own.

California grudgingly agreed to limit its use. Though Arizona continued to complain about being bullied, Congress approved the Boulder Canyon bill in late 1928. And in the early summer of 1929, President Herbert Hoover declared the legislation effective, making the Colorado River Compact official and clearing the way for construction of a great wall of concrete, its smooth surface brilliant in the desert sun.

CHAPTER 5

Dam Nation

IT WAS 1931. WALL STREET HAD COLLAPSED, AND MASSES OF THE unemployed queued in breadlines. But thirty miles from the sleepy little railroad town of Las Vegas, Nevada, a monumental effort was underway, intended not only to domesticate the wild Colorado and harness it for power, but also to restore the Bureau of Reclamation's reputation and lift the spirits of a downtrodden nation. Amid sands of barren desert, America was rebuilding belief in itself by constructing the largest dam on earth.[6]

No single private company had the resources to create the colossal structure. Firms joined together in a consortium called Six Companies to take on the monumental task. Constructing the biggest dam ever built by anyone, anywhere, meant jobs. Lots of jobs. Armies of the unemployed with their families in tow flooded the desert before the project began. They came in cars if they had them; they came on foot. They came with everything they owned, hoping for a chance to reconstruct their lives. Squatters who massed in the desert by the thousands pieced together a makeshift village. Dubbed "Ragtown," it sprawled along the banks of the Colorado. At night its inhabitants clustered around fires with flames that sawed the chilly air; by day they baked inside tents. The temperature in their sun-stricken encampment consistently climbed to 120 degrees, and it soared as high as 143 during a period of record-breaking heat. The

---

6 Confusingly, the dam was built in Black Canyon but was called Boulder Canyon Dam or Boulder Dam and was later renamed Hoover Dam.

air shimmered and the world warped in this fevered land. Desert cliffs and boulders seemed to wobble and bend, as if viewed through bad glass. Food spoiled. Mothers swaddled their babies in wet sheets to cool them. Men clawed at riverbanks in search of water beneath the mud and sand. Dysentery spread through the camp, where the only toilets were reeking trenches powdered with lime. From this rude metropolis emerged a store. A baker and a barber. A church opened its doors, and then a school. A post office. A newspaper that chronicled life in the town began circulating. Sandy ruts widened to become named roads. Like the mountain gold camps and boomtowns that had appeared virtually overnight from a hint of yellow metal, Ragtown burgeoned in a heartbeat from the promise of jobs. Hungry masses packed themselves into ramshackle hovels, making soup of whatever food scraps they could scrounge. Scorpions arched their jointed tails as their prey of spiders and centipedes squirmed in their pinchers. The bare feet of boys and girls pressed into the mud of the riverbanks as they explored their new world and spied on its strange creatures, its hopping kangaroo rats and skittery lizards that slithered past their toes. While children with empty bellies played, their mothers tended homes made of cardboard and tin and their fathers trudged toward the dam site in search of jobs.

The Hoover Dam high scalers were steel-nerved men in bosun's chairs that hung suspended from ropes of braided hemp hundreds of feet above the floor of Black Canyon. Blasting walls with dynamite and then using crowbars to pry off the stones that shook loose, the high scalers smoothed rock faces where the concrete dam would join the cliffs. Like circus acrobats, they swung back and forth, ropes and harnesses holding them as they danced from site to site in a crazy vertical world of canyon walls. Using jackhammers they drilled holes and stuffed them with sticks of dynamite; they dodged away from the explosions and then pendulumed back to scrape off flaking stones that tumbled toward the void below. The high scalers were not issued hard hats. To protect themselves from rocks raining down from above, they made their own head protection: cloth hats coated with hot coal tar that cooled to hardened shells. Though all this dynamiting and dangling in empty space with rocks hurtling down was intensely dangerous, scaling was perhaps a better gig than many others. The high scalers could, at least, breathe. The tunnelers were not so fortunate. They gagged on noxious fumes, and their eardrums cracked from the noise.

Some of the laborers at the dam site died in explosions and rock falls and in deadly spells of heat that split apart the linings of their throats and turned their blood to putty. The workers' disgruntlement with the dangerous conditions swelled until they went on strike, demanding safer working environments and decent housing with adequate drinking water.

Strikebreakers with clubs and guns descended on the site, and within a week the standoff ended. Summer's blast-furnace temperatures cooled in autumn, and tempers too seemed to simmer down. The government built Boulder City for the workers and their families, replacing the squalid shanties of Ragtown with a settlement of cottages that offered some measure of dignity and comfort. Running water, electricity, the green grass of public lawns: Boulder City had amenities that lifted the spirits of the beleaguered laborers struggling to raise a mammoth curtain of concrete in the desert.

To create a dry dam site, two cofferdams were built of gravel, sand, and rock. One was located upstream from the worksite, the other downstream, and the space between them was drained with pumps. The river, blocked by the upstream cofferdam, flowed into diversion tunnels that emptied out below the downstream cofferdam. To gouge the diversion tunnels into solid rock, gasoline-powered trucks and machinery chugged through stone passageways, flooding them with carbon monoxide that sickened men whose fate it was to breathe poisons while they burrowed through the gloom. The tipsy high wire act of the scalers, whose death loomed below them as they swung in the fresh air, seemed pleasant by comparison. Some men drilled in dank tunnels; others mucked debris from the floors. To prepare a solid foundation for the dam, some workers scraped the silty riverbed down to bare rock, scorpions crunching under their boots, eyes stinging with sweat and dust as they worked in the suffocating canyon. Some men ran electricity through cables; some poured freshly batched concrete into giant wooden forms.

The more than three million cubic yards of concrete needed to build the dam—enough to pave a two-lane highway from San Francisco to New York City—required two mixing plants to be built at the site, the construction of a railway that ran nine trains with specially designed cars, and the invention of an intricate system of aerial cableways that transported twenty-ton steel buckets across the canyon and suspended them above the work zone.

Concrete, as it hardens, creates chemical reactions that generate heat. Had the concrete been poured all at once into one seamless slab, so much heat would have been generated that more than a century would have elapsed before it completely cooled, slumping, cracking, and crumbling all the while. Engineers figured out that they could pour small batches of concrete into blocks, stacking these atop each other as they worked their way upward—more than thirty thousand blocks in all. But even these blocks would stay hot too long and crack as they slowly cooled, so a refrigeration plant was built on site and steel pipes were placed in the concrete to circulate chilled water.

Block by block, column by column, section by section, the dam rose to towering height as workcrews clambered back and forth and up and down in a brutal ballet on scaffolding and catwalks and rickety lifts. Rumors of workers entombed in the dam's concrete linger to this day, though these are myths and nothing more. The structural imperfection caused by a soft human body lodged in the hard concrete would have weakened the dam, which engineers would not allow.

The pace of construction was pushed relentlessly forward by chief field engineer Frank Crowe—known as "Hurry-Up Crowe"—and the dam was completed two years ahead of schedule. While Lake Mead filled behind the concrete wall, the rising waters covered Ragtown, and the remnants of the tent camp vanished beneath a reservoir such as the world had never seen. On September 30, 1935, the dam was dedicated by President Franklin Roosevelt, who declared, "This morning I came, I saw and I was conquered, as everyone would be who sees for the first time this great feat of mankind."

The official death count when the dam was completed reached 112—though many tunnel workers with lungs poisoned by carbon monoxide were diagnosed with pneumonia by company doctors so the company wouldn't have to pay compensation claims. These men were deemed to have died from "natural causes" and weren't added to the official tally.

Hoover Dam combined the principles of both an arch dam and a gravity dam. Bending upstream toward the great pressure of the water it holds back, the curved crest of the concrete arch is squeezed and compressed, strengthening the structure as it transmits the water load to the canyon wall abutments. The dam also resists the force of the water pressure with gravity, which pulls the massive structure toward its base—thicker than the lengths of two football fields. Put simply, the weight of the dam keeps it from tipping over.

The decision about what type of dam to build is a product of psychology as well as engineering principles. Arch dams can be built of slender slabs because the shape of the structure provides such strength. But the sight of these startlingly thin eggshell walls holding back floods can be disturbing to the public. Hoover's appearance of massive permanence due to the thick wall of its gravity dam design, combined with the reassuring curve of its arched construction, was believed to inspire the public's confidence as it gazed upon this modern wonder of the world.

When completed, Hoover Dam stood at 726 feet, taller than a sixty-story building, twice as high as the record holder it had surpassed when it earned the superlative of world's tallest dam. It contained more material than the Great Pyramid at Giza. Its weight was such that it deformed the crust of the earth and could generate its own earthquakes.

After the dam's diversion gates were closed, the wild river that had once carried Powell's dories on bucking currents was replaced by a tamed flow metered through valves. Americans journeyed to the desert to stare awestruck at the dam and the caged lake it held. They stood atop the airy crest peering down into the canyon at the steady churn of water exiting the tailrace. Destitute and nagged by fading hope, they gazed at this concrete miracle in the wilderness and felt their faith restored. T. S. Eliot referred to the Mississippi River as a "strong brown god—sullen, untamed and untractable." Though the Colorado carried only one-thirtieth the flow of the Mississippi, it was far wilder, crashing through canyons along its rambunctious course. The Colorado writhed like a red beast, carving the desert with restless thrashings. But now it lay stilled in a slack pool, its sinewy brawn held in check by a dam rising tall as a skyscraper in a wilderness no more.

Michael Hiltzik, in his book *Colossus: Hoover Dam and the Making of the American Century,* contends that the profound changes that occurred in America during the post–World War II period really began with Hoover Dam. When the dam was completed, the United States, in Hiltzik's words, "was transformed from a society that glorified individualism into one that cherished shared enterprise and communal social support." Though the project had been launched under the Republican administration of Herbert Hoover, President Roosevelt saw the dam as a tangible symbol of his New Deal, which he designed to counteract the nation's economic collapse. The dam generated jobs, provided cheap power and reliable irrigation water, and kept the public safe from ferocious natural forces. It served as the prototype for many public works projects to come. It also spawned global construction titans such as Bechtel and Morrison Knudsen, and it heralded an era of collaboration between the federal government and private industry to remake the West's watercourses on a staggering scale.

The dam's facade, with its minimal ornamentation, its celebration of machine-age design in clean and soaring concrete lines, and its sculpted turrets that merged seamlessly with the bold planes of its face, was an exemplar of 1930s art deco style—the largest piece of public art on the planet. Winged bronze statues reaching heavenward atop the dam offered a narrative of triumph. Surely a nation that had erected something so magnificent would rise again. Certainly a country that could conquer the desert with a dam such as this was destined for greatness. Regardless of the cost of the dam in dollars and environmental detriment, it did wonders for the spirit of a cowed America. A symbol of rebirth sculpted in concrete, the megadam served as a source of wonder and pride when the nation desperately needed a boost. Bigger dams would be built, but few would ever be as important to the psyche of a nation.

⸺⸺

Aside from the opportunity to build Hoover Dam, the Bureau of Reclamation gained greatly from the Great Depression. President Roosevelt, eager to create jobs with public works projects, encouraged the Bureau to balloon into an enormous agency that fast-tracked dam after dam, ushering in what have become known as the "go-go years" of federal reclamation. As it became painfully clear to even the most ardent irrigation boosters that water projects couldn't pay for themselves and power-producing dams were the real future of the agency, private electric utilities and some politicians of a conservative bent fulminated against the projects. But the Bureau polished its promotional skills and sold reclamation as something the country sorely needed to create work and farms and growth. Most important, it reminded the nation that it had a mandate to control nature, to domesticate the West's wildlands by wringing water and power from its rivers.

The Dust Bowl, one of the greatest manmade catastrophes ever, furthered the drive to wrest control of the West from nature's arid grip. For the first three decades of the twentieth century, there had been enough moisture on the High Plains for farms to eke by. Cattle grazed the plains down to dead sod in places, and vast stretches of shortgrass prairie were converted to whiskered stalks of wheat. The root systems of the native grasses had evolved to hold the soil in place and trap moisture, even during times of high wind and no rain. But an ecosystem of bison and prairie plants that had developed through millennia of droughty weather was replaced with a moneymaking machine of water-dependent beef and wheat, the demand for which had risen dramatically during World War I. Intensively plowed fields were left bare in winter and their stubble was burned, allowing the crumbly soil to easily erode.

And then came the inevitable drought, and the wind. With nothing holding topsoil in place, sheets of it were peeled from the wounded ground and carried away in gusts. Dirty winds became increasingly abrasive as they gathered grit, forming avalanches of windborne dirt, building as they blew. The High Plains were scoured bare and an apocalypse of roiling black clouds filled the air. Skies turned dark as night, and dirt rode the jet stream all the way to Europe. Shafts of golden wheat crumbled like ash. Stock tanks overflowed with drifting soil. Piles of sand tilted fenceposts toward the ground, and dead trees creaked in the wind. People who didn't wear wet handkerchiefs across their mouths when they ventured outside risked choking to death on dust. Roaring gusts rattled shutters and banged doors of abandoned houses, and farm machinery sat rusting beneath a red sun that burned dimly in the haze-stricken sky.

Calamity forced the depopulation of the dry western plains as great hordes of humanity packed up everything they owned and fled the Dust Bowl. Ragged bands of nomads found their way to California's Great Central Valley, which stretches some 450 miles from the Sacramento River Valley in the north, beset by an overabundance of water that caused disastrous flooding, to the San Joaquin River Valley in the south, a fertile plain rarely dampened by rain. To the west of the wide-spreading Central Valley rises the Coast Range. The snow-slathered Sierra Nevada hover on the eastern edge.

Though there was little surface water for irrigation in the San Joaquin Valley—where most of the Okies who fled the Dust Bowl settled—an aquifer lay beneath the crackly soil. The farmers in the region sank wells deep into the thirsty earth and pumped it with abandon. Their fields turned green while the underground reserve of water shrank. Marshlands once visited by birds in clouds so dense they darkened the sky, and a savannah of scattered oaks and blonde grasses that had been crowded with tule elk and grizzly bears, were reduced to a few isolated remnants, like displays in a zoo.

The California legislature, loath to let agricultural wealth disappear as wells gulped the aquifer dry beneath the San Joaquin Valley, approved a mammoth irrigation plan in 1933. The Central Valley Project was designed to capture two-thirds of the state's runoff and relocate rivers of mountain snowmelt through many hundreds of miles of canals that snaked through desert lands. The project was byzantine in its complexity, staggering in its scope. Unable to finance the scheme because of the Great Depression, California encouraged the Bureau of Reclamation to take over. FDR turned it into the largest public works project in America. The flow of the San Joaquin River slackened as it was diverted toward fields, and chinook salmon with their blushed sides and savagely hooked jaws all but disappeared from the Sierra Nevada foothills. Canneries chained shut their doors as agricultural empires began a period of storied productivity.

By the time the Okies began pouring into the San Joaquin Valley, dams were being erected around California, altering the state's plumbing so that food and fiber could grow in dry lands and jobs could be created for the destitute. Shasta Dam, which blocked the upper Sacramento River and stalled its timeless flow, would stand taller than the Washington Monument. Armies of laborers were required to raise it. But so great was the mass of unemployed humanity in America, and so low were the nation's spirits, another monumental public works project was needed to generate jobs and to show the world that America was capable of achieving great things. FDR dreamed of a humongous dam holding back the waters of the West's greatest river—one that pushed more than ten times the flow of the Colorado through the channeled scablands of Washington State, a landscape carved by ancient floods when ice age dams burst apart.

No river as large as the Columbia had ever been impounded by people. Because of its steep gradient, tight canyons, and prodigious volume, the river's potential for hydroelectric power was enormous. The rich soils that surrounded Grand Coulee, which President Roosevelt and the Bureau of Reclamation were eyeing as a dam site, were perfect for agriculture. Most important to the president, he believed the elephantine dam would create many thousands of jobs through its construction and through the farmland it would bring into production.

As pointed out by historian Paul Pitzer in his book *Grand Coulee*, the local industrialists and politicians who spent many years promoting the project, though deeply resentful of the federal government's power to intrude in the affairs of states, reluctantly accepted that only the government could build a dam as big as the one they wanted.

The tremendous cost of such a project in a region populated by jackrabbits and rattlesnakes and a handful of farmers made Congress hesitant to finance the wildly ambitious enterprise. But the president had been given special powers to fund emergency projects that would help alleviate the national economic crisis. FDR allocated money for a dam, and a fifty-story wall nearly a mile long rose from the river's bed. Workers who had built Hoover Dam reeled at the size of it. Hailed as the Eighth Wonder of the World when it was completed in 1941, the dam contained enough concrete to build a sidewalk around the world's equator. All the pyramids of Giza could fit within its base, and to this day it is still the largest concrete structure in the United States. The dam put an end to the greatest runs of spawning salmon in America, pitching into steep decline the salmon-dependent cultures and economies of Native American tribes that harvested the fish with dipnets and spears. And by harnessing the energy of the flowing water, the dam generated more power than a million locomotives, providing the electricity to win World War II.

Airplanes by the thousands were needed to defeat Germany and Japan. Aluminum was used to manufacture the airplanes. It takes a lot of electricity to make aluminum. Ergo, every bit of the enormous surplus of hydroelectricity being produced by the Grand Coulee Dam (the small cities of the Northwest couldn't come close to consuming all of it) was used by the defense industry as warplanes rolled off assembly lines. The dam's generators chugged day and night, shaking the powerhouse as American pilots in aluminum planes did battle in the theaters of Europe and the Pacific. And when scientists swarmed to Los Alamos, New Mexico, to build the atomic bomb that would end the war, plutonium-239 was produced at the Hanford Nuclear Reservation, a secret government complex along the Columbia River in Washington. Creating plutonium-239, the material that allows atomic bombs to wreak widespread destruction, requires enormous amounts of energy. Hanford's plutonium production reactors were powered by Columbia River water.

Woody Guthrie fused genuine pride in American ingenuity with propaganda when the Bonneville Power Administration paid the unemployed folk singer to write a series of songs about the Grand Coulee

Dam. His lyrics immortalized it as "the mightiest thing ever built by a man." Along with the Grand Coulee Dam, other monumental dams rose throughout the West, including several megaprojects on the Columbia, and the Fort Peck Dam on the Missouri River in Montana—at the time the most massive structure in the world save the Great Wall of China. By the middle of the 1930s, five of the largest structures on earth were being built on the rivers of the western United States. In one of America's grimmest periods, as the economy crumbled and people lost confidence in themselves and their country, dams provided jobs and the hydropower needed to win the war. For all the criticism they now evoke, the breathtaking dams of the Great Depression years played an essential role in saving America from chaos and despair. Building them ushered in an era of rampant water project construction that has caused no end of problems. But to not have built the dams may have caused bigger problems. Not just the West but all of America profited from the era of great dams, for they were dreams made real in concrete and steel. Had America not realized those dreams, it would likely be a very different place today. It is easy to look at Hoover and Grand Coulee and see a river stilled, or a run of salmon extirpated. But the people who raised those dams, by their vision and their labor, helped stop the nation from slipping into an abyss so dark that no amount of wild beauty would have mattered.

Before the Wall Street Crash of 1929, row upon row of low-slung houses had been razed in New York City and from their ruins soaring towers were conceived. As the Empire State Building with its spire poking above America punctuated the confidence and prosperity the country enjoyed in the 1920s, so the concrete elevations of the West's great dams became emblematic of a downtrodden nation in the 1930s that had not lost all hope, a nation convinced it could rise again. The skyscrapers of Manhattan had been built with private capital by entrepreneurs when the economy was booming. The dams of the West, by contrast, were constructed as public works projects funded by the government when America was mired in the Depression. But after the nation's economy turned around following World War II, still the giant dams kept coming, one after another, dams by the dozens for several decades, and all of them financed by tax dollars.

~~~

The Corps of Engineers came late to the dam-building party in the West, but it was determined to join. The construction arm of the US Army, the Corps of Engineers is divided into two branches, one military, one civilian. The projects carried out by the civilian branch morphed from modest tasks such as clearing rivers of driftwood to redesigning waterways so that barges could float safely above their beds. While the Bureau was diverting the West's scant water so crops could grow in the desert, the Corps was drying out soggy land in the East so it could be farmed. Discouraging people from settling where there was either too much water or too little water was never part of the national discussion. America believed it could build anything, could engineer its way around nature's lethal scarcity and deadly overabundance. One of the main tasks of the Corps became flood control, which it initially pursued by building levees. The most effective way to prevent rivers from damaging property is, of course, to not allow development in floodplains. But to an agency made up of engineers, modifying human behavior to fit the natural world is antithetical to the mission. Engineers want to build.

To further discipline unruly rivers and stop their disorderly flows from spreading destruction, the Corps began building dams. Lots of dams. Soon it was building dams at a pace that made the Bureau of Reclamation take note, and when the two bureaucracies locked their sights on the same undammed rivers of the West, trouble began.

Until the Great Depression, the Corps rarely strayed west of the Mississippi. But the western United States had a wealth of prime dam sites, and the Corps wasn't content to let the Bureau of Reclamation have all the fun and gain all the glory. The West's rocky, treeless terrain and bouts of violent rainfall and snowmelt make it particularly prone to flooding. Rivers that most of the year yield a trickle through empty beds suddenly swell to epic torrents that wash away entire towns. The Corps intended to put a stop to this destruction by building dams. And the catch was this: If the Corps built a dam for the purpose of flood control, the water it stored could be used for irrigation—and it didn't cost farmers a dime. Bureau of Reclamation water was cheap, subsidized both by hydropower and taxpayers. But Corps of Engineers' water was flat-out free. And this did not go unnoticed by irrigation farmers.

The owners of megafarms in the Tulare Basin of California's Central Valley wanted all the water of the Kings River for themselves. If the Bureau of Reclamation built dams on the river, the agency would encourage new farms to use the water. And the big growers would, at least in theory, be prohibited from using the cheap irrigation water because the Reclamation Act limited the size of farms that could benefit from its projects. But if the Corps of Engineers built the dams for flood control, there would be no restrictions on how the water was used. Agribusinesses would be able to slurp up as much as they wanted to fatten their profits.

When the Bureau began feasibility studies on the Kings River, the Corps went to Congress and asked for money to study building its own dam on the river. As explained by political scientist Arthur Maass in *Muddy Waters*, the battle for dominion in the Tulare Basin between the two bureaucracies brought Congress, the president, and Californians into conflict by forcing them to choose sides. The Corps began constructing on the Kings River an emergency flood control diversion of dubious necessity. It made sure the structure diverted water to big growers at no cost, giving them a taste of what would come their way if the Corps could chase the Bureau away. The White House backed the Bureau, but the Corps defied the president's will and continued to push the case for flood control on rivers that threatened no people or property when they overflowed. The swollen rivers simply filled up shallow lakes that were a nuisance to growers when the waters rose high enough to prevent them from planting all of their fields.

The Bureau at least made a pretense of building projects that benefited small farms. But the Corps, unabashedly pandering to the nation's largest irrigation farmers, some of whom owned spreads that sprawled over twenty thousand acres or more, won the battle with the Bureau and dammed the Kings and other rivers in the Tulare Basin. It provided, for a token fee, a windfall of water for rich growers with land monopolies, allowing them to expand their already spectacular productivity and tighten their control of California's agricultural wealth. Former secretary of the interior Harold Ickes wrote, "No more lawless or irresponsible Federal group than the Corps of Army Engineers has ever attempted to operate in the United States, either outside of or within the law."

Paul Taylor, an economics professor at the University of California at Berkeley, spent considerable time and energy trying to get the US government to follow the letter of the Reclamation Act. The legislation had been designed to prevent land and water monopoly in the West, and to foster family farming by limiting the water landowners could receive from federal reclamation projects to an amount sufficient to irrigate 160 acres. But the pleas of Paul Taylor and others fell on deaf ears. The 160-acre limit was evaded with abandon, allowing agricultural land in California that benefited from taxpayer-funded water projects, whether built by the Bureau or the Corps, to be concentrated into large estates.

When the Bureau's Central Valley Project was completed, the Southern Pacific Railroad, the largest private landowner in California, became the largest beneficiary of the largest water project in history. Corporations such as Exxon and Getty Oil operated megafarms irrigated by taxpayer dollars. Big government had financed the waterworks that allowed big business to flourish. When President Jimmy Carter ordered an investigation of the Westlands Water District in the Central Valley, not a single 160-acre family spread envisioned by the originators of the reclamation movement could be found. And the growers were paying about a quarter of the cost to bring water across California to their fields, which were producing each year more than a billion dollars' worth of crops. Hundreds of millions of taxpayer dollars had been gifted to a fortunate few—who happened to offer a significant source of campaign contributions to politicians.

While subsidized water was being used by some of the wealthiest farmers in the world to grow subsidized crops that the federal government was paying people in other parts of the country not to grow, wetlands in the Tulare Basin dried up and were replaced by cottonlands. Tulare Lake, the largest freshwater lake west of the Mississippi and among the world's oldest lakes, disappeared when the Corps dammed the rivers that fed it. Agribusinesses planted crops across its dry basin and then flooded their fields with water that was virtually free. Rows of perfectly plowed cotton spread along Interstate 5 in a land where it never rained in summer. The Central Valley became one enormous factory farm cranking out an embarrassment of fiber and food. The world's largest transformed landscape, the valley's vast acreage was tended by gigantic pieces of machinery that rose up and tilted and lowered and swiveled like strange species of saurian beasts. These mechanical creations, spawned from studies at the publicly funded University of California, increased the profits of the valley's growers, while communities of farm laborers in the heart of the richest agricultural region in the world remained mired in poverty.

With its victory in California's Tulare Basin under its belt, the Corps was in the West to stay. And the dam-building boom spread across arid lands, accelerating ever faster as the Bureau and the Corps battled it out to see who could claim the best western dam sites first. They reached something of a truce on the Missouri.

A clumsy oaf of a river, the Missouri had a bad habit of smashing and drowning everything in its path as it staggered back and forth across its floodplain. The Corps proposed the Pick Plan, which called for low dams downriver to control floods and improve navigation. The Bureau's Sloan Plan, which the agency hurried to complete after catching wind of the Corps' plan, called for high dams on the upper river to generate hydropower that could subsidize money-losing irrigation projects. Unable to choose between the two alternatives, Congress approved the Pick-Sloan Plan, which allowed both agencies to build nearly every structure they desired. One hundred and twelve dams rose to paralyze the flow of the burly Missouri and its wandering tributaries. The entire basin was riprapped, channelized, and diverted with earthen walls and poured concrete until it was turned into a gigantic piece of plumbing.

Herbert Hoover described the efforts of the Bureau and Corps as a "great hodgepodge of duplication, overlapping, and unbelievably extravagant planning." If there was a motto the two dueling agencies shared, it was this: Dam first, ask questions later. There were no environmental impact reports, no detailed studies to assess economic benefits. No public comment periods, no revised alternative implementation strategies. The dam-building bureaucracies preferred to pile up concrete instead of paperwork. Everything that could be dammed was quickly dammed. In the name of settling barren lands with small farms, in the name of feeding the nation or the world, in the name of flood control, in the name of improved navigation, in the name of enhanced fish and wildlife habitat—in the name of whatever happened to sound good at the time—river after river found its path blocked with a concrete barrier, and many of these streams were sliced into so many sections by the waterworks of the Bureau and the Corps that their wild flows were tamed to tidy pools.

Along with the monumental structures raised by the Bureau and the Corps, other dams were constructed by private enterprise. Though not nearly as massive, the modest structures had tremendous impacts on economies and ecosystems throughout the West. Take the case of the Elwha River, which spills from the glaciated peaks of Washington State's Olympic Peninsula toward a cobbled delta in the Strait of Juan de Fuca. In the primordial forests of spruce, fir, and cedar through which the river runs, the trees wear beards of moss and water drools from their tips. The river once throbbed red, silver, and green with salmon and other anadromous fish—fish that spend most of their lives fattening in the salty sea and then return to spawn in the freshwater rivers where they were born. The Elwha roars down chutes it has blasted through chunks of basalt. This watery violence forced chinook salmon to grow exceptionally large and strong, some reaching legendary proportions of one hundred pounds. The upper reaches of the river were rich with gravel bars where fish spawned in prolific abundance. The meaty, muscular creatures that surged upstream were capable of leaping waterfalls ten feet high. They were central to the diet and culture of Native Americans who lived along the river, and their decomposing carcasses fertilized the earth. From soil dark with decayed matter that maggots had stripped from their bones, flowers sprang in bright bouquets.

In 1908, an entrepreneur put an abrupt end to the bounty of the Elwha that fought its way upriver with hooked jaws and thrashing tails by erecting a shoddily constructed dam. Its base blew apart, emptying the reservoir in a deluge that smashed everything in its path. When the floodwaters receded, people picked fish from the crooks of trees, and the hole in the dam was plugged with conifer branches and concrete. The dam powered a lumber mill that provided jobs and generated electricity to light up the homes of Port Angeles, and finned torpedoes bashed themselves against concrete when they found the path to their ancestral spawning grounds blocked. Salmon populations crashed from hundreds of thousands of fish—concentrations so thick that when they ran upriver you couldn't see the streambed—to a few stray stock reared in hatcheries scrambling to stave off extinction. Bears that had once gathered along the Elwha to feast on spawning fish, their chins slick with salmon fat, disappeared into the last scraps of forest wrapped in moss and shadow.

The Colorado River Compact and Boulder Canyon bill paved the way for the population of California's southern coastal plain to swell as droves of Americans scampered toward the desert. Arizona watched this growth with increasing bitterness. The chafed state claimed California's success came at its expense, for the palmy glitter of Southern California grew from liquid that was rightfully Arizona's, it insisted. Arizonan negotiators wrestled with Californian representatives over a Lower Basin compact to divide the waters of the Colorado River but reached no agreement.

Arizona, which continued to covet its neighbor's water, asked the Supreme Court to intervene. And in 1930 there began a series of *Arizona v. California* cases, the first three of which did not provide Arizona the redress it believed it was due. Tensions escalated between the two states in 1934 when Arizona governor Benjamin Moeur, known for his dramatic flair, sent the National Guard to the Colorado River. Vowing to stop California from completing Parker Dam, which was being built to divert water into an aqueduct running to Los Angeles, the governor dispatched a hundred troops with machine guns "to repel an invasion." The troops traveled by truck to the town of Parker. The dam site was another eighteen miles upriver; to carry themselves to the battlefield, the guardsmen commandeered a ferryboat, which promptly ran aground on a sandbar. One of the men caught a deadly case of pneumonia—the conflict's only casualty. The *Los Angeles Times* sent a "war correspondent" to cover the rumpus. He mockingly dubbed the ferryboat passengers Arizona's Navy. In 1935 Congress passed legislation authorizing Parker Dam, putting an end to The Great Colorado River War.

To Arizonans, Hoover Dam was less an icon of hope for the nation than a symbol of their state's weakness and defeat—a reminder sixty stories tall of their humiliation. After the towering structure was completed in 1935, the following year power from hydroelectric generators was transmitted to Los Angeles, and the city spilled across the desert in a luminous sprawl. By 1941, Colorado River water surged through the aqueducts of the Metropolitan Water District and into the thirsty maw of Southern California, and farmers in the Imperial Valley drenched fields with their portion that flowed through the All-American Canal. As Arizona watched the cities and farms of its neighbor grow, its California envy swelled. Feelings of inadequacy hardened Arizona's opposition to California's water use. The jealous state wanted an enormous canal of its own.

While California was completing the infrastructure that would allow it to binge on water and power from the Colorado River, the cities of Tucson and Phoenix were spreading across the scorching sands and xeric shrublands of the Sonoran Desert. Bayonets of yucca leaves and spiky arms of cholla were paved over with slabs of fresh cement, and saguaro tall as trees and with flowers that bloomed yellow in the night were bulldozed to make way for blacktop that turned soft in the baking sun. Little elf owls that hunted white-footed mice in the moonlight moved on. Gila monsters lumbered toward new locales, forked tongues flicking from their venomous snouts, beaded scales showing patterns of orange and pink against black backgrounds, like strange maps of the desert.

Treasures of water stored in hidden vaults beneath the sand were raided for their riches. Vast stores of wetness had been deposited during the last ice age, when what are now deserts were covered with lakes. Arizona's metropolises drew down these aquifers faster than the region's meager rainfall could recharge them. The earth beneath streets and buildings began to buckle and sag. Along desert washes cottonwoods a century and a half old stood skeletal against the sky, their branches bare of leaves. Wells ran dry and pumps coughed to a halt. Not only were Phoenix and Tucson frantic for water—power supplies were also strained by the state's sizzling growth. In 1939, Arizona asked for emergency electricity from the Bureau of Reclamation, which agreed to the request and ran power lines from Hoover Dam to the dimly lit cities in the desert.

Arizona knew that by accepting power from Hoover Dam it would compromise its stalwart opposition to the project and to the Colorado River Compact. Private utilities in Arizona didn't want to compete with cheap public power, but the state was desperate for electricity. Likewise, Arizona's need for an immediate solution to its water woes overcame its idealistic stance against the dam. Thirst trumped principles as Arizona, eager to tap into federal funding for water projects of its own, ended twenty-two years of opposition and ratified the Colorado River Compact in 1944. Now in bed with the feds, Arizona's leaders worked with the Bureau of Reclamation to create a diversion project to help relieve their lust for water.

Just before Arizona relented and ratified the compact, the United States and Mexico engaged in diplomatic fisticuffs over the Colorado River. Mexico and the United States had sparred over Colorado River water for decades; they had also traded punches over the flow of the lower Rio Grande. Increasingly the separate controversies over the two rivers converged. Some of the water sent to California's Imperial Valley in the old canal that ran through Mexico had been diverted to the fields of Mexicali, turning the bone-dry basin into one of the country's most productive agricultural regions. After the All-American Canal was completed to siphon off water from the Colorado above where the river crossed the border and flowed into the Mexicali Valley, and following America's announcement that it would build a diversion project on the lower Rio Grande, Mexican officials grew eager for a resolution. The United States, warily watching Mexico's increased use of Colorado River water and worrying about its neighbor's future plans—which would surely involve more use now that the river's flow was regulated by Hoover Dam—came to the bargaining table intent on finding a solution.

In 1944 Mexico and the United States signed a treaty. Mexico was guaranteed 1.5 maf annually, less than the amount the United States thought Mexico was using at the time. Californians, believing Mexico was only entitled to the amount it had used before Hoover Dam was constructed, and fearing the extra water would come from their state's share, were incensed. They opposed congressional approval of the treaty. The other six basin states, worried that delays in implementing the treaty would allow Mexico to guzzle more water and claim prior appropriation rights, causing the water apportionments of the Colorado River Compact to become moot, yelled for immediate ratification. Even normally combative Arizona endorsed the treaty. Texas was satisfied with the treaty's allocation of Rio Grande water and became a staunch supporter of swift ratification. President Roosevelt, eager to repair America's image as an imperialistic bully in Latin America with the Good Neighbor Policy, and anxious to build alliances with World War II allies, pushed for ratification.

California, in its opposition to the treaty, stood alone. But like a kid in a schoolyard surrounded by a mob cajoling him to slap his own face, California finally succumbed to the pressure of the other states and the White House and reluctantly put its support behind ratification. The US Senate approved the treaty in 1945. Mexico's Senate soon followed suit and voted its approval, and an uneasy peace prevailed at the border.

Colorado became the first Upper Basin state to start to see its reclamation dreams realized. In 1937 Congress granted approval to build the Colorado–Big Thompson Project. The transmountain diversion moves flow from the headwaters of the Colorado River on the western side of the Rocky Mountains to the eastern side, where most of the state's population lives on semiarid plains with rivers so scrawny they make visitors from wet places scoff. Developing Colorado's cities near the state's major water supplies, though eminently logical, would have taken all the fun away from engineers. The Colorado–Big Thompson Project uses electric pumps to lift water up the western slope; when the water is dropped two thousand vertical feet down the eastern slope it cascades through six power plants, generating electricity. The project spans 250 miles and consists of twelve reservoirs, eighteen dams and dikes, and a 13.1-mile-long tunnel bored through the granite of the Continental Divide, as well as canals, pipelines, transmission lines, substations, and various other structures. Rube Goldberg, who once worked as an engineer for San Francisco's Water and Sewers Department, could not have invented a more complicated scheme to move water from one place to another. Built between 1938 and 1957, the Colorado–Big Thompson Project allowed the Bureau of Reclamation to showcase its prodigious talents. This engineering *tour de force* provided an artificial river that allowed the Front Range region to grow far beyond the meager amount of water supplied by nature on Colorado's eastern plains. Some said the project was a work of pure genius. The historian David Lavender called it a "massive violation of geography."

Before Colorado and the other Upper Basin states could fulfill the rest of their reclamation wishes, first they had to wait for a feasibility study authorized by the Boulder Canyon Project Act. Delayed by World War II, the study was finally released by the Bureau of Reclamation in 1946. It concluded that while many projects were technically possible on the upper reaches of the Colorado, the river was too lean to supply them all. The Bureau could not approve any more projects until the Upper Basin states sorted out how to distribute their Colorado River allocation among themselves.

Compared to the bitter bouts between Arizona and California in the Lower Basin, relations upstream were a regular lovefest. The Upper Basin states quickly forged an agreement. Uncertain about how much water would remain after meeting their obligations to the Lower Basin and Mexico, they formed a compact based on percentages: Colorado was entitled to 51.75 percent, Utah to 23 percent, Wyoming to 14 percent and New Mexico to 11.25 percent. The Upper Colorado River Commission was created to monitor the water use of each state and to enforce reductions if deliveries sent to the Lower Basin and Mexico depleted supplies. The agreement, known as the Upper Basin Compact, was approved by the legislatures of the Upper Basin states in 1948, and by Congress a year later. Let the building binge begin, shouted the Upper Basin states.

Southern Californians, seeing water development upriver as a threat to their supply, were up in arms. But the real battle that ensued was not between states. Instead, it pitted the dam-building bureaucracy of the federal government against a movement in America that would soon swell into a force powerful enough to profoundly alter water laws and policies in the West.

CHAPTER 6

What We Have Lost

WHEN JOHN WESLEY POWELL LED HIS FRAIL FLOTILLA DOWN THE Colorado River, smashing rapids and crushing waterfalls pounded his wooden boats and tore at their gunwales. But he also found calm stretches of water where his dories were carried on languid currents and drifted through peaceful canyons. When his party floated near what is today the border of Utah and Arizona, they entered a place where the river lay flat and glassy and deer sipped from pools along its mossy shores. Ferns were strung across rock faces painted pink and vermillion and mottled with the dark oxidation known as desert varnish. Each ledge held a hanging garden of greenery. Pictographs covered the walls, telling stories from another age. Side canyons pinched together and then opened into valleys lush as jungles. When the men shouted, their voices bounced back from every direction. Light beamed down through narrow slots, ricocheting around sandstone caverns and towers like fractal patterns in a fairyland. Powell named the place Glen Canyon. For the next eighty years it remained essentially the same. Only a handful of rugged adventurers discovered its treasures—the gurgle of streams in its side canyons, the rich patinas of its walls.

$$\sim$$

After World War II, America's economy boomed and the nation left the poverty and desperation of the era of Hoover Dam behind as it raced forward toward a promising future. The United States had the money and momentum to build big in the West. Echoing those who had once invoked Manifest Destiny when pushing to develop arid lands, and reinforcing the idea that taming the tumble and rush of rivers was less about money and more about a national mandate to control nature, the Bureau of Reclamation issued a report that called for the development of water projects in the Upper Basin of the Colorado. It effused, "Tomorrow the Colorado River will be utilized to the last drop. . . . Here is a job so great in its possibilities that only a nation of free people have the vision to know that it can be done and that it must be done. The Colorado River is their heritage."

Hoover Dam had controlled the lower Colorado, allowing California to tap the river's bounty. Now the Upper Basin states, emboldened by the Bureau of Reclamation's feasibility study, shouted for a megaproject of their own so they could satisfy their water desires. Their representatives in Congress introduced a bill to authorize the Colorado River Storage Project. This engineering spectacular would create dams of Brobdingnagian proportions on the upper reaches of the Colorado and its tributaries, allowing Wyoming, Colorado, Utah, and New Mexico to make full use of their apportionment of 7.5 maf. (As mentioned, the Lower Basin states of Arizona, Nevada, and California had also been apportioned 7.5 maf, and California had wasted no time putting the water to use.) The project was also promoted as necessary to subdue a rogue river that flowed in perpetual rage: The public was told that the dams would put a stop to property destruction and loss of life by preventing the river from overrunning its banks. Turning the upper Colorado into a series of slackwater lakes would allow the large-scale irrigation needed to make lands of sagebrush and dust fat with food, and it would provide the power to light up cities in the wilderness. This sort of activity was at the time promoted as conservation—in the sense that water would be saved for human use instead of being allowed to slip wastefully toward the sea. In those days the worst nightmare of a water "conservationist" was a river's flow that served no practical purpose. Irrigating a field or turning a turbine, flushing a toilet or flowing from a tap: Every drop had to be put to some productive end—every drop had be *used*. The US Postal

Service once issued a first class stamp with a picture of a dam and the word *conservation*.

In this sense, the Bureau of Reclamation was an army of conservationists. Its engineers were ready to raise dams anywhere, everywhere, to conserve rivers, ensuring that no drop of water in the West would escape human use. It had become an organization of serial dam builders. Only a handful of rivers in the West, such as the Yellowstone, still flowed freely from mountain snowfields to the sea, and the Bureau had plans to dam them too. The Bureau was building, building, and it would not stop building until every river was blocked.

The weight of water held back by dams in the western United States is such that it has sped up the earth's rotation and moved the planet's axis. These shifts are not enormous, but they are measurable. The dam-building frenzy that began with the Bureau of Reclamation remaking the waterscape of the West has changed the very tilt and speed of our planet as it tumbles through the void.

———

At 710 feet—more than half the height of the Empire State Building— Glen Canyon Dam would be one of the largest construction projects in human history. And it would form one of the planet's most extensive manmade lakes, the placid waters of which would bury labyrinthine canyons and remains of an ancient culture. A web of transmission lines would send electricity from generators at the dam to a five-state grid. New towns would boom and a multimillion-dollar tourism industry would rise in a landscape forever altered. And the reservoir, Lake Powell, would hold the deepest hue of blue in a desert of blood-red rock.

Two men occupy the center of the Glen Canyon Dam story: Floyd Dominy, commissioner of the Bureau of Reclamation who oversaw the building of the dam, and David Brower, director of the Sierra Club. The former was cigar-puffing and brash, a man with a booming voice and an evangelical zeal for bringing water to the parched West; the latter was a shy butterfly collector and lover of untrammeled mountains who'd made it his mission to preserve America's last wild places. One man wanted to build a dam in Glen Canyon; the other wanted to stop it from being built. Their battle was a clash of wills, but more important, it was a duel of ideas. The impassioned efforts to keep rivers and the landscapes they drain in an untamed state begin here, in one of twentieth-century America's epic battles over the fate of a natural resource.

Floyd Dominy, raised on a dryland Nebraska farm during the Dust Bowl, was appalled by water that managed to reach the sea without serving people. He was a man hell-bent on damming everything that flowed. Unlike most Bureau commissioners before him, Dominy hadn't been trained as an engineer. But he understood how power worked in Washington. Forging alliances, cultivating key partnerships, and crushing enemies, Dominy dominated the world of water in the West. Under this western waterlord's leadership, the Bureau provided absurdly cheap water subsidized by taxpayer dollars to landholdings that far exceeded the size limits laid out in the Reclamation Act. In *Cadillac Desert*, Marc Reisner quotes Dominy: "Half of our projects were insolvent.... On top of that, there were practically no requirements.... Any fool could sign up and get on a Reclamation farm and use whatever intelligence he had cheating the government. When the projects began to go bankrupt, [the former commissioners] were afraid to expose them..... We were illegally delivering water all over the place. Payments were way in arrears and no one was doing a damn thing about it. I think we were violating the law at least as often as we were not violating it."

Western senators and congressmen in cowboy boots and snap-button shirts, while holding forth about freeing their people from the tyranny of the federal government, hungered for development in their sparsely populated and poor states, and they welcomed a federal project that in today's money would have a price tag of a billion dollars or more. Water was the key to growth in the West, and states didn't have the financial resources to build projects big enough to control the Colorado. Democrats, Republicans, independents: They all loved reclamation, regardless of the nation's rising environmental awareness. Some of them, such as

Morris Udall of Arizona, even managed to blend environmental advocacy with ardent support of big water projects.

Environmental safeguards were virtually nonexistent. There was no Environmental Protection Agency, no environmental impact statements. A gargantuan water project was proposed, approved, and built—business as usual. Everyone anticipated that the Colorado River Storage Project, which included dams at Echo Park on the Green River and Glen Canyon on the Colorado River, would move forward like a freight train. Even President Eisenhower, who had campaigned on a platform of rolling back Franklin Roosevelt's New Deal liberalism, which he decried as "creeping socialism," embraced the project. The nation had confidence and cash in spades, and the Colorado was a wild river that needed to be conserved at any cost.

But the Bureau of Reclamation had miscalculated when it decided to build a dam at Echo Park. Located just below the junction of the Yampa and Green Rivers in Dinosaur National Monument, the proposed dam site was just fine with the neighboring town of Vernal, Utah, which would enjoy a robust economic boost from the project. One member of the community declared in congressional testimony that he'd told an anti-dam advocate, "did it ever occur to you that we might not want to be saved? We want to be dammed."

But the proposed dam raised the hackles of environmentalists who had a very different idea of what it means to conserve a river: Flooding a national monument was not their idea of conservation. After World War II, as population had soared and technological advances had transformed landscapes, concern over development gobbling up wilderness areas arose, and grassroots movements to preserve wild places began to spread across America. To an increasing number of Westerners, a worthy use of water was to leave it where it was. To contain freely flowing water in an artificial receptacle for agriculture or flood control or a city's spigots was, to these advocates of protecting wild nature, a waste of a perfectly good river. And the deserts through which the rivers ran in stony solitude and immense silence were not wastelands to be reclaimed, but storehouses of treasure, where rare streams glittered with mica as they glided beneath the cauldron of the sun, where dragonflies with metallic bodies and iridescent eyes shuttled between springs on diaphanous wings, where lean coyotes yelped and howled their songs.

The Sierra Club, founded in 1892 by legendary conservationist John Muir, had failed to stop San Francisco from building a dam that drowned part of Yosemite National Park. At roughly the same time Los Angeles began draining the Owens Valley, the thirsty city of San Francisco had followed its rival to the south's lead and extended an aqueduct 134 miles away, into a majestic glacial valley through which a wild river flowed. In meadowy fields between faces of polished granite, mariposa lilies honeyed the air and birds filled it with song. Waterfalls spread veils of mist throughout the valley. Silver firs and sugar pines rose from skirts of dirt around rock masses that soared so high clouds bumped against their brows. The reservoir that filled behind Hetch Hetchy Dam in Yosemite National Park flooded this landscape beloved by John Muir, despite his passionate objections.

When the Echo Park Dam near the confluence of the Green and Yampa Rivers in Dinosaur National Monument was proposed, Sierra Club director David Brower was ready to make a stand: no more dams in national parks and national monuments. But the dam at Echo Park was a "cash register" project designed to generate power to pay for the dam-building spree on the upper Colorado and its tributaries, and the Bureau of Reclamation would not easily back down.

Opposing water projects was regarded by many Westerners to be, if not subversive and un-American, then downright nutty—why would someone *not* want to conserve water in dry country? But Walter Prescott Webb, a distinguished historian of the West, published an article in a 1957 edition of *Harper's* entitled "The American West: Perpetual Mirage," in which he argued that draining the national treasury to convert arid lands to gardens was lunacy. His was a lonely voice in the desert wilderness, and the opprobrium that was piled upon him by defenders of federal irrigation efforts made clear the West's fierce love of taxpayer-funded waterworks. Increasingly, however, some members of the public began questioning the nation's obsession with putting walls in front of everything wet that moved. David Brower was one of them. He led the Sierra Club in a battle against the Echo Park Dam. By attacking the Bureau's math with what he called "ninth grade arithmetic" when he testified before Congress, he exposed some serious errors in its calculations. He also distributed films and ran ads in newspapers and magazines to educate people about what would be lost if Dinosaur National Monument was flooded.

The reservoirs that rise behind dams smother living rivers beneath standing water and kill or drive away most occupants of rich bottom-lands. If the proposed project in Dinosaur National Monument was built, cliffs that stood like fairytale battlements and parapets would be drowned, and quarries dense with Jurassic-age bones would disappear beneath the reservoir. Mule deer would flee to higher ground, and the hiss and cry of mountain lions would be replaced by the dead silence of dammed water.

One of the Sierra Club films stated, "We all know that progress must move forward. . . . Certainly we can ask progress to walk around and not through our garden—our national parks." The Sierra Club campaign caught the attention of the public, which let Congress know it wasn't pleased with the idea of its parks and monuments drowning beneath floodwaters. Never before had so many citizens of the United States been so fired up about an environmental issue. Some members of Congress, afraid that opposition to flooding Dinosaur would put the entire Colorado River Storage Project at risk and endanger the other dams they hoped would bring wealth to their districts and states, backed away from the dam at Echo Park. Eventually the Bureau of Reclamation scrapped its plans for Echo Park so the rest of the project could move forward, and paleontologists were left to chip away at the strata of an ancient riverbed turned to stone and littered with the bones of giants that once walked the earth.

To help persuade the Bureau to leave Dinosaur National Monument alone, Brower didn't oppose Glen Canyon Dam. He had never been to Glen Canyon. He didn't know what was there—few people did. A hand-ful of river outfitters guided trips there for adventurous souls who craved immersion in wild canyon country, where they could be swallowed by the desert and float along on lazy currents while listening to the laughter of side streams that bounced in bubbles and froth down stony troughs. But there were no nearby towns or paved roads, and most people had no inkling of the treasures Glen Canyon held in the fastness of its hidden wilds. They knew nothing of its meandering bends where canyons erupted in riots of color, its hidden passageways through stone walls, its random stabs of light that fell on sandy floors, its long beaches that curved against the shores, its petroglyphs and pictographs, its ruined cities of the ancients.

Brower later changed his mind and wanted to fight Glen Canyon Dam after he saw its beauty firsthand. But the Sierra Club, satisfied that the Bureau of Reclamation had agreed not to dam Dinosaur National Monument, and not wanting to further antagonize the Bureau by battling with it over a little-known area that lacked national park or national monument status, ordered Brower to stop his opposition. "Glen Canyon died, and I was partly responsible for its needless death," Brower wrote. "Neither you nor I, nor anyone else, knew it well enough to insist that at all costs it should endure. When we began to find out it was too late."

Glen Canyon is composed not of solid granite like the canyon where Hoover Dam had been built, but of sandstone and shale, and its flaky geology played into political theatrics as Glen Canyon Dam was debated in Congress. A California congressman, quite pleased that conservationists had killed the dam at Echo Park, and hoping to scuttle plans for a dam at Glen Canyon so the Colorado River could flow downstream unmolested and allow his state to continue putting its surplus to use, dropped a chunk of shale he'd gathered from Glen Canyon into a glass of water. His colleagues watched it dissolve while he warned that a giant concrete wall sited in such an unstable area would lead to disaster. He spoke of slumping abutments and a dam collapsing atop crumbled footings as the piece of shale in his glass turned to mud. Following this presentation, a supporter of the dam dropped a core sample of sandstone from the site into another water glass. Upon finishing his argument in favor of the dam, he drank clear water while the stone rattled against the sides of his glass.

In 1956 Congress approved the Interstate Highway System, knitting the nation together with roads; the same year it also passed the Colorado River Storage Project Act to regulate the West's wildest river. There were a few dissenters in Congress, but there was so much momentum behind the Bureau of Reclamation's urge to erect new dams, such terrific force driving America's desire to build bigger and higher, a giant dam had to rise. The Bureau, under Dominy's leadership, erected many grand projects simply because it could. Its engineers dreamed of building structures that would drop the jaws of all who gazed at their creations. And in 1956, construction on a dam that would hold eight trillion gallons of water in a desert wilderness began. In an interview for a 1997 PBS documentary, Dominy said, "I have no apologies. I was a crusader for the development of water. I was the messiah."

Identified by the US Geological Survey in the late 1940s as the most remote place in the lower forty-eight states, Glen Canyon country was made of sandy tablelands and fractured stone broken into bulky shapes and stretched in slender spires, like the remains of ruined cathedrals. Naked rock so brightly colored it seemed painted by an artist on acid filled the earth to every edge. Seussian towers stained pink and orange wore drooping hats of caprock. All around lay wrinkled sheets and plump domes of slickrock, sandpapery in texture, and so named because the metal shoes of horses and mules slid over its surface. The boots of surveyors slipped across the slickrock and trudged through sand, and each time these engineers with measuring tools escaped the laser of the sun by ducking beneath a lip of stone, they were pestered by deerflies. The sky blazed with white heat by day; at night the breath of workers smoked in the cold moonlight.

The dam site lay within a deep and skinny canyon with the Colorado River roiling along its floor. The nearest town was Kanab, Utah, eighty miles away. Workcrews drove two hundred miles to get from one side to the other. The tough terrain burned out the clutches of jeeps and rubbed their tires bald. The worksite required that a bridge reaching across the rift that held the river be built, as well as roads and a town to house twenty-five hundred workers. A New York–based corporation, Merritt-Chapman & Scott, submitted the winning bid for the project and was awarded the contract by the Bureau of Reclamation, which thought its bid absurdly, impossibly low. Construction soon began.

The desert's cracked and undulating terrain, made up of petrified sand dunes and the beds of eroded seas, was wrapped in blacktopped roads, and the red gashes of canyons were crossed with steel bridges. Workers shuttled back and forth across the enormous cleft that held the Colorado on a jury-rigged footbridge made of chain-link fencing laid on cables. Seven hundred empty feet yawned beneath them as they welded and riveted the highest steel arch bridge ever constructed. The river lay in the depths below, a narrow strip of muddy red with white etchings of foam, and the roar of it came crashing up between chasm walls. The footbridge swayed in the wind and bounced with the weight of steelworkers. Safety nets were stretched below to catch men who tumbled from the beams of the bridge as it was being assembled across the void. Some workers, done with their shifts for the day, would leap into the nets for a jolt of adrenaline.

When the steel arch bridge was finished, curious gawkers walked across, peering into shadows to see the place where a cement barricade would be wedged in the gloom below. Laborers at the dam site seemed as tiny as toy soldiers to onlookers gazing down. The entire enterprise inspired awe. That humans could build such a thing, and in a howling desert wilderness no less, was almost as shocking as landing a man on the moon. Citizens stood on that vertiginous span watching the dam rise, and some of them believed there was no end to America's greatness, no limit to what it could create.

After Arizona and Utah finished fighting over where the city for workers would be sited, the Navajo Nation traded the US government a bleak sweep of rock near the gorge for oil-rich land in another locale. The gridwork of a town took shape atop a mesa, and soon the blank map of Glen Canyon country was marked with the scribbles of roads. The town of Page, Arizona, swelled with ten thousand people—workers and their families—the world's largest trailer park. This metropolis of metal boxes in the American outback had a big tin building that held a school, and it had a grocery store and a beauty salon, but there were no forests or fields, just clumps of saltbush and the occasional piñon or juniper, stone and wind and sun. And the sand, always the sand. From the edges of windows it drifted into trailers, and each time a door was opened, a blast of it scratched across the floor.

High scalers rappelled down from the rims of the gorge, dangling by ropes as they blasted rocks and pried apart the spalling walls where the sides of the dam would be slotted in the keyways. Stones they set free fell bouncing and tumbling into the shadows below. Some workers too tumbled downward, falling to their deaths. And blasting and burrowing into the cliffs to carve out a diversion tunnel was no less dangerous.

In the summer of 1959, the project skidded to a halt and the town of Page shut down as the workforce went on strike. The company that had won the contract to build the dam with a shockingly low bid had razor-thin margins. It wanted to save money by stopping the hardship bonuses it had been paying out to employees before the town of Page was finished. Now that the workers had a permanent town with regular services, no more hardship pay was merited, the company reasoned. The workers were having none of it. The economy was in a postwar upswing, and construction jobs were not in short supply. Page emptied, the trailer court boomtown turning to a ghost town. Merchants went bust and shuttered their shops. Lights went dim in the desert, and coyotes wandered empty streets lit by the stars and the moon.

Eventually the strike was resolved, and the smell of wet concrete filled Glen Canyon, covering the resiny scent of pine. From the dam site the great structure began to rise. Boys and girls crept toward the railings of the bridge and stared down on the backs of birds. Ravens rode columns of updrafting air and then they tumbled and dived. The concrete blocks of the dam locked together—a giant Lego tower assembled below the erector set of the metal-beamed bridge. The joy of children building things for the sake of building them—their love of assembling complex structures simply because they can—is as beautiful as the wind that carves a sandstone wall, as stirring as flowers that burst from cracks in desert rock. The child in all of us built Glen Canyon Dam because we could; now the adult in us wonders what we have lost.

Around the time dam construction began at Glen Canyon, archaeologists journeyed upstream to do their dusty work. Trowels and brushes in their patient hands, they sifted through the remains of a world that rose and fell in the prehistory of the Colorado Plateau. The Anasazi, now often referred to as Ancestral Puebloans, left clues to their lifeways in the labyrinth of canyons. They had farmed fields of corn, beans, and squash, manipulating water to succor urban concentrations of people in the desert. They built multistoried dwellings of mortared sandstone and wood beams that stood clustered in the sheltered alcoves of canyon walls. Their culture achieved a dazzling fluorescence between about AD 900 and 1100, and then, beginning in the middle of the twelfth century and extending into the thirteenth century, they abandoned their stone cities. They migrated and eventually became the modern Pueblo people of New Mexico and Arizona. The exact reasons for the exodus from their desert cities are unknown. Scholars speculate that a long and brutal drought forced the collapse of their society by straining their resources and causing warfare and cannibalism.

Maybe there are no lessons here for us. The Anasazi made little dams of stones and sticks and dug shallow ditches. Our dams and aqueducts are huge. We have the technology to survive drought, we tell ourselves as we gaze with reassurance upon our concrete monoliths beneath skies that were generous with rain for centuries but then turned stingy as the climate tipped toward a period of wicked dryness that ended a civilization.

As Glen Canyon Dam neared completion, teams of archaeologists scoured the canyons soon to be entombed beneath Lake Powell. In boats, on the backs of mules, and on foot, they salvaged what they could in what was, at the time, the largest archaeological project ever undertaken in the United States. Hidden beneath the wide brims of hats to shield their faces from the sun, they sifted through fragments of chert piled up in places where the Anasazi had worked their arrowpoints. At night these searchers lay their bedrolls on the sand of the canyon floor, next to the river's purling current, beneath the Pleiades burning blue and luminous in the desert night. Some stars shook loose from the firmament and shot down the sky, and there were showers of stars, so many falling they could not be counted. Some of the water on Earth came from frozen comets and icy asteroids crashing into the young planet. Our world formed hot and dry, a lifeless desert. Ice from space helped fill the oceans and feed the hydrologic cycle, in which the sun lifts water from oceans and land, and the moisture returns as rain and snow. Water moves across the globe, circulating in a nourishing flow that allows a thin layer of life to take hold on the crust of the world. The Hopi, modern-day descendants of the Anasazi, are stewards of springs and dancers of rain. To their way of thinking, the liquid that passes in and out of the cells of our bodies, the water that came from the cosmos and flows through desert stone, is an opening to another world and belongs to every living thing.

The archaeologists in Glen Canyon were forced to high ground when the Colorado and its tributaries swelled from storms. Flash floods chased them through a maze of canyons. Stone hallways ended in corners and closets and craggy walls, and twisted corridors opened into chambers with their ceilings set at odd angles and their floors strangely canted, like a demented mansion in a dream. Vaulted roofs had skylights through which sunlight fell like cords of golden rope. In this otherworldly setting the archaeologists discovered stashes of pottery, sandals, tools, entire walls of rock art, toeholds chipped in cliffs leading from the riverbed to the rimrock above, and intact dwellings that had not been entered by humans for six hundred years. They came upon scene after scene from prehistory and endless relic troves. Many thousands of artifacts, along with the accompanying photos, notes, and maps of researchers, were deposited in museums in Flagstaff, Arizona, and the University of Utah. The dwellings and rock art could not be moved from their desert sites. When the reservoir finally began to fill, waves would lap against them and slowly they would drown.

While the archaeologists were staving off dehydration, heat exhaustion, and hypothermia as they hurried to save and record what they could, workcrews at the dam site poured more than ten million tons of concrete through the frozen depths of winter and in the scalding days of summer. Sparks from welding guns added white-hot heat to temperatures hovering near 120 degrees, and men working shoulder to shoulder slumped unconscious in the hellish oven of the canyon. Ice was added to the warm pudding of concrete in summer so it could cool and set when poured. During a winter cold snap, freshly batched concrete had to be wrapped in electric blankets to prevent it from freezing.

Rockslides crashing down canyon walls, shrapnel from explosions hurling through the air, snapped safety ropes: There was no end to the dangers the workers at the dam site faced. And as the crews toiled to raise the structure, real estate developers touted beachfront property. They said Lake Powell would have two thousand miles of shoreline—more than the entire West Coast of America. Skeptics wearing the red dust of the desert in their hair stared at endless expanses of rock dotted with juniper and prickly pear, wondering if such a lake could really exist in this dry place.

River rats floated the Colorado through Glen Canyon before the wild landscape was erased, trying to get one last look at waterfalls that plashed in emerald pools, slot canyons painted with murals of mineral stains, sandstone sculpted into bridges and windows, turrets and domes, gardens of bonsai-like Gambel oak, and purple and cream columbine watered by dripping springs. Many who saw Glen Canyon before it was submerged declared it more beautiful than Grand Canyon, though its beauty was more subtle and lay in its details. In his essay "Glen Canyon Submersus," Wallace Stegner wrote, "Awe was never Glen Canyon's province. That is for the Grand Canyon. Glen Canyon was for delight."

With rising waters threatening to slip into Rainbow Bridge National Monument and fill the channel beneath the largest natural stone span on Earth, a strange scenario unfolded. Environmentalists advocated for a system of dams, diversion tunnels, and diesel pumps to be built in roadless wilderness to protect Rainbow Bridge. Secretary of the Interior Stewart Udall argued that constructing roads and infrastructure would damage the fragile environment simply to stop a tongue of lake water from lapping beneath the bridge. He proposed expanding the boundaries of the monument and turning it into a vast preserve of wild beauty. David

Brower was not swayed and demanded a system of waterworks be built by the Bureau. He went to Washington to plead that the reservoir be stopped from filling until the national monument could be protected with dams and pumps. But Dominy and others in the Bureau had finished raising Glen Canyon Dam and now they were determined to close the diversion tunnels as scheduled. It was their job to bring water to the people of the desert, and they weren't about to stop now. Dominy held nothing but derision for the burgeoning environmental movement in America, and he said of the wild Colorado that it was "useless to anyone." Brower called Glen Canyon Dam "America's most regretted environmental mistake."

After the diversion tunnels were closed, the Colorado started piling up behind the concrete barrier. And for the next few years the waters rose, inundating Glen Canyon and flooding side canyons. Coyotes trotted for the last time through gullies red as wounds, and bobcats chased lizards among pale cottonwoods while rising waters licked at their trunks and then lifted upward toward their leaves.

Eventually slack water backed up 186 miles to the San Juan and Escalante Rivers, turning arid canyonlands to inland sea. The Anasazi sites, the fountains that spouted from cliffs into pools of dusky jade, the hidden glens laced with maidenhair and monkey-flowers, the vaulted grottoes—all of this disappeared beneath a body of water that spread like an amoeba, its pseudopods reaching into every crevice and cleft as it gobbled the desert.

Lake Powell became a vacation mecca as marinas were built along its squiggly shoreline. Visitors to the area each year had been counted in the hundreds; after the lake filled, they numbered in the millions. Once hikers who wanted to see Rainbow Bridge had been forced to trudge their way across twelve miles of corrugated countryside after a multi-day float trip on the river. Now people roared toward it in powerboats across a smooth lake of wondrous blue, its surface painted with swirls of oil from engines. The town of Page and other dozy hamlets near Lake Powell boomed as a half-billion-dollar-a-year tourism industry was born. People came to water-ski and fish for bass with gobs of worms dangled from the decks of houseboats. Some came to gaze awestruck at the white concrete triumph of Glen Canyon Dam, and some came to leap from its crest. People who committed suicide by jumping from the top were shredded as they bounced along the dam's downstream face—the concrete slab wasn't as vertical as it appeared but instead sloped gently toward the power plant sited at its toe.

To memorialize the world that had drowned in silent flood beneath the reservoir, the Sierra Club published *The Place No One Knew*, a book featuring the work of Eliot Porter, one of America's most renowned wilderness photographers. Porter's lovely photographs depicted the landscape before the dam was built. The Bureau of Reclamation responded with a publication of its own: *The Jewel of the Colorado*. In this exaltation of engineering triumph and recreational opportunities for multitudes that became available after the dam was completed, Floyd Dominy wrote, "There is a natural order in our Universe. God created both man and nature. And man serves God. But nature serves man. To have a deep blue lake where no lake was before seems to bring man closer to God." Both books were as balanced as a person holding a bowling ball in one hand and a cotton ball in the other.

In 1969, a few years after Glen Canyon Dam was completed, President Nixon took office and ordered FBI investigations of top federal officials. The report on Dominy revealed a history of sexual escapades that resulted in his removal as commissioner of the Bureau. At roughly the same time, Brower was accused of financial recklessness and insubordination by board members of the Sierra Club and was booted out of his directorship.

New Yorker writer John McPhee managed to talk Dominy and Brower into spending time together on Lake Powell and sharing a descent of the Grand Canyon just before their downfalls. In his book *Encounters with the Archdruid*, McPhee relates the banter that ensues when the two nemeses explore Lake Powell by powerboat and float the Colorado in a rubber raft. Surrounded by the strange striations of rock walls rising a mile in the sky, the men form an unlikely friendship as each appreciates the other's notion of beauty, be it the blue fjords of a dam-made lake, or a wild staircase of waterfalls stepping down the travertine plunge pools of an undisturbed canyon. But still they cling to their opinions, one man expressing the beliefs that raised one of the nation's last great dams, the other advocating the ideas that made the environmental movement a force to be reckoned with in America. Development versus preservation, tamed reservoir versus turbulent river: The contrasts could not be starker, and they illustrate one of the great debates of our time, articulated by two men passionate about the positions they staked out and defending them as they float the river, their raft punching through the chaos of foaming waves and frothing holes.

As it turns out, Glen Canyon Dam is sited too far downriver to serve the water needs of the Upper Basin states, and very little volume is diverted from Lake Powell for water supply. The dam and other projects in the Upper Basin were built ostensibly to aid farmers. But the region's altitudes are high enough to severely restrict the growing season. Winters come early and linger late. In an article in *Reader's Digest* titled "Dollars into Dust," former governor of Wyoming Leslie Miller argued that an acre of land watered by the Colorado River Storage Project would cost at least $2,900 to irrigate but be worth less than $150. The loopy economics of the project prompted the *New York Times* to opine, "It would of course be possible to grow bananas on top of the Rockies if one wanted to spend the money; but the question is, could not this money be spent more advantageously elsewhere?"

Another argument the Bureau of Reclamation offered for building the dam was to regulate the river for the benefit of downstream users, preventing catastrophic floods and storing up water to ensure a steady flow. But floods menaced no one in the uninhabited canyonlands below the dam; at worst the Colorado threatened a few scattered settlements in the desert. Building a shield over America to protect it from meteors would have made more sense.

And because of water steaming from Lake Powell's surface, its storage effect on the overall river is negligible—or even nonexistent, according to hydrologists. The reservoir doesn't add water to the river; it causes loss of water volume due to evaporation. Some scientists now argue that emptying Powell and pumping water underground into aquifers where it can't vanish in the dry air would provide more effective storage. But problems abound with storing water underground: There are no engineering and construction jobs to build enormous concrete structures; politicians can't pass legislation authorizing billions of dollars worth of projects; and dam tour guides trained in the use of double entendres, who have been getting laughs from tourists for years by saying "This will be the best *dam* tour ever," have to transition into jobs guiding less glamorous Aquifer Recharge Basin tours.

Glen Canyon Dam was designed to produce hydroelectric power. When the desert sun blazed down on the cities of the Southwest and air conditioners switched on, dam managers released more water, producing power to be sold at peak rates. The hydroelectricity sales of the Glen Canyon cash register dam subsidized money-losing water projects throughout the Upper Basin, forcing the river to pay the cost of its confinement. The dam was the result not of sound economics but of politics. And those politics stem from laws that evolved in the gold-mad days of the West.

Glen Canyon Dam allowed the Upper Basin states to store water and release the exact amount they were obligated by the Colorado River Compact to deliver to the Lower Basin. Absent the dam, during wet years excess water would spill down the river unused by the Upper Basin; and in times of drought, California could issue a "compact call" that would force the Upper Basin to meet its downstream delivery obligations—even if doing so meant the Upper Basin had to cut into its own consumption. Glen Canyon Dam was built to solve these problems for the Upper Basin. If the Compact had required the Upper Basin to deliver *half the flow* of the Colorado in low water years, rather than a *fixed amount*, the burden of drought would have been spread equally between the basins and there would have been no need to build the dam. Lake Powell is, in essence, an "aquatic bank" engineered to fulfill the terms of a legal agreement based on an artificial allocation scheme of water payments made at an arbitrary boundary. The dam is a monument to the consequences of ignoring John Wesley Powell's plans to settle the West based on the facts of hydrology, instead of recklessly sectioning its rivers and governing them with rules based on politics, not science. And the reservoir held back by the dam was named by the Bureau of Reclamation, with no irony intended, in Powell's honor.

Congress's support of dams on the upper Colorado and its tributaries stirred to action Arizonans—who wanted projects of their own and worried about being denied their share of water in the deserts of the Southwest because of all the new infrastructure that was being planned in the Upper Basin. Arizona introduced to Congress a bill that would authorize the Bureau of Reclamation's plan to build the mammoth Central Arizona Project (CAP), a 336-mile-long aqueduct system to send Colorado River water uphill to Phoenix and Tucson. The cities were sucking their aquifers empty at a frightening pace while artificial lakes in their suburbs shimmered in the sun. Arizona senator Barry Goldwater, famous for championing the cause of conservatism, said of the taxpayer-funded CAP, "It has to be built, and if it's not, this valley is going out of business."

California objected to CAP, arguing that Arizona would be using more water than the amount it had been allotted by the Colorado River Compact. Arizona, of course, disagreed. Congress refused to approve CAP until Arizona and California quit squabbling about how much water each state was allowed to use. Arizona, watching states in the basin above it, California to its west, and Mexico to its south all moving forward with water projects, grew increasingly anxious to begin work on one of its own. And once again Arizona turned to the Supreme Court, filing suit in 1952.

The trial that followed is among the most complex, contentious, and costly in the history of the Supreme Court. After five million dollars were spent, fifty lawyers participated, hundreds of witnesses testified, thousands of pages of transcripts were recorded, and eleven years elapsed, the Court finally announced its opinion in 1963.

Bewildering almost everyone by basing its five-to-three decision not on the 1922 Colorado River Compact but on the legislation passed in 1928 known as the Boulder Canyon Project Act (which authorized the construction of Hoover Dam and the All-American Canal), the Supreme Court declared that Congress hadn't suggested how to divide the waters of the Lower Basin when it passed the legislation. Instead, it had authorized the secretary of the interior to implement the scheme—which limited California to an apportionment of 4.4 maf and ensured 2.8 maf for Arizona, plus all the water in its tributaries. (Nevada received a paltry 300,000 acre-feet. At the time Las Vegas was a scruffy settlement; no one fathomed it would morph into a metropolis bright with neon cowboys and racked with savage thirst.)

Though the Court's reasoning was unexpected, its decision cemented Arizona's claims to almost everything the scrappy state had fought for and failed to secure in its negotiations of the Colorado River Compact. The compact, which had originally been conceived as a means to avoid long and costly litigation between states, had resulted in one of the longest and most expensive court battles in US history. There is no end to irony when it comes to water in the West.

Californians, outraged at the outcome of the epic court battle, squawked that the decision trampled states' rights. They pointed out that in the past, water rights between states had been agreed upon by compact or determined by the Supreme Court. Now, based on the Supreme Court's decision, Congress could apportion water rights, and had, according to the Court, done exactly that. This was a new development in the ever-increasing complexity of the West's water laws, and it pleased California not a bit.

Another shocker delivered by the Court was its decision to give responsibility for adjusting water allotments both between states and within states, in times of surplus and shortage, to the secretary of the interior. This turned upside down the time-honored tradition of states determining water rights for users within their borders. Now the secretary of the interior would be the arbiter of water rights disputes between states and even inside their borders when the water under question came from federal reclamation projects. The Court based this decision on the constitutional power of Congress to regulate navigable waterways. It also indicated that the constitution's "general welfare" clause, which grants Congress the power to "lay and collect Taxes, Duties, Imposts, and Excises, to pay the Debts and provide for the common defense and general Welfare of the United States," could be invoked to extend the power of Congress to regulate water rights on non-navigable streams.

The 1922 Colorado River Compact negotiations, aside from originally being conceived to limit the length and cost of court battles, had been intended by states to remove the threat of federal involvement in the water affairs of the West. But the 1963 Supreme Court decision resolved more than forty years of legal conflict by dramatically increasing the federal government's control over the Colorado River. In a scathing dissent, Justice William O. Douglas sharply criticized the majority for giving the government "a power and command over water rights in the 17 Western states that it never has had, that it always wanted, that it could never persuade Congress to grant, and that this Court up to now has consistently refused to recognize . . . the life-and-death power of dispensation of water rights long administered according to state law."

Regardless of the legal repercussions for states that drank from the Colorado River, the decision thrilled Arizonans, who could now push forward their water project to fend off the thirst of the cities and farms they planned to spread across sun-cooked sands.

Pleased too were Native Americans, who prior to the latest *Arizona v. California* case had not had their needs or rights factored into the metrics of water allotment in the West. When Arizona filed suit with the Supreme Court in 1952, the federal government had included its lawyers in the case to protect the water rights of American Indians on reservations in the Lower Basin, and to ensure sufficient water for national forests, national parks, and other federal lands.

The Court, when issuing its decision in 1963, referred to a 1908 Supreme Court decision, *Winters v. United States*. In the *Winters* case, the Court had settled a dispute over the use of Montana's Milk River by determining that when Congress created the Fort Belknap Reservation

117

it had implicitly set aside water rights so the reservation lands could be farmed. Even though nonnative settlers had perfected their water rights under Montana state law (water rights are "perfected" by exercising a water right permit and putting the water to beneficial use), the water rights of Native Americans on the Fort Belknap Reservation were senior, and thus had priority.

Citing the 1908 *Winters* decision, the Supreme Court in 1963 decided that the five reservations along the lower Colorado River included rights to use water. When the government of the United States created the reservations, the Court reasoned, it intended for the people who lived on them to raise crops; and the ability of these arid lands to support agriculture is tied directly to water. And, according to the Court, the states in which reservations were located had to provide the amount of water necessary to fulfill the tribal water rights. These rights, which became known as "Indian reserved water rights" or "reserved tribal water rights," trumped the hoary doctrine of prior appropriation at the heart of western water law. Native Americans suddenly went from being offstage and ignored in the West's water drama to becoming major actors.

The amount of water to which Native Americans were entitled was based on the "practicably irrigable acreage" of their reservations, which created disagreements for decades about how the acreage was to be quantified. Courts also interpreted Indian reserved rights as entitling a tribe to use enough water to establish a "permanent homeland." Lawyers are still busy arguing over what this entails. Non-Indian water users, grumbling about Indians stealing their water, pressured the government to avoid diverting streamflow to Indian homelands and away from thirsty cities and farms. Endless litigation ensued, and much of the water that legally belonged to Native Americans continued to flow down western rivers to be tapped by other users.

Even if Native Americans won their water rights cases in court, they often couldn't use their legal share of water because they didn't have the money to build the pricey diversion projects necessary to irrigate their land and deliver drinking water. Often they found themselves with rights to "paper water" but with no "wet water." And people on reservations across the West who had been awarded water rights worth fortunes still found themselves hauling buckets of drinking water from faraway springs and disinfecting the contaminated liquid with bleach. Native Americans in some cases relinquished their water rights in exchange for water infrastructure they urgently needed. For instance, in 1957, the Navajos, the largest tribe in the United States, traded their priority rights to the flow of the San Juan River for congressional approval of the Navajo Indian Irrigation Project. Aside from needing water storage and diversion infrastructure, the tribe was in dire need of money and jobs. It bargained away even more of its water rights for the construction of a coal-fired power plant on its lands, providing revenue and employment for its people. Many Navajos later complained of government subterfuge and claimed their tribe had not been fully informed about the value of the water rights they had given up. The Navajo Nation, split between New Mexico, Arizona, and Utah, and bisected by the Upper and Lower Colorado River Basins, engaged state governments and federal agencies in legal battles over water of numbing complexity.

After more than a decade of negotiation, in 2010 the Navajo Nation's water rights were quantified for the Lower Colorado River Basin. The landmark settlement with the federal government "attempts to resolve a 142-year-old dispute over water distribution" and will provide clean running water to tens of thousands of Navajos. Previously, the Navajo people had battled among themselves over how to negotiate a water rights settlement, which, according to an article in *High Country News*, led to slashed tires and loosened lug nuts on vehicle wheels, a nefarious plot with poisoned cough drops, and rumors of witchcraft. The recent agreement has created a schism within the Navajo Nation, with some members accusing other members of signing away too many water rights. Non-Navajo critics of the agreement complain that too much water—about 600,000 acre-feet per year, twice the annual allotment of Nevada—will flow to a small group of people.

The federal government once forced Native Americans to settle on reservations and tried to turn them into farmers. Now some of them are farming, and all of them want the water they were implicitly promised by the government. Reserved tribal water rights that have yet to be quantified have been called a "sleeping giant" and a "wild card" that could potentially force the entire Colorado River Compact to collapse.

In 2004, the Gila River Water Settlement Act left a community of fewer than twenty thousand people in control of enough water to supply half of Arizona's population. Pima and Maricopa Indians, who had scratched out a living growing cotton and food in the desert and running casinos after having their resources stripped from them in a series of broken treaties and promises, and who had first gone to court in 1925 to secure water rights, were suddenly powerbrokers on par with the water czars of Phoenix. After the tribes along the Gila River flood their commercial citrus groves and fill their tilapia ponds with their allotment, they will lease the rest of the water they were awarded to Phoenix at a price fixed by the terms of their settlement. A steady flow of money from the leased water will enter a reservation stricken with poverty, unemployment, and health epidemics caused by disintegration of the people's traditional lifestyle—which was based on sustainably farming the floodplains of the Gila River before whites arrived with their treaties and water laws.

The 1963 *Arizona v. California* Supreme Court decision, along with establishing Indian reserved water rights, also established federal reserved water rights. The Court reasoned that when lands were set aside by statute or executive order to create national parks, forests, wildlife refuges, wilderness areas, and military bases, water rights were also implicitly set aside to fulfill the intended purposes of the reserved lands. These federal reserved water rights had priority over other users' water rights that were perfected after the federal lands were established.

Indian reserved rights and federal reserved rights shuffled western water law in a profound way. Users who had been at the front of the line, having acquired senior rights by first putting the resource to beneficial use, suddenly found themselves behind Native Americans and the federal government, which had in many cases leapfrogged to the head of the line.

Congress had in the past deferred to the states with regard to water laws. The 1963 Supreme Court decision marked something of a turning point—federal laws began to displace state water laws. Legislation passed by Congress establishing water rules and regulations accumulated, fundamentally changing the way water was managed in the West.[7] As the role of the federal government flipped from financing and building large infrastructure projects to protecting water resources from environmental harm, states' rights advocates railed against what they saw as the heavy-handed control of the government, and environmentalists applauded measures taken to safeguard the West's rivers.

States face the same dilemma as tribes: Water allotted by court decree doesn't instantly flow from faucets. Structures of concrete and steel must first be built, and someone has to foot the bill. Before Arizona could put to use the share of Colorado River water it had been ensured by the 1963 Supreme Court decision, its representatives had to persuade Congress to authorize CAP—a project as costly as a space mission. California had a huge contingent in the House of Representatives, and its politicians did everything they could to stall the project. Tapping the national treasury to bring water to the desert wasn't the root of California's opposition. Rather, the Golden State's belligerence toward CAP was based on the growing realization that the 1922 Colorado River Compact—and the entire Law of the River—had been built around a false figure: The 16.4 maf of water estimated as average annual flow at Lee's Ferry had been inflated by nearly 3 maf. Given how precious every drop of water is in the West, this miscalculation was something like NASA launching a probe toward Mercury and landing it on the moon by mistake.

With the river being stretched thin from development in the Upper Basin, the Mexican treaty, and Indian claims, California wanted to quash

---

7 This spate of federal legislation included the Wild and Scenic Rivers Act of 1968 (protecting wild rivers and scenic rivers from development); the National Environmental Policy Act of 1970 (requiring all federal agencies to prepare environmental impact statements); the Clean Water Act of 1972 (regulating water pollution); the Endangered Species Act of 1973 (protecting imperiled species from extinction); and the Safe Drinking Water Act of 1974 (ensuring drinking water free of hazardous contaminants).

its Lower Basin rival's megaproject. It was, however, willing to work out a deal. In exchange for dropping its opposition to CAP, California required that its apportionment of 4.4 maf of Colorado River water be given priority. CAP would move forward, but Arizona, because of its junior water right, would have no guarantee that it would receive the amount of water it wanted. The deal meant that Arizona would suffer the brunt of droughts. Arizona, grossly underrepresented in Congress compared to California, had little choice but to accept. Desperate to shore up water supplies for cities it hoped would swell within its borders, the state that had proved prickly as a saguaro when it came to water deals reluctantly agreed to the compromise—which allowed California to gain back some of its power over Colorado River water it had lost in the recent Supreme Court decision. In the scrum to distribute water in the West, the number of votes possessed by districts and states had become as important as the doctrine of prior appropriation, interstate compacts, and court decisions. Bigger cities meant more votes. More votes meant more water projects. More water projects were needed to make the cities grow. Anyone who pointed out that all this smacked of insanity had an ice cube's chance in Death Valley of being elected to public office.

The faulty data that had been used as the basis for the Colorado River Compact, the Mexican treaty, and Indian water rights claims all provoked the Upper Basin states, who worried there wouldn't be enough water in the river for their own diversion projects. In his novel *The Milagro Beanfield War*, John Nichols portrayed the machinations of New Mexico's politicians: "They had also sweated, plotted, finagled, begged, twisted and driven their way to what they felt was their state's fair share of Colorado River Basin water. . . ." In exchange for their support of the bill authorizing CAP, New Mexico and other Upper Basin states tacked on additional projects that would deliver water to their populations. All this legal wrangling resulted in a bill authorizing projects for which, in all likelihood, there would not be enough water. The Colorado was being diverted from every direction, and each drop was taken and turned into money. What was left of the river dribbled into the sandy wastes of a desertified delta before it reached the sea. The Colorado was becoming a "deficit river" with more demands placed on it than its meager waters could fulfill.

As feuding fiefdoms put aside their differences to unite against a common enemy, Colorado River Basin politicians joined forces to battle the specter of the vanishing river that sustained them all. They added a provision to the CAP bill that directed the Bureau of Reclamation to start looking at other sources of water to supplement the Colorado. The Columbia River, which rises in Canada among peaks swaddled in cloud, carries a fortune of melted snow through the high deserts of Washington and Oregon. Its vast wetness quickened the pulse of states in the Interior West. Panicky Pacific Northwest politicians, aiming to avoid a water grab, tried and failed to remove the measure from the bill. But they did succeed in including a ten-year ban on studies to determine the feasibility of bolstering the Colorado's flow with water from other river basins.

Conservation was never mentioned. If the rivers of the western United States were all spoken for, then there were icebergs to be towed down from Alaska, or the Yukon could be made to run in reverse and piped to the desert Southwest, or water from the Mississippi could be lifted uphill with nuclear power plants to drench the high plains of West Texas—no scheme to add to the region's water supply was too outrageous. Atomic bombs were detonated to test if nuclear explosions could excavate canals through mountains. So confident were residents of the West that technology could deliver an inexhaustible supply of water, many cities did not even meter its flow. Limiting the amount of water people used to flood their yards so grass could grow amid cactus and sand? That was un-American. Reducing the six gallons of potable water it took to flush a toilet? That made as much sense as a plaid tiger.

The embattled CAP bill faced further opposition from environmentalists, who fought two proposed dams that would be sited near the Grand Canyon, one above it, one below. The dams would generate hydroelectric power to pay for CAP and to move water uphill toward central Arizona. And their headwalls would flood wild landscapes of Grand Canyon National Park and Grand Canyon National Monument. A bitter and protracted struggle reminiscent of the fight over Echo Park ensued, pitting those who wanted to preserve the natural terrain of Grand Canyon country against those who wanted to develop the Colorado River to moisten the dust-dry fields of the Grand Canyon State and supply its thirst-crazed cities. *Life* magazine and *Reader's Digest* ran articles that opposed the dams, and the Sierra Club published a book, *Time and the River Flowing*, which celebrated the wild Colorado in the Grand Canyon. It also ran ads in the *New York Times* and the *Washington Post* that declared, "Now only you can save the Grand Canyon from being flooded . . . for profit."

The IRS, at the behest of a congressman riled by what he perceived as the Sierra Club stretching the truth about the damage the dams would do, informed the organization that its tax-exempt status might be suspended because it was trying to influence legislation (organizations that lobby must pay taxes). When the public caught wind of this, it was not pleased. It saw the goliath of the IRS bullying David Brower and the little organization he led, which simply wanted to defend an iconic part of the nation's heritage. And Brower and the Sierra Club, buoyed by a rising tide of support for their cause, did not back down. The next ad they ran questioned whether other beloved national parks such as Yellowstone were in peril from the Bureau of Reclamation's dam-building spree; and another ad, responding to the Bureau's contention that dams would make it easier for the public to view the beauty of the Grand Canyon up close, asked, "Should we also flood the Sistine Chapel so tourists can get nearer the ceiling?"

The American public, which had a hard time placing obscure dam battlegrounds such as Echo Park on a map and wasn't entirely clear what was at stake should these places disappear beneath reservoirs, knew the majesty of the Grand Canyon. Many had been there on family vacations; many more planned to one day travel to this classic landscape. The thought of a national treasure being damaged by water projects struck a great many Americans as scandalous. While Bureau of Reclamation commissioner Floyd Dominy was out of the country, the dams were hurriedly deleted from the bill. They were replaced by a coal-fired power plant at Page in northern Arizona to provide the power to pump water from the

Colorado over the Buckskin Mountains to central Arizona. The final version of the CAP legislation was approved by Congress in 1968, authorizing more than a billion dollars' worth of projects. Today that amount of money might barely cover the cost of the environmental impact statements and the plans to address the safety concerns of workers. After the legislation was finally passed, the funding needed to complete the construction extravaganza was divvied out in a trickle, its flow slowed by concerns about insufficient water in the Colorado and the environmental consequences of such a colossal system designed to reroute the river. But the coal-fired Navajo Generating Station at Page was built. Coal was strip-mined from the scalped earth of a deposit at nearby Black Mesa. Cooling water was drawn from Lake Powell, and power lines were strung high above Navajo hogans, many of which didn't have electricity. The plant sent a pall of pollution across the Southwest, obscuring the view of the Grand Canyon, as well as shrouding several other national parks. Environmentalists celebrated their defeat of Grand Canyon dams while squinting through a haze of sulfur skies.

CAP, originally budgeted to cost around $832 million, set the Bureau of Reclamation back $4.7 billion—the most expensive waterworks in the agency's history. When CAP water finally flowed from Tucson's taps in 1992, its minerals corroded plumbing and stripped rust from iron pipes. Water from faucets ran orange, and residents gagged on the taste. Tucson voters overwhelmingly passed an initiative prohibiting the city from using CAP water—which the state had fought to secure for half a century while insisting that its cities and farms were in danger of drying up and blowing away—until it could be made as pure as groundwater raised up from wells. Many years of tinkering with the Colorado River's chemistry ensued as its salty waters were blended with Arizona's well water, the mining of which was emptying the state's aquifers. Meanwhile, the CAP water was used to flood fields of surplus crops, where it steamed to nothing in the dry heat beloved by snowbirds fleeing cold, damp places and cramping desert cities with their influx.

While the CAP drama was playing out, the United States once again found itself at odds with Mexico over the Colorado River. This time the issue was salinity. The treaty signed in 1944 had guaranteed Mexico an amount of water but had nothing to say about its quality. The pre-dam Colorado River had been salty enough to corrode the teakettles of pioneers. But once its flow was used for irrigation, repeatedly flushing salts from the soil, and once pure water began evaporating from giant reservoirs to further concentrate salts in the Colorado, the heightened salinity levels caused increasing friction between the United States and Mexico until the conflict threatened to combust.

Water in southern Arizona's Wellton-Mohawk Irrigation and Drainage District was repeatedly poured on fields, each time gathering salts as it drained from the soil. Eventually the contaminated water began killing crops. Congress authorized the Bureau of Reclamation to bail out the farmers who were causing the problem. In 1961 a channel was completed that routed the supersaline wastewater out of the Wellton-Mohawk basin and into the Colorado River just above the border with Mexico. When the salt-poisoned flow headed south, it killed vast acreage of Mexican crops. Famine loomed and farmers rioted. Mexico growled that it would make the United States face the World Court. This threat, combined with Mexico's discovery of oilfields in its offshore waters and fears that the irate nation would withhold petroleum in reprisal, prompted the United States to act. In 1973 the United States and Mexico signed what became known as Minute 242 of the International Boundary and Water Commission, an agreement that limited the average annual salinity of the water sent to Mexico. And in 1974 both houses of Congress passed the Colorado River Basin Salinity Control Act. The legislation authorized salt-control projects in Colorado, Utah, and Nevada, and it called for a $260 million desalination plant, one of the largest on the planet, to be built near Yuma, Arizona.

Government subsidies had encouraged farmers to bring marginal lands of salt-laced soil into production and to use water inefficiently, dumping it with abandon on their fields because it was so cheap, flushing salt into the river until its waters were too poisoned to use. Now the solution to the problem, a complicated piece of technology with a price tag of more than a quarter of a billion dollars, would be financed not by the people who were contaminating the river, not by Westerners with hands rough from working the land and necks creased by sun. The cost would be covered by taxpayers across the nation.

As the physical and social realities of the West were subsumed by myths and legends, so the flow of the Colorado River, with each compact, court decision, legislative act, and treaty, was replaced by the Law of the River. With prior appropriation as its basis, western water law created a mad scramble to be "first in time, first in right"—the six most powerful words ever spoken in the West. Each city, state, and country that coveted the waters of the Colorado was so worried about someone else using water first and claiming the right to continue using it, they maneuvered as quickly as they could to tap the river's flow, no matter the economic consequences, regardless of the environmental repercussions.

The 1922 Colorado River Compact softened the sharp urgency of prior appropriation somewhat, but the Boulder Canyon Dam Act ushered in an era of megaprojects designed to store massive amounts of water and shunt it to dry places. The Bureau of Reclamation used federal expenditures to create some of the largest public works projects in human history, infrastructure that transformed the Colorado from a marauding river to a watercourse tamed and drained. Ten major dams and eighty major diversion projects stored four times the river's annual flow and redistributed the liquid wealth throughout the arid West, turning trackless wastes into burgeoning cities and some of the planet's most productive farms. The Colorado became an enormous hydraulic machine; each dam and diversion was a cog in a carefully calibrated system. Reengineering the Colorado put a stop to the swollen waters of spring that had once delivered soil, seeds, and moisture to the river's floodplain. Trees along the shores turned to dead sticks of timber. Fields starved of the silty floodwaters that had replenished nutrients were doused with chemical fertilizers that forced food to grow. The Colorado rarely reached the sea, and the river's delta, once one of the world's great wetland ecosystems, morphed to a Martian landscape of naked beds that wrinkled and cracked in the sun. Communities of indigenous people who had lived in the delta region for a thousand years teetered toward collapse when the fish they relied on lay gasping in mud.

Some believe dams should be built by any means necessary and at any cost, so important they are to the West, a land of drought and drenching snowmelt that gathers in thunderous flood. Others believe not a single dam should ever have been raised, and even Hoover was a colossal mistake. Perhaps the truth, as it so often does, lies somewhere in the middle. Dams are not inherently good or bad; they are the product of people's thinking writ large, and as such, sometimes they are incandescently brilliant, sometimes tragically flawed.

Stand atop a dam and feel its solid permanence. Gravity pulls the concrete of the pyramidal structure toward the bedrock at its base. See the curved arch that directs the great pressure of the water against the bulky cliffs that flank the dam. Hear the powerhouse rumble far below. Enter it and walk across metal grating that vibrates with the roar of the dynamo. Listen to the water tumble down the penstocks and rush through the spiraled piping of the scrollcase; see the liquid push against bladed wheels that turn the turbine's shaft and spin the magnets of the rotor, building the current to set a city aglow. Reach your hand toward the polished casing of the turbine. Feel the energy within. That the human mind can conceive of a structure to hold back a river and generate such power is staggering. In a once wild land of treeless prairie and endless sand, cities now shimmer in the night.

Tour guides at dams love to talk about tonnage of concrete and kilowatt hours of power. America's dams are impressive, to be sure, but the reengineered watercourses of the West are sublime rivers the same way McDonald's food is haute cuisine. For an increasingly large segment of the American public, dams have come to symbolize misplaced faith in harnessing natural resources. The great faces of concrete now evoke an era of engineering excess, when the nation's wild bounty—its plains that shuddered beneath the hooves of bison, its rivers crammed so full of salmon a person could walk across the water on their backs, its skies thrumming with the wings of waterfowl—was ravaged in the name of progress and replaced with factory farms and shopping malls. Large growers and their political supporters persuaded the country to raise walls of spellbinding size to control the flow of water. Their efforts yielded thousands of dams that plugged the rivers of the West, spilling water across the wasteland, bringing forth life from stone. While the banks of rivers were grazed bare by cows, the desert grew a green fur of grass to mimic the lawns we left behind in rainier places. We ate salad in winter. We watched fountains cough precious water into the sky. Restless and wanting more, we left our freshly paved cities to traipse back into the last patches of wilderness and found them barren of bison and salmon and birds. And now the winged statues above Hoover Dam seem not so much narratives of triumph over nature as mementoes of a blind faith in dams, a misplaced belief in their potential to help forge a perfect world. Glen Canyon Dam is just another concrete slab in the desert, one more attempt to fill the world with awe. The novelty wore thin long ago. The shining dream of technological utopia grows dim in the glare of the West's suburban streetlights. Now multitudes flock to the halls of Congress clamoring for the barricades to come tumbling down, for the rivers to run free.

Chapter 7

When Dams Fall

It was 1972. The Bureau of Reclamation had a staff of nearly twenty thousand and an annual budget of half a billion dollars. The Bureau was searching for places to put new dams, but there were few decent sites left—almost every location that made some economic sense had already been dammed. For Bureau engineers to keep themselves in business, however, they had to keep building. So a place was chosen on the Snake River Plain, a land of cinder cones crumbling beneath a cobalt sky.

The mountains of northern Idaho pull moisture from storms, and the valleys are lush with several shades of green. But most of the population of Idaho is in the south, on the dark volcanic plain along the Snake River. The Mormons who settled this land diverted small streams to water their fields. Then the Bureau of Reclamation built dams on the Snake, allowing large-scale irrigation. Potato farming exploded. Idaho once boasted more millionaires per capita than any other state, thanks to the loose, sandy, potato-friendly soil—and thanks to the Bureau's taxpayer-funded waterworks. But the soil loved by spuds is porous and doesn't hold water, so large flows had to be pumped to the potato fields. Idaho farmers lusted for more water that could soak more soot-colored soil and grow more potatoes. They wanted a dam. And they wanted the federal government to pay for it and build it.

First came a drought, and then a flood, and then Uncle Sam built a dam: the story of the West. A dry spell in 1961 and 1962 cooked Idaho's fields to a crisp, and the following winter floodwaters swelled beyond the banks of the Snake River and busted bridges apart, turning them to splintered wood and tangles of steel. Neither the drought nor the flood was particularly devastating, but they created enough drama for dam proponents to push forward their proposal. They built nearly unanimous support across southern Idaho's Mormon potato kingdom, and soon the Teton Dam was authorized.

Because Congress had passed the National Environmental Policy Act in 1969, directing the Bureau to state publicly the effects of its projects, the agency was forced to file an environmental impact statement on the Teton Dam. As explained by Marc Reisner in *Cadillac Desert*, the Boise-based *Idaho Statesman*, the state's major newspaper, got hold of the document, and with the help of an Idaho environmental watchdog group with many scientists as members, they analyzed the Bureau's statistics and tore the project apart. Most of the lands the dam would benefit were already being drenched with irrigation water. The costly dam would provide wealthy potato farmers with cheap water they could use to supplement the already prodigious amount they were pouring into the leaky soil in one of the most arid regions of America. A newspaper based in Idaho Falls, a town near the site of the proposed dam, railed against creeping socialism in its editorials while aggressively promoting the project. When irrigation statistics failed the dam's boosters, they claimed the structure was for flood control.

"Facts," John Wesley Powell wrote, "are to be collected as preliminary to the construction of a reservoir system. To neglect the essential facts is to be guilty of criminal neglect." The Snake River Plain, where Bureau engineers sited the Teton Dam, is paved with fissured ashflows and lava from a time when magma rose up from the glowing innards of the earth and punched through the crust to cool. The eruptions of these supervolcanos, whose collapsed remains formed the cracked and blistered plain along the Snake River, were some of the greatest cataclysms in the planet's history. Liquid fire still rises toward the surface of the nearby Yellowstone Plateau, triggering earthquakes as the whole unsettled region, adrift on a molten dome, buckles and tilts. Before construction began in 1972, the US Geological Survey raised questions about the safety of building the dam on brittle rock in an area frequented by seismic convulsions. But the project's momentum was a bus without brakes. The Bureau was committed. The Nixon White House, focused on shoring up congressional support for opening China and other foreign affairs initiatives, appeased Idaho's members of Congress by not blocking the project. And in an Idaho court, appeals by environmentalists were shot down like so many clay pigeons.

Cracks in a cliff against which one of the dam abutments would be built were filled with grout. But the largest cracks—some big enough to hold a pickup truck, or a Winnebago, or maybe even a house—swallowed up great globs of grout and still they couldn't be filled. Voids that large had the potential to let water escape the reservoir and erode the volcanic buttresses that held the dam in place, or they could turn the earthen dam itself into mudholes and mire. But the project manager decided to press on with construction, and the dam was completed according to schedule. Towns in the floodpath below knew nothing about the deeply fractured rock. The Bureau had a perfect track record, and no one seemed concerned that the dam would fail. It employed the finest engineers on the planet and had created half the manmade wonders of the modern world. The Teton Dam was modest in stature compared to the Bureau's masterworks on the Colorado and Columbia Rivers.

The earthfill wall of Teton Dam, made by compacting successive layers of dirt and gravel, spanned more than three thousand feet between canyon walls. At the beginning of October 1975, the Teton River found its path blocked and began to pile up its waters behind the earthen dam. In the following months, winter storms snagged on the Teton Mountains, a range of toothy peaks, some as sharp and pointy as incisors, a few as blunt as molars, and all their crevices and cavities packed with snow. The snow melted quickly in the hot spring sun. Water raced down terraces of stone, finding the fastest way into canyons, engorging the Teton River with runoff. Though Bureau safety protocol dictated that the dam should be filled slowly so problems could be monitored and corrected, the dam's main outlet works, designed to allow excess water to be released from the reservoir, weren't yet operational—only the auxiliary outlet works had been completed. With so much snowmelt flooding into the reservoir and no way to release it all, the water level swiftly lifted. Observation wells drilled in land downstream from the dam revealed a precipitously rising water table. This could have been interpreted to mean the reservoir was seeping water at a dangerous rate, undermining the stability of the cracked volcanic walls that anchored the dam in place. But the phenomenon was explained away by Bureau engineers as a harmless response to pressure changes caused by the reservoir filling.

In early June 1976, when the reservoir was almost full, small leaks spouted from the canyon walls. And then a wet spot appeared on the downstream face of the dam. The wetness spread, finally erupting in a muddy fountain. Bulldozers pushed debris into the hole but couldn't plug it, and from the widening gap gushed torrents of glop. The sheriffs of counties downstream were told to evacuate everyone in the river's path.

In the reservoir, a giant whirlpool circled near the dam's edge. As if spiraling down a drain, water was quickly falling from the basin, dropping straight through the dam, turning its earthfill insides to mush. On the dam's downstream face, two bulldozers continued shoving boulders and stones into the spewing sinkhole. But the maw suddenly opened wide, swallowing both machines an instant after their operators leapt to safety. The crest of the dam sagged into the reservoir. Then a great chunk slumped and fell apart, releasing a flood with the energy of an atomic bomb.

A tourist standing on the canyon rim captured the image by video camera: A wall of liquid violence surged along the riverbed and spread across the plain downstream in a frothy slather. As radio broadcasts warned people in the floodpath that the dam had failed, they fled to high ground. Wilford, the town sited nearest the dam and low enough to be inundated, was hit first. Observers said the wave bearing down on the town looked like a cloud of dust. Houses were ripped from their foundations. Trees snapped in half. The floodwaters tumbled trailers and cars in a brown tumult that rushed through town gathering dead cows and all manner of debris in its grabby flow. Carpets of topsoil were peeled from the ground, turning the wave at the leading edge of the waters to muddy ooze as it rolled into Sugar City. The crest diminished as the flood headed on toward Rexburg, but still it packed enough of a punch to break apart a lumberyard, setting logs free, which hurled toward a gasoline tank.

The tank exploded, and slicks of flaming gas spread across the water like brightly swirled paisleys. Citizens watched the spectacle from the hills above, reciting scripture as the town was engulfed in fire and flood.

When the floodwaters subsided and the fires died to a few licks of flame and curls of smoke, townspeople tottered through the wreckage, sinking in mud up to their hips, their noses and mouths covered with bandannas to mask the stink of rotting plants and animal flesh mixed with the foul slurry. Clouds of flies and mosquitoes rose from stagnant pools. Seagulls appeared from distant shores to feast on the insects. The flocks of seagulls in Idaho were seen as a sign, and irrigation farmers began lobbying for a new dam to be built. God, they decided, wanted the dam so much He was willing to send seagulls to mitigate the destruction caused by the first failed attempt.

For more than three decades, interest in raising another version of the dam has lingered, though many people who witnessed the carnage caused by the collapse hesitate to support it. Citizens of Rexburg, the town that absorbed the brunt of the disaster, are mostly opposed to the idea. But agriculture has a powerful voice in Idaho, and the shouts of irrigators for cheap water are growing louder. In 2008 the Idaho Legislature appropriated $400,000 to study building another Teton Dam.

The cause of the dam's collapse is not completely understood, but geologists have concluded that a combination of factors—the permeable soil used to construct the dam's core and the fissures in the cliff abutments—allowed water to seep into the earthen dam, softening it from inside.

Regardless of the reason for its failure, a dam that had been touted as necessary for flood control had caused a billion dollars worth of flood damage. More land than the amount the dam would have made bloom from irrigation was dead, stripped of topsoil down to bare rock. But the handful of farmers who stood to benefit most from the dam owned property on a raised bench that hovered over the denuded landscape; their fields were not harmed by the flood. Before the dam construction began, those wealthy farmers, perched safely above the river plain, had been pumping groundwater from an aquifer to saturate their potato fields and they had enjoyed bounteous harvests. The dam would have provided them with some supplemental water to grow their profits, nothing more. On the plain below, eleven people were dead, thousands of lives were in turmoil, and entire towns lay in ruins.

⁓

The pork barrel of American politics sloshed with water. Ever since the Reclamation Act was passed in 1902, bringing a dam home from Washington was a sure way to get reelected. Members of Congress voted for dams that weren't in their districts because they knew that if they supported someone else's dam now, sooner or later they might have a dam of their own that would provide a bonanza for their constituents: Farmers, construction contractors, engineering companies, and the recreation and tourism industries would all benefit. And the politician who delivered the dam would be rewarded with votes. It was not unusual to find appropriations for dams contained in an Omnibus bill—a single document accepted in a single vote by Congress, but which bundles together several unrelated pieces of legislation. An education bill might have a dam project buried deep within its fine print. Welfare reform legislation might contain a water project or two. Dan Beard, former Bureau of Reclamation commissioner, said that without using pork barrel water projects in the legislative process, the Civil Rights Act never would have passed.

Beginning in the 1970s the absurdly large subsidies associated with dams began to be revealed. Richard Wahl, an economist who worked for the Department of the Interior, exposed the government giveaways and questionable accounting methods that enabled irrigators to avoid paying their share of the capital expenses and the cost of the operation and maintenance of dams. He calculated that the federal treasury would recoup only 14 percent of the total construction cost of Bureau of Reclamation irrigation projects—the rest of the cost was borne by taxpayers, amounting to a bill of many billions of dollars for the boondoggled public.

An aficionado of whitewater canoeing and the recipient of an engineering degree from the Naval Academy at Annapolis, President Jimmy Carter found himself uncomfortable with the dam-everything-at-any-cost mentality that pervaded Washington when he took his place in the Oval Office in 1977. As governor of Georgia he had personally scrutinized a water project proposal from the Corps of Engineers and found both the numbers and concern for the environment sorely lacking. The methodology used to compute the cost-benefit ratio struck him as downright fraudulent; he used his gubernatorial powers to veto the dam. And so began his opposition to the American pork barrel brimful of ill-conceived water projects. And so began his political undoing.

Congress, preaching temperance from a barstool, stalled what it derided as wasteful welfare programs while fast-tracking projects that would cost hundreds of millions of dollars to deliver subsidized water to handfuls of wealthy farm businesses. Throughout the twentieth century, rarely did someone in Washington who wanted to get reelected question the fiscal sanity of projects whose costs to taxpayers outweighed their benefits to society. Nor did anyone comment on the moral irresponsibility of such projects. Water projects were sacred and untouchable. They lay outside the traditional dichotomies of conservative and liberal, left and right. Democrats professing their support of the working man voted for dams that delivered free water to agribusiness leviathans. Republicans yammering about people pulling themselves up by their bootstraps voted for water projects that turned tax dollars into entitlements. Dams were, if not loved by all, at least accepted by most as a necessary part of American politics.

In *Cadillac Desert*, Marc Reisner quotes Robert Edgar, who served in the House of Representatives from 1975 to 1987 and boldly attacked pork-barrel water projects throughout his political career:

> *The old-boy network comes to you. . . . They say, "You've got a water project in your district? You want one? Let us take care of it for you." Then they come around a few months later and get their pound of flesh. You actually risk very little by going along. You get a lot of money thrown into your district for a project that few of your constituents oppose. In return, you vote for a lot of projects your constituents don't know or care about. . . . Then everyone wonders why we're running such big federal deficits, and they cut the social programs, which must be the culprit.*

This was the environment in which President Carter, who had never served in Congress, took aim at water projects in 1977. After packing his cabinet with conservation-minded and cost-conscious staff, he attempted to make good on his campaign pledge to balance the federal budget by the end of his first term in office. He delivered to Congress his infamous "hit list," which identified nineteen water projects he found deplorable because of poor cost-benefit ratios, safety concerns, and environmental consequences. Philip Fradkin noted in his book *A River No More* that one especially pernicious project, Fruitland Mesa, "would have benefited sixty-nine ranchers, at an investment of $1.2 million per landowner."

Making clear his intention to reform water policy, Carter stated, "In the arid West and across the entire nation, we must begin to recognize that water is not free—it is a precious resource. . . . The cornerstone of future water policy should be wise management and conservation." Wise management and conservation went over in the West like lead balloons filled with lumps of granite.

Carter's hit list coincided with a brutal period of drought. Arizona's cotton crop was brittle with thirst, California's fields lay crisp beneath a pitiless sun, Colorado's mountains were bare of snow. Westerners were in no mood to have their water projects taken away. They called Carter's attack on their waterworks the "War on the West" and the "George Washington's Birthday Massacre." Even politicians who had opposed dams in the past, such as California governor Jerry Brown, and politicians who had expressed their support for reforming the Bureau of Reclamation and the Corps of Engineers, such as Arizona congressman Morris Udall, demanded their water projects back. Irrigation farmers with political clout were furious. Congress was, almost to a member, livid. Simmering hostilities between states threatened to flare up into full-blown fires. Arizonans feared that crafty Californians were scheming to snatch their water. To calm them, California's members of Congress promised they would vote to get the Central Arizona Project restored so that western states could maintain their unity against the federal government—which had no business meddling with the West's water. Unless, of course, it was building dams and aqueducts. The water establishment in the West—that is to say, essentially the entire West—shook and shuddered when it read of the projects slated for elimination. The Bureau of Reclamation and the Corps of Engineers frothed and fumed. Carter suddenly found himself with few friends and surrounded by enemies.

Carter's principled stand backfired terribly, alienating him from members of his own party who saw their hopes of reelection dashed as they lost their ability to bring home dams from Washington. Even the press, ever critical of pork barrel politics, turned against him. He was depicted as an environmental extremist and a rube who didn't understand the ways of Washington. In the end, every project he opposed save one was built, and his hastily conceived hit list threatened his entire domestic agenda.

Shaken by the Teton Dam disaster and stirred by Rachel Carson's seminal work *Silent Spring* and other exposés that made clear the costs of environmental degradation, more Americans were beginning to view dams not as monuments of their civilization but as monstrosities that turned living arteries to lifeless plumbing. The American people were ready to weigh the value of wild streams against concrete structures that choked streamflow for the benefit of industries bloated with government subsidies, and there was inexorable movement toward stopping the building bonanza of public works projects in the West. But Carter, by brazenly attacking the water establishment, made little headway. Washington wasn't ready to give up its addiction to dams just yet.

Marc Reisner asserts that Carter's western water debacle was as big a factor in his one-term presidency as the hostage crisis in Iran. Though Carter failed to reform pork barrel water politics, he did pave the way for his successors to take on Congress and the "water lobby"—the farmers, developers, engineers, construction workers, and so on who pushed for ever more water projects—and cut fiscally wasteful dams from the federal budget. President Ronald Reagan, reveling in his reputation as a bona fide Westerner, appointed arch-conservative, development-friendly Coloradan James Watt as secretary of the interior, spreading fear and loathing in the environmental community. Reagan staged press conferences at his Santa Barbara ranch to announce plans to slash away at the fat federal government, and Westerners cheered. But when he got down to the business of cutting spending to trim the budget deficit, he proposed that states share in the cost of their water projects, and bulldozers sputtered to a halt.

Echoing a cost-sharing proposal that Carter had championed, Reagan required states that wanted new dams to put up some of the money for the projects. Congress and the water lobby were stunned. States reeled at the prospect of reaching into their own pockets to pay for water projects—in the past, the federal government hadn't required them to pay a dime before construction began. (California had paid the tab for its enormous State Water Project, one of the most expensive public works projects in history, but California was a special case: Its economy had grown larger than the economies of all but seven of the world's nations.) Reagan threatened to veto, as Carter had, any legislation with water projects that were not financially sound. He experienced pushback, of course, but he was a savvy politician. Fiscal conservatives in his administration forged an alliance with environmentalists to support cost sharing, effectively putting the kibosh on colossal water projects financed by the federal government. Reagan never slapped the water establishment in the face with a hit list, and the shouts of outrage that had echoed in the halls of Congress during the Carter administration quieted to muted grumblings during the Reagan years.

By the time President Clinton was helming the country, the national mood around dams in the West had changed, so much so that in 1993 Clinton appointed Dan Beard, an avowed environmentalist, as commissioner of the Bureau of Reclamation. "I came to Reclamation with one purpose," Beard told Marc Reisner in an interview published in *High Country News.* "To make us more environmentally sensitive and responsive to the needs of the contemporary West. . . . The Bureau's future isn't in dams. The era of dams is over."

Before being appointed commissioner, Beard had made his mark on the Bureau while serving as a congressional staffer. He had helped write the Central Valley Project Improvement Act legislation, which was signed into law by President George H. W. Bush despite the strident protests of growers in California. Public outrage over images of birds hideously misshapen by selenium and other poisons that had been concentrated by intensive irrigation practices provided momentum for revising water policy. The legislation, encompassing everything from reserving flows for wildlife and fisheries to restructuring pricing to more faithfully reflect water's true cost, initiated the most extensive reforms in the Bureau's history.

Beard, who succeeded a long line of crazy-for-dams commissioners such as Floyd Dominy, made one of his acts as the leader of the Bureau to pare down its staff; it was reduced to less than a quarter of what it had been during the FDR-Truman dam-everything-that-flows days. And the people Beard did hire were often biologists and ecologists instead of engineers. He said that the Bureau had to "become an environmental agency moving away from dam-building and into water-resource management."

Before Beard arrived at the Bureau, a dam-building fever had infected countries across the globe. The Bureau, after damming damn near every stream in the western United States, had begun securing contracts to build international megaprojects and had helped raise concrete walls around the world. Many Bureau engineers enjoyed lucrative careers in engineering firms after leaving their government gigs. Beard, after his stint at the Bureau, went to work for the National Audubon Society—and he even joined the ranks of the antidam advocates of the world. As recounted by Fred Pearce in his book *When the Rivers Run Dry*, Beard marched with protesters in Japan and shouted through a megaphone, "This is one of the most awful dam projects I have ever seen—and I've seen some."

A Salt Lake City doctor who had visited Glen Canyon as a boy, and as an adult found himself distressed by this paradise lost beneath Lake Powell, founded the Glen Canyon Institute. The Institute, which refers to the offending body of water as "Reservoir Powell" to stress its artificiality, has the stated mission "to restore a free-flowing Colorado River through Glen and Grand Canyons." David Brower, former director of the Sierra Club, after deciding that damming Glen Canyon was an enormous mistake, joined the Glen Canyon Institute and began advocating the draining of Lake Powell. The Sierra Club adopted this position too. The Glen

Canyon Institute and the Sierra Club contend that all the functions of Glen Canyon Dam can be performed by Hoover Dam. They point to a Bureau of Reclamation study that found that 1 maf of water—enough to meet the annual domestic needs of four million people—is lost from Lake Powell through seepage into the surrounding stone and evaporation into the desert sky. This renders the reservoir's storage function negligible, they argue. Open the gates, drain the lake, let the canyon recover, they insist. The Glen Canyon Institute and the Sierra Club don't advocate destroying Glen Canyon Dam. Instead, the structure would stand as a monument to, depending on one's position, the determination and grit of those who raised it, or the arrogance and recklessness of the bureaucrats who drowned a wild canyon, burying its beauty beneath a sluggish lake abuzz with powerboats. Of course, not everyone agrees. Colorado senator Ben Nighthorse Campbell referred to pulling the plug on Lake Powell as "a certifiable nut idea."

The throngs of boaters who cruise Powell's blue waters lapping against red bluffs see draining a perfectly good body of water, accessible for all, so it can be replaced by a canyon available to only a handful of the hardiest hikers, as lunacy at best, and at worst a threat to their liberty that will prod them to take up arms. Arizona now has more boats per capita than any other state. The inland sea of Lake Powell, though the product of a concrete wall 710 feet tall, seems as natural to the people in the region—and to the fish that live in its waters and the wildlife along its shores—as if the hand of God had built it.

Nature did once dam the mighty river. A million years ago or more, great gouts of lava coughed through a crack in the crust of the earth, creating a wall taller than Glen Canyon Dam. Water backed up behind the lava plug, forming a lake that lifted higher and higher until finally it poured over the top and tore the dam down. Lava Falls, a rapid in the river, is what remains of the gigantic blockade.

Nature can rearrange a landscape by moving massive amounts of material, but without the talent of Reclamation engineers, who pour concrete in perfect arches to resist the push of water and build spillways to relieve the pressure, natural dams come tumbling down. In time, manmade dams too will fall, though the process of their undoing is much slower—slower from people's perspective, anyway. Nature's patience is inexhaustible, and all rivers eventually remove whatever stands in their path. The Colorado did, after all, excavate the Grand Canyon. Through millennia of relentless wearing down, the river sawed through rock and gnawed at soil. Sometimes slowly, grain by grain and pebble by pebble, and sometimes in great cataclysmic bursts of flood that sent boulders rolling, the river moved away mountains of sediment until it had gouged a trench three hundred miles long, fifteen miles wide, and a mile deep.

In 1983, Glen Canyon Dam nearly came tumbling down. After winter blizzards buried the Rocky Mountains, a soggy spring stacked up more snow and saturated it with rain. A quick zap of heat in May obliterated the thick snowpack so quickly meltwater couldn't soak into the dusty lunar landscape of the desert but instead slid downhill in torrents, overfilling each gully and basin, swelling creeks until they spilled beyond their banks. Streams stampeded down the streets of Salt Lake City, and hillsides turned to sloughing muck. People scurried toward safety, their footprints oozing shut behind them. Mudslides shoved houses off their foundations. Runoff flooded toward the Colorado, and the engorged river poured into Lake Powell. By early June the reservoir was full, but still it rose a vertical foot and a half per day along its two thousand miles of shoreline. The piping of the outlet works at the dam was opened to spill excess water, and the power generators were run at full tilt to release as much flow as possible. But still the reservoir rose.

For the first time since Glen Canyon Dam had been constructed, spillways purged water so that Lake Powell wouldn't flow over the dam's crest, destroying the power plant sited downstream. Like the overflow drain on a bathtub, spillway portals near the top of a reservoir prevent water from rising too high. When the spillway gates of Glen Canyon Dam were lifted open, water surged under their lower edges into tunnels drilled in cliffs at the edges of the dam, and the flow was released into the river below. Clear water from the lake poured into the spillways; ruddy water carrying chunks of debris vomited out. The entire dam shook and shuddered.

The spillway gates were closed, and when inspectors were lowered down the tunnels in a little cart to have a look inside, concrete linings three feet thick showed holes as big as houses. Water had torn through the reinforced concrete of the tunnels and was eating away at the soft sandstone bedrock behind them, moving in pressured blasts toward the dam abutments that held the structure in place. If the dam failed, it would release a flood that would likely topple downstream dams like dominoes as it pushed toward the sea. The solution to preventing this apocalyptic flood? Plywood.

The dam operators attached sheets of plywood, known as flashboards, to the top of the spillway gates. This increased the height of the gates by four feet, allowing the lake some room to rise a little higher. Makeshift flashboards were holding back nine trillion gallons of water. Plywood was preventing the largest dam disaster in human history.

Runoff from melting mountain snows continued to flood the Colorado River above Lake Powell, and rainstorms added to the surge. The level of the lake crept closer to the crest of the dam, and water rumbled and roared as it smashed through the spillway tunnels. Tearing their concrete linings and ripping apart the surrounding rocks, the water in the stressed spillways created a mad symphony that could be heard from miles away. The dam shook so hard manhole covers popped open. Water spouted from leaks in the quaking concrete. Vibrations threatened to rattle the turbines in the power plant loose. Chunks of concrete and sandstone the size of refrigerators blasted out from the ends of the spillways. One of them sputtered and then stopped shooting water. Dam operators, their teeth rattling as one of the largest slabs of concrete on Earth shook like a toy, ramped up the flow, hoping to dislodge whatever was blocking the spillway. The gamble paid off: Water erupted from the end of the tunnel as it cleared itself of debris.

So much water was dumping from the dam that floodwaves slapped into the Grand Canyon, flipping rafts and chasing campers on drowned shores to higher ground. Sediment scoured from the riverbed darkened the swollen waters as helicopters dropped into the canyon to lift people out.

The plywood flashboards were replaced with ones made of steel, and the reservoir level continued to rise, climbing to seven feet below the crest of the dam. Then the level steadied. And finally it began to fall. The spillways were in ruins, but the dam had held: just barely, thanks to a few pieces of plywood purchased from a local supply store. Maybe whoever bought the plywood picked up a roll of duct tape too, just in case things got really crazy at the dam.

As pointed out by James Lawrence Powell in *Dead Pool*, the reason for the predicament was not so much nature as money. Dam managers had ignored reports by the National Weather Service about high temperatures causing above-average runoff. They could have let water out of the reservoir to be ready for the coming floodwaters, but they chose not to. Peak power rates come later in the summer, and managers wanted the dam as close to full as possible to maximize profits. Leaving plenty of empty room in the reservoir for the runoff would have risked letting the level of Lake Powell dip too low to enjoy the bonanza afforded by air conditioners humming in Phoenix in the heat of summer. This is a dam dilemma. Reservoirs should be emptied so they can safely stop floods; they should be allowed to fill to their rims so they can generate maximum power. The latter imperative often takes precedence, and dams that were sold to the public as necessary for flood control become potential creators of floods. This is a dirty secret of dams.

━━◆━━

Edward Abbey didn't care as much about the conflicting imperatives of dam managers as he did about the sheer ugliness of a dam intruding in a wild paradise. In his 1968 book *Desert Solitaire*, while floating through Glen Canyon with a friend in little rubber boats, their stomachs full of catfish and cold river water, their minds pleasant with pipe tobacco and the idyllic scenery gliding by—red walls painted with mineral mosaics, ferns and flowers growing from wet seams of rock, side canyons with waterfalls tumbling in spray and thunder—Abbey fantasizes about "some unknown hero with a rucksack full of dynamite strapped to his back" blowing up the dam. He imagines the rapids created from the rubble will be named "Floyd E. Dominy Falls."

Abbey served as the mouthpiece for a movement that looked at the deserts of the West and saw in their aridity not a defect of nature that needed to be corrected but something to be celebrated. In *Desert Solitaire* he wrote:

> *"This would be good country," a tourist says to me, "if only you had some water."*
> He's *from Cleveland, Ohio.*
> *"If we had water here," I reply, "this country would not be what it is. It would be like Ohio, wet and humid and hydrological, all covered with cabbage farms and golf courses. Instead of this lovely barren desert we would have only another blooming garden state, like New Jersey. You see what I mean?"*
> *"If you had more water more people could live here."*
> *"Yes sir. And where then would people go when they wanted to see something besides people?"*

In Abbey's iconic 1975 novel *The Monkey Wrench Gang*, which coined the ecological sabotage term "monkey wrenching," the main characters scheme to float a houseboat full of explosives to Glen Canyon Dam and blow it apart. The radical environmental group Earth First! formed in part because of the book and adopted Abbey as something of a patron saint. In 1981, Earth First! pranksters draped a piece of wedge-shaped black plastic that tapered to a point down the face of Glen Canyon Dam, making it look as though a crack had split the concrete. Abbey, speaking to a crowd assembled to watch the shenanigans, said, "Surely no manmade structure in modern American history has been hated so much by so many for so long with such good reason as Glen Canyon Dam."

Naturalist Craig Childs doesn't spend words railing against dams but instead praises desert water in its natural state, lovely for its scarcity, and for the crushing force of its sudden floods. To Childs, water that pools and flows through lands of stone and sand is perfect as it is, something to respect and revere. In his book *The Secret Knowledge of Water*, he writes, "I stood at the edge of the waterpocket, where much of the desert dropped off below, showing pockets of even greater size, and lifted my arms straight into the sky. Beads came down my body. This was abundance."

~~~

A river picks up whatever it can, including grains of soil and sand. The bare earth through which so much of the Colorado steeply flows doesn't have trees and plants to anchor it, and moving water cuts it and crumbles it and tumbles it downstream. Once, the Colorado shaped the earth beneath it, pushing land toward the sea. And through the seasons it fattened up and skinnied down, its rate of flow ranging from swellings of more than 300,000 cfs during spring runoff to meager flows of 10,000 cfs or less after the mountain snows had melted.[8] When the diversion tunnels of Glen Canyon Dam were closed in 1963, the river below the concrete bulwark began to change. From a warm, muddy flow that fluctuated through the seasons with ancient rhythms, it became a chilly stream clear as gin as water drawn from deep in the reservoir was released, and it rose and fell on a daily tide determined by the energy demands of Phoenix. The native fish, which had once been so abundant that pioneers pitchforked them from the river and piled them on their fields for fertilizer, were unable to adapt to the new river conditions. They crashed in number. The Colorado pikeminnow, the bonytail, the razorback sucker, and the humpback chub were shoved to the edge of extinction.[9] Perhaps these species should be saved if for no other reason than their names sound really cool, but earnest biologists who want to reverse the changes caused by the dam have a more serious agenda.

As the turbidity of the river below Glen Canyon Dam declined, sun streamed through the water, allowing new plant life to thrive. Gone was the decomposing matter that had served as the river's main source of energy; in its place strings of algae feathered greenly in the current.

---

8 Cubic feet per second—cfs—is a standard measurement of a river's flow. A cubic foot is like a box of water that measures one foot by one foot by one foot. The number of these "boxes"—each one the equivalent of about 7.5 gallons—that pass a given point every second is measured as cfs.

9 The pikeminnow, formerly known as the "squawfish," was renamed for reasons of political correctness—but its minnow moniker is a bit misleading because it grows as long as a person's leg.

Populations of aquatic insects and crustaceans prospered, and nonnative species of sportfish were introduced. The cold, clear flow of the tailwater below the dam and running downstream to Lee's Ferry became one of the finest fisheries in North America for rainbow trout—a species that University of Colorado professor Anders Halverson calls "an entirely synthetic fish."

According to Halverson, more than a century ago American leaders worried that industrialization had diminished men's masculinity, weakening the nation. In response, the government stocked rainbow trout across the country to provide anglers with a quarry they could capture and kill to hone their manliness and thereby strengthen democracy. In 1962, the government went so far as to dump poison into the Green River, killing all native fish for a stretch of 450 miles so the river could be restocked with the rainbows that would save American males from turning into sissies as they ventured into the wilds to hook some feisty trout.

As the rainbows in the Grand Canyon ate the young of native fishes, bald eagles with their curved beaks and razor talons dropped from the sky to gorge themselves on the trout. Swarms of insects hatched in the modified environment, swirling in profuse clouds. Swifts and swallows dipped and skimmed along the water, hunting the abundant bugs. Waterfowl fattened on the rich buffet of insects, and peregrine falcons feasted on these bloated birds. The river's web of life had been rewoven.

Tamarisk, commonly known as salt cedar, thrived along the subdued Colorado below the dam. A water-loving Eurasian shrub with feathery leaves and pink flowers, tamarisk had been brought to America as an ornamental and was later used for erosion control. Its deep roots drink from the water table, and it spreads in dense clusters, crowding out native cottonwood and willow. Though some animal species such as the southwestern willow flycatcher do just fine in the tamarisk thickets, the new environment tips away from biodiversity toward monoculture. Uniform jungles of tamarisk that fluff into canopies as tall as thirty feet dominate the banks of rivers throughout the West.

Before the dam was built, high seasonal flows had deposited sand in sinuous beaches and bars along the river's edges. But when those silty floods vanished, the stream's architecture changed. Tamarisk bound together the banks and beaches of the river, but the tangled roots couldn't completely stop erosion. Daily fluctuations in power-generating releases from the dam ate at clumps of mud and silt. Beaches disappeared, to the dismay of river runners and campers, and to the detriment of the wildlife that had evolved to live along the sandy margins of the shore.

The humpback chub, a member of the minnow family roughly the size of a trout and named for the prominent hump behind its head, spawns in slow-moving water. When the sandbars in the river started disappearing, the turbid backwaters that had formed behind them vanished, and the humpback chub too began to disappear.

The Endangered Species Act requires the government to take steps to prevent the humpback chub's extinction. But the chub is of no use to the sportfishing industry below Glen Canyon Dam, and efforts to save it and other native fishes by killing trout leave many anglers tipping back their hats to scratch their heads. The warm, silt-thick water that humpback chubs require is poison to rainbow trout, which crave the clear, cold currents of dam-released flows. A rainbow will readily take the nymphs and dryflies of anglers, stripping line from their reels as the muscular fish plunges through rapids and breaks the surface of the river in athletic leaps, stripes of color flashing on its silvery sides. Replacing this regal sportfish with an overgrown member of the minnow family with a hump that huddles in muddy pools—this is a tough sell to fishing fanatics who collectively spend the GDP of a small nation to stand in the tailwater below the dam and feel rainbows tugging at the ends of their tight lines.

The humpback chub is not beautiful in the way that a rainbow trout is beautiful, but three million to five million years of evolution in the turbulent world of pre-dam Colorado River canyons have provided it with an impressive array of features. Aside from its hydrodynamic hump and large, fanlike fins that steady its streamlined body in the Colorado's powerful currents, the species developed, in lieu of keen eyes that work well in clear water, sensitive chemoreceptors that help it hunt prey in the murk. But the humpback chub's support group barely extends beyond biologists. This piscine Quasimodo seriously lacks charisma. It doesn't have trophy antlers or pretty feathers or cuddly cubs. Have You Hugged a Humpback Chub Today? is not a bumper sticker likely to appear on Subarus in the West. The homely fish has, however, managed to retain the services of attorneys to defend its interests in the nation's highest courts.

In the mid-1970s the Bureau of Reclamation tried to increase the power generation of Glen Canyon Dam, setting off a cascade of legal battles. Environmental groups, demanding scientific studies of the effects of power generation on the stretch of river below the dam, took the Bureau to court, and won. The Bureau was forced to fund the Glen Canyon Environmental Studies office. And in an attempt to slow erosion, daily fluctuations in the river's release were reduced by cutting electricity generation during peak power hours. In 1992 Congress passed the Grand Canyon Protection Act, adding a new twist to the Law of the River. The legislation directed the Interior secretary to manage Glen Canyon Dam in a way that protects natural and recreational values. This provided further momentum for releases from the dam that gave precedence not to human needs for water and power but to mimicking the natural cycles of the river. In 1995 a team of scientists completed an environmental impact statement that was the most detailed study ever conducted on the downstream effects of a dam. And after public hearings garnered many thousands of comments reflecting widespread interest in restoring the natural ecosystem, the Bureau, attempting to undo some of the changes wrought by the dam, released into the river below Glen Canyon Dam the oxymoron of a "managed flood."

Sand and silt were stirred up and redeposited in beaches and bars. Clusters of tamarisk remained, clinging stubbornly to the flooded banks. The filaments of algae that thrive in the clear water, and the nonnative fish that thrive on the little creatures that feast on the algae, survived the deluge. The sky still seethed with hatching insects, and the river was fat with trout. The fishing industry was pleased that its artificial world of biological bounty was still intact. Beaches that formed along the shores soon washed away. To say that the Grand Canyon ecosystem had been restored by this controlled flood and the ones that followed would not be accurate. To say that the managed floods were like putting Band-Aids on bullet wounds might be a bit closer to the truth.

What was noteworthy, however, was the motivation behind creating the artificial floods. The volume of water released exceeded the amount the power plant could use to spin its turbines. Water was being put to "beneficial use," in the parlance of western water law, by being released into the river to enhance "instream flow"—water flowing within the stream channel.

Historically, the West's water laws and practices evolved to promote "offstream use"—taking water out of stream channels. The laws were weighted toward the individual's right to remove water from a stream for private gain, which often came at the expense of the public good of leaving water in rivers to support ecological, aesthetic, and recreational values. As economies across the West surged, streams were dammed, ditched, and diverted until their beds were nearly bare. Many rivers became toxic trickles because they didn't carry enough volume to dilute poisons and flush themselves clean. And each diversion for an offstream use, whether to grow crops or make steel or send drinking water to city taps, reduced the amount of instream flow available for supporting fish and wildlife populations, nourishing riparian vegetation, and promoting recreational pursuits such as boating, camping, fishing, and bird-watching—or simply leaving water in channels carved through rocks raised up from the cellars of time. To some people, these instream uses of water started to seem more important than cheap slabs of beef. To others—especially those profiting from raising beef on irrigated pasture—these uses seemed ridiculous at best, a threat to their way of life at worst.

In the second half of the twentieth century, a major shift in attitudes and beliefs across the West led to a reevaluation of the worth of rivers, and maintaining instream flows was increasingly seen as a beneficial use of water. Aside from federal legislation such as the Grand Canyon Protection Act, which called for dam operators to manage the Colorado to enhance the health of the ecosystem, state laws reflecting the new attitudes toward the use of rivers were passed. Montana, for example, enacted legislation in 1973 allowing the state to maintain minimum instream flows to protect fish, wildlife, and water quality. As one result, about 70 percent of the annual flow in the Yellowstone River's upper basin was reserved by the state to remain instream for the benefit of the aquatic ecosystem.

In 2009 Interior Secretary Ken Salazar supported the use of more controlled floods at Glen Canyon Dam. "We must find a way," he said, "to protect one of the world's most treasured landscapes, the Grand Canyon, while meeting water and clean energy needs in the face of climate change." The Bureau had throughout its history benefited from the talent of some of the brightest minds in the world. Its engineers and technicians, however, worked under the assumption that they were correcting defects of nature with their dams and diversions, and they operated without scientific scrutiny of the changes to riverine and riparian environments caused by their projects. The first controlled flood released by the Glen Canyon Dam brought scores of hydrologists, biologists, and geologists into the Grand Canyon, observing, sampling, measuring, and recording. By applying rigorous scientific analysis to the river's structure and ecosystems, they assessed the effects of the controlled release. The scientists concluded that the efforts to simulate pre-flood flows weren't entirely successful in rebuilding the river because the vast majority of nutrient-rich sediment that is needed to form beaches and sandbars lies trapped behind the dam. Sending silt from the reservoir into the river is a possibility, but according to the Bureau of Reclamation, this would require a $100 million pipeline—a giant piece of infrastructure designed to reverse the changes caused by a giant piece of infrastructure.

The little beaches that formed as a result of the artificial floods have slumped back into the river. The humpback chub still struggles to find warm and murky pools nestled behind sandbars where it can spawn. And now a new threat pushes it closer to extinction: A tapeworm from Asia has infested the waters of the Colorado and is killing the last of a species that evolved over millions of years to survive the Colorado's muddy floods. A rapidly heating climate, of all things, may be its best hope of survival.

Beginning in October 1999, the Upper Colorado River Basin entered a period of protracted drought, one of the most severe in the past few centuries. Blades of grass poked up from the scanty mountain snowpack. Spring runoff reduced from torrents to trickles. The Colorado River shrank into its bed, leaving muck to dry on its nude banks. Clouds brought dry rumbles of thunder but no rain, and Lake Powell, full during the summer of 1999, began to drain. By 2005 the reservoir was a mere one-third full. Boat ramps lay stranded hundreds of yards from where water lapped the shore, and marinas sat beached and empty on mudflats cracked like shattered crockery. The surface of the reservoir sagged to near the elevation of the generator intakes. Had the extreme dryness continued for a few more years, power production would have ceased entirely. James Lawrence Powell points out in his book *Dead Pool* that experts were caught off guard by the drought because they had failed to account for the effects of climate change. Global warming is already affecting the West, he asserts, and Lake Powell's precarious drop in 2005 toward "dead pool," at which the level of a reservoir falls below its lowest outlet and prevents water from being released downstream, was a harbinger of things to come.

As drought pulled the level of Lake Powell down, the sun-heated surface water that spilled out from the dam was warmer than the water released from chilly depths when the reservoir was full. Scientists hypothesized that since the warmer water was closer in temperature to the river's natural flow, the humpback chub had been given a boost and its numbers had improved. Climate change, by wrecking the reservoir, was restoring the river to a more natural state.

❧

Even as the nation's enthusiasm for building big water projects was fading, Two Forks Dam was proposed on the South Platte River near Denver. Along with supplying the city and its surrounds with water for faucets and lawns, the $1 billion project would have strangled downstream wetlands in Nebraska, where sandhill cranes and endangered whooping cranes soar on wind currents toward the sheltering wetness to fatten on snails and grain. During their annual migration, the cranes arrive in chevron after chevron. There are so many they darken the sky as though storm clouds have passed before the sun, and the sound of their voices and the beats of their wings blend together in a thundering babble.

Had the dam been built, it would also have buried Cheesman Canyon beneath several hundred feet of water. In pine trees along the canyon walls, bald eagles with wingspans longer than a person is tall build nests that weigh as much as a ton. Peering out from beneath the bony over-hangs of brows that shade their eyes from the sun, the eagles search the boulder-strewn flow of a fishery crowded with trout. The dam proposal met with protest not from eagles but from anglers; the director of Colorado Trout Unlimited called the stretch of river that would be drowned "our holy water." Fishing enthusiasts were joined in their opposition to the dam by birders, biologists, and bunches of other citizens unwilling to trade wild places for more water supply. Denver, which planned to pay for the project itself without federal funds, came within a hairsbreadth of securing the necessary permit to begin construction. But in 1990, at the eleventh hour, the Environmental Protection Agency used its authority under the Clean Water Act to veto the project.

Denver was forced to turn to conservation and efficiency to make up for the shortfall of water supply caused by the dam's cancellation. The city installed water meters so consumers were conscious of the amount they used; it raised water rates to discourage consumption; and it made cash payments to businesses that implemented efficiency measures. Scuttling the dam project to protect a stretch of wild river and instead enacting a plan to save water was viewed by many as a crucial turning of a corner. Once in the West we built soaring dams that would have dazzled kings and dropped the jaws of pharaohs. Now we install waterless urinals.

———

Politicians used to make appearances at dam dedications and wax eloquent about man taming nature. Today they are more likely to show up wielding ceremonial sledgehammers and speaking of returning a river to its natural state. Dan Beard, the former Bureau of Reclamation commissioner turned anti-dam campaigner quoted by author Fred Pearce in *When the Rivers Run Dry,* summed up the shift:

> *[The decisions to build dams were] political, benefiting particular politicians or their benefactors rather than solving a problem. In our experience at BuRec [Bureau of Reclamation], the actual total costs of completing projects exceeded the original estimate typically by 50*

*percent. And the actual contribution made to the national economy by
these dam projects was small in comparison to the alternative uses that
could have been made with the public funds they swallowed up. We are
now spending billions of dollars to correct the unanticipated impacts
such as lost fisheries, salinized soils, and desiccated wetlands.*

The West is in the throes of a dam-removal mania as intense as the
dam-building frenzy that once gripped the region. The concrete ram-
parts that were viewed as magnificent engineering achievements are now
seen as impediments to the free flow of rivers. And often there is more
value assigned to the fish and wildlife that thrive in an intact ecosystem
than there is to a dam's capacity to store water and produce hydropower.
Three federal acts—the Clean Water Act, Endangered Species Act, and
National Environmental Policy Act—are now as important to the assessment of whether a dam should be left standing or torn down as are its
power-generating revenues and acre-feet of irrigation water. Recreation
also factors in. It's hard to imagine the engineers who raised the mighty
walls of Hoover and Shasta in an effort to end the Great Depression
and produce the power to win World War II worrying about whether
rafters would have waves in which to dip and brace their oars, but that's
the world we live in now. The fun of kayakers and the survival of salmon
are weighed against bushels of corn and megawatts of electricity. And in
the calculus of water's worth in the New West, streams are sometimes
deemed valuable for their aesthetic merit alone.

From Henry David Thoreau to Annie Dillard, from Aldo Leopold
to Rick Bass, America's most celebrated nature writers have been drawn
to moving water. It is only a matter of time before some clever environmentalist tallies the dollar value of books sold that have been influenced
by wild rivers and adds that metric to the spreadsheet; in the meantime,
countless thousands visit the banks of braided streams, drawn to the weave
of their currents in search of inspiration and peace, seeking experiences
that can't be found in the cockpits of powerboats roaring across reservoirs.

Throughout the West dams are scheduled to be torn down. Once,
Congress passed legislation to authorize and fund construction of dams;

now it writes bills to hasten their removal. Washington State's Department of Fisheries estimated that salmon runs that had disappeared due to dams on the Elwha River were costing the people of Washington half a million dollars a year. Before the dams rose, the Elwha and its tributaries had been crammed full of all five species of Pacific salmon—chinook (or king), sockeye (or red), coho (or silver), chum (or dog), and pink (or humpback)—as well as steelhead, coastal cutthroat trout, and bull trout. After the dams were built, the fishing was good but the catching was bad. The Elwha River Ecosystem and Fisheries Restoration Act of 1992 authorized the US government to acquire the two dams on the Elwha and decommission and demolish them. The river, much of which lies within Olympic National Park and is still relatively pristine, is scheduled to have its free flow restored so that fish can surge upstream to fuel the local economy.

While dismantling a dam can be relatively straightforward—pack it with explosives and blow it apart, or tear a hole in it with the yellow teeth of a backhoe—restoring a river is never simple. When dams come down, sediment is released that can damage water treatment plants and fish hatcheries and spread trapped contaminants and invasive species through the watershed. In the case of the Elwha, removing the dams may allow exotic brook trout, now sequestered downstream, to compete with native bull trout upstream in Olympic National Park.

To safely remove the Milltown Dam near Missoula, Montana, it took more than two decades of litigation, study, planning, remediation, and restoration. First, sediment contaminated with arsenic, copper, and other heavy metals had to be removed so the toxic mud wouldn't poison the Clark Fork River when the earthen wall of the dam was breached. Mining waste that had washed into the Milltown Reservoir had backed up behind the dam, forming part of the West's largest Superfund complex. More than three million tons of polluted sediment were scooped up and hauled away by train. As the dam was slowly dismantled and drained, pent up waters trickled through a channel constructed by environmental engineers, and the freed flow joined the current downstream.

The Klamath River, born in the snowfields that plaster the smoking cones of Oregon's Cascade Range, and emptying into the Pacific Ocean along Northern California's coast, once provided prime spawning habitat for salmon and steelhead. But dams and irrigation diversions to croplands and pastures upstream blocked migrating salmon and shriveled the lower Klamath. Fish populations plummeted, nearly forcing the closure of commercial salmon fishing along seven hundred miles of Oregon–California coastline. Indian tribes, conservation groups, and commercial fishermen demanded the dams come down; farmers rioted when their irrigation water was diverted to protect fish. Into this war came Vice President Dick Cheney, who personally intervened to make sure water was returned to the farmers in the growing season of 2002, causing the largest fish die-off in the history of the West. Tens of thousands of salmon rotted along riverbanks, and Native Americans watched as the creatures that sustained them suffocated in airless pools.

The superlatives of water in the West have shifted from creating the biggest structures on Earth to the equally monumental task of destroying some of those structures. When a private company that owns four hydro-electric dams on the upper Klamath applied to have them relicensed, the United States Fish and Wildlife Service and the National Marine Fisheries Service required the installation of expensive fish ladders. Renovating the dams to comply with the decision would cost far more than removing them, and the power they generated and water they stored for irrigating sugar beets and alfalfa fields didn't create enough revenue to justify the investment. The company entered into an agreement with Oregon, California, and the federal government in 2008, clearing the way for what the *Washington Post* has called "the largest dam-removal project in world history."

Along the Columbia's 1,240-mile length, nineteen dams create a series of reservoirs backed up against each other, leaving only forty miles of river to freely flow. The Columbia's waters once ran silver and red with salmon and steelhead. The fish swarmed upstream in congregations so dense their bullet heads and thick tails merged together in masses of pulsing and slippery life. We will never again know that abundance. But perhaps future generations will see the crimson and chrome flash of a few salmon and steelhead pushing their way into foaming currents, hurtling themselves up waterfalls as they return from the sea to the swift-flowing rivers that snake through wild mountains. Whether some of this bounty will be restored on the Snake River, the Columbia's largest tributary, is one of the most contentious issues in the West. From 1962 to 1975, at the tail end of America's dam-building era, the Snake River was incarcerated behind four dams so that grain could be barged downriver all the way to the Pacific Coast, turning the lower Snake River into a shipping channel and transforming Lewiston, Idaho, located more than four hundred miles from the Pacific, into a seaport. Former secretary of the interior Bruce Babbitt called it "a maniacal idea." Railroads with capacity to transport grain already ran along the river, but this didn't give the Corps pause. That lakes in central Idaho frothing with spawning fish and circled over by ospreys and eagles would be emptied as the great runs collapsed concerned them not at all. The Corps piled the fish on barges and hauled them through the dams, but that didn't stop the Snake River coho from going extinct and the Snake River chinook and sockeye from ending up on the endangered species list—forcing the federal government to come up with a plan for their survival. Indian tribes, irrigators, conservation groups, the Corps of Engineers, the Department of Energy, the Department of Transportation, and industries in Idaho continue to argue about what is best for the river, the fish, and the region's economy, and talk of "damolition" elicits emotions that run the gamut from elation to rage.

Speak of tearing down the walls that block the runs of salmon on the Snake River and see a glint of hope in a tribal member's eye.

"Mention breaching the dams in the wrong bar and you can end up in the hospital—or worse," a Lewiston local told me.

David James Duncan, author of the fly-fishing cult-classic novel *The River Why*, in an interview in which he discussed spending time with a PBS *Nature* crew in search of wild salmon in Idaho, said, "An enormous female spring chinook swept into the crystalline wilderness water and spawning gravel at the tail of the pool. . . . I went nuts. Then the [film crew] saw her, caught on to the one in a million miracle of it, and went nuts too."

⟿

Water in the West can be manipulated to create both fabulous fortunes and desperate poverty. Nowhere is this divide more apparent than in California's Imperial Valley. After the US government built the All-American Canal in the 1930s, from its end gushed wealth. Federal law prevented landowners who received water from reclamation projects from holding more than 160 acres, and it required the owners to live within fifty miles of their property. Many farms in the Imperial Valley, however, had sprawled well beyond the size limit, some reaching three thousand acres. Instead of complying with reclamation law by selling off excess land and moving onto their property, Imperial Valley's landowners, to avoid acreage limits and residency requirements, launched a series of legal battles that lasted fifty years. In 1980, the Supreme Court found for the landowners, allowing absentee growers with enormous farm operations to use taxpayer-subsidized water in the Imperial Valley. Water in nearby San Diego costs about twenty times what it does in the Imperial Valley, and the cheap water allows agribusinesses to harvest bountiful profits. The valley produces a billion dollars' worth of crops annually. But the wealth does not trickle down to workers. A lot of the labor in the fields is provided by people living across the border in Mexicali—they are bused in to work for the day, bused back out at night. Imperial County has the highest unemployment rate of any county in California, along with the highest percentage of people on welfare and the greatest number of families living below the poverty line.

Though a work of fiction, John Nichols's *The Milagro Beanfield War* revolves around the very real issue of social damage caused by the West's distribution of water. The book imagines an impoverished Hispanic community in rural New Mexico in the 1970s beleaguered by government bureaucrats and business tycoons who have devised policies and projects to dewater the town's ditches, turning scarce liquid into money. Nichols's novel evokes actual government-sponsored water projects, such as Elephant Butte Dam on New Mexico's Rio Grande River, which benefited Anglo agribusinesses while devastating the cultures and economies of traditional Hispanic farming communities nourished by hand-built acequias.

Nichols writes, "But then one day Joe suddenly decided to irrigate the little field in front of his dead parents' decaying west side home . . . and grow himself some beans. It was that simple. And yet irrigating that field was an act as irrevocable as Hitler's invasion of Poland, Castro's voyage on the *Granma*, or the assassination of Archduke Ferdinand, because it was certain to catalyze tensions which had been building for years, certain to precipitate a war."

Problems abound with building new water projects—lack of good sites, as well as the tremendous expense and environmental impacts in these times of already overburdened budgets and shrill objections to altering natural landscapes and harming fish and wildlife habitat. Environmental review processes are so long and tedious, requiring years of scientific study and legal procedures, few people have the patience and time to see a project through to completion. And federal agencies, states, and private investors can rarely put up the capital to fund a megaproject that may drag on for several decades before it is completed. The emphasis now is less on creating infrastructure and more on developing fresh approaches to conserving water and using it efficiently. New water megaprojects do, however, occasionally rear their gargantuan heads—especially in times of drought. There are still plenty of politicians who would love to deliver a pork barrel full of water to their constituents, plenty of civil engineers who fantasize about taking rivers from their natural beds and routing them through mountains penetrated by tunnels, plenty of construction companies that would be pleased to pour gigatons of concrete.

The passage of the Grand Canyon Protection Act, the cancellation of Denver's Two Forks Dam, the restoration of salmon runs in the Pacific Northwest—these may seem like permanent victories for the environment. But a severe drought could prompt water managers to revert to a system that makes the use of rivers for municipal and agricultural water and power the priority and ignores directives to maintain instream flow for the benefit of fish and boaters. A ban on building dams doesn't guarantee they will never be built; it means they will not be built *right now*.

Ten years from now—twenty, thirty, fifty years—the thirst of the West's cities could be so ravenous that appeals to preserve a wild landscape may not be enough. A wonderland of stone amphitheaters and pinnacles, of buttresses and pavilions may not be enough. A world where cliffs painted in bands of vermillion and crimson flare with color when the sun is low; where wild sheep with nautilus horns and nimble hooves climb slender ledges toward the sky; where swallows circle and swerve above streams ponded by beavers; where rafters pull their oars against whirling currents as they ride the crests of waves and plunge steeply toward their troughs; where campers bed down on beaches and listen to the music of flowing water—all this may not be enough. And the rivers will once again be made solely to turn turbines and flow from city taps.

CHAPTER 8

The Wealth Below

BENEATH THE PARCHED SURFACE OF THE WESTERN LANDSCAPE LIE oceans of water. This liquid plentitude is sometimes squeezed between layers of impermeable rock. When a well is bored into these wet depths, liquid overcomes gravity as it rushes to the place of lowest pressure and pushes upward toward the opening—an artesian well. It may even flow like a fountain, or a pump can be used to bring groundwater to the surface, where meadowlarks spread their melodic songs across the windy silence of the plains.

The Ogallala aquifer, also known as the High Plains aquifer, stretches between central Texas and southern South Dakota, and from eastern Colorado almost to Iowa, covering an area larger than the state of California. This bounty lies beneath eight states: South Dakota, Wyoming, Nebraska, Colorado, Kansas, Oklahoma, New Mexico, and Texas. Above this aquifer the size of Lake Huron is a treeless expanse of land, vast stretches of which are as level as a floor. A dry region of fertile soil, the High Plains once supported shortgrass prairie, a multitude of bison and antelope that browsed the grasses, bears and wolves that stalked them, and bands of Plains Indians who roamed the land on horseback feasting on the shifting richness as the seasons changed, retreating to moist and sheltered riverbottoms when the summer sun scorched the plains or winter blizzards raged. No permanent civilizations took hold on the southern High Plains, no agriculture. But now, thanks to groundwater pumping, this semiarid prairie supports fields bursting with thirsty crops of alfalfa, cotton, and corn.

The mystery of springs that slithered from holes in the ground led to the realization that a fortune of water swelled below the pioneers' feet. Stored in the sediment of primeval valleys and long-vanished riverbeds buried beneath the High Plains, meltwater from the great ice sheets of the Pleistocene lay waiting to be pumped. Once brought to the surface, it could irrigate the loess soil—rock ground by glaciers to mineral-rich silt, distributed by the wind, and anchored in place by grass. Groundwater, unlike surface water, is not rapidly depleted by drought. Rivers shrivel when the skies don't offer rain, but the Ogallala aquifer was the product of continent-size glaciers; a few seasons' worth of dry weather wouldn't make the fossil water disappear. But 200,000 wells perforating the plains would.

First the buffalo were exterminated and the Native Americans who depended on them were herded onto reservations; then the native grasses of the plains were overgrazed by cattle. Homesteaders plowed up the sod and made a go of wheat farming during the wet years that coincided with a demand for grain during World War I. Windmills turned the relentless gusts that roared across the plains into power to raise up meager amounts of water for crops and cattle. Then came the Dust Bowl with its clouds of topsoil blackening the sky, and an exodus ensued. Oil and gas brought people back. And then came wells of another sort: Beginning in the 1940s, centrifugal pumps run by power line electricity replaced windmills with creaky vanes and skeletal towers, and water stored for three million years in subterranean vaults was hoisted up through holes drilled into invisible depths. Hydropower dams on western rivers provided cheap electricity to run the pumps that lifted the Ogallala's liquid treasure from darkness below, and the abundant water allowed farmers to transform the land from crackly brown to green. The greenery, as anyone who has flown above the Great Plains knows, exists not only in a patchwork quilt of squares and rectangles but also in discs—great circles of verdure seen from on high. Each round patch is serviced by a center-pivot sprinkler made of a pipe, usually a quarter of a mile long, and mounted on wheeled towers. Nozzles spray water as the system rotates in a manmade circle of rain.

Groundwater pumped from the Ogallala allowed a parched region to be transformed into "a food production facility a quarter of a continent wide," in the words of author William Ashworth. This agricultural powerhouse supplied so much food that the surplus was exported around the globe. In some years of extraordinary bounty, three quarters of the wheat traded on the world market was grown with Ogallala water. Among the geometric shapes of High Plains fields sprawled cattle feedlots and beef-processing plants. Fueled by the new wealth of this breadbasket of the nation, towns sprang up around the flourishing fields. The High Plains region now accounts for 30 percent of the nation's irrigated agriculture and produces 40 percent of its beef. Crops and livestock, people and towns: All of it grew from buried waters. And those waters, which once seemed inexhaustible, are shrinking. The corn, soybeans, wheat, beef, and cotton we're consuming are drawing down the Ogallala. The grain and meat and fiber we're growing to send to other countries are emptying our nation's largest aquifer. We are, in effect, eating the Ogallala, wearing it, exporting it.

After center-pivot sprinklers were developed, the water table in many areas of the High Plains started to fall, and as early as 1970 some wells that reached down into the Ogallala's wetness began to go dry. As with nearly all aquifers in the West, the vast lake of the Ogallala is in danger of being sucked to a puddle as pumps empty it faster than rainfall can recharge it. To make crops and towns grow, many billions of gallons are withdrawn each day—over the course of a year this adds up to more water than the entire flow of the Colorado River. In the High Plains region and throughout the West, aquifer replenishment is a process almost as slow as that which weathers a jagged mountain down to a gentle hill. What takes nature millennia to fill, humans mine in a matter of decades. Some experts fear the Ogallala could disappear entirely within twenty to thirty years, leaving dry hollows beneath the earth upon which so much farmland stands.

"Ruin is the destination toward which all men rush, each pursuing his own interest in a society that believes in the freedom of the commons," wrote Garrett Hardin in 1968. More than forty years later, the commons of the Ogallala is being overused to the point of collapse. Everyone sees the tragedy coming, but each farmer is afraid that if he doesn't use the maximum amount of water that he can extract, he will lose out because others will make use of it instead. This disincentive to conserve creates a "race to the bottom of the aquifer."

Improving the efficiency of irrigation systems helps slow the aquifer's atrophy, as does switching from thirsty crops like cotton to plants that need less water, such as sunflowers. But even with these changes, groundwater is still pumped faster than it is replenished. Farmers concerned about being subjected to draconian pumping limits set by state or federal government have voluntarily formed local groundwater management districts. These grassroots organizations have been somewhat effective in reducing the amount of Ogallala overdraft by implementing rules such as mandatory water metering and spacing out wells, yet the aquifer continues to shrink. And the areas of the High Plains that still have ample Ogallala water are now being inundated by new dairies that want to enjoy the bounty while it lasts. When the water does finally run out, there is always the hope of a government bailout.

The laws regulating groundwater extraction are simpler and more permissive than the convoluted and restrictive legal system surrounding surface water. The West's water laws evolved before people understood that groundwater and surface water are not separate systems but are joined in one hydrologic cycle. And because aquifers were assumed to be inexhaustible and their movements beneath the surface of the earth too mysterious to measure, few legal restrictions arose to limit extraction. The doctrine of "reasonable use" and the "rule of capture" that govern much of the West's groundwater tend to sanction a free-for-all. The jumble of state laws, management plans, and permitting systems that regulate groundwater have not always evolved to keep pace with increased understanding of the interconnectivity of groundwater and surface water, or with the accelerating scarcity of the resource. On the Texas High Plains, for instance, farmers who grow water-gulping cotton are entitled to as much water drawn from the Ogallala as they can use. They are limited in the amount of water they consume not by legal restrictions but by the size of the pumps they thrust into the ground. The person with the biggest pump gets the most water. Texas is filled with big pumps, and every year there is less water.

Forcing water, which weighs more than eight pounds per gallon and is heavier than oil, farther toward the surface demands extra energy. Even in the best of times when groundwater supplies are plentiful, pumping water requires prodigious amounts of power. After the Ogallala is drained to the point at which pumping is cost prohibitive, using dryland farming techniques to raise wheat and other plants that need relatively little water is a possibility. But yields for dryland farming are much lower than with irrigated agriculture and are entirely dependent on rainfall—in droughty years there will be dwarfed crops, and should the skies turn really miserly with rain, there will be no harvests at all. As if all this weren't grim enough, a warming climate will increase evaporation and transpiration, depleting soil moisture, which will force farmers to use more water to grow the same amount of crops.

Unrestricted mining of the Ogallala's clear gold is unsustainable in the extreme, and everyone now knows this. Short-term riches are being reaped at the expense of long-term sustainability. Boomtowns built on an exhaustible supply of water will one day go bust. The question is when, exactly, the underground water supply will be so diminished that agriculture will have to be abandoned and the prairie will turn from green back to brown. When the water is finally used up and farming on the High Plains fizzles out, not only will most of the people leave, but along with them the soil could disappear. When the roots of dead crops wither and release their hold on the friable soil, and drought turns the land to dust and wind scours the earth, the prairie topsoil could once again, as in the days of the Dust Bowl, be blown eastward to blacken skies all the way to the ocean.

Creating a "Buffalo Commons," a system of nature preserves that would attract tourists and their dollars by rewilding sections of the Great Plains with native grasses and forbs browsed by buffalo, when first proposed in 1987 by East Coast academics, seemed about as likely as, say, the invention of time travel machines, or western states agreeing on how to share water. But with the Ogallala's depletion almost certain to make irrigated farming on the High Plains go the way of the Pony Express, a Buffalo Commons is beginning to seem to more and more residents of the region a viable solution to ecological decline and economic disintegration.

For now, people continue to haul in bounteous harvests of crops, and towns wrapped in white picket fences huddle beneath an immensity of sky. Farmers tinker with the water, reusing some here, using a bit less there, but still the ancient wetness is sucked from the gravels and sands that have stored it through the ages.

⸺

Dams and canals that were built to relieve strain on the groundwater of California's Central Valley—which was being drained to supply the richest agricultural region in the world—allowed more agricultural lands to be put into production. Whether unintended, or by design, this led to more aggressive pumping to irrigate the new fields, forcing the water table even farther down into empty pits beneath the ground. Oak trees that had stood greenly in robust and brilliant leaf turned to dead snags when they failed to reach their roots deep enough to drink from the shrinking supply of water.

What liquid remains in the aquifers that underlie the Central Valley's river basins is still being drained by overzealous pumping—especially in times of drought, or when environmental restrictions limit the amount of surface water diverted out of rivers and sent to fields. And yet, groundwater extraction in California is not required by state law to be monitored or regulated. A farmer in Tulare, California, told a *New York Times* reporter, "I don't want the government to come in and dictate to us, 'This is all the water you can use on your own land.' We would resist that to our dying day."

NASA announced in 2009 that its satellite data revealed that the amount of water sucked from beneath the ground in the Central Valley in the preceding six years could almost fill Lake Mead. Land in the San Joaquin basin, located in the Central Valley's southern end, has subsided fifty feet as the water table drops deep enough in places to make pumping infeasible, threatening the area's cotton and canning tomatoes, iceberg lettuce and pistachios—a cornucopia of fiber and food that includes some fifty crops that help to feed and clothe the nation.

Stores of groundwater all over the West are in trouble. The aquifers that lie beneath Arizona are being stressed by overdraft—water is being pumped out twice as fast as rain and mountain snowmelt can replenish them. And overpumping, aside from depleting groundwater, can collapse the formations that store water. When the liquid is sucked out, the weight of the earth above crushes spongy rock, permanently reducing an aquifer's ability to hold water. California's Central Valley aquifer system, its hollow spaces squashed by great mounds of sinking ground, has already had its storage capacity reduced by as much as half. And when land above dewatered aquifers subsides, buildings can be damaged. Shifts in the ground caused by water pulled from the earth beneath structures can make them tilt and tumble. Railroads bend and bridges break. Pipes burst open and canals crumble. Fissures split the ground like earthquake faults, cracking open roads; signs are posted that warn motorists of the danger with graphics of cars plummeting into clefts.

In coastal areas, saltwater can flood cavities beneath the ground emptied by pumps, contaminating freshwater supplies. The quality of a rapidly draining aquifer often worsens as pure water filtered through the centuries is infused with contaminants released by the drying basin: Toxins such as arsenic and radon lurk in the lower layers of the aquifer—the heat deep down in the earth dissolves them. And shrunken aquifers are less effective at diluting pollution such as agricultural runoff and sewage.

Though problems with using groundwater abound, tapping water from aquifers is often far more enticing to cities, farms, and industry than using surface water. Groundwater is prevalent across the West, even in the most arid regions that are spritzed by a few inches of rain in a year and have no rivers or streams. Surface water requires dams and diversion projects so it can be stored and delivered, sometimes across great distances. Substantial amounts of it are lost to evaporation and seepage, and it is often contaminated with salt and muddied with silt. Groundwater requires only a pump to pull up a steady flow. No dams and canals, no evaporation or seepage. And usually no salt or silt—just pure watery goodness.

The science of groundwater hydrology is rapidly advancing as researchers measure the size of aquifers and their rate of recharge. Scientists are investigating the link between groundwater and surface water and studying the consequences of depleted aquifers not just for farming, but for plants and animals. Life in dry lands throughout the West relies on rare springs, streams, and wetlands. When the aquifers that feed these oases are drained by human use, whether for a city's taps or for the tanker trucks of a company hawking healthful spring water in bottles, balance can quickly tilt toward disaster for the flora and fauna that depend on the liquid sustenance.

Once along the Santa Cruz River, the Tohono O'odham (People of the Desert) farmed squash, corn, and beans in the loamy soils of the floodplain. Corridors of cottonwood, willow, and mesquite thrived along the riverbanks, and birds and wildlife were abundant in this ribbon of life that wound through hot sands. To pioneers in the Southwest, few sights were as sweet as the river's smooth glides and glistening pools fringed with green plants and trees. But as the aquifer that drained into the river was tapped to quench the thirst of Tucson's growing population and to meet the ferocious needs of open-pit copper mines, pecan orchards, and fields of Pima cotton, the water table dropped, drying up the Santa Cruz. Crops the Tohono O'odham had planted along the riverbanks turned brown and crackly. Woodlands wizened and their birds moved on, searching the desert for places of moist relief among living trees. Tortoises and rabbits set off into broiled wastes to seek out new oases. The tracks of deer vanished in the chalky soil, and mountain lions retreated deep into shadowed crags in search of hidden seeps.

Elsewhere in Arizona, a raucous battle is being fought over the San Pedro River. From mountain snows in Mexico, a tinselly maze of streams springs forth. After spilling down canyons in silver threads, the San Pedro spreads across an alluvial basin that meanders into Arizona. Along its winding course grow gallery forests (woodland corridors that line the banks of desert rivers). The San Pedro River Valley, once boggy with water stored behind beaver dams, changed dramatically when the animals that are second only to humans in their ability to manipulate rivers were exterminated and their dams were dynamited to eliminate breeding grounds for malarial mosquitoes. But the San Pedro is one of the last rivers in the Southwest undammed by humans. Galleries of cottonwoods with their leaves of acid green and willows with their pliant branches still stand astride its waters, providing sanctuary for more than 350 species of birds—nearly half of all the avian species in the United States. And the bounty of this natural paradise in the Sonoran Desert doesn't end with birds: two hundred species of butterflies, sixty-five species of reptiles and amphibians, and more than eighty species of mammals, including the jaguar with its tapestry of spots and silky paws that fall silently among the trees—the San Pedro's gallery forests harbor endless riparian riches. In the Western Hemisphere, only a few tropical rainforests boast more biological diversity.

In 1988 Congress created the San Pedro Riparian Natural Conservation Area, establishing a federal water right that has priority over all subsequent state water rights. Hydrologists, developers, politicians, and environmentalists are locked in rancorous debate over how water sucked from the ground will affect the flow of the San Pedro. Beaver have been reintroduced so their dams can shore up water to nourish wildlife during droughts, but there is no greater force on earth than thirsty people. As suburban accretions fill the Sonoran Desert, the San Pedro moves closer to becoming a bed of barren sand like the Santa Cruz, and the survival of its trove of biological treasures tucked amid the lacy shade of gallery forests grows increasingly tenuous.

Springs that burble up in the Grand Canyon to support rare plants, butterflies, and snails are affected by groundwater pumping in a city seventy miles away. Farmers in Idaho who rely on surface water watch their supply diminish when groundwater is pumped by farmers who draw from the aquifer. Scenarios such as these are receiving increased scientific scrutiny and attention from water managers and lawmakers. Idaho, for example, hired hydrologists to create a sophisticated computer model that shows how water moves through the aquifer and across the land,

and the state crafted policies to treat its groundwater and surface water as one interconnected system. This didn't put a complete stop to the wars between farmers who pump and farmers who divert streams, but it did create a scientific basis for managing the resource and for adjudicating disputes.

An even more daunting task is getting states to agree among themselves on scientific principles and legal guidelines to regulate groundwater extraction. Robert Glennon, in his book *Water Follies*, describes internecine conflicts over western groundwater:

> *Colorado rails against Nebraska for failing to curb groundwater pumping and cites this as a reason why Colorado should not be required to release flows for the protection of endangered species in Nebraska. Nebraska sanctimoniously attacks Wyoming for permissive groundwater rules and simultaneously deprives Kansas of water owed under interstate compacts. New Mexico demands that Colorado account for reduced flows under the Rio Grande Compact, but New Mexico allows groundwater pumping that violates its obligations to Texas under the Pecos River Compact. Texas complains about New Mexico's groundwater pumping but chooses not to curb pumping from the Edwards Aquifer under the doctrine of capture.*

Developing a system that manages groundwater in the West in a sustainable manner is as easy as standing blindfolded on a greased bowling ball while removing a straitjacket and solving differential equations. But it is something we must summon the will to do. If each party sucks up as much water as it wants, acting to satisfy its own self-interest without safeguarding the long-term viability of aquifers, attorneys specializing in groundwater law will be out of work, and civilization in the West will hang by the thin thread of drought-stricken streams.

CHAPTER 9

The New Normal

THE DUST BOWL OF THE 1930S, WHICH FORMS THE BACKGROUND FOR John Steinbeck's novel *The Grapes of Wrath*, forced millions of people to migrate as black blizzards of soil choked the sky. In the 1950s a searing spell of heat and dryness again devastated the West, and desperate ranchers fed cattle with skin stretched tight across their ribs a mix of prickly pear cactus and molasses. A drought in the late 1980s that forced California to implement water-saving measures and fueled wildfires that charred Yellowstone National Park is considered the costliest natural disaster in US history.

The paleoclimatic record puts these droughts in perspective by reconstructing patterns of precipitation and streamflow in the West far beyond the skimpy century or so of rainfall records we've compiled. The conclusions are enough to make one pack up and head east to a cypress swamp in Mississippi, or maybe a houseboat on Lake Michigan. The worst droughts we have endured in our brief occupation of these lands west of the 100th meridian are not at all unusual—and droughts of much greater ferocity have created infernos of crispy dryness and withering heat that would pose a profound challenge to our civilization. Our desert cities are as fragile as Fabergé eggs. Take away water and they crack and crumble.

Paleoclimatology, the study of the past climate, cannot predict future droughts, but it can help us anticipate what's in store by illuminating the natural flux of moisture and dryness through a previous span of many hundreds, or even thousands, of years. Instead of relying on observed

171

measurements of precipitation and streamflow, paleoclimatologists use "proxy data," or substitutes for rain gauges and other instruments, to infer what the climate was like in the past. The proxy data can be found buried in the sediment of sand dunes and lakes and hidden in the middens of pack rats; the most useful proxy data is preserved in tree rings.

Dendrochronology is the dating and study of the growth rings in trees. Annual tree growth across much of the western United States is limited by the amount of moisture available. A dry year results in a narrow growth ring; a wet year leads to a wide growth ring. The correlation between the width of tree rings and measurements of annual precipitation is remarkably robust, allowing researchers to use tree ring measurements to reconstruct the climate and streamflow of the West before records were kept. Dendrochronology and other paleoclimate studies reveal that dry spells as severe as the calamitous 1950s drought have parched North America several times a century over the past three hundred to four hundred years. According to the National Oceanic and Atmospheric Administration's Paleoclimatology Program, "When records of drought for the last two millennia are examined, the major 20th century droughts appear to be relatively mild in comparison with other droughts that occurred within this timeframe."

Scott Stine of California State University at Hayward reported in *Nature* that by carbon dating the preserved wood of trees that grew in the dry beds of rivers and lakes and then died when the water levels rose, he discovered that droughts lasting more than a century at a time prevented any substantial runoff from leaving the Sierra Nevada. California's major urban centers depend on this runoff for their water supply. Stine also determined that the twentieth century was one of the wettest in the past four thousand years. California, according to Stine, presents "a classic case of people building themselves beyond the carrying capacity of the land," which is defined by dry periods, not wet ones.

We now know for certain that civilization in the American West gained a foothold during a wet climatic period—what scientists call a "pluvial." In our day-to-day lives, what we construe as normal amounts of precipitation are narrow constructs that form, essentially, a failure of our imagination to see ourselves and our cities and farms placed within the vast span of time, throughout which the blistered land we now inhabit has been so dry for such long periods, the brutal droughts that dehydrated the West in the twentieth and early twenty-first centuries seem soggy by comparison.

Superimposed on the natural variability of drought cycles in the West is anthropogenic (human-caused) climate change. Testifying before the National Research Council, Richard Seager, a geophysicist at Columbia University's Lamont-Doherty Earth Observatory, cautioned that all the models being produced by climate scientists' supercomputers were reaching the same conclusion, one of impending dryness. But the dearth of moisture will be different from the droughts of the past, noted Seager. Driven by rising concentrations of greenhouse gases in the atmosphere, the dry lands of the Southwest will become even dryer. And hotter. Much hotter.

In 2007, the Intergovernmental Panel on Climate Change (IPCC) issued its Fourth Assessment Report, to which twenty-five hundred scientists from 130 countries contributed. One of its many unsettling predictions is that, under a moderate greenhouse gas emissions scenario, temperatures in the western United States over the remainder of this century will increase 3.8 to 10.6 degrees Fahrenheit. Seattle will be as warm as Sacramento is now. Missoula will have the climate of present-day Denver. Phoenix will be an inferno that makes Death Valley seem mild. The snowy keeps of mountaintops will unfreeze, blizzards will become rainstorms that steam to nothing in the sun, and the new "normal" in the West will be what we used to call "drought."

A megadrought similar to the one that forced the collapse of the Anasazi civilization could become the region's new climatology. A study published in 2010 in the *Proceedings of the National Academy of Sciences* points to a sixty-year drought that seared the Southwest during the mid-twelfth century—the worst drought in the region in the past twelve hundred years—as an analogue of what is in store as greenhouse gases ratchet up the heat. The comparison is not perfect, however, noted the study's lead author, Connie Woodhouse, in an interview with the *New York Times*. Temperatures in the future will rise higher than those that occurred during the medieval dry spell that coincided with people abandoning their cities in the desert.

When moisture is abundant, there is little talk of the dangers of drought. But when crops wilt and swimming pools can't be filled because cities under siege of dry weather have issued restrictions on water use, the public moves swiftly from apathy toward hair-on-fire panic. Ranchers call their state representatives and complain of thirsty stock. Suburbanites spy on neighbors who secretly water their brown grass. Governments enact emergency plans to divvy out the dwindling resource. Pundits announce that "peak water" has come and gone. Almost everyone agrees the system is broken and must be fixed. More dams are the answer, some yell; conservation will solve the crisis, others howl. Better coordination between local, state, and federal agencies is essential, many insist. And then one day cumulonimbus clouds swell blackly and thump the ground with rain, and the debate over how to manage future droughts diminishes as quickly as a summer thunderstorm along a baking plain. Human cycles of indifference and panic in response to shifting patterns of precipitation are far more predictable than the vagaries of changing weather.

A brutal drought that stretched from 1986 to 1993 depleted California's reservoirs, dropping them to half their normal level. Water rationing in cities ensued. But more people poured into the state, shrinking available water to a trickle. Ground above empty aquifers collapsed, and millions of acres of crops perished when water managers constrained the flow needed to sustain them. Produce prices spiked all over the nation. Cities across California stopped people from filling pools. Citizens started turning off their faucets when they brushed their teeth. Restaurants served food on paper plates with plastic sporks to skinny down their water use by avoiding dishwashing. Dead trees dried to brittle sticks of fuel. Wildfires engulfed canyons and consumed forested hills surrounding cities, and pricey homes combusted. Helicopters were fitted with buckets for scooping water from swimming pools to douse the flames because the lakes and reservoirs from which they usually drew water had drained to puddles. And then raindrops rinsed dust from the leaves of withered trees. Storms brought relief to the crisp deserts and crackly hills, and California returned to business as usual. People refilled swimming pools that humidified the dry air, and new residents continued to surge into the state, which made no plans to limit growth by linking it to existing water supplies. There was talk of dragging icebergs from Alaska down the coast so citizens of San Diego could wash their cars.

In 2007, the National Research Council, an arm of the National Academy of Sciences, released a report about the consequences of climate change for the Colorado River Basin. The report describes "a future in which warmer conditions across the Colorado River region are likely to contribute to reductions in snowpack, an earlier peak in spring snowmelt, higher rates of evapotranspiration [evaporation and transpiration], reduced late spring and summer flows, and a reduction in annual runoff and streamflow." Researchers at the Scripps Institution of Oceanography predicted in 2008 that Lake Mead and Lake Powell, the two largest reservoirs on the Colorado, designed to store water supplies for times of drought, both have by 2021 a 50 percent chance of drying out. A study published in 2009 by the same researchers concluded that by 2050, roughly 60 to 90 percent of the time the Colorado won't be able to meet its scheduled deliveries to the people who rely on it. Another study, also published in 2009 and conducted by University of Colorado researchers in response to the startling conclusion of the 2008 Scripps study, found that climate change and overuse could, if current management practices continue, cause as much as a 50 percent chance of Colorado River reservoirs emptying by 2057. There seems to be a building scientific consensus that unless we change our ways, we are, to put it scientifically, screwed.

Most climate models project a 10 to 30 percent reduction in runoff in the Colorado River Basin by mid-century. But the Bureau of Reclamation, insisting that "additional research is both needed and warranted," hasn't incorporated information from tree ring studies or climate change science when forecasting streamflow for the Colorado River Basin. Author and distinguished scientist James Lawrence Powell, in his book *Dead Pool*, writes that guidelines to manage the Colorado River based on the Bureau of Reclamation's projections "are like a Potemkin village of water planning," and he demonstrates that when streamflow models incorporate the best science, they "project the reasonable possibility that within two or three decades, the Colorado River system of dams and reservoirs could fail."

In the summer of 2010, shrunken Lakes Mead and Powell were circled by bathtub rings ten stories tall, where high water left mineral stains on canyon walls. Sprigs of grass and bushes sprouted from cracks in the rock caulked with dirt, and the *New York Times* reported that Lake Mead was "receding to a level not seen since it was first being filled in the 1930s, stoking existential fears about water supply in the parched Southwest." The region's eleven-year drought, the most severe in over a century, threatened to drop the level of the reservoir below a critical demarcation line, triggering an emergency plan that would have reduced water deliveries to Arizona and Nevada.

The plan is part of a 2007 agreement signed by the secretary of the interior and the Bureau of Reclamation commissioner and hailed as the most important document in western water law since the 1922 Colorado River Compact. Based on Bureau of Reclamation streamflow projections, the plan to manage the Colorado River was crafted around the dubious assumption that the volume of water in the river will conform to historic measurements and not be substantially diminished by climate change in coming years. The plan allowed for Nevada to build a new reservoir in California so that Las Vegas could tap more of the Colorado's flow. It encouraged augmenting supplies by building desalination plants, transferring water from agriculture to cities, and tapping supplies in other river basins. It created guidelines for managing the two linchpins in the system, Lakes Mead and Powell, drawing down one while the other refills, and distributing the shortage among the seven member-states. Western water officials lauded these measures. An optimist might say the plan signaled a new era in cooperation among the Colorado River Basin states. A cynic might call it rearranging the deckchairs on the *Titanic*.

Drought is often defined as a lack of precipitation over an extended period of time, but drought occurs whenever a diminished water supply cannot meet the demands placed upon it. Along with warmer temperatures, another threat to the West's snowpack that will lead to drought is a loss of reflectivity. Winds gusting out of the deserts of the Southwest blow brown clouds toward the mountains. Dust that settles on the mountain snowpack makes it melt early because the dark particles absorb the sun's rays instead of reflecting them back into space, as bright snow does.

A study conducted by the Snow Optics Laboratory of the University of Utah concluded that in 2005 and 2006, snow in Colorado's San Juan Mountains that was covered in dust melted up to thirty-five days earlier than a clean snowpack would have. In the spring of 2009, snow in the San Juans melted forty-eight days earlier than usual when the Rockies were blanketed with layers of reddish-brown dirt borne on storms that swirled up from the Colorado Plateau at the Four Corners region (where Arizona, New Mexico, Utah, and Colorado meet at one point). Water managers in southern Colorado and New Mexico scrambled to empty reservoirs in preparation for the early spring deluge. Then, as the level of the San Juan River plummeted in summer, Colorado water officials struggled to meet their obligations to divert flow from the San Juan to relieve the dried-out cities of New Mexico.

When snow melts early, the growing season for mountain vegetation begins sooner, and water returns to the atmosphere through evaporation and through transpiration from plants—instead of flowing into rivers. A study conducted by the University of Colorado found that heavy dust loading of the snowpack has caused the Colorado River to reach peak spring runoff on average three weeks earlier, and to lose about 5 percent of its water each year. The amount robbed from the river is enough to supply Los Angeles for eighteen months, according to Brad Udall, co-author of the study and director of the Western Water Assessment. In a news release, Udall said, "By cutting down on dust we could restore some of the lost flow, which is critical as the Southwest climate warms."

In the spring of 2010, I spoke with residents of Buena Vista, Colorado, about dust that had darkened the snowfields of the surrounding mountains, triggering early runoff in the Arkansas River. They blamed the dust on brown storms that had blown in from the Gobi Desert on the other side of the globe. Though particles can come from as far away as China, scientists have determined that the Colorado Plateau is the main source of dust storms in the Rockies. Disturbances to the desert topsoil's delicate crust by grazing, agriculture, mining, and recreation expose loose dust, which lies on the ground until windstorms carry it away. Renewable energy development in the West threatens to further disrupt desert soils. The wind turbines, arrays of solar panels, geothermal plants, and new transmission lines that are being planned to deliver clean energy to cities all have the potential to create dirty winds.

Airborne soot from automobiles and coal-fired power plants poses an additional reflectivity problem for the snowpack. A study conducted by the US Department of Energy's Pacific Northwest National Laboratory on the Rockies, Sierra Nevada, and Cascade mountain ranges found that tiny particles emitted from the tailpipes of vehicles and industry smokestacks settle in the snow-covered mountains. Like a layer of dust, the dark soot absorbs sunlight instead of reflecting it, melting the dirty snow more rapidly than clean, white snow.

And to further complicate things, when dust and soot accelerate the melting of the snowpack, the dark ground underneath is exposed. The soil and rock absorb more of the sun's energy, which could increase regional warming. The melting snow speeds up its own rate of melting—an example of what scientists call a "positive feedback." Dust storms and soot not only melt the snowpack sooner and reduce the amount of runoff; they are potential sources of climate change, which further shrinks the snowpack—and all of this, of course, leads to conflict over decreasing water supplies. How we treat our soil and air affects our water and influences how we treat each other. As John Wesley Powell pointed out some 120 years ago, all things in watersheds are connected.

Chapter 10

Tainted Waters

THE WEST IS AT WAR WITH ZEBRA MUSSELS AND QUAGGA MUSSELS, HARD-shelled animals the size of fingernails that hail from Russia and Ukraine and were introduced into the Great Lakes in the ballast of ships. Their razor-edged shells that fend off predators slice open the hands and feet of people playing in lakes, and the little mollusks cling to all manner of submerged surfaces, encrusting everything from buoys to beer cans to boat engines. They reproduce explosively, causing millions of dollars in damage by clogging the intakes to water treatment facilities and power plants. Inspectors prowl lakeshores examining the undersides of trailered boats and issuing warnings and fines to keep the invasive species from spreading through western rivers and reservoirs. The pesky mollusks are already in Lake Mead and are starting to gum up the intakes of Hoover Dam's power plant and the pipeline that sends water to Las Vegas.

By gobbling phytoplankton, the first link in food chains, the mussels wreak havoc on native ecosystems. Because the mussels are filter feeders, however, they can consume vast quantities of sewage and fertilizer, cleansing water bodies of pollution—an increasingly pervasive problem in the West.

But the problem doesn't end happily with these alien bivalves that act as little livers. After the mussels take heavy metals and toxins from the water, they excrete the chemicals and metals in pellets that sink to the lake floor and are sucked up by bottom-feeding fish, which in turn are eaten by predators. Poisons accumulate and move up the food chain, ultimately flooding into the bodies of fishermen and bird hunters. The mussels' feeding habits also change the chemistry of water to favor blooms of cyanobacteria (blue-green algae), which produce toxins that can sicken people. A critter the size of a nickel could contaminate the West's water supplies by tipping a delicate balance.

⸻

While leaps forward in engineering were making possible wonders of the world such as Hoover Dam, advances in chemical manufacturing, agriculture, and hardrock mining were poisoning rivers and aquifers throughout the western United States. During World War II, the federal government raced to establish manufacturing plants and military bases in the West. The focus was on winning the war, and safely disposing of waste was, understandably, not a priority. Chemicals with unpronounceable names, and some with names so long they have to be shortened to acronyms, have made Superfund sites of many of the West's water sources, reducing supplies of safe drinking water.

Perchlorate, a component of rocket fuel used for the space shuttle and military weaponry, can make people's thyroids go haywire and interferes with the brain development of fetuses and children. It turns up in drinking water throughout the western United States. It is in wells in Pasadena, for instance—NASA's Jet Propulsion Laboratory is nearby. Perchlorate is leaching from a chemical manufacturing plant in Henderson, Nevada, thirty miles south of the Las Vegas Strip. Despite expensive cleanup efforts to stop the poison from spreading, it continues to seep into the Colorado River, tainting the drinking water supply for some twenty million people downstream in Nevada, Arizona, California, and Mexico.

MTBE (methyl tertiary butyl ether), a fuel additive used to boost octane that replaced lead when it was banned, leaks from underground storage tanks at gas stations. A possible human carcinogen at high doses according to the Environmental Protection Agency (EPA), the polysyllabic poison has found its way into aquifers, causing, for example, Santa Monica to shut down several of its wells.

TCE (trichloroethylene), an industrial solvent once widely used in dry cleaning and for degreasing metal parts, has been linked to kidney cancer and Parkinson's disease, and it threatens the West's water supplies. It is seeping, for instance, from a former Atlas missile site into Cheyenne, Wyoming's, groundwater.

If you are a corn farmer, ammonium nitrate fertilizer is the greatest invention since irrigation. Following World War II, fertilizer made from petrochemicals was dumped on fields with abandon, allowing crops to grow in such abundance farmers were buried beneath a surplus. Fertilizers rich in nitrates dissolve in water. This solubility allows plants to draw the nutrients up through their roots; it also allows the fertilizer to wash from the soil into rivers and lakes. Nitrates that make corn grow tall and sag with tasseled ears cause algae to spread in clotted mats. Algal blooms block sunlight from reaching other organisms, and when the algae die, the bacteria that decompose them reduce the amount of dissolved oxygen in the water. This creates dead zones of viscous slime where no fish or other aquatic organisms can live—a process called "eutrophication," which, aside from disrupting aquatic ecosystems, can interfere with water treatment. Phosphorus fertilizer also causes eutrophication when it washes into rivers.

Fertilizer and a whole host of pesticides and herbicides have polluted water while providing a never-ending banquet of food. The same is true of factory farms. Enormous feedlots produce a bounty of poultry, beef, and pork. But runoff fouled by fecal bacteria, along with hormones, antibiotics, and arsenic (arsenic, added to poultry feed to kill parasites and increase the growth of chickens, is excreted from the animals and is a recognized cancer-causing agent), renders water unusable. People will be well fed when they fight over what is left of the West's clean water.

"Nonpoint source" pollution (pollution that comes from diffuse sources, such as runoff from agricultural fields) is the leading cause of water pollution in the United States. It is difficult to regulate. The Clean Water Act addresses "point source" pollution (discharge that comes from a single location, such as the outflow pipe of a chemical factory) and leaves nonpoint source pollution control up to the states—something that works better in theory than in practice. Bruce Babbitt, former governor of Arizona and former secretary of the interior, writes in his book *Cities in the Wilderness,* "In the more than thirty years since the Clean Water Act was enacted, no state yet has produced a meaningful plan to clean up and restore its waters by managing land uses." Across the western United States, septic systems seep sewage, cities' wastewater treatment systems overflow, and municipal landfills leak liquid made up of everything from decaying garbage to decomposing rats, filling our water with a fetid stew of nasties. Nitrates in human waste reduce the oxygen-carrying capacity of babies' blood (known as "blue baby syndrome" because their skin develops a bluish tint). *E. coli* finds its way into drinking water supplies, causing gastrointestinal distress so severe it can kill. And parasites such as cryptosporidium cause dangerous diarrhea in the hardiest of guts.

Utah's Great Salt Lake has some of the highest levels of mercury ever measured by the US Geological Survey. The toxic metal shows up throughout the lake's food chain, from brine shrimp (marketed as Sea-Monkeys in comic books) to eared grebes and cinnamon teal. No one is certain where the mercury originated. Sources that range from coal-burning power plants to dental fillings burned in crematoriums have been fingered as possible culprits of putting mercury into the atmosphere of the West. Mines that use cyanide leaching and ore roasting to gather specks of gold seem a likely source. Duck hunters, positioned at the top of the food chain, worry about mercury short-circuiting their central nervous systems when they eat their prey from the Great Salt Lake. Even in places that boast what seem like pristine waters, such as the mountains of northern Idaho, mercury pollution has prompted advisories for pregnant women and children not to eat fish caught from local lakes and streams lest they risk birth defects and brain damage.

In 2010 the EPA mandated lower mercury emissions from cement plants. To meet the reductions, wet scrubbers are required, but they use large quantities of water. The EPA is poised to crack down on mercury emissions from coal-fired power plants in 2011. More wet scrubbers, more water use. Water that isn't used up by scrubbing will be tainted with less mercury. In the world of western water, nothing is ever simple, and lunch is never free.

Scientists recently discovered that wildfires release large amounts of mercury. The volatile metal, which is bound to carbon atoms in plants and trees that have absorbed it from the atmosphere, is spewed back into the air as vapor when forests burn. The mercury gas swirls on smoky currents before falling into western waters, where it is converted to toxic methyl mercury.

Wildfires are increasing in frequency and intensity as the West heats up and the snowpack melts earlier—and as populations of bark beetles explode. The mountain pine beetle thrives in the West's new climate. An antifreeze-like glycerol secreted in its blood protects it from cold. In the past, long periods of frigid weather froze the beetles regardless of their glycerol and kept their populations in check; now, with warmer winters and longer summers, the beetles are reproducing in numbers so great they are decimating trees throughout the Rockies, leaving little wounds in drought-weakened pines that leak sap as the beetles bore into the bark. Swaths of dead trees have turned entire mountain slopes the color of rust, and in time the crackly fuel will go up in flames.

A healthy forest is a filtration system and a giant sponge, soaking up snowmelt and rain and then slowly releasing water cleansed of pollutants into rivers and streams. When forests are devastated by fire or pathogens, runoff dumps down their denuded floors. Ash, dirt, and debris washes into rivers and reservoirs, clogging them with silt. Entire slopes can slump downhill in mudslides that fill water sources with muck. And without trees to shade mountain slopes, the snowpack melts more rapidly, swelling streams, causing flash floods. Fire retardant dropped from slurry bombers to fight conflagrations is a chemical mixture toxic in watercourses; in 2010 a federal judge ordered the US Forest Service to file an environmental impact statement on its use.

Bark beetles kill trees and the dead wood burns, releasing carbon that heats up the climate, allowing the beetles to thrive and kill more trees—a positive feedback. More mountain pine beetles means more fires, which means less usable water, which means more competition for dwindling supplies—which, of course, means more conflict. Such is the precarious balance of the West's most precious resource that a beetle the size of a grain of rice can lead to water wars.

More bad news is that in the warmer, drier climate of the West, forest regeneration seems to be slowing. Scientists worry that mountain slopes blackened by fire are exchanging their char for greenery at a pace more sluggish than in the past. The good news is that forest managers have developed techniques to prevent fire-scarred land from fouling watersheds, such as building sedimentation ponds and installing fabric fences to catch eroded earth before it reaches streams and reservoirs, and aerially reseeding naked slopes to speed revegetation. Technology to battle the mountain pine beetle with pheromones and pesticides is being developed, but in the meantime, millions of acres of dead trees spread across the West from Montana to New Mexico, providing fuel for fires that race through crisp canopies and leave in their wake mud and ash and mercury.

Mining is a major source of tainted water throughout the West. Consider gold mining. Forget about picks and pans, nuggets and lodes—the great veins played out long ago. What remains are microscopic gold particles embedded in massive tonnage of ore that must be torn from mountains in gashes and pits, crushed by the truckload, piled in heaps, and soaked with a mist of cyanide to tease out hidden gold. With the help of cyanide, one ounce of yellow metal might be recovered from a hundred tons of smashed rock—a mountain of rubble rises for a necklace of gold.

A teaspoonful of cyanide can kill a person; weak concentrations in streams can inhibit fish reproduction. Open-pit cyanide-leach mines are deadly to birds and wildlife that drink from them, and when the mines release their poison into streams and rivers through spills, dam overflows, and runoff, cyanide can eliminate the entire food chain. From plankton to aquatic insects, from trout to osprey, all life dies for several miles downstream.

Montana's Spirit Mountain, a sacred site where the soil was once tamped down by the feet of Assiniboine and Gros Ventre tribal members during vision quests and prayers, was taken from them in a treaty so it could be mined for gold. The earth was gouged open and poisoned by cyanide spills—and by drainage as potent as battery acid.

When ore that contains abundant sulfide minerals, such as the material that was dug up at the Zortman-Landusky open-pit gold mine at Spirit Mountain, is exposed to air and water, it produces sulfuric acid. Metal sulfides are dissolved in chemical reactions as complicated as the legal systems that govern western water, and they create environments nearly as toxic. The process of acidification and metal contamination is accelerated by bacteria known as extremophiles, life forms that thrive in hostile conditions.

Lawyers from the State of Montana and the EPA helped the tribes fight back against Pegasus Gold Corporation, which pioneered the use of cyanide heap-leach mining at the Zortman-Landusky open-pit operation. Cyanide and acid drainage laced with arsenic, cadmium, chromium, and copper had seeped into nearby streams and groundwater, killing aquatic life and contaminating supplies of drinking water for towns on the Fort Belknap reservation. One of the tribal members said of Pegasus, "They destroyed this place, took their gold off in armored trucks and left us a wounded mountain spewing poison on the people the mountain was stolen from."

A lawsuit brought against Pegasus for violating the federal Clean Water Act resulted in a large settlement and an order that the company immediately make safe the poisoned water flowing onto the reservation. Pegasus did finance some remediation efforts. But according to the *Washington Post*, the company gave $5 million to its executives and then declared bankruptcy, leaving behind a toxic mess for the taxpayers of Montana to clean up and "water [that] may need to be treated forever."

When Montana's citizens voted in 1998 to ban new gold mines in their state from using cyanide, Canyon Resources, a Colorado-based company that operated mines in Montana, filed lawsuits seeking hundreds of millions of dollars in damages. A Montana district court ruled against it. The company appealed to the Montana Supreme Court and lost. The company challenged the cyanide ban in federal district court and lost. It appealed to the US Supreme Court, which declined to take the case. Challenges to repeal the initiative in state legislative sessions also failed. Montana state law still prohibits the development of new open-pit cyanide-leach mines, providing hope for environmentalists who want to ban cyanide-leach mining throughout the West.

Their hope is tempered, however, by the proposed Pebble Mine project in the headwaters above Alaska's Bristol Bay, a tundra wilderness braided with rivers and pocked with ponds. All the bounty that the Columbia River system once held, the Bristol Bay watershed still boasts: Wild salmon teem in the tens of millions. The proposed open-pit gold and copper mine, sited near critical spawning habitat for the world's largest sockeye salmon run, would entail five earthen dams, the largest of which would exceed China's Three Gorges Dam in size. Pebble Mine supporters point out that demand for copper is soaring because it is a key material in wind turbines and photovoltaic cells—copper mining means clean energy. Critics fear copper sulfide could seep into the watershed and put an end to one of the world's last great fisheries.

In the mountains of Crested Butte, Colorado, a mining company has its eyes on one of the planet's richest deposits of molybdenum. Known as "moly" for short, molybdenum is added to steel to create high-strength alloys used in products as diverse as mountain bikes and surgical instruments. Mining moly from Red Lady, so named because the peak's face is rouged by the rising sun, will make the shareholders of Thompson Creek Metals Company and US Energy Corp a mountain of money. But the townspeople of Crested Butte are having none of it. A former mayor of Crested Butte said of big mining companies, "They'd rape us and leave us bleeding."

Share a ski lift chair with a resident of Crested Butte, and she'll tell you that James Cameron has spent a lot of time in town and his film *Avatar* was inspired by the tale of this Rocky Mountain Shangri-la's epic struggle with mining developers, which began in 1977 and rages to this day. Crested Butte is dependent on tourism and outdoor recreation, and almost to a person its citizens insist that mining moly would add nothing of value to their economy—the jobs would be filled with people from out of town, the profits would be sent to faraway places, and extracting the metal would taint the peaceful mountain paradise with noise, dust, and a spaghetti tangle of roads. But the main issue, as always in the West, is water.

Thompson Creek Metals Company plans to build two large dams to store material left over from mining in the town's sole watershed. If the tailings leach toxic chemicals into the water, the contamination could keep tourist dollars out of Crested Butte and send the locals off to ski and bike and live in more pristine environs, leaving the town's lovely Victorian buildings, raised during silver and coal booms and abandoned during busts, and then colonized by ski bums and gentrified by jetsetters, to house moly miners who will have to drink water trucked in from outside the trashed watershed. The mining company has assured everyone that its techniques are perfectly safe and is moving ahead with plans to extract Red Lady's moly. But citizens of Crested Butte point out that mining in the area has already left a legacy of poisonous waste. Below the proposed moly mine is a water treatment plant that filters heavy metals leaching from tailings left over from former extraction efforts, and less than a mile from Red Lady is a dormant mine so contaminated it made the EPA's Superfund list. Moreover, the Molycorp molybdenum mine in New Mexico made a Rio Grande tributary, the Red River, cloudy blue with acid drainage, and heavy metal poisoning downstream turned people's hair white.

Nearly twenty years ago Crested Butte lost a court battle when a state judge prohibited the town from stopping a mining company's exploratory drilling on the grounds that it threatened its water supply. That company abandoned its plans because of a crash in the molybdenum market. But Thompson Creek Metals Company took its place, and the longest-running mine battle in the West drags on, one of many debates raging across the region about trading a few decades of economic benefits for water problems that could last a thousand years.

Uranium booms that supplied nuclear bombs and power plants have produced a heritage of radioactive waste. According to the Grand Canyon Trust, when the Atlas Minerals Corporation, which ran a mill on a bank of the Colorado River to process yellowcake uranium mined around Moab, Utah, was forced to pay the cleanup costs of radioactive sludge in an unlined pond in the river's floodplain, it declared bankruptcy. Toxins from the slimy waste seep into an aquifer that discharges into the nearby Colorado River. And floods threaten to wash the poisons directly into the river, which supplies drinking water for some twenty-five million people downstream. Southern California's Metropolitan Water District, responsible for delivering Colorado River water to about nineteen million customers, measured increasing levels of radioactivity at its Colorado River intake but lacked the technology to remove uranium. Though it couldn't prove where the radioactivity was originating, it suspected the Atlas tailings were the cause and clamored for their removal from the riverbank. Atlas offered to put dirt over the radioactive pile. When this sophisticated plan was rejected by federal agencies, Atlas folded its tent in Utah and began mining gold in Bolivia, leaving behind a $5.25 million bond for cleanup. But the cost of removing sixteen million tons of uranium mill tailings to keep them from continuing to bleed radioactive waste, heavy metals, and ammonia into the Colorado River could reach $1 billion.

Along with all the obvious poisons in the West's water are contaminants more subtle but perhaps just as damaging: endocrine disruptors. These chemicals in the environment that mimic hormones cause male fish to develop female sexual characteristics. Eventually endocrine disruptors lead to population collapse when there aren't enough males left to reproduce with the overabundant females. For the few remaining male fish in search of a female to have sex with, the odds are good but the goods are odd.

In clear-running creeks that tumble out of mountain wilderness and then pass by wastewater treatment plants, researchers have found downstream from the plants cosmetics, shampoos, soaps, plastics, pesticides, and pharmaceuticals, including chemicals used in contraceptives. All of these estrogen-related substances, which are flushed down toilets and drains, cause hormonal changes that trigger fish feminization, altering both reproductive systems and behavior. In one experiment, a researcher discovered that fathead minnows exposed to estrogenic compounds found in common household cleaners couldn't reproduce successfully because they didn't defend their territory from other males, who invaded the nests of the feminized fish and ate their offspring.

Some scientists fear feminized fish are the canary in the coal mine.

They worry that even if trace amounts of estrogenic chemicals can't alter people's endocrine systems, cocktails of the chemicals could wreak havoc with physiological development, resulting in changes such as girls entering puberty earlier and reduced sperm counts in men. According to David Norris, a University of Colorado physiology professor who has documented fish feminization in rivers, the buildup of endocrine-disrupting chemicals in the environment "has the potential of feminizing humans," and he believes that solving the problem is going to require changing what products we purchase.

Researchers are also finding in water supplies increased concentrations of drugs ranging from caffeine to antidepressants. Antidepressants interfere with signaling mechanisms in the brains of fish, causing them to swim slowly away from predators. No word yet from scientists on whether fish turn jittery when coffee is poured in their water.

Most wastewater treatment plants were not designed to remove the complex chemicals now appearing in our rivers and streams. Improvements such as reverse osmosis filtering and ultraviolet treatment are required. When the city of Boulder, Colorado, recently upgraded its wastewater treatment facility, the feminization of male fish decreased dramatically downstream from the plant in Boulder Creek, where gender-bending fish that swim sluggishly through drug-infested waters have been the subject of much recent study.

The federal Safe Drinking Water Act requires municipalities to test their water for contamination, but private wells are often unregulated. From _E. coli_ to MTBE, from cyanide to selenium, poisons of every type can lurk in our public water supplies and private wells, along with a complicated soup of hormone-disrupting substances that scientists are still trying to make sense of, and which are neither regulated by EPA standards nor monitored in drinking water. Even if we were to suddenly stop dumping and leaking waste into the environment, toxins would still turn up in our water supplies, for water is in constant motion. Rushing through streams, creeping through aquifers where plumes of poison slowly spread, the liquid that sustains life is forever circulating both above ground and below it, and poisons released into the environment decades ago and forgotten could find their way to a spigot tomorrow. Purchase a filtration system for your home if you'd like, but many chemicals aren't removed by the treatment process.

And stocking up on bottled water isn't much help either. The Natural Resources Defense Council, after conducting a comprehensive four-year study of bottled water that detected synthetic organic chemicals, bacteria, arsenic, and other contaminants in one-third of the samples, concluded, "Bottled water sold in the United States is not necessarily cleaner or safer than most tap water." The EPA, which regulates tap water, doesn't enforce bottled water regulations; the Food and Drug Administration (FDA) does. FDA regulatory loopholes exempt the majority of bottled water sold in the United States from safety rules, and the regulations that do apply to bottled water are weaker than EPA regulations for tap water.

But the bottled water industry, by cleverly using images of sparkling glaciers and pristine mountain springs to convey a perception of purity and safety, and by playing upon people's fears by shouting slogans such as "Tap water is poison!", has convinced consumers they need to pay four times the cost of gasoline, or up to ten thousand times the cost of tap water, for something that is no more pure or safe than what flows from their faucets virtually free. And a lot of bottled water is actually just treated tap water that has been put into bottles. Peter Gleick goes to great length in his book *Bottled and Sold* to show that the bottled water industry—currently enjoying a sales bonanza fueled by one of the most successful marketing campaigns in American history—relies on smoke and mirrors. Aside from consuming large amounts of energy, generating huge quantities of waste, fostering neglect of public water systems, and dewatering springs that sustain aquatic ecosystems, bottled water provides a product no better in safety or flavor than tap water. Brand managers are giggling at the gullibility of the public, and companies such as Nestlé, Coke, and Pepsi are laughing all the way to the bank.

To supplement the sober ruminations of water specialists, the comedic duo of Penn and Teller engaged in some shenanigans that further drive home the point that when it comes to bottled water, we've been sold a bill of goods. As part of an episode of *Bullshit!* that aired on Showtime, in a blind taste test, New Yorkers choose the flavor of New York City's tap water (some of the finest in the world, as explained by the modern-day muckraker Elizabeth Royte in her book *Bottlemania*) over the taste of bottled water. And in California, Penn and Teller have an actor pose at a trendy restaurant as a "water steward" bearing a menu of imaginary brands based on silliness such as French names and tropical rainforest spiders. The steward fills plastic bottles from a hose on the patio. When he serves the purported pricey bottled water to patrons inside, they babble like mountain brooks about the fine taste and satisfying mouthfeel.

CHAPTER 11

Silt, Salt, and Civilization

THE LEGENDARY ASSYRIAN RULER QUEEN SEMIRAMIS WAS SAID TO HAVE had inscribed on her tomb, "I constrained the mighty river to flow according to my will and let its water to fertilize lands that had before been barren and without inhabitants." With the completion of Hoover Dam and Glen Canyon Dam, American ingenuity had figured out how to control water on a scale unprecedented in human history, fulfilling a dream of total mastery that had spanned millennia. But in the words of Donald Worster, "Reclamation . . . is a technological stunt that, as the experience of other irrigation societies shows, cannot be indefinitely sustained. . . . Despite all efforts to save the system, it breaks down here, then there, then everywhere." Our engineers still have not solved the two problems that have bedeviled all irrigation societies since the dawn of human civilization, whether they rely on hand-dug ditches or computer-controlled waterworks: silt and salt.

The great irrigation civilizations of the world soared high and then came tumbling down as silt clogged their canals and salt poisoned their soil, turning their fields to dust. Sumer rose and fell on the Mesopotamian plain, and Babylon was built atop its ruins. Along with the dazzling ziggurats of these vanished kingdoms stand dull mounds of mud that clogged the water conduits. Armies of slaves could not dig them clean and keep the liquid flowing. What water did reach the fields eventually frosted the land white with salt. Harvests of wheat declined; yields of barley, a crop more tolerant of saline water, increased. And when the soil became saltier yet, all farming failed, and fields stitched with green rows of crops turned to tan wastes of desert.

Egypt escaped the fate of Sumer and Babylon by practicing a unique form of irrigation agriculture. The Nile swelled above its banks each summer, spilling into basins to renew the fertility of the land. When the floodwaters receded, the Egyptians planted crops. They had no need for extensive systems of aqueducts, and silt was a blessing instead of a curse—their crops flourished in the nutrient-rich soil washed of salt by the river. While the once populous cities of the Mesopotamian plain lay empty and in ruins, Egyptian civilization continued for thousands of years.

The natural system of irrigation along the Nile was not interrupted until the Aswan High Dam was built. Completed in 1970, the giant structure radically transformed the river's flow. Gone were the annual floods with their replenishing silt. The river deposited its sediment in the reservoir behind the dam, starving the fields below. Hydroelectricity generated by the dam powered factories built to manufacture fertilizer, which farmers dumped on their fields to make up for the missing nutrients. Diseases such as schistosomiasis and malaria proliferated in the stagnant river basin, and beneath the red Egyptian sun, vast quantities of irrigation water evaporated, leaving salty residue to cover fields no longer flushed clean by the river's yearly flood. Now the fields are losing their fabled fertility. Land once watered by the natural rise and fall of the river, land that sustained a civilization in the desert for thousands of years, is covered with white scabs of salt where nothing grows save weeds.

<hr />

The Colorado River basin was once buried beneath salty waves. And then the seas drained and were replaced by swamps, which eventually gave way to dry lands where dust rose in dervishes and sand lay humped in dunes. The great dams and diversion works of the American West allowed a green veneer to grow atop dun-colored desert—a thin layer of life atop so much salty waste.

Much of the West's irrigated farmland lies above a sheet of clay, the residue of the vanished seas. Water, an excellent solvent, percolates into soil laced with alkaline elements such as calcium, magnesium, and sodium; water dissolves these substances, which were deposited over millions of years by marine sediments and are commonly known as "salts." When the salty water dribbles down to the impermeable layer of clay, it has nowhere to go. It stalls against the hardpan of the ancient seabed, and then the saline liquid rises back up to where the roots of plants thread their way through soil. Salt in high quantities is poison to plants. It prevents them from absorbing essential minerals, strangling them of the nutrients they need.

When irrigated land in the West turns salty, farm yields decrease, and high-value crops such as fruits are replaced with salt-tolerant plants of lower economic value, such as alfalfa. After fields have been caked by brine, more irrigation water is used to flush the soil clean. If the soil becomes waterlogged and saline liquid lingers in the root zones of plants, tile drains can be placed beneath the ground to move the contaminated water away—but they are expensive to install and they simply send the problem to another place. When rivers shrink, as they will continue to do across the West as the climate warms and cities and farms divert their flow, less water is available for dilution, and salts become more concentrated. Reservoirs also increase salinity. In a process somewhat similar to distillation, pure water evaporates from the surfaces of reservoirs, leaving behind dissolved minerals. Salt can contaminate drinking water supplies, rendering the liquid unfit for humans, and it can turn aquatic habitats for plants and animals into lifeless saline soup.

Hard water—water that contains high amounts of dissolved minerals such as calcium and magnesium—causes soaps and detergents to produce less suds. It provides dietary calcium and magnesium and prevents toxic metals such as lead from leaching out of pipes, but it can corrode appliances and form scaly deposits that destroy plumbing and damage water treatment facilities. Making excessively hard water suitable for domestic use requires costly water-softening measures that use an ion-exchange resin to replace calcium and magnesium ions with sodium ions. Incidentally, ruthless marketers have recently been using science-babble to persuade people that they need to buy "ionized" or "alkalinized" water. This quackery harks back to the "rain follows the plow" pseudoscience that helped settle the frontier.

Swaths of alkaline soil white as snow are spreading across the basins and plains of the West, causing fields that have been forced by reclamation engineers to bloom to now undergo a process of desertification, by which nature reclaims them, turning arable land to salty waste that cannot grow food. Scientists have genetically modified plants to tolerate saline soil, offering a potential solution to the sterile white crusts. Drought-tolerant crops are also being bioengineered, leading some optimists to predict that technology will lead us out of our current crisis. But scientists caution that the salinity of soil and the aridity of the American West are increasing to a point at which no amount of tinkering with plants will allow them to be coaxed to life in the blast-furnace heat and plant-strangling salt. Denial isn't just a river in Egypt, as Mark Twain observed. It flows through the American West.

Beneath the streets of Phoenix lie the ruins of canals. These crumbling ditches are what remains of an irrigation system created by one of the most startlingly advanced preindustrial civilizations on earth. Spanish conquistadors who journeyed through present-day Arizona in the 1600s found tribes of Pima and Tohono O'odham Indians that had reoccupied desert lands long abandoned. The Native Americans called the people who had built cities there before them *Hohokam*, meaning "all used up."

The first white explorers to wander into the Salt River Valley saw the remains of buildings clustered around platforms, and within these ruins they found ballcourts and trash heaps piled with pottery shards. Branching out from the river were networks of canals that spanned the valley, connecting villages. This evidence of widespread irrigation in the past, along with the irrigation methods of modern Pima farmers, inspired pioneers in the area to create their own irrigation-based community. Legend has it a drunken Englishman tottering on the edge of an antique canal imagined Phoenix rising from the ashes of Hohokam civilization and gave the city its name.

Since the Hohokam had no written language, archaeologists now scratch at the dirt, searching for clues to help them piece together the puzzle of this vanished society. People began migrating into the Salt and Gila River Valleys at roughly the time of Christ. On hills overlooking the Salt River, the Hohokam built adobe villages. They planted seeds in soil that had been soaked by floodwater when spring runoff swelled the rivers, spilling them beyond their banks. And then at some point, maybe as early as AD 50, the Hohokam began stacking stones and brush in streams to make check dams (small dams built across minor channels) that stored water and nutrient-rich silt until the temporary structures were washed away in floods and then rebuilt. They also began constructing ditches near the rivers to irrigate corn, beans, and squash.

From AD 600 to 900 the Hohokam expanded their irrigation system to include not just little ditches along rivers but immense conduits of massive permanence on par with Roman masterworks—they reached dimensions of twenty miles in length, eighty-five feet in width, and twenty feet in depth. These monumental structures, which the Bureau of Reclamation would have been proud to build, were capable of moving vast quantities of water. The largest one irrigated ten thousand acres of land—the American West's earliest public works project.

With the frenetic expansion of the freeway system around Phoenix and excavation for skyscrapers ripping up desert soil and exposing numerous ruins, researchers are gaining more insight into the Hohokam's waterworks. The canals were wide where they opened to the river; they tapered to narrower passageways to accommodate for flows diminished by seepage, evaporation, and water spread across fields. By designing the canals to grow smaller as the flow lessened, and by carefully calibrating their drop, the water's velocity was held constant—which was critical to the longevity of the canals. If the water raced through too quickly it would erode their sides and floors; if it flowed too sluggishly, dirt particles would accumulate and cause clogging. Erosion required repairs; silting required digging the channels clean. These problems were avoided with sophisticated engineering.

The complexity and scale of this irrigation system rivaled those built in Egypt and China. At the height of Hohokam civilization, with water moving through an engineered grid of canals and flowing in measured rates through a labyrinth of laterals and ditches, satellite cities sprawled outward from the mighty urban core. One can imagine that the citizens who enjoyed the bounty flowing from this highly organized network didn't spend much time pondering their civilization's eventual decline. The canals constructed by Phoenix city planners match almost precisely in gradient and location those built by the Hohokam.

The canals were excavated entirely by hand. Laborers used digging sticks and hoes with stone blades to pry loose the hard earth. Dirt was hauled away in baskets. Not only did the initial construction of canals require enormous amounts of human labor, but flood damage, which occurred frequently, demanded further expenditures of effort. Designing, building, and maintaining such an elaborate irrigation system, as well as meting out the water and monitoring its use to prevent conflict, required complex social organization. Indeed, all "hydraulic civilizations," societies organized around the storage and distribution of scarce water, from Sumer to Hohokam, maintain power and control by creating bureaucracies that monopolize the water supply. Historian Donald Worster writes in his provocative and influential book *Rivers of Empire* that the American West "can best be described as a modern hydraulic society, which is to say, a social order based on the intensive, large-scale manipulation of water and its products in an arid setting. . . . The hydraulic society of the West . . . is increasingly a coercive, monolithic, and hierarchical system, ruled by a power elite based on the ownership of capital and expertise."

Researchers think the great platform mounds built by the Hohokam, some standing at the heads of major waterworks and others rising in regular intervals along the canals, served as the headquarters for administrators—from these airy heights they oversaw the system that controlled the flow of water. Other researchers hypothesize that the mounds served some spiritual purpose, and religion played an important role in the construction of the monumental waterworks and the society organized around them. Regardless, after some fifteen hundred years of flourishing agriculture and urban life in the Sonoran Desert, the Hohokam civilization vanished. First floods ravaged the region, and then a drought shriveled the

Colorado to its lowest flow in hundreds of years. Some scholars point to salt accumulation in the soil due to intensive irrigation as the cause of the collapse of Hohokam civilization. No matter the extent of their canals, no matter the sophistication of their society, there was too much water and then there wasn't enough. The priests and technocrats atop the mounds looked down upon the parched and salt-crusted land. And they could do nothing but lead their people out of the desert.

Phoenix rose from the dust-clogged canals of the Hohokam and built conduits greater yet, hulking pieces of piping to slake the cavernous thirst of a city that was said to be growing by two acres an hour in the mid-1990s. Within its sprawling precincts could be placed Paris, Rome, and Manhattan. Rows of houses marched into the smoggy distance of what real-estate developers dubbed the "Valley of the Sun." Air-conditioned shopping centers spread among the arroyos, and big-box stores covered the desert's cryptobiotic crust. Now the region's climate is heating up and the distant mountains are wrapped in thinning robes of snow. The Central Arizona Project, its control room blinking with computer screens like central command at NASA, is in danger of running dry due to an extended drought. And it has become fashionable in environmental circles to compare the fate of Phoenix to that of the Hohokam.

———

Pioneers quipped that the Colorado River was "too thick to drink, too thin to plow." Before it was dammed, the river's turbid currents carried past a single point each day enough silt to fill a line of trucks stretched across the continent's width. The Mississippi is crystal clear compared to the Colorado, which excavates, carries, and deposits seventeen times more silt than the Big Muddy. The Colorado is a giant conveyor belt, endlessly moving sediment as it erodes the land in one area to build it up in another. Where the undammed river once branched into braided channels that spread fanwise into the sea, silt piled up in a delta more than a mile thick. In some places the sediment lies some twenty thousand feet deep, the height of the tallest mountain in North America.

When a river is blocked by a dam, it builds its delta not in the sea but in the reservoir behind the obstruction, and substances like mercury and selenium it once flushed along its length and purged in floods lie trapped in thickening silt. The Río Colorado, which means Red River or Colored River, was named by Spanish explorers for the ruddy hue of its waters. But the flows that exit dams along its length are now clear because the river deposits its burden of silt in reservoirs, turning them to tubs of poisoned mud. Sonar studies have revealed a wide delta at the inlet of Lake Powell and a wedge of silt piled up against the dam. Eventually Lake Powell and Lake Mead will clog completely, as all reservoirs do.

The dams of the West were designed to hold water, not mud, which weighs much more than water. When former Bureau of Reclamation commissioner Floyd Dominy was asked what the Bureau's plan was for dealing with a sediment-clogged Lake Powell, he responded, "We will let people in the future worry about it." But as James Lawrence Powell demonstrates in his book *Dead Pool*, an extended drought due to a warming climate drained Lake Powell early in this century, and the shrunken reservoir could fill with silt not in some comfortably distant future projected by bureaucrats at the federal government's Office of Sedimentation, but in our children's lifetimes. David Haskell, former Science Center director for Grand Canyon National Park, contends that Glen Canyon Dam needs to be dismantled before it causes a catastrophe. "In about 60 years, the sediment will build up to a point where the dam could break," says Haskell. "Models of a dam break show a 500-foot wall of water scouring every living thing out of Grand Canyon."

Before it was dammed by humans, the Colorado dumped so much silt in front of itself, sometimes it found its path blocked by sediment and was forced to cut new channels as it shoved its way toward the sea. Changing course, it set out across broad reaches of land, scouring the earth until stone turned to sand, impounding reservoirs the size of Lake Mead as it built its own levees and dams. Mark Twain wrote of the Mississippi, which engineers were trying to yoke, "ten thousand River Commissions, with the mines of the world at their back, cannot tame that lawless stream, cannot curb it or confine it, cannot say to it, 'Go here,' or

'Go there,' and make it obey; cannot save a shore which it has sentenced; cannot bar its path with an obstruction which it will not tear down, dance over, and laugh at."

Hoover Dam and Glen Canyon Dam and a slew of other structures now straitjacket the Colorado's flow and store its silt. Robbed of the grit and floodwaters it once used to abrade its bed and blast boulders out of its way, the river's slow work of shaping the land has come nearly to a stop. But only for a time. All that silt backing up behind the concrete slabs must go somewhere when the reservoirs are finally filled with mud, and so must the river's force. In time the patient river will find a way out from behind its walls. We can tap its power and divert its flow, but in the end it wanders where it wants to go.

CHAPTER 12

Water in the Twenty-First-Century West

AGRICULTURE

The Rio Grande River begins in ice-skimmed headwaters atop the Colorado Rockies. It runs down slopes of huddled pines, their branches flagged by wind, and it rolls through valleys braised by sun. Harvey Fergusson wrote of the Rio Grande region in 1933, "It is a land where water has always been scarce and therefore precious, a thing to be fought for, prayed for, and cherished in beautiful vessels." Nomadic Native American hunters and gatherers settled near the river to raise crops, and fields along its banks have been farmed continuously for more than six hundred years. When the livestock of white settlers trampled the desert soil's fragile crust, narrow gullies widened into gaping arroyos and the river filled with mud. Now the lower reaches of the Rio Grande turn each year to a trickle, and fields of crops fade to dusty scrub.

Once a wide-flowing watercourse that bloated with runoff to threaten towns along its banks, the Rio Grande was subdued in 1915. A Reclamation Service dam built upstream from the city of El Paso in West Texas put a stop to floods and allowed water to be stored for irrigation. But mud began to clog the reservoir behind the dam, and a brown slurry spread upstream, slipping over levees, waterlogging fields. The Army Corps of Engineers took charge, removing the twists from the river, straightening it, engineering it into submission.

The river's flow was divvied up by international treaties between the United States and Mexico, and by the Rio Grande Compact, an interstate agreement between Colorado, New Mexico, and Texas. When people in New Mexico decided the river didn't satisfy their needs, they made it bigger by transferring flow from the Colorado River watershed to the Rio Grande watershed. Diversion dams and siphons sent water beneath the Continental Divide through a tunnel complex so vast it "almost defies comprehension," in the words of law professor and author Charles Wilkinson. Still it wasn't enough. Now the Rio Grande is overappropriated—there are more claims to the water than there is water, and El Paso and nearby farms suck the river dry. Downstream from El Paso and its twin city in Mexico, Juárez, is a stretch of the Rio Grande that has been dubbed the "Forgotten River." A concrete canal that replaced the river's bed is mostly bare, and its naked flanks bake in the sun of the Chihuahua Desert. The bottom of the concrete trough holds an ooze of green slime. Litter lies in a colorful scatter. Against so much grim concrete, the trash seems festive, as if a carnival is taking place, or a parade is passing by. Freeways stretch along the canal and tall fences fortress its sides, separating the United States from Mexico.

A treaty signed in 1944 between the neighboring nations obligates Mexico to deliver in its tributaries a minimum amount of water annually. The water is supposed to flow into the Rio Grande for use by the United States—regardless of drought. The area of northern Mexico through which the tributaries flow was sparsely populated when the treaty was signed; now it is full of shantytowns and croplands. When drought desiccated the region in the first few years of the twenty-first century, Mexico fell behind on its quota, prompting Texas farmers to demand reparations of $1 billion for crop losses. Rainfall ended the drought and tensions eased as swollen mountain streams bolstered the Rio Grande. But another drought is now wilting crops and turning fields to sun-cracked crust. The tributaries in northern Mexico are under increasing strain as Mexican farmers use more of the water to irrigate their fields.

Crazy with thirst, the city of El Paso is buying up local farms so it can own the rights to their water. Cattle ranches are turning into water ranches, and farmland is reverting to desert. What water is left is being directed toward the city. And the dehydrated metropolis is pumping underground water as fast as it can, much faster than rain will recharge it. To make efficient use of its dwindling resource, the city is lining canals that divert water from the Rio Grande to stop them from seeping. But seepage replenishes the aquifer. By conserving water diverted from the river, there will be less water to pump from the ground.

Below El Paso, the Forgotten River stretch of the Rio Grande receives tributaries that reinvigorate the diminished watercourse, turning the stinky sewage goop that slides along the concrete trench into something that once again resembles a river. In the painted canyons and sculpted badlands of Big Bend National Park, the Rio Grande forms a muddy flow that sometimes drops so low it strands whiskered catfish, leaving them flopping on gravel. The river stalls in reservoirs built in its lower basin to supply agricultural fields. Most of the water drawn from these impoundments goes to farming in the subtropical Rio Grande Valley, where plump grapefruit with ruby flesh bend the boughs of trees. Cotton blooms in white abundance, and flooded fields steam in the sun. What is left of the exhausted Rio Grande dribbles through hot sand. Some years it doesn't reach the Gulf of Mexico. The last of its moisture evaporates from stagnant pools, and stones rattle like bones in the river's dry bed.

There is a building consensus that agriculture, on the scale it is practiced now along the Rio Grande and throughout the West, is doomed. As cities swell across the deserts and plains, there just isn't enough water to go around. Most of the water that growing metropolises will need in coming years will be taken from irrigation. As cities raid rural areas for their water, cotton growers in California's San Joaquin Valley may have to find a new business, one that doesn't rely on the American taxpayer to provide water in a desert to grow a thirsty crop that is subsidized by the federal government. And ranchers in Wyoming may have to recognize that *The Virginian* is a fine story, but land covered in sagebrush and dust is not the most logical place to raise the nation's beef.

The cowboy is firmly ensconced in America's iconography, though the facts are often trampled like the packed earth beneath the hooves of cattle. Today's hero of the rangeland rides off in the saddle of his ATV, heading into the smoggy haze of the western sky to collect his government subsidy. The corporate rancher who sucks from the federal water teat is protected by symbols born when the first cattle were driven north from the haciendas of Mexico and Americans told themselves stories of who they were and what they believed. From these stories of rugged individuals living lives of freedom and representing the best of the American character grew a sprawling system of federally subsidized water. The subsidies allowed farm and ranch businesses to use the lion's share of the West's most precious resource with little regard for the costs of delivering it to dry lands.

Growing food demands enormous inputs of water. According to the Water Education Foundation, it takes about 118 gallons of water to grow a pound of corn. In his book *When the Rivers Run Dry*, Fred Pearce notes that the 250 to 650 gallons of water it takes to grow a pound of rice exceeds the weekly water use for many households. According to *Newsweek* magazine, "The water that goes into a 1,000 pound steer would float a destroyer." Figures for the amount of water needed to produce one pound of beef vary from an astonishing 1,801 gallons (according to *The Economist* magazine) to an almost unfathomable 12,009 gallons—that's more than 100,000 pounds of water, or fifty tons, for a pound of beef! (The cow doesn't drink all that water, of course—most of it is used to grow the grass and grain fed to the animal over the course of its lifetime.) According to David Pimentel, a professor of ecology and agricultural science at Cornell who calculated the 12,009-gallons figure, you could go two years without taking a shower and you wouldn't save as much water as you would by not eating one pound of beef. This might be worth considering the next time you are taking a shower, or eating a hamburger. And that glass of milk you just drank with your hamburger? The US Geological Survey's Water Science for Schools website calculates sixty-five gallons of water in order for you to wear a milk mustache after draining the delicious beverage. Start adding up the water used for meals and you get the picture—it takes high-rise dams and giant pipelines to grow your dinner in the West.

When it comes time to pay for these projects, the cowboy is seldom to be found. But silt from the erosion caused by his cattle can be found clogging the rivers of the West. The federal government has numerous times tried to mitigate range damage by reforming western grazing policy, beginning with the Taylor Grazing Act of 1934. But in the 1990s, a report by the Bureau of Land Management and the Forest Service said riparian areas on public lands were in their "worst condition in history," mainly because of grazing. Soil sloughs into watercourses of the West, and the native grasses and flowers that once covered their banks give way to bare scabs of dirt and thickets of weedy plants that cut and slash at bare legs like forests of wire and knives.

Agriculture, which predated the growth of cities in the western United States, snatched up senior water rights and now claims about 80 percent of water used across the region. Agriculture in Nevada uses some 90 percent of the state's water yet generates fewer jobs statewide than a single Las Vegas mega-resort. California's farms use more water in a year than Los Angeles could slurp up in half a century. But even with government subsidies, growing crops and raising livestock in the West are tough businesses, and when cities offer farmers and ranchers more money for the right to use their water than they can make growing alfalfa to feed cattle, sending their water to cities makes good economic sense. With population growth in western cities outstripping water supplies and a lull in the construction of huge federal water projects, city water managers are scrambling for solutions; buying up agricultural water rights offers a quick fix.

Western states have been passing legislation to make the sale and transfer of water rights easier so their cities can grow. Many economists applaud such transfers, arguing that they facilitate a free market in water, a commodity that has been mismanaged by the federal government into a terribly inefficient system based on illogical subsidies for crops already in surplus, which are often bought at a loss by the government. Cotton grows like a weed in the wet climate of the Deep South. Thanks to federal commodity price support payments, devised during the Great Depression as a stopgap to stabilize small family farms but continuing to this day, cotton is also grown in the deserts of the Southwest, where it gulps enormous amounts of irrigation water, which, of course, is heavily subsidized by the government. The more one learns about water in the West, the farther one falls into the rabbit hole. While China introduces capitalism into its countryside, the rural western United States remains firmly entrenched in what looks an awful lot like a command economy.

Robert Glennon, in his book *Unquenchable*, explains that growers in California use 80 percent of the state's water but their contribution to the gross state product is a mere 2 percent. One acre-foot of water used to grow alfalfa generates about $60; the same amount of water used in the semiconductor industry (which uses purified water to clean and cool microchips) generates roughly $1 million. Peter Gleick, director of the Pacific Institute, a nonpartisan think tank that focuses on water issues, writes in *Scientific American*, "Supporting 100,000 high-tech California jobs requires some 250 million gallons of water a year; the same amount of water used in the agricultural sector sustains fewer than 10 jobs—a stunning difference." Glennon, Gleick, and others argue that the glaring disparity between water's worth in agriculture and technology industries favors a vigorous trade in water rights. This argument, however, is not unlike the one Los Angeles used to convince President Theodore Roosevelt that water from the Owens River would be better put to use by a burgeoning metropolis than by a bunch of rubes in a rural valley who wanted to raise fruit.

More buying and selling of water rights could restore some sense to how water is used in the West, many argue. The free market is the cure, they insist. Environmentalists generally approve of the transfers, because when cities purchase agricultural water rights, they avert the need to build more dams and diversion projects, leaving natural landscapes intact. And water rights can be bought by environmental groups to protect instream flows for the benefit of fish and wildlife. Moreover, many environmentalists maintain that damage caused by livestock, which overgraze grasslands and trample and degrade riparian zones across the West, will disappear as water is directed away from the chambered stomachs of cows and into the pipes of cities. Anti-livestock advocates across the water-scarce region celebrate a future in which raising cattle on dry plains will be as out-moded as whaling in the world's oceans, and the myth of the cowboy as noble steward of the land will seem as relevant as Santa Claus.

But when farms and ranches sell their water rights to growing met-ropolitan areas, local food production decreases. The biggest losers in the transfer of water from farms to cities, aside from the rural communities that wither and die when their tax base disappears because no crops or livestock are being raised, are urban locavores who want to eat fresh food grown nearby. A city can quench its thirst today with the water rights of farmers, but what of its hunger tomorrow?

Glennon and others contend that as more water rights are transferred from farm to city, farming productivity will not necessarily decrease. American farmers are innovators. Forced to make due with less water, they find ways to get "more crop per drop." They replace lower-value crops like alfalfa and cotton with higher-value, less water-intensive crops like almonds and broccoli; they line irrigation canals to stop seepage; they install soil-moisture monitors that help them avoid overwatering; they laser level their fields to prevent irrigation water from draining away; they switch from wasteful flood irrigation (simply letting water run from ditches onto fields) to more efficient drip systems that deliver water near the root zones of plants, minimizing evaporation and runoff. Where the cows and the icons who now ride in the plastic saddles of ATVs to herd them will fit into all this will not be clear until the dust of the market scramble for water rights settles.

Historian Hal Rothman wrote, "No American city has ever ceased to grow because of a lack of water, and it's unlikely that Las Vegas will be the first." The only obstacle to securing water supplies, Rothman argues, is cost. And lack of money is not a problem that plagues Las Vegas or other booming cities of the West. Aurora, a fast-growing suburb of Denver with a big bank account, looked around the state for solutions to preventing a water famine and found cash-poor farmers in the Arkansas River Val-ley south of Denver who were water-rich and willing to sell their rights. Aurora shelled out $50 million and boosted its water supply by 30 per-cent. Though this helped stave off Aurora's water crisis and brought some struggling farmers much-needed money, one newspaper in the Arkansas Valley dubbed the Aurora water manager who orchestrated the deal "the Baron of Darkness." Journalist Allen Best notes, "Colorado's self-image is grounded in pastoral pleasantness. Buying farms for their water is only a step above selling your sister into the sex trade."

When farmers and ranchers succumb to the water vultures circling their land and sell their water rights to cities, their spreads are often devoured by suburban sprawl. Not only does food production stop, but a pretty piece of open space becomes a shopping mall. And the scenic value and the environmental worth of farmland and ranchland, which can provide critical habitat for wildlife and protect soil and watersheds, is lost. Some farmers and ranchers see their way of life as sacrosanct; they are about as likely to sell their cash crop of water to the Babylon of a big city, no matter how much they might profit, as Muslims are to close down Mecca and open a liquor store in its stead to make some money.

As farms and ranches give way to parking lots and office towers, cities are forced to find more water for their growing populations. The conurbations of Southern California and Phoenix serve as cautionary tales about cities that grow so fast and so far that they consume all their open space, their boundaries blending into amorphous spreads of asphalt and concrete that smother the land. And now other places in the West, such as Colorado's Front Range, are experiencing similar explosive growth. Denver, the "Mile Dry City," and its satellite cities are spreading toward each other, burying farms and fields beneath swelling grids without discernable centers. The borders merge into one thirsty megalopolis, and the rancher with his cattle and subsidized water—and open space—suddenly is no longer a villain to many chagrined environmentalists. Overgrazed land ruins watersheds, but land covered in blacktop does even more damage.

Regardless of the dangers of sprawl, it is difficult to make an argument for using the bulk of a western state's water supplies to grow low-value crops that glut the national market. Take the case of alfalfa. Used mainly as feed for cows, alfalfa requires more water than many other crops and generates less revenue per acre than, say, fruits or vegetables. It is easy to grow in water-rich states such as Wisconsin; in deserts it requires astounding amounts of irrigation water. Summer temperatures in California's Imperial Valley regularly push past 110 degrees, evaporating large quantities of water. The alfalfa that is grown in summer is of lower quality (less nutritional value for livestock) than what is produced in cooler temperatures—and requires much more water.

When irrigation began in the Imperial Valley, water diverted from the Colorado River was plentiful and cheap and no one worried about wasting it. Enormous quantities were dumped on fields in the hottest days of summer, and a lot of the water ran into the Salton Sea. It flowed through unlined canals, seeping into the earth, and farmers didn't have gauges to monitor how much they used. Nobody seemed to mind—there was enough to go around. But then San Diego grew mad with thirst.

In what is considered the largest water trade in US history, in 2003, after nine years of tense negotiations, litigation, and political intrigue, California's Imperial Valley Irrigation District agreed to transfer more than 30 maf of water over seventy-five years to San Diego County. Interior Secretary Gale Norton declared, "With this agreement, conflict on the river is stilled." Seldom have sillier words been spoken in the West.

California, which had been slurping up surplus flow of the Colorado River beyond the state's 4.4 maf annual allocation, made the transfer as part of an agreement to satisfy the federal government that it would scale back its use of water from the Colorado and live within the means allotted to it by the 1963 *Arizona v. California* Supreme Court decision. The Imperial Valley was paid handsomely for its water by San Diego, and the city also footed the bill for lining irrigation canals so it could use the water that was conserved. San Diego got to quench its thirst with Colorado River water, and California moved closer to abiding by the Law of the River. On the surface, the transfer seemed like a good deal for everyone, but it generated controversy that continues to this day. Some Californians grumbled about the massive amount of money the absentee agribusinesses in the area earned simply by implementing conservation measures that were desperately needed anyway, allowing farmers to lounge on beaches and "raise martinis instead of alfalfa." Some residents of the Imperial Valley complained that the money wasn't nearly enough to compensate them for the decrease in agricultural productivity and job losses caused by the water transfer. Though most of the land in the valley is owned by wealthy corporations, the people who work on the farms are some of the poorest in the state of California. Farm workers and small business owners in the area feared the agribusinesses would take the money and run, leaving the community devastated. Residents of the Imperial Valley, worried that their way of life and their economy would be threatened if they gave up some of their water rights, voted down the transfer.

The Department of the Interior got into the mix by deciding that water in the Imperial Valley was not being put to beneficial use because it was being wasted with sloppy irrigation practices. Secretary Norton, in a move she compared to laying cards on the table during a poker game, announced that the amount of Colorado River water sent to the Imperial Valley Irrigation District would be reduced. She wasn't bluffing. The Department of the Interior cut California's water allotment, marking the first time the federal government curtailed a state's use of Colorado River water. Imperial Valley residents believed they were being bullied by the State of California and by the feds into selling their water to San Diego. Eventually valley residents succumbed to the pressure, and claiming a gun was being held to their heads, they reluctantly approved the transfer. And water that had grown crops in the desert grew green lawns in San Diego.

When Imperial Valley growers fallowed some of their fields (left the land unplanted) and started irrigating more efficiently, runoff into the Salton Sea decreased, lowering the level of a body of water that provides critical habitat for a bounty of birds—more species than are found in the Everglades. The Salton Sea, artificially created when the Colorado River was rerouted, provides sanctuary for avian species that have abandoned wetlands drained by developers. And now, as agricultural practices in the Imperial Valley are improved to waste less water, the Salton Sea is becoming saltier and drying up, putting migratory waterfowl at risk and exposing polluted shoreline. The naked soil cooks in the sun to dust as soft and dry as talcum powder, and the dust is scattered by windstorms, potentially spreading particulates laced with selenium, pesticides, and other poisons into people's lungs. Imperial County already has the highest rate of childhood asthma in California. Air pollution resulting from the Imperial Valley–San Diego water transfer became the subject of a federal lawsuit soon after the deal was signed. The transfer agreement has been dragged through several courts, and there is no end to conflict in sight. A system of dikes with a jaw-dropping price tag of nearly $9 billion has been proposed to save the Salton Sea for birds and to dampen the poisoned dust.

Long before people schemed to reengineer the Colorado River, bodies of water filled the Salton depression and then dried out and disappeared as the restless river changed its course. The latest manmade Salton Sea is smaller than its natural predecessors. Tide marks made by mineral salts and calcified shells ring the mountains around the valley, evidence of vast inland seas that filled the basin brimful, offering a watery haven for life before the liquid evaporated into the dry sky. Our tampering with the ecosystem there has occurred on an infinitesimally small section of a sprawling timeline, geologic eons in which mountains rise and crumble and seas gather and drain.

It is easy to say that Imperial Valley farmers growing low-value alfalfa by drowning their fields in water that searing heat turns to vapor in the desert is a poor use of a dwindling resource. It is much harder to figure out how to reform the agricultural policies and water laws that have allowed this to happen. Corporations like to receive ridiculously cheap water so they can get rich from agribusiness ventures. Politicians like to make powerful agribusiness interests happy so they can get elected and reelected. Most of us just turn on the tap and never give a thought to the water that comes out. Until, one day, it doesn't. Then we might start asking why the Colorado River is being drained to grow alfalfa, one of the nation's most abundant crops, in one of the hottest places in America, with water that is subsidized by taxpayers and used by companies that control some of the largest landholdings in the country. And that steak we just ate, which came from a cow gorged on alfalfa grown in the roasting summer sun, could be hard to swallow without a glass of water to wash it down. Suddenly water is worth any price, for without it nothing else matters.

GROWTH, MARKETS, AND MONEY

Boulder, Colorado, located where the Great Plains rise up in wrinkled foothills to meet the Rocky Mountains, is the only city in America to own a glacier. This sparkling chunk of ice nestled in a mountain bowl was acquired by the city to protect the purity of its water supply. In 1959, Boulder's voters approved the "Blue Line," which restricted city water service to below a contour line of elevation near the base of the mountains, helping to put the kibosh on unlimited population growth. Citizens were motivated more by concern about their quality of life being damaged by development than by fear of using up all the meltwater from their glacier and exhausting other water sources. Nevertheless, this was an early effort to link land use to water supply—something as new and strange to denizens of the American West as Facebook is to the Bushmen of the Kalahari. (The nomadic Bushmen, by the way, are perhaps the most adept people on the planet at surviving water scarcity.)

In the past, the West experienced unrestrained growth as governments across the region approved subdivision after subdivision with no regard for the limits of water supplies. But as new sources became more difficult and costly to develop, some municipal governments stopped handing out building permits like lollipops at a bank teller's window. When a drought shrank the snowpack in the Sangre de Cristo (Spanish for Blood of Christ) Mountains near Santa Fe, its life-giving flow turned to a random trickle. The city responded by requiring developers to secure water rights for their proposed projects before they could receive building permits. There was plenty of grumbling from developers. To speed the permitting process along and reduce the risk of developers getting stuck with water rights to projects they couldn't build, the city created a "water bank" that allowed it to deposit water rights it had purchased without attaching them to a specific project. Developers could save the rights until they needed them for a project, or they could sell the rights to other developers who needed water for their own projects. This is a far cry from the use-it-or-lose-it principle that had guided water law in the West from the time of the gold rushes onward. Now, instead of obtaining the rights to water by getting to a stream first and putting its flow to beneficial use, developers could purchase and sell water rights in a market that turned them to abstract assets without regard to whether the water was actually being used. By breaking with Western water rights tradition, and by linking development directly to the existing water supply, Santa Fe created a system better suited to issues of water scarcity and urban growth than the water rights system that had guided mining and the agrarian settlement of the frontier.

The parsimony of the Mormon pioneers, who carefully used water they diverted with their backbreaking labor, gave way to the profligacy of the highest per capita use of water in the nation when the Central Utah Project, originally intended by the federal government to help farmers, was redesigned to sate the water appetite of urban areas agglomerating along the busy Wasatch Front. Conservation and recycling helped relieve stress on Salt Lake City's water supply. But to check its reckless use of water, the city also addressed growth. For developers to obtain building permits, they were required to prove that they owned water rights sufficient to serve the homes they planned to build. But there is no surplus water in Utah: Every drop is already accounted for. The only way developers can obtain water for their projects is to purchase the rights from existing users—which means that increasingly valuable water rights are transferred from the ditches of farms to the taps of new housing developments.

Former secretary of the interior Bruce Babbitt stated, "Without water markets, we can't solve the problem of meeting the future water needs of the West." By transferring agricultural water to industrial and commercial enterprises, water markets like those that emerged in Santa Fe and Salt Lake City reduce waste and move a scarce resource toward its most productive uses. The markets bring water consumption in line with the West's changing economy—water moves from corn to real estate, from alfalfa to computer chips. Markets that transfer water between states and between the upper and lower basins of the Colorado River are more complicated and controversial, but many believe they are essential for solving the West's water conundrum.

Some want to take the idea of markets a step further and privatize public water supplies. Commodifying something so crucial for life, however, is hugely contentious. Advocates of water being treated as a human right rather than a commercial product, such as Maude Barlow, author of *Blue Covenant* and appointed the first senior advisor on water issues to the United Nations, believe that water should be made safe, affordable, and accessible for everyone. Barlow insists that privatization creates a "water cartel" that deprives citizens of their basic right to use freshwater. Barlow and others working for what they call "water justice" maintain that it is the proper role of government to store, protect, and deliver water. That the track records of federal agencies and state governments with regard to managing the West's life-giving resource are marginal at best—and arguably downright abysmal—doesn't dampen the enthusiasm of Barlow and others of her mindset for keeping businesses out of the water supply.

Government supervision of the region's most precious resource for the good of the people is a fine idea. The reality, however, is that throughout the history of the American West, the federal government and state governments have distributed water with little regard for democratic principles or sensible economics, and elected and appointed officials have consistently directed water toward powerful interests. As a people we have mismanaged our water supplies, and whether they are municipally owned or manipulated by commerce doesn't seem to matter as much as the basic human drive to maximize individual wealth and power, even at the expense of a vital resource's ruin. This impulse is more powerful than market mechanisms, more potent than democratic institutions, for it is the product of billions of years of evolution: Nature has designed us to destroy nature. Countering this impulse will take more than free enterprise or government policies. It will take education—lots of education. Until each of us understands our role in the tragedy of the commons, and until we evolve beyond what our selfish genes have programmed us to do, we will continue to trample and raid the resources that sustain us, including water, the most important commons of all.

Water cannot be provided for free, because even though it falls from the sky, filtration systems and pipes do not. There is a cost to treat water and deliver it to people, and this cost must be paid either through taxes or fees. Most economists and environmentalists agree that water in the West is simply too cheap: Its low price doesn't reflect its scarcity or its external costs to society, such as salt contamination, subsidence, and damage to riverine and riparian ecosystems. They point out that cheap water encourages waste, and water in the West, where the resource is rare, has historically cost users less than in the East, where water is relatively abundant. The West's water quandaries are caused by pricing, they argue. If beer were being sold for a penny a bottle, stores would run out of beer. Forced to pay more for water, whether by the law of supply and demand in a marketplace or by government decree, consumers cut back on their use. Case in point: Tucson, frightened by a plummeting water table in the 1980s, implemented a tiered billing system that charged more per gallon as water use increased; the city's per capita water consumption dropped by more than forty gallons per day. But some people argue that water *should* be cheap because access to it is an unalienable human right.

The solution is something of a middle way. Prices can be mandated to remain low for the amount of water needed to fulfill basic daily needs such as drinking, cooking, flushing toilets, and washing clothes. For amounts beyond that threshold, which are most likely used for watering lawns, filling swimming pools, and so on, the price can be increased to levels that discourage consumption and more realistically reflect the paucity of water in the West and the high costs to society of collecting and distributing the resource upon which our lives depend.

Food production, of course, depends on water. Many critics of the federal government's water policies in the West argue that taxpayers, who have funded the construction and operation of dams and diversion works, have received nothing for their dollars. Sandra Postel, for instance, refers to western irrigation systems as "all for the benefit of the few and at taxpayer expense." That is not entirely accurate. In exchange for funding the subsidies that allowed the farming and ranching industries to make money by splashing water on their fields, taxpayers received benefits such as fruits and vegetables in winter, compliment of the warm climes of Arizona and California. Most important, the American public was provided with a super-cheap supply of food. If agribusinesses were forced to pay the true cost of water, then burgers, fries, and cola would cost consumers considerably more. Our federal policies of subsidizing water for large farm businesses are partly to blame for the spread of obesity and heart disease. These epidemics create windfalls for the pharmaceutical industry, which benefits from people who need medication, and the petroleum industry, which profits from overweight people who consume more fuel. A fast food nation runs on cheap water.

ENERGY

Water and energy are inextricably linked. Next to agriculture, the energy industry is the largest user of water in the United States. And the water industry consumes enormous amounts of energy. According to the EPA, running a faucet for five minutes uses about as much energy as burning a sixty-watt lightbulb for fourteen hours.

A lot of energy is consumed making water potable and treating effluent to meet environmental standards. Whether pumping water from aquifers, lifting it uphill, or delivering it to homes and businesses, energy is needed to move the liquid. And water is not light, a fact to which anyone who has lugged a watering can through a garden or worn a hydration system while hiking can attest. In California, the largest single user of energy is the State Water Project, an elaborate system of dams, aqueducts, pipelines, and pumps, featuring one extraordinarily energy-gobbling section that hoists water nearly two thousand feet over an entire mountain range.

Producing the fuel that runs our nation—petroleum, natural gas, and coal—requires a lot of water. The fuels have to be mined and refined, processed and transported, and water is used at each stage for everything from cooling drill bits and flushing rock cuttings from oil wells to creating coal slurry that can flow through pipelines. Most power plants produce steam to spin turbine generators, a process that consumes some water; but the bulk of the water needed for converting fuel to electricity is used for cooling. Because of water's high specific heat index—meaning it can absorb a lot of heat before it starts to get hot—it is an excellent coolant (which is why we use it in car radiators). Power plants, whether coal, natural gas, nuclear, or biomass, consume copious amounts of water for cooling when fuel is combusted. According to a report by Western Resource Advocates and the Environmental Defense Fund, in 2005 thermoelectric power plants in Arizona, Colorado, New Mexico, Nevada, and Utah consumed a volume of water roughly equal to the combined water use of Denver, Phoenix, and Albuquerque. If you are worried about the rivers of the West running dry, switch off the lights. If you want to save energy, turn off the tap.

Developing clean energy technologies such as wind and solar, aside from reducing the greenhouse gas emissions that are heating up the climate, will lessen our reliance on water-guzzling power plants, freeing up supplies for thirsty cities.

The problem with wind and solar, however, is that they are intermittent—we can't predict when the sun will shine or the wind will blow. They produce power at the pleasure of nature, not in accord with the needs of people. Sometimes when cities are pulling the most energy from the grid the air is still or clouds pass over the sun. The solution may be energy storage technology known as "pumped hydro." But the solution could create more problems for the region's water supplies.

When wind is screaming across the Wyoming plains at night and air conditioners are quiet, or when sun is beaming down on the deserts of California but there is still plenty of juice in the grid, energy from spinning wind turbines or photovoltaic panels can be used to lift water from one reservoir to a nearby reservoir sited at a higher elevation. Then, when the wind isn't blowing or the sun isn't shining but energy is needed, the water can be released to spin hydroelectric turbines as it drops back down toward the lower reservoir. The projects, however, usually require building new reservoirs and transmission towers, which can have tremendous environmental impacts. And when natural bodies of water are used, pumped hydro can harm water quality and aquatic environments by altering rivers and lakes. Some projects that have been proposed call for pulling billions of gallons of groundwater out of desert aquifers so the liquid can be sloshed back and forth between reservoirs to store energy. Using wind and solar to power the West's cities could shift water use away from cooling power plants to filling reservoirs with fossil water drawn up from wet tombs beneath the ground, exposing it to the evaporative energy of the sun. There is no simple solution to the West's water-energy-climate puzzle, a complex and teetering three-dimensional creation, each piece of which has the potential to collapse the entire structure when you grab it and jiggle.

In the race to demonize dams, the environmental movement often ignored the benefits of hydropower: It is renewable, and there are no problems with disposing of nuclear waste or with coal emissions fouling the air. Generating hydroelectricity uses water but doesn't consume it—water spins turbines and then returns to the river. But as the rivers of the West dry up, they will lose capacity to produce hydropower, and we will be forced to rely increasingly on burning fossil fuels.

To say that hydropower is "clean" or "green" is not entirely correct, however. Dams are actually major sources of greenhouse gases. As trees and other plants that are drowned beneath rising reservoirs decompose, and as the vegetation that grows in the water and washes into it rots, carbon dioxide and methane are created. These gases enter the atmosphere when they bubble up to the surface of reservoirs and when water is released downstream of dams.

Hydropower in the West is associated with dams that form giant reservoirs and generate electricity by building up enormous hydraulic heads to spin turbines. But renewable energy can also be produced through small, run-of-the-river hydroelectricity projects that don't require dams. Instead, they use the constant throb of a river spilling down its bed to generate electricity. On a stream in the West with a steep drop, water can be diverted into penstocks to turn turbines and then returned to the river channel downstream, providing power for local communities without the environmental disturbances caused by large dams.

In many places in the West, water drips down stone gullets, dropping toward the molten basement of the world, where the water is heated by magma and gathers in steaming chambers to rise back up as the pressured breath of geysers and the sulfurous belching of hot springs. A complex of geothermal power plants known as The Geysers, located in the mountains above Northern California's wine country, produces enough electricity to meet the power needs of San Francisco. The largest geothermal development in the world, The Geysers uses wells to capture steam created by the heat of the earth's core; the steam drives turbines to generate electricity. But most of the steam is lost to evaporation, depleting the boiling groundwater from which it rises. In the late 1980s, steam at The Geysers began to fizzle out, threatening to stop the turbines from spinning. A pipeline was built to send treated wastewater from nearby Santa Rosa to recharge the geothermal reservoir. Thanks to the city's sewage, power production continues to this day.

Tapping geothermal energy resources near Yellowstone National Park, while potentially providing clean, green energy, could pose a threat to geysers such as Old Faithful. Yellowstone's iconic geysers are supplied by reservoirs of underground water boiled by volcanic magma. Hot water and steam squeeze through fractures in rock that reach beyond the boundaries of the park. Geysers are sensitive to nearby groundwater extraction and geothermal energy development. Companies that sink wells into the hydrothermal plumbing that supplies the geysers can find themselves in conflict with groups trying to protect Yellowstone's turbulent ejections for their scientific and scenic value—and for their economic benefit to industries that help tourists dispose of their dollars.

Corn is an ingredient in so much of what we eat, from soda to steak. Now politicians in places thick with cornstalks are making it part of our fuel. But corn-based ethanol demands a lot of water, both in growing corn, a water-gobbling crop, and in turning the corn into fuel. According to Cornell professor David Pimentel, about seventeen hundred gallons of water is consumed for every gallon of corn ethanol produced. Growing corn to power our engines will require shifting water from food production to fuel production. We may find ourselves driving ethanol-fueled SUVs to grocery stores with empty shelves.

Wyoming, nicknamed "the cowboy state" and bearing a bucking bronco on its license plate, is in the midst of the largest mineral boom in its history. The development of coalbed methane (a form of natural gas extracted from coal deposits) has provided a bonanza for energy companies and earns far more revenue for the state than cowboys contribute.

But according to the Powder River Basin Resource Council, it poses "the greatest environmental and cultural threat Wyoming has faced in decades."

The Powder River Basin, once the floor of a shallow sea, is now rolling prairie stretching across southeast Montana and northeast Wyoming from the Black Hills to the Big Horn Mountains. Life that once thrived greenly in ancient swamps now lies bricked and black beneath the ground. Tucked inside these snug beds of coal and held in place by water pressure are stores of methane. After the water is removed, the trapped gases escape toward the surface. Wells that reach into gassy coal seams extract groundwater, which is often thick with salt, at rates of one hundred gallons a minute, pumped by roaring jet engines that power compressor stations. Untreated saline water that is discharged into drainages and spread across fields damages crops and natural landscapes, which turn to white crusts that glisten in the sun. The pumping also drains aquifers, drying up household wells and stock tanks. Environmentalists and ranchers joined ranks to oppose the discharge of contaminated groundwater into the Powder River Basin; the coalbed methane industry responded by building enormous plastic-lined pits to evaporate the salty wastewater. In 2010, a Montana State District Court judge ruled that dumping wastewater from coalbed methane development into evaporation pits is not a beneficial use of water and therefore violates the Montana Constitution. In the Powder River Basin and throughout the West, legal battles over water supplies used to develop energy rage on.

Fracking (hydraulic fracturing) is the process of forcing fluid laced with chemicals into the ground to crack open shale deposits and release natural gas. The chemicals used include known carcinogens, such as benzene. The Energy Policy Act of 2005 exempted fracked wells from federal regulation under the Safe Drinking Water Act, leaving it up to states to regulate fracking operations. The FRAC Act (Fracturing Responsibility and Awareness of Chemicals Act), introduced to both houses of Congress in 2009, would repeal the exemption, bringing fracking under federal regulation and requiring drilling companies to disclose the chemicals they mix with water and sand and inject underground. The industry currently keeps this information secret, maintaining that it needs to protect the proprietary technology of its fracking fluids—something of a "special sauce." The gas industry opposes the FRAC Act legislation and maintains that fracking is safe, state oversight is sufficient, and restoring EPA regulation will result in a spate of lawsuits that could cripple an industry that is providing the nation with potential energy independence and a fuel far cleaner than oil or coal.

Gasland, a 2010 documentary film made by a banjo-strumming hipster in a gas mask, relates the poignant stories of people in, among other states, Colorado, Wyoming, and Texas, who suffer from severe health problems they believe are caused by fracking. Though not a polished piece of investigative journalism, the film packs an emotional punch, especially with scenes of tap water allegedly polluted with fracking fluid bursting into flames when it flows from household faucets.

The EPA has launched a far-reaching federal scientific study of how fracking affects drinking water, the results of which will most likely determine the fate of the FRAC Act. In 2011 the *New York Times* reported that, based on internal EPA documents, wastewater from fracking is often contaminated with radioactivity that poses a threat to drinking water supplies. Regardless of whether hydraulic fracturing poisons water, it consumes an enormous amount of the increasingly scarce substance. Water is directed away from irrigated fields toward drill rigs as farmers transfer their liquid assets to energy companies. Food gives way to gas as the suburbs of the West are festooned with lights.

The Green River Formation of Colorado, Utah, and Wyoming contains by some estimates nine times the amount of petroleum buried beneath Saudi Arabia. The black gold is locked inside rocks known as oil shale; extracting the oil demands complicated technology such as heating the shale underground with electrodes—and it requires staggering amounts of water. According to a report released by the US Government Accountability Office, five hundred gallons of water may be needed to produce a barrel of oil. A study by Western Resource Advocates, a Colorado-based nonprofit law and policy organization, concluded that energy giants such as ExxonMobil and Chevron own water rights to divert and store enough water to meet the annual needs of millions of Colorado residents. Should an oil-shale boom ensue and the energy companies tap the water they own the rights to use, the economy and culture of the Upper Colorado River Basin could be transformed, with agriculture sharply curtailed and growth in cities at a standstill while rural areas metamorphose into clanking, fuming industrial zones that slurp up an enormous share of the Colorado River. A future in which streams are reduced to bare beds while oil is cooked out of the stony ground is conceivable—and legal. The oil companies accumulated their priority water rights largely by purchasing them from ranchers. This might give pause to those who argue that market forces are a panacea for the West's water woes.

RUNOFF, RAIN HARVESTING, AND RECLAIMED WASTEWATER

The endless freeways, parking lots, and rooftops of the West's metropolises aren't conducive to capturing water. Rainfall rolls across the hard surfaces, rushing toward impervious trenches, filling concrete ditches and drains with torrents in a matter of minutes. And when meanders are removed from reengineered rivers and their flow is squeezed into narrower bounds, all the water hurries through straight channels. It cannot wander downhill, pooling in wetlands, sinking into the soil, filtering into aquifers. While the concrete walls that line the Los Angeles River prevent flooding by sending stormwater from infrequent but intense rains speeding into the San Pedro Bay, the parched city survives on water pumped in from rivers hundreds of miles away.

Across Southern California, urban runoff is a major source of pollution on the coast—and runoff can occur even beneath sunny skies that haven't known rain clouds in months. In Santa Monica, all sewers lead to the sea. When the sprinkler systems of the rich and famous leak, when their pools are drained and the hired help hoses down their sidewalks and washes their cars, the water is captured and sent to the state-of-the-art Santa Monica Urban Runoff Recycling Facility (SMURRF) for treatment inside a building with a hip façade that is more art gallery than public utility. After the cigarette butts, dog poop, pesticides from lawns, oil from driveways, and other pollutants that befoul the city's pretty beaches are filtered out, pathogens are killed with ultraviolet radiation, and the treated water is then used to irrigate parks and medians, and to flush toilets in dual-plumbed buildings. The more runoff that cities in dry environments treat and reuse, the less water they have to import from distant sources.

Urban planners across the West are designing cities that are more porous, both to decrease flood danger and to boost water supplies. They are replacing traditional paving with pervious concrete. Instead of using pipes and drains to carry stormwater away as swiftly as possible, they are creating cisterns and basins to capture the runoff so it can be used to irrigate parks. And floodwater is directed toward fields, gravel pits, and other places where it can percolate into the ground, recharging aquifers.

Some green urban builders are installing catchments on roofs to capture rainwater for uses such as watering gardens and flushing toilets. Harvesting rain reduces peak stormwater flows that flood sewer systems. It also allows the conservation of potable water put to non-potable purposes.

Individuals are getting in on the rain harvesting movement by using infrastructure ranging from a bucket under a gutter to catch water for a tomato plant, to complicated tanks and filtration systems that turn runoff spilling from roofs into drinking water for families. In some places in the West, however, gathering rainwater can result in a hefty fine—illustrating how water laws that worked well in the 1800s don't always mesh with a modern environmental ethos.

Each drop of rain falling through the sky has already been allocated to a user. The right to use the drop may have been perfected under state water law more than a century ago, and the owner of the right may live hundreds of miles from the rooftop upon which the drop splats. Leave the hose running between rinses while you wash your car and you won't run afoul of the law; but if you gather a pailful of rainwater and pour it on your tomato plant, look over your shoulder for a water cop. You will be preventing those raindrops from entering the watershed (water poured on the plant will evaporate from soil and transpire from leaves), depriving people downstream from the surrounding creeks and rivers of their rights to use their apportioned amounts of streamflow. The doctrine of prior appropriation comes crashing up against the imperative to conserve scarce water.

Colorado recently made it legal for some homeowners to harvest rain and snow from their roofs, and rainwater renegades began emerging from the shadows beneath their dripping gutters. There are efforts underway to alter water laws around the West to bring them in line with the changing needs and ethics of the region. But some old-school Westerners in bolo ties will not abide new age hippies in hemp shirts filling vessels with rainwater to splash on their herbs—they see this as a slippery slope to eliminating the time-honored tradition of prior appropriation.

Tucson is encouraging its citizens to gather rainwater. Santa Fe made catchment devices mandatory for new dwellings. But in Utah and Washington (with the exception of Seattle), harvesting raindrops is still a crime. Scofflaws slip cisterns beneath their eaves and hope for a water revolution in the West.

━ ⌒

The New River formed from 1905 to 1907 when a break in an aqueduct below the border in Mexico created a stream that spilled into the Imperial Valley and flowed to the Salton Sea. As the bustling border city of Mexicali exploded with growth in the following decades, and as cities across the border in the United States discharged their sewage into the river, its flow ran rancid with human feces, slaughterhouse filth, and a foul broth of industrial and agricultural poisons. The river forms a handy conveyance for trash: People and industries dump their garbage without restraint into the unsanitary stream of sewage. Animal carcasses bob between tires, toilet paper unfurls in the current, and plastic bottles form logjams miles long. Billows of foam born from phosphate detergents blow off the river, spreading contaminants into nearby communities, and mosquitoes and flies rise in pulsing clouds from the banks. The river is so toxic it is said to eat the flesh from the bones of murder victims that are tossed into it, and it is rumored to strip the paint from cars that are abandoned in its caustic flow. In the summer, when temperatures push toward 120 degrees, the stench from the liquid in the fetid lagoon induces vomiting in passersby. Signs along its shores warn people not to get too close, but desperate migrants in Mexico clutch inner tubes and plastic bags filled with dry clothes and ride the river's currents past US border guards, who don't brave the water to give chase. The river is full of salmonella and the viruses that cause hepatitis, dysentery, typhoid, and polio. The level of fecal coliform bacteria in its flow is off the charts, and when the river, after picking up selenium and pesticides as it pushes through the Imperial Valley, reaches the Salton Sea, it causes algal blooms and creates breeding grounds for botulism and cholera. From the "Salton Sewer" wafts the stench of decaying fish and rotting birds.

The New River is now slime-green goop and toxic sludge, but it is wet, and in the West that counts for a lot. A wastewater treatment facility, financed jointly by Mexico and the United States, is being built in Mexicali to clean up one of the planet's most poisoned rivers. A source of international tension for many years because of its pollution, the river, when finally brought up to basic human health standards, will create disputes over water rights. Mexico plans to reclaim some of the water south of the border to use in greenbelts, which will reduce the flow into the Imperial Valley, creating friction with people who want the reclaimed water to nourish the Salton Sea, home to some of the best bird habitat in the West.

"Reclamation," the process of reclaiming something from loss or a less useful state, originally was defined in the West as damming rivers that wastefully dumped their waters into the sea and diverting those waters to dry lands to make them fruitful. Today the word *reclamation* is used in relation to wastewater that is recycled and put to productive use: It is "reclaimed."

Greywater, which is wastewater generated from laundry, dishwashing, bathing, and so on—and is not to be confused with blackwater (sewage from toilets)—can be recycled on site for landscape irrigation: "from showers to flowers."

According to the EPA, more than 4.8 billion gallons of water goes down the toilet each day in the United States. Effluent from sewage treatment plants (containing a mixture of both greywater and blackwater) is one of the West's largest potential sources of freshwater. After being treated, the effluent can be reused for industrial applications such as cooling power plants, for irrigating parks and golf courses, and for flushing toilets—dual systems with purple pipes for reused water keep it separate from potable water.

In places where water supplies are extremely limited in the West, effluent is sometimes purified to a point at which it can be added to the drinking water supply. California's Orange County Water District operates one of the largest and most technologically sophisticated reclamation plants in the world. The $480 million project uses an advanced assemblage of microfilters and membranes, along with hydrogen peroxide and ultraviolet light, to turn sewage into water as clean as if it had been distilled. The treated water is injected underground to prevent saltwater intrusion and to supplement aquifers from which drinking water is drawn, lessening the county's dependence on outside water sources, which are becoming increasingly costly. There was widespread public discontent with adding treated sewage to the drinking water supply of one of the wealthiest residential areas in the United States. But practical economics trumped the visceral "yuck factor," and the treatment plant's space-age technology (astronauts drink water recycled from urine) now serves as a model for some of the water-starved cities of the West.

When it comes to wastewater, what happens in Vegas does indeed stay in Vegas. The city flushes its treated wastewater into Lake Mead to the north; it draws out its drinking water along the lakeshore farther south. Because the wastewater has passed through the natural filter of the lake's enormous volume, citizens don't balk at the thought of drinking it. Proposals to route treated wastewater more directly into drinking water supplies, however, are usually met with staunch opposition. In San Diego, "indirect potable reuse" of wastewater projects—similar to what Orange County is using—have twice been voted down by disgusted citizens. Critics deride these projects as "toilet to tap."

Cloudcroft, perched high in the mountains of New Mexico, didn't have a choice—it ran out of water. Hauling emergency water supplies into town in trucks was noisy, polluting, and prohibitively expensive, so the little resort town with the nation's highest golf course began purifying its wastewater with an advanced membrane technology that removes everything potentially harmful to people, including pharmaceuticals. The highly treated effluent is discharged into a manmade reservoir from which the town draws its drinking water—about half of Cloudcroft's drinking water supply is purified wastewater.

Though perfectly safe, guzzling a glass of cleansed wastewater that was recently swirling around a toilet bowl gives people pause. But each molecule of water we drink can be traced back more than four billion years to the planet's formation. Every drop has moved through oceans and rivers and aquifers, has filtered through plants and animals and people from when the world began. Molecules in that glass of water you just drank passed through the kidneys of a brontosaurus—and through the kidneys of Aztecs and Mongolians and Bostonians, through the bladders of priests and poets and thieves. Each drop of water in the Colorado River is used an average of seventeen times. But when the path from toilet to tap is so direct that there is no large body of water in between—no lake or river in which the tainted water can seep back into soil and sand and mix with trillions of other water molecules to dilute its filth and then emerge, in our minds, cleansed—our instinct is to register disgust. This survival mechanism is rooted in our evolution and buried deeply in our brains. But overriding it with reason is necessary: The survival of our desert civilization in a region heating up and drying out may depend on it. The effluent that pours out of wastewater treatment plants is one of the West's largest and most reliable water supplies, and reclaiming it on a large scale would go a long way toward alleviating the region's water worries.

WATER PROJECTS

Though we have entered the post-dam era, some throwback megaprojects continue to be built. Take the case of Colorado's Animas–La Plata project, a waterworks scheme first dreamed up in the 1930s when farmers along the La Plata River in southwestern Colorado found themselves with fertile fields and not enough water. Not to worry: Wayne Aspinall, Democratic congressman from a rural Colorado district and chair of the

House Interior Committee, finagled a deal. Aspinall's constituents were quintessential Westerners—fiercely independent people who insisted the federal government spare no expense to help them maintain their fierce independence. Arizonan politicians who had struggled for decades to get approval for their Central Arizona Project would find their efforts blocked by Aspinall unless they supported his five pet water projects, including Animas–La Plata, which benefited a handful of hay farmers in one corner of Colorado. And thus was authorized a scheme of eye-popping complexity and financial lunacy, described by *U.S. News and World Report* as the "last surviving dinosaur from the age of behemoth water schemes."

The $710 million project called for the Animas River to be dammed, diverted, sucked up by siphons, pumped one thousand feet uphill, and then delivered to a few La Plata landowners who wanted to grow alfalfa. Thousands of dollars in irrigation costs for each acre would produce a few hundred dollars worth of crops. The project would return to taxpayers thirty-six cents for each dollar spent. Daniel Dreyfus, a planner for the Bureau, admitted to Marc Reisner in an interview in 1981 that when the Office of Management and Budget killed Animas–La Plata, he had to "jerk around the benefit-cost numbers to make the thing look sound." In 1994, a study by the inspector general of the Department of the Interior found that the project was "not economically feasible."

Exposing the bogus numbers game didn't stop the project, but it took a new twist when Indian water rights became an issue. In 2000, to avoid costly litigation with the tribes of the Southern Ute Reservation and the Ute Mountain Reservation, the federal government promised most of the project's water to the tribes—who had paper water rights dating back to the 1800s, when their reservations were created by Congress, but no wet water. The project was scaled down, but it is still a behemoth, and it is being built right now. It has been dubbed "the dam that won't die" and "Jurassic Pork." To thwart America's enemies who might tamper with the project, the federal government allocated $2 million after 9/11 to protect the construction site. Safe from terrorists who would do harm to America's economy, a dam and diversion works of ludicrous cost and little benefit are taking shape as in the days of old.

Each time the cities of the West face a water shortage, "the treacherous allure of the grandiose solution," in the words of Charles Wilkinson, insinuates its way into problem solving. In 2002 the state of Colorado suffered a brutal drought. A meager snowpack caused streamflows to sink to their lowest levels in more than one hundred years of recordkeeping, and tree ring studies showed the episode to be the driest period in more than three hundred years. As the mud of empty reservoirs fractured into geometric shapes, Denver began to entertain ideas of building enormous waterworks to compensate for its liquid shortfall. Known as "big straws," these pipelines would bring water from distant places to relieve the dehydrated city. One of the most ambitious schemes was thought up by a Colorado rancher and former mining engineer who proposed building a two-story twelve-hundred-mile pipeline to deliver water from the Mississippi River to Colorado's Front Range so that the thirsty metropolitan centers would leave western Colorado's water alone. Another extravagant big straw is the brainchild of aptly named entrepreneur Aaron Million, who has proposed building a 560-mile pipeline to send water from the Flaming Gorge Reservoir on the Utah-Wyoming border to Colorado's Front Range. A proposal for a shorter straw would suck water from the Yampa, one of the last rivers in the West with no major dams or diversions, a river that doesn't rush through arrow-straight canals and still has time to meander and pool, a river in which wild creatures, some of them endangered, still slither and swarm. Water from the Yampa would be pumped through a 250-mile pipeline to the cities of eastern Colorado, where the dry plains touch the mountains and the mountains reach upward toward the sky.

Denver, determined to become the Los Angeles of the Rockies, is the fourth-fastest-growing major county in the United States. Cul-de-sac cowboys are crowding into this twenty-first-century boomtown, and Denver Water, which is responsible for supplying 1.3 million people in the mushrooming metropolitan area, insists there is no way around building new infrastructure to store and divert water. It says a water shortfall will begin in 2016 and then grow steadily worse. Half of the shortage can be eliminated through conservation, it predicts, but more water supply will still be needed. Suburbs filling with people fleeing California are sucking aquifers dry and clamoring for more storage projects to stave off a crisis. Environmentalists insist that more conservation is needed—building more dams and diversion pipelines will simply trash and squander what little is left of wild nature in the state, turning rivers that tumble over cobbles into sterile delivery systems in which water is guided through pipes and along lifeless concrete trenches. Denver Water counters that it incorporates the concerns of all stakeholders, including environmentalists, into its plans, and it has been vigorously promoting conservation all the way back to 1936, when it advertised on street trolleys asking people to save water. But conservation, it asserts, is not enough. Residents are xeriscaping their yards.[10] The city is also reusing sewage to provide water for some of its projects. And still the metro area needs more water.

One proposal floated by Denver Water would modify an existing structure rather than build an entirely new one. Gross Reservoir Dam in the Rocky Mountain foothills would be raised 125 feet, nearly tripling its capacity to cache flow taken from the upper reaches of the Colorado River Basin on the western slope of the Rockies and diverted to the Missouri River Basin on the eastern slope. No new plumbing would be added to the Rockies; more water would be routed through the existing pipework and stored in an expanded mountain tub to be tapped by the city below. Anglers and environmentalists have reluctantly supported the project, even asking for the dam to be made larger so that a constant flow of water will wet the bed of South Boulder Creek below the dam. The stream is often drawn down so low in winter that fish die in frozen pools. If the reservoir is expanded, rainbow trout transplanted from tributaries of the Pacific Ocean in North America and Asia, along with brown trout, natives of Europe and Asia with brassy sides and spots of red and black so pretty they seem painted, will survive the winter when Denver drinks from the creek. But the flow along the Continental Divide will be further altered—water nature destined to run to the Pacific will be routed to the

---

10 Derived from *xeros*, the Greek word meaning *dry*, xeriscaping uses drought-tolerant plants appropriate to the climate. This water-saving technique was pioneered in Denver.

231

Atlantic. People settled where there wasn't enough water, and they continue to move rivers across mountains.

Citizens of rural communities on the state's wet western slope argue that Denver should do more to conserve. They grumble that drenching green lawns in the metropolis on the crispy plains should be outlawed before the city snatches more water from the already stressed Colorado River headwaters, where fish will turn belly up in warm and stagnant flows. And citizens of the eastern slope worry that bull elk with nostrils steaming in the mountain air and heads canted back will lead their harems away from the disturbance at the dam site. Water bills are bouncing back and forth in the state legislature, and an environmental impact statement for the proposed reservoir expansion is being prepared by the Army Corps of Engineers. It remains to be seen if the old saw about water in the West flowing uphill toward money will once again prove true. Though to be precise, Denver lies at an elevation lower than that of the rivers it wants to remove from timeworn channels and send across the Continental Divide to flow from its spigots.

The future of water projects in the West may be ones that, rather than transporting water across vast distances between basins, make more efficient use of water within basins. Take the case of Prairie Waters, one of the most innovative water projects built in the United States in recent years.

In 2002–2003, as the city of Aurora in the Denver metro area watched its drought-withered water reserves dwindle to less than a nine months' supply, it grew desperate for relief. Instead of going to the mountains and trying to buy up water rights and building a reservoir and pipeline, it created in its own backyard the $650 million Prairie Waters Project on the South Platte River, where it already owned water rights. Aurora and other cities dump their treated wastewater into the South Platte River. Aurora's Prairie Waters Project uses wells next to the riverbank thirty-four miles downstream from the city. Water is drawn up through the gravelly ground, providing natural, energy-saving filtration. The water is pumped into basins where it percolates through more sand and gravel for additional cleansing, and then it is piped back toward the city's reservoir for final purification with chemicals and ultraviolet light at a high-tech treatment plant. So,

Aurora draws water from the river, uses it, treats it at a wastewater plant, and releases it back into the river; downstream it draws the water out of riverbank wells, sends it back to the city, purifies it to potable standards, and uses it again—a renewable water loop.

By recycling water over and over, Aurora doesn't have to rely on shrinking mountain snowpack and depleted aquifers; nor is it forced to bloody its knuckles battling over water rights. The Prairie Waters Project breaks the cycle of water wars between dust-dry metropolitan areas on Colorado's Front Range and water-blessed rural communities on its western slope. Environmentalists who don't want new dams built and watersheds depleted praise it. Farmers who don't want their communities to give up water rights to cities applaud it. Prairie Waters was the first big water project authorized in Colorado since the federal government's Animas–La Plata boondoggle, and it was paid for by Aurora. The city raised residential water fees and issued bonds to cover the costs. The project was completed ahead of schedule and almost $100 million *under* budget. Because Washington is no longer footing the bill to build megadams, states and municipalities must now solve their own water infrastructure problems. The future of water projects in the West may lie not with federally financed pieces of giant infrastructure that carry water from faraway places, but with innovative technological solutions that allow water to be used within communities as efficiently as possible. Prairie Waters is not as sexy as Hoover Dam, but it works.

RAINMAKERS

Schemes to add more water to the West's supplies abound. Cloud seeding, which has been around since the 1940s, is known in Bureau-of-Reclamation-speak as "precipitation augmentation." A cloud seeding pioneer dumped granules of dry ice (frozen carbon dioxide) out of a surplus warplane over California's Sierra Nevada to induce the clouds to let go of their moisture. Cloud seeding was used during the Vietnam War to increase rain over the Ho Chi Minh Trail, turning it to glop that bogged down the enemy; and in the 1970s the Bureau of Reclamation launched Project Skywater, in which ground-based generators blew plumes of silver iodide into the air above Colorado's San Juan Mountains. When water supplies in the West are reduced by drought, irrigation districts, cities, and ski resorts pay private contractors millions of dollars to spray chemicals with lattice structures similar to ice over propane burners on the ground, ignite them in flares dropped from airplanes, or fire them into the sky with artillery guns. The chemicals, by attracting droplets of moisture, squeeze about 10 to 15 percent more rain or snow from storms than would fall naturally—so the theory goes.

Despite some promising results, the scientific community has not reached a consensus on the efficacy of cloud seeding, largely because it is impossible to replicate the "success" of a cloud-seeding experiment. If a storm dumps two feet of snow on mountain slopes after clouds have been seeded, it is difficult to prove how much of that amount, if any, was caused by the chemicals and how much would have fallen without them. Skeptics dismiss cloud seeding as nothing more than a "modern day rain dance." But many water officials in the West are convinced cloud seeding boosts precipitation, and they use the technique because it is much cheaper than building dams or buying water from a distant watershed and transporting it. While some people worry that humans shouldn't be tampering with the weather, others point out that we have been modifying the weather on a much larger scale ever since we began burning fossil fuels and creating airborne pollution, and the West's reservoirs already influence the weather around them by adding moisture to the air.

Because cloud seeding can potentially cause more rain or snow to fall in one area, leaving less moisture to precipitate in another place, the practice leads to water wars. In the early 1990s, farmers in eastern Montana, after seeing North Dakota's cloud-seeding planes flying overhead and watching a worsening drought shrivel their crops, accused North Dakota farmers of stealing their rain. The Montana Board of Natural Resources and Conservation refused to give North Dakota a permit for cloud seeding. North Dakota sued; a Montana judge sided with North Dakota. The Montana legislature responded by passing a law requiring costly environmental studies and an expensive bond before any cloud seeding project could take place, effectively putting a stop to cloud seeding in the state.

Glaciers in northwestern Wyoming's Wind River Range, the most extensive in the American Rockies, have been the focus of much recent attention. Glaciologists are carefully monitoring their mass and measuring their shrinkage, peering into their crevasses and poking at their snouts. The Wind River glaciers store frozen water that is melted by the sun's energy and distributed downhill by gravity into the Big Horn–Yellowstone drainage systems, which sustain everything from trout to towns across large sections of Wyoming and Montana. A study program of cloud seeding is being conducted to try to increase the amount of snow that falls on the glaciers, receding rapidly due to climate change.

To further augment water supplies in the West, experimental polymer films have been spread across the surface of reservoirs to reduce evaporation, and phreatophytes—plants that live along riverbanks and tap into the water table with deep roots—have been removed to cut down on water lost to transpiration.

It was once thought that tamarisk used far more water than the native riparian vegetation such as the cottonwood and willow that it displaces, but this has recently been shown in studies not to be the case. The emphasis of tamarisk eradication efforts has shifted from increasing water supplies for cities and farms to restoring streamside ecosystems. But the endangered Southwestern willow flycatcher likes the pesky shrub, and the West's war on tamarisk has created conflict with bird lovers, who look for the drab little bird around the pink blooms of tamarisk and listen for its song of *fitz-bews* and *breets*, its calls of *whitts* and *brrr-kitters*. Efforts to eradicate the dense thickets of tamarisk have included bulldozing, burning, flattening the tough shrub with mechanical tree crushers, chainsawing it down to stumps that are painted with herbicide just above its iron-hard roots, and loosing species of Asian beetles to devour its lacy leaves. But in the reengineered river basins of the West, tamarisk jungles continue to thrive, providing critical nesting habitat. Groups advocating for the rare flycatcher filed lawsuits that invoked the Endangered Species Act, putting a halt to a US Department of Agriculture biocontrol program that aimed to introduce nonnative beetles to kill the nonnative plants that furnish shelter for the native bird. It is now illegal to transport the beetles across state lines. With water in the West, the truth is often stranger than an *Onion* article.

———

"Water, water, everywhere; Nor any drop to drink," laments the sailor tormented by thirst and surrounded by the salty sea in Samuel Taylor Coleridge's "The Rime of the Ancient Mariner." Some in the West believe the region's water salvation will be achieved through desalination. Others say that's about as likely as the legend of unicorns purifying water with the tips of their horns. Desalting plants require silly amounts of energy to operate, and when nuclear power fell out of favor with the public, support for desalination all but dried up. Aside from the tremendous expense of desalination in dollars, its costs to the environment—by burning coal, oil, and other fossil fuels—is enormous. Climate change increases the need for desalination; desalination drives climate change.

The simplest form of desalination is distillation. Seawater is heated until it evaporates, separating salts from the steam, which is then condensed and collected. This method demands cost-prohibitive amounts of power. But reverse osmosis technology, which uses high pressure to push water through membranes, filtering out salts and other dissolved minerals, has undergone rapid advancement in the past few decades; its energy requirements and costs have dropped dramatically.

After the United States placated Mexico by promising to stop sending Colorado River water poisoned with salt across the border, workcrews broke ground on the Yuma desalination plant in 1975. But budget cuts slowed construction to a crawl, and a long stretch of unusually wet weather made the need for the plant less pressing. After taking nearly seventeen years to complete, the plant finally began operations in 1992. Salty water that had drained from farms outside Yuma collected in a concrete canal that directed the liquid toward the desalination plant. Water pretreated to strain out solids was forced through pipes filled with reverse osmosis membranes to remove salt; then the desalted water was sent by sluiceway to the Colorado River and flowed toward Mexico. All systems go. But after only eight months, the quarter-billion-dollar plant was shut down due to engineering flaws and damage caused by a flood. A period of relatively abundant moisture in the Colorado River Basin reduced the plant's usefulness, and it was put on "ready reserve" status. The United States, in order to meet its obligations to Mexico, sent flow from Lake Mead south of the border. The salty irrigation runoff that the plant was supposed to treat was carried away from farms by a canal that empties into the Sonoran Desert in Mexico.

The saline wastewater dumped in the desert created an artificial wetland, the Cienega de Santa Clara. Cattails replaced cactus and creosote, providing sanctuary in this accidental nature preserve for endangered species such as the Yuma clapper rail, a marsh bird the size of a chicken whose call sounds like human hands clapping, and the desert pupfish, a tiny species that can survive in water hotter than 110 degrees and which chases after rival fish nipping at their tails like a puppy—hence the name. The Colorado River, before being pinched off from its floodplain by levees and dams, and before its lower reaches were drained to a sick trickle that tinkles toward the Sea of Cortez, had nourished vast wetlands. The resurrection of life in the dead delta was heartening to advocates of restoring the region from a lunarscape of barren mudflats to the rich ecosystem it had once been, a place where beaver busied themselves in the marshes and jaguars prowled pathways through jungles of grass. The revived wetland was a remnant of what Aldo Leopold, who had paddled a canoe through green lagoons crammed full of mullet and crowded with cormorants, willets, and teal, called "this wealth of fowl and fish." Saline drainage from irrigation continued to be diverted into the Mexican desert, growing the Cienega larger, increasing its aquatic bounty, and this watery wilderness in a dry land became a critical stop for migrating birds along the Pacific Flyway.

Southwestern states have recently been pressuring the Bureau of Reclamation to reopen the Yuma desalting plant to relieve Lake Mead, whose waters are being depleted by a lengthy drought. Environmentalists, however, are pleased by the thought of the plant never running again. If it were to operate at full capacity, the agricultural runoff now being channeled into the desert, creating a fragile paradise for birds and fish, would be treated and diverted to the Colorado River for delivery to Mexico so it could be spread across tilled fields and piped to Tijuana. An ooze of thickened brine left over from the desalting process would flow into the Cienega de Santa Clara. The wetland would turn to saline goop, and its rare birds and fish would vanish.

In 2010, the long-shut Yuma plant started desalting water. Operating at only 30 percent of capacity, the plant is undergoing a test run scheduled to last twelve months. The cost of this test: $23 million. That the farmers who created the salinity problem are not picking up the tab goes without saying. Running the plant is so expensive the Bureau of Reclamation is considering as a more cost-effective alternative paying the farmers to not grow crops. If the farmers stop contaminating the water by using it for irrigation, it could be sent to Mexico without being treated. Either way, whether the plant operates or the salty fields are fallowed, the resurrected wetland could vanish in the desert, a faded mirage, a brief glimpse of an ecosystem reborn.

The city of Santa Cruz, located on the northern edge of California's Monterey Bay, found itself in dire straits in 2009 as drought dried up its surface water and seawater threatened to swamp its overdrawn aquifer. It ran a yearlong pilot project at a desalination plant. In addition to using reverse osmosis technology, the plant experimented with a "slow sand" technique, which filters saltwater by letting it soak into small silos of sand, trapping the salt. The city declared the test run a success and may be moving forward with building a larger permanent plant. Fisheries biologists are thrilled: The plant will allow flow to remain in the San Lorenzo River during droughts. Desalination might stop the city's water crisis and save salmon, but because the process is so energy intensive, local environmental groups have vigorously opposed it. Instead of building a fossil-fuel-burning, greenhouse-gas-generating plant, they advocate more conservation to bring water use in line with a sustainable yield from the aquifer that supplies the city. Some opponents of the project fear that increasing the water supply will encourage more growth, threatening the area's quality of life. The project may threaten residents' pocketbooks—water rates in Santa Cruz could rise steeply to cover the cost of the plant.

Desalination is not cheap, and cheery thoughts by Panglossian prognosticators about desalination technology ending the West's water troubles must be (prepare to groan at the pun) taken with a grain of salt. Desalting ocean water requires plants that occupy large spreads of land, consume enormous amounts of energy, kill marine life at the base of the food chain when the water is sucked in and treated, and produce briny waste that can disrupt ocean ecosystems and harm freshwater supplies when released into the environment. Pumping desalted water inland to cities sited far from coasts raises the already considerable cost and environmental footprint. But technological advances have in the past few decades been steadily lowering the price of desalted water. Desalination promoters point out that the West's freshwater supplies will become increasingly expensive as demands on the resource spiral upward, and the costs of desalinating seawater will continue to drop as technology improves. "If we could ever competitively—at a cheap rate—get fresh water from salt water," commented President John F. Kennedy, "that would be in the long-range interest of humanity, and would really dwarf any other scientific accomplishment."

Some in the West still see desalination as the Holy Grail of water. The days of dams may be done, but the faith that technology will free us from nature's constraints is with us still. Desalination dreamers see a future in which ranks of plants arrayed along the West Coast, powered by solar panels and wind farms and using emerging desalination technologies such as forward osmosis, carbon nanotubes, and biomimetics, overflow with freshwater—freeing Denver, Salt Lake City, Albuquerque, Las Vegas, and Phoenix to slurp up the entire flow of the Colorado as they swell with limitless growth.

A more modest application of desalination technology is for purifying brackish groundwater, a process that uses less energy than forcing saltier ocean water through membranes. In Texas everything is indeed bigger: El Paso recently constructed the "world's largest inland brackish water desalination plant." No word yet on whether China is trying to one-up us in this coveted infrastructure category by building a bigger one.

CONSERVATION

Author Sandra Postel contends that improved water conservation is humanity's "last oasis." Conservation was not on the minds of the farmers who first diverted streams. Under traditional western water law, if water was not being put to beneficial use, the rights to use it were snatched up by those next in line—the "use it or lose it" principle. Leaving water instream was not considered a beneficial use, and across the West bare riverbeds lay alongside lush fields. Why would a farmer conserve water if by doing so he risked losing the rights to the water he saved? Many western states responded to this disincentive to conserve by enacting laws that broadened the concept of beneficial use to include conservation. Some allowed water saved by farmers and ranchers to be leased or sold. Some gave landowners who donated their water to help protect rivers an income tax credit—providing an alternative to selling their water to cities.

In the past, when a city in the West ran short of water, the solution was to find new rivers or aquifers to empty, or to buy water rights from rural areas. But as supplies of freshwater dwindle through a combination of climate change, contamination, and overuse; as environmental regulations increase the difficulty and cost of securing new sources; and as urban areas meet resistance from farmers and ranchers unwilling to sell their water, cities are turning to conservation and enhanced efficiency to help relieve their thirst.

Albuquerque, located in New Mexico's high desert and sprinkled with eight inches of rain a year (an afternoon shower's worth in Alabama), bulged from a dusty outpost into a bustling city. Powered by high-tech luminaries such as Intel, which uses a lot of water to manufacture the silicon wafers that run our world, Albuquerque's economy expanded, and the water table fell. Believing the aquifer from which it drew its sustenance held unlimited stores, the city was removing water three times faster than it was being replenished by rainfall and snowmelt. The ground sagged and pumps sputtered. Faced with few options to snare new water supplies from outlying areas, doing more with less became the order of the day. In 1995 the city implemented one of the most aggressive water conservation programs in the country. It offered rebates to people who installed low-flow toilets and showerheads in their homes and rewarded residents who replaced water-gobbling grass with drought-tolerant landscaping. It paid homeowners to take classes on reducing outdoor water use and offered incentives for harvesting rainwater. It used treated wastewater to irrigate golf courses and parks. It raised water rates to decrease demand, and it printed on all monthly water bills comparative usage data so residents could see how their water consumption stacked up against that of their neighbors. These measures reduced household use in ten years from a wasteful 250 gallons per capita per day (gpcd) to a more austere 177 gpcd, and education and incentive programs continue to lower Albuquerque's household consumption closer to the current national average of about 100 gpcd.

Because residents of Boulder, Colorado, had been especially vigilant about conserving water, in 2010 the city was left with a gaping hole in its coffers. Less use by citizens meant less money was billed to water consumers, which meant less revenue for the city, which meant there was a shortfall to fund repairs to the city's aging water infrastructure—including a tank that had leaked 120 million gallons of drinking water over the past ten years. The tank dumped precious liquid into the ground while the City Council debated raising water rates to make up for the budget shortfall. And conscientious citizens continued to faithfully follow the city's water conservation tips, such as shoveling snow from sidewalks onto the base of trees and not flushing toilets after every use. The hippies in Boulder, a city where more Tibetan prayer flags furl in the wind than American flags, adhere to the principle of "if it's yellow let it mellow, if it's brown flush it down."

———

One of the most powerful tools for conserving rivers and protecting water supplies does not require ascetic sacrifice. It does not come from political circuses and bruising legal battles over water rights. Nor does it rely on space-age technology. It involves land trusts: private, nonprofit organizations that work to preserve land and water through the use of easements. According to The Nature Conservancy, "Conservation easements conserve watersheds and aquifers, helping ensure a clean supply of water for public use."

A conservation easement is voluntarily sold or donated by a private landowner to either a large organization such as The Nature Conservancy, which has more than one million members and has protected more than five thousand miles of rivers worldwide, or to a local organization, such as the Jackson Hole Land Trust, which among other achievements has protected streams in Jackson Hole, Wyoming, that harbor critical spawning habitat for Snake River fine-spotted cutthroat trout. The transfer of an easement creates a legally binding agreement that limits harmful uses and restricts development to preserve the property's natural resources. The land remains privately owned. Landowners often continue to live on the property, and in exchange for giving up development rights they receive cash payments or tax benefits. The public receives benefits such as pure water and habitat that flourishes with fish and birds.

One of The Nature Conservancy's most notable successes is the 132-mile, free-flowing Blackfoot River, which ambles through a valley in western Montana carved by glaciers in an age when frozen water gouged its way across the land. The river's trout that stir in green depths and hold steady in the current with swaying fins inspired Norman Maclean to write the classic fly-fishing novella *A River Runs Through It*. Along the valley's timbered slopes, the footprints of people are fewer than the wild tread of elk, and grizzly bears mark their territories by clawing the bark of trees. When moose step their stilt legs through wetlands in the valley bottom, sandhill cranes and trumpeter swans open their wings and shake the air. And when you walk toward the water, birds rise in ones and twos and bunches, so many they dim the sky, and what light there is shines through their feathers as they pass above in bright squadrons. Tilt your face toward the sky, and you can feel the wind of their passage on your cheeks.

The ranchette subdivisions that have filled so many mountain valleys throughout the West, often straining water supplies and polluting watersheds, are absent in the Blackfoot Valley, due largely to landowners working together with The Nature Conservancy to permanently protect with conservation easements almost fifty miles of river and more than one hundred and ten thousand acres in the watershed. The area remains much as it was when Norman Maclean cast his flies into the riffles and pools of a river that runs through one of the West's storied landscapes sculpted by waters.

CRISIS

Workcrews in Nevada wearing raincoats are drilling around the clock through fissured rock spurting water. Their boots sticking in the gluey floor of a tunnel beneath Lake Mead, they are blasting and mucking out a moist cavern through which they will direct a boring machine into the darkness ahead. The reservoir that straddles the Arizona-Nevada border and supplies most of the water for Las Vegas is less than half full. If its level drops much lower, one of the two intake pipes that Las Vegas currently uses to suck water toward its hotels and casinos will fill with air. The new intake the city is scurrying to put in place will prevent an immediate crisis, but the larger problem is that too many straws are sucking from a shrinking puddle, and Lake Mead may never fill again.

Las Vegas, Spanish for "the meadows," once offered an oasis to cottonmouthed travelers. Though it receives an average of three inches of rain a year, about the same as the Sahara, and is surrounded by bald plains tufted with bunchgrass, its springs nourished Native American and Spanish traders, along with Mormon settlers, ranchers, and a railroad depot. But the population of the boomtown soon exceeded the capacity of its water supply, and bringing relief to this city nagged by chronic drought has been a struggle ever since. As mentioned, Nevada is entitled to only a small share of the Colorado River's flow, because when the Colorado River Compact was signed in 1922, no one imagined the metastatic growth that would take place in Sin City. The hard stars that once punched like bullet holes through the black of the desert night are now dulled by glaring neon. Towers thrust skyward, and fountains fill the dry air with burbling song. The city is running out of water, yet people keep coming. One of the fastest growing cities in America, Las Vegas is ground zero for the West's water crisis.

Patricia Mulroy, Las Vegas's water manager, is known for her out-spokenness and her stylish clothing and coif. Blending European fashion with bare-knuckles western water brawling, she is widely respected across the parched frontier. Mulroy has been seeking new water sources for her city for more than two decades. She offered to build desalination plants for San Diego and Tijuana in exchange for some of their apportionments from the Colorado River. She proposed building, in exchange for more rights to the Colorado River, a new reservoir in Southern California to capture unused water allocated to farmers. She planned to construct a $2 billion pipeline to bring water into the city from aquifers that underlie rural counties in the wild basin-and-range terrain of eastern Nevada and western Utah, but locals screamed of a water grab similar to Los Angeles seizing the lifeblood of the Owens Valley. She forged an agreement with Arizona to store surplus Colorado River water in Arizona's aquifers, but that deal dried up when a drought did away with any extra flow in the river. She imagined a megaproject diverting some of the Mississippi River to her water-starved city, but contentious hydropolitics and environmental concerns rendered this a pipe dream.

Realizing that new sources of water wouldn't come easy, even with the city's surplus of cash, Mulroy, long known for her ardent support of unfettered growth, launched a nervy plan to conserve water. She aimed to change the culture of a desert metropolis famous for its gauche fountains and faux Venetian canals. Enacting measures that ranged from imposing water limits on golf courses to restricting the number of hours people could water their lawns, she tackled the issue of outdoor water use—which accounts for the vast majority of the city's usage. The plan had sticks in the form of fines for misbehavers who didn't comply with the new rules, and it offered the carrots of monetary rewards for homeowners who ripped up their grass and replaced it with plants adapted to drought—known as a "cash-for-grass program" (not to be confused with movements to legalize and tax marijuana). Casinos were encouraged to use reclaimed water in their fountains. Innovations in hotels such as on-demand water heaters, which provide instant hot water so taps don't have to run and waste water down the drain as it slowly warms, and aerating showerheads—which mix air with water to make bathers feel as if they are standing beneath a luxurious spray befitting a Vegas hotel instead of being teased by an unsatisfying trickle—further decreased water use. The efforts were successful. Though people kept pouring into the metropolis in the Mojave, the city's overall water use dropped. But the population of Las Vegas is projected to double by 2035, and the city will most likely need to tap new sources of water no matter how much it conserves.

Mulroy has spoken of challenging the Colorado River Compact. To other states in the Colorado River Basin, this is a frightening prospect because the Supreme Court, which would settle the dispute, could reduce their allotments of water. But Nevada, with its paltry 4 percent apportionment of the river's flow, has little to lose and may go for broke and try to force the Law of the River to be rewritten in its favor.

At this point in the story, it is customary to make a joke about Vegas's odds of solving its water crisis. What are the chances of such a joke being funny? Don't bet on it.

～～

St. George, Utah, once a little Mormon agricultural community in Washington County based on cotton, and then blasted with nuclear fallout during atomic bomb testing, has turned into a popular retirement destination. Now one of the fastest growing metropolitan areas in the United States, Washington County wants to stick a pipeline in Lake Powell, despite the shrinking volume of the reservoir, despite all the claims on the Colorado's flow. New cities and suburbs frantic to find water could prove the biggest challenge to seemingly invincible western water law.

Daniel McCool, a professor of political science at the University of Utah, has said, "The law of the river is hopelessly, irretrievably obsolete, designed on a hydrological fallacy, around an agrarian West that no longer exists." In a New West of urban archipelagoes, we still rely on water laws developed when covered wagons crossed the plains. Agricultural interests and old cities hold the senior water rights and stand at the front of the line, while new metropolitan areas are stuck at the back and have to squabble over scraps. But their populations are surging, along with their political power. The great thirst of these cities of tomorrow could pose a challenge to prior appropriation as legal systems devised in the nineteenth century slam into twentieth-century infrastructure and twenty-first-century economics and climate change.

Between 1920 and 2000, the population of the seven states in the Colorado River Basin grew more than 750 percent. From energy production to preserving wild rivers for fish and rafters, uses for water not envisioned in the 1922 Colorado River Compact strain the West's most crucial resource. Some argue that we should cut the Gordian knot of western water policy by dispensing with the Law of the River and begin anew. They think the Compact should be thrown out and fresh agreements should be forged that reflect actual streamflows rather than the faulty numbers upon which the original agreement was based, and they argue for an overhaul of western water law to base it on need and appropriate use rather than the priority system. To their way of thinking, cities brimming with people and the burgeoning tourism and high-tech industries need water most, and flooding alfalfa on arid plains and cotton in deserts are not suitable uses of dwindling water supplies. In 2008 Arizona senator John McCain ignited a firestorm while running for president when he said that the Colorado River Compact should be renegotiated. "Over my dead body," retorted Colorado senator Ken Salazar.

Those opposed to overhauling western water law claim that doing so will result in Armageddon because the survival of the West rests upon the complexly intertwined rules that evolved to govern the use of water. Those who advocate rebooting the system insist that leaving the Law of the River intact is a sure path to apocalypse. And the river rolls on, carrying in its diminished flow a burden of silt and salt, pooling slackly in impoundments, trickling in a poisonous ooze toward the cracked mud of its delta.

~◆~

A shrinking snowpack that melts earlier in spring, aside from causing trouble for cities, farmers, and power companies by decreasing the amount of water stored in reservoirs in summer months, will harm the tourism industry—one of the main economic drivers of towns throughout the West. Ski resorts, anticipating less snow on their slopes, plan to ramp up their artificial snowmaking efforts. But making snow requires lots of water. Less snow also means lower streamflows for whitewater rafters and kayakers in the spring and summer, and less water for fish and wildlife, decreasing the yields of hunters and anglers.

Glacier National Park draws hordes of visitors to its gateway communities in Montana, supporting more than four thousand jobs and contributing as much as $1 billion a year to the state's tourism economy, Montana's second largest industry. A study by the Rocky Mountain Climate Organization and the Natural Resources Defense Council concluded that over the past decade the park has warmed twice as much as the planet as a whole. While the namesake glaciers melt, the turquoise hues of its alpine lakes fade, its streams shrink to more sluggish flows, and the fate of the park's panoply of charismatic megafauna—its moose, elk, mountain goats, bighorn sheep, grizzlies, black bears, mountain lions, lynx, wolves, and wolverines—becomes increasingly uncertain. Many of the small glaciers are already gone; the larger ones are melting quickly and will disappear within the next few decades. No plans have been announced to rename the park, though "The Place Where There Once Were Glaciers National Park" is one possibility that has been bounced around on Montana barstools.

"Touch water [in the West] and you touch everything," John Gunther wrote in 1947. In the New West, where skyscrapers rise from ranchland and the semiconductor industry tries to tap the flow of ditches that irrigate alfalfa fields, water is still the most important substance, and the battle to control it is at the heart of so much of what happens here. Short of science suddenly developing cold fusion or some other source of clean, cheap, limitless energy to power desalination plants, there is no quick fix for the West's water problems, no silver bullet. As certain as death and taxes, nature's stinginess with water in the region will continue to nag its inhabitants throughout the twenty-first century. The trouble that results from increasing demand on a decreasing resource might be mitigated with sensible policies, but the trouble will always be there. It is present in monstrous dams and canals that have rearranged the scant liquid the climate allows in this dry place. It exists in pipes and lawns and pools of those who flock to this sunny land of epic scenery. Most of all, the trouble is planted deep in the mindset of a people who have filled the vast and wild spaces that one bearded soothsayer, after sober observation and careful study, declared could never sustain settlement on a massive scale. The Hohokam did not have written records, so we are left to sift through the ruins of their world and wonder was there a John Wesley Powell among them—someone who looked at the West and saw not the hydraulic superstructure of human invention, not the wealth and power that rests on technology's fragile footings in the desert, but the land, the thirsty land beneath it.

———

Jared Diamond explains in his book *Collapse* that the sudden decline of Anasazi civilization at Chaco Canyon was not due simply to drought. What ended six centuries of prosperity in chaos and cannibalism was the impact of severe dryness on a landscape denuded by people who had grown attached to lavish lifestyles in the desert and were not prepared to meet the challenges of a changing climate. Cue the images of fountains in Las Vegas and swimming pools in Phoenix.

Speak of climate change and most people think of cities on the coasts slipping beneath the sea, polar bears stranded on shrinking ice floes. But while the Arctic thaws and oceans rise, mountain snowpack in the West shrinks and the cities on the plains below run short of freshwater. What will happen when more demands are placed on the Colorado River than what spills down its bed and is held in its reservoirs? The Law of the River does not cover drought, has nothing to say about climate change. If farmers sue cities, and cities sue states, and states sue the federal government, and the United States and Mexico sue each other, the legal tangles that govern water in the West could become more convoluted—or they could unravel. A depopulation of the desiccated lands west of the 100th meridian could occur. Instead of Okies with mattresses strapped to the roofs of their model Ts rattling away from the Dust Bowl toward California, yuppies with kayaks and skis shining in the racks of their Outbacks and Tacomas, and suburbanites with their electronics and pets packed into their Expeditions and Escalades, will cram western interstates as they retreat back east to moister climes. Only the lawyers will be left behind to argue among themselves over what remains of the rivers. Farmlands revert to sagebrush and sand. Cities slump into empty aquifers, their towers cracking as they lean, canals filling with dust. The West's motherboard of lights goes dim in the desert night, and tumbleweeds wheel their way down empty streets.

Or maybe not. There is a point at which a problem tips toward a crisis that is tumbling toward disaster. Right now we have a problem. A big problem. The West's most important resource is drying up, and people are filling the region like bargain shoppers racing to a clearance sale. What we do about the problem of increasing pressure on decreasing water supplies—from the technologies we devise that conserve water to the laws we write to govern its use and to manage population growth—will determine our future in this dry land. Developing a water sustainability plan for the West is something of a moon shot: It will take our nation's best and brightest economists, legal experts, urban planners, municipal water managers, and so on working together to determine a path forward.

While there is no room for complacency, there is also no need for hysteria. For all the talk of the West's water wars, more ink has been shed than blood, and disputes over water rights have been settled far more often in courtrooms than on battlefields. Aside from laws, our civilization is built on science. If we pay attention to the conclusions of our best scientists and create a legal framework that incorporates their projections about how much water will be available in the coming years, and that reflects our contemporary economy and values, we most likely won't go the way of the Anasazi. At least not yet.

A report released by the National Oceanic and Atmospheric Administration in 2010, to which more than three hundred scientists from 160 research groups in forty-eight countries contributed, concluded that "the warming of the climate system is unequivocal." The overwhelming consensus of climate scientists is that humans have caused the climate to change; but the cause, in terms of water management in the West, is not important. What is important is that the region is heating up, and west of the 100th meridian the effects are already being felt as snowpack reduces and reservoirs shrink. Political leaders and water managers must first accept this and then begin to adapt. The situation is serious but not drastic because the vast bulk of water use in the region—80 percent or more—is devoted to agriculture. And, as pointed out by water sustainability guru Peter Gleick, nearly 50 percent of the agricultural water used in California is for "inefficient flood-irrigation." The crisis lies not so much in our dwindling water supply as in our inept management of the resource.

Shifting some water away from agriculture will free up new supplies for the region's burgeoning cities. Low-value crops such as alfalfa are going to have to go in many arid areas of the West, as are water-demanding crops such as cotton. There is no reason to provide government subsidies to growers so they can use enormous amounts of water to raise thirsty crops—of which the nation already enjoys a surplus—in droughty deserts and plains. Reforming the agricultural subsidy system, including both artificially cheap water and price supports for crops easily grown in wet climates, though politically difficult due to the tremendous power wielded by the western agricultural lobby ensconced in Washington and determined to continue handouts for rich landowners and corporations, is a crucial first step in coping with the West's shrinking water supplies.

In these days of bloated federal budgets and a skyrocketing national deficit, momentum is building across the political spectrum to reform farm policy, often drawing together an unlikely coalition of fiscal conservatives and environmental activists, all of whom agree that our system of crop subsidies is as outdated as a landline phone network. Regarding California's Westlands Water District, Environmental Working Group noted, "When U.S. taxpayers' annual expenditure of $10.8 million in crop subsidies is taken into account, the cost of continuing to farm Westlands' 250,000 troubled acres becomes exorbitant." The Heritage Foundation, an ultra-conservative think tank, wrote, "Farm subsidies have become America's largest corporate welfare program." And from the libertarian

Cato Institute: "Far from 'saving the family farm,' federal agricultural subsidies are environmentally destructive corporate welfare, with more than 70 percent of aid going to the largest 10 percent of agribusiness." Gutting subsidies should be approached with caution, however. Stopping subsidized water from flowing to small farms in the West could put them out of business (their margins are narrow as it is, and many of them wobble on the brink of bankruptcy each year). Charging farmers the true price of water in the West could cause farming to be concentrated even more than it is now with industrial agribusiness, which leads to the problems of food monopolies and crop monoculture when the diversity fostered by small farms disappears, as detailed by Michael Pollan in *Omnivore's Dilemma*. And if water were to become too expensive even for agribusinesses in the West and farming were to be profitable only in areas where crops can be grown without irrigation, the nation's food supply would be more geographically constrained, and thus more vulnerable to natural disasters. To feed the West's crowded cities, food would have to be shipped in from wet regions, consuming fossil fuels—which require enormous amounts of water to extract and refine.

It is easy to say we should put an end to subsidized water and price support payments for farming and ranching in the West, but can we live with the consequences? Treating water as a mere saleable good, instead of something special and outside the laws of supply and demand because its liquid nourishment is essential to our survival, could mean that we turn up at farmers' markets in Santa Fe and San Francisco, in Boise and Bozeman, and find them empty, while supermarkets bulge with fruits and vegetables and meats flown in and trucked in and sent by train as the last of the West's farms and ranches are covered with tract homes and outlet malls.

If we are going to continue to subsidize water to protect farming and ranching in the West, where do we want that water to flow? Toward industrial growers of corn and soybeans and concentrated animal feeding operations that pollute water sources and make us sick? Or do we want the subsidized water to run through the ditches of family-size farms that feed their communities with nutritionally rich fruits and vegetables, and with meat, eggs, and dairy products from animals that range freely across the pastures of the West? Reforming the West's water subsidy system for agriculture could not only help stave off the region's water crisis, but it could also affect the food supply, altering the way we eat and preempting ballooning health care costs. If the torrent of taxpayer-funded water that flows to agribusinesses that churn out corn syrup were diverted to small farms raising produce, an organically grown Palisades peach at a farmers' market might cost less than a can of Coke at a convenience store. And Type II diabetes might be less of a scourge than it is today. Changing the West's water subsidy system could make waves that ripple all the way to hospital beds.

Cities, for their part, could stop guzzling so much water for landscaping—at least half of their overall use. Swapping lush lawns for xeriscaping would go a long way toward freeing up enough water for the West to weather the crisis. James Lawrence Powell, in his book *Dead Pool*, argues that reducing the percentage of water used for agriculture from 80 to 70 percent in the Colorado River Basin, and slashing city water devoted to landscaping from 50 percent to 5 percent, would provide an additional 2.7 maf per year—almost 20 percent of the Colorado River's annual flow. And millions of additional acre-feet could be added to the West's water supply by implementing conservation and efficiency programs that encourage simple water-saving measures such as the installation of low-flow fixtures in homes and businesses. These modest steps would free up enough water for the West to survive as it is today, relatively intact, even as its aquifers are pinched and its rivers get skinnier. More aggressive strategies, such as designing dual plumbing systems in cities so that reclaimed effluent rather than potable water could be used to flush toilets and irrigate landscaping, would go even further toward preventing the exhaustion of the region's water supplies.

The problem, however, is this: Surplus water in the West has always led to new growth. Increasing the water supply has resulted in increased demand. William Mulholland, speaking about his city's plunder of the Owens Valley, famously declared, "If we don't take the water, we won't need it." Southern California wasn't unexpectedly inundated with people. While Los Angeles was sending its boosters across the country to promote the city's charms and trigger a population boom, its water seekers were hurrying to dip pails in rivers hundreds of miles away, securing a surplus that the new citizens could slurp dry after they arrived. And when the city overflowed with people, to accommodate the new masses, municipal leaders scrambled to get infrastructure such as roads and sewers in place while at the same time scheming to purloin more water for the next population boom. This may seem a reckless way to build cities in the desert, but in the western United States it's what passes for urban planning.

While the cities of the West drink, rivers and aquifers shrink. Metropolitan areas newly rich from the tax dollars of transplants who have flocked to their job-rich sprawls have no desire to stop this bonanza. They don't want to vex their citizens with talk of restricting growth to levels that are sustainable given the region's limited water—these citizens simply don't want to hear it. We want sun and open space and powder snow. Leave tree rings to scientists, let the water managers worry about how to shore up supplies. We will surf our skis through the fluffy whiteness of mountain slopes and drift our boats down crystalline streams. It could be many years yet before the rivers run dry, and we will all crowd into paradise as long as water still flows from the taps.

If shrinking water supply is the elephant in the room, then growth is a mastodon playing a bass drum. California's Department of Finance projected in 2007 that the state's population, now about thirty-seven million, will rise to some sixty million by 2050. If the water freed up by conservation and by shifting use away from agriculture and landscaping is gobbled up by explosive population growth, the West will be right back where it started—in crisis. The region needs to peg its growth to water supplies. In terms of water resources, sixty million Californians is about thirty million too many.

A study published in the *Proceedings of the National Academy of Sciences* in 2010 concluded that in order for Phoenix to achieve water sustainability in 2030, policy action will be necessary—even without climate change reducing water supplies. Most irrigated outdoor landscaping and private backyard pools may have to be eliminated, communities may have to be planned in dense urban concentrations rather than in neighborhoods of suburban sprawl, and growth may have to be limited to 50 percent of projected levels.

Growth, according to Donald Worster, is a word that for some Americans "is more sacred than God or country." The idea of government limiting growth is repugnant to the rugged individualists of the West. But those rugged individualists have been swilling at the federal water trough for more than a century. And as Bruce Babbitt points out in his book *Cities in the Wilderness*, the US government has been guiding land use in the western United States since the Reclamation Act of 1902, which gave bureaucrats the authority to allocate scarce water. By deciding where water should go and not go with subsidized water development, the federal government determined the shape of the modern urbanized West. Phoenix, for example, became the population center of Arizona because the Bureau built dams with taxpayer dollars in the state's richly watered high country and set aside rights to most of the flow for Phoenix and its stark surrounds. On lands that look as if they haven't known moisture since the Mesozoic Era, a sandy outpost swelled into a federally planned metropolis. As the saying goes, "Arizona grows where water flows."

To scream that states' rights should prohibit the government from combating unsustainable city overspill in arid regions is disingenuous at best—federal water management in the West, since 1902, has served as the most important form of land-use planning in the region. Adjusting the planning to include limits on growth could be done with a carrot-and-stick approach similar to the way federal highway funds are withheld from states that don't raise their minimum drinking age to twenty-one. Western states that adopt policies that tie growth to their water supplies would be eligible to use water from federal projects and to receive federal money for water infrastructure development and flood control; states that refuse to stop their growth from exceeding the limits of their water supply would not.

The use of federal money for water development could also be linked to protecting rivers. Babbitt, commenting on the Clean Water Act's ability to prevent pollution but not protect instream flows, writes, "This is rather like a legal system that prohibits spraying graffiti on a building, yet says nothing about burning the structure to the ground." Babbitt argues for extending the reach of the Clean Water Act to prohibit streamflows from dropping below a hydrologic "bright line"—a minimum level necessary to maintain aquatic ecosystems. The bright line for each river would be determined by scientists, as with California's Sacramento River, where biologists identified the minimum seasonal flow needed to protect what remains of the river's salmon runs. With Babbitt's plan, states that implemented instream flow programs to protect rivers would be eligible to receive federal money for water infrastructure and flood control; those that depleted their rivers below a sustainable level would not.

The attitude of many environmentalists who see the federal government as the solution to rehabilitating the West's trashed watercourses is something along the following lines: Let the rugged individualists howl about a heavy-handed government messing in their affairs—the biggest welfare queens in American history tend with their machinery and migrant labor vast acreage of potato patches and alfalfa fields in the West, all of it watered with taxpayer dollars. The people of America purchased the dams that control the flow of the West's rivers; in increasing numbers they are asking for their rivers to run full and free in their ancient channels, where salmon sniff their way toward natal waters when they return from the sea. The public is asking for its rivers to hold pure water uncontaminated by the debris and poisons caused by overcut forests, overgrazed grasslands, and reckless mining.

We insist on more salmon and clean, free-flowing streams, but then we open our taps without considering where the water comes from, or the consequences of letting our faucets run. How we use water in our daily lives determines, to a large extent, the fate of the West's rivers. If we are sloppy with water use in our homes and businesses, streams will languish and aquifers will atrophy. To use water carefully and sparingly is to understand the relationship between our taps and the sources that supply them. It is to promote the health of the watersheds that sustain us. It is to acknowledge that every glass of water we drink is a gift, every garden we grow a blessing.

The water crisis in the West has been caused not only by bad policies and poor planning but by the wasteful water use of citizens. Government policies and Herculean efforts to build dams and pipelines won't end it. What will keep the West's water crisis from becoming a catastrophe is millions of people installing low-flow plumbing fixtures in their homes and businesses. Millions of buckets of rainwater harvested for backyard gardens. Millions of faucets turned off for a few moments when parents teach their children how to soap and rinse their hands. And millions of parents taking their children to the shingled banks of rivers to hold in their hands the jeweled cases of caddisfly larvae as the backs of leaping fish flash in the sun and kingfishers call from the sedges.

Most of us have grown used to monitoring and curtailing our energy consumption, in part because of pricing that discourages wasteful use— and in part because of concern over the impact our actions have on the environment. And we are increasingly paying attention to how the food we eat affects the world around us. Wendell Berry's famous formulation "eating is an agricultural act" is reaching a wide audience as Michael Pollan and others help spread the food movement through America. Many of us are now starting to understand that each time we consume a meal we are involved in farming: When we purchase food we are voting with our dollars, sending signals to the marketplace about what kind of agriculture we support and how we want the planet's resources to be used to grow, produce, and deliver the things we eat.

Using water is an ecological act. Just as food doesn't simply appear in cellophane packages in grocery stores, water doesn't just flow from our faucets. We sip from wild rivers, we bathe in ancient aquifers. If we choose to luxuriate in long showers and gorge ourselves on feedlot beef, it should come as no surprise when the West's riverbeds turn dry as gravel roads. We should expect the skeletons of fish to bleach in the sun and marshlands once riotous with birds to fall silent. Each time we let sprinklers hiss across lawns we send a signal to politicians and water managers that we need more dams and diversions to bring us more supply. Each time we tear up water-hungry turf and replace it with plants that thrive in dry climates, we vote for wild streams.

But conservation and improved efficiency measures, whether mandated by governments or voluntarily adopted by citizens, can only do so much. Eventually, if the West continues on its present trajectory of rampant growth, it will run out of conservation, just as it has run out of good dam sites—and then the region will have to face the insuperable limits imposed by nature. At some point politicians in the West are going to have to find the courage to rise above partisan posturing and to take on powerful agribusiness interests and squabbling cities and states. They are going to have to tell the truth, which is simply this: A region with limited precipitation cannot support unlimited growth. And the public in the West is going to have to pay attention. Phoenix probably won't turn to ashes like the Hohokam civilization, but its future may not include green fairways and gushing fountains. Its citizens may have to stop pretending they are in a Costa Rican rainforest and accept that they live in a desert, and a desert is very dry. Residents of California's metropolises may have to put aside their self-congratulatory belief in their environmental progressiveness and take responsibility for the widespread damage the cancerous growth of their cities has caused, and continues to cause, the waterscape of the West. And all of us, whether we live in Marin County or Cheyenne, in Missoula or Los Angeles, need to look through the smog of our self-righteousness and start conserving more water and paying more for the water we do use. We need to stop blaming the Bureau of Reclamation, politicians, city planners, water managers, environmentalists, farmers—everyone and everything but ourselves—and make fundamental changes to the way we live. Even more to the point, perhaps we need to adjust how we think about our right to live wherever we want, even in places that lack the water to sustain us.

Whether we plant our yard with bluegrass or cover it with cacti, whether we leave the hose running while we wash our car or conscientiously turn off the tap each time we brush our teeth, all of us who live in the West are complicit in its aquifers emptying and its rivers running dry. By choosing to make lives for ourselves west of the 100th meridian, we are part of the problem. We each have a water footprint, and however lightly we might tread, footprints in the desert leave a mark.

Peter Gleick, the dean of water experts, sees two trails diverging in the droughty years ahead: a "hard path" and a "soft path." The hard path relies on dams, aqueducts, and pipelines that transport water over vast distances to provide new supplies. The soft path, which Gleick and many other of the nation's leading water experts follow, is an integrated, sustainable approach that emphasizes conservation and efficiency and learning to live within the limits of the land rather than trying to replumb it on a grand scale. Developing decentralized infrastructure is part of this approach. And for those who tread this soft path, John Wesley Powell's vision of the management of watersheds by resident citizens is a guiding principle. Protecting aquatic ecosystems is assigned as much importance as developing water supplies for people. Pricing water to reflect costs to the environment and to discourage waste is seen by soft-path proponents as key to distributing the vital resource equitably and using it efficiently.

Wendell Berry, in his essay "A Native Hill," writes that in early America we developed this basis of our economy: "When faced with abundance, one should consume abundantly." In the West, when faced with scarcity of water, we created abundance with the world's largest dams so that we could consume abundantly. We built cities according to blueprints that had no relationship to watersheds, and we relied on technology to supply the *sine qua non* of life. We kept faith in a fever dream of growth. We convinced ourselves the chimera of a technological utopia was real, and we let ourselves believe that increasingly audacious feats of engineering would allow us to ignore nature's limits. And yet, for all our ingenuity, all our heroic efforts to construct systems of siphons and pumps, canals and dams, we have managed to irrigate only a small portion of the deserts and plains that make up the American West. We can move water from one river to another, we can transport it hundreds of miles through scrubland and sand, but in the end we cannot magically create more of it.

Though some still clamor for bigger dams and longer pipelines and desalination facilities along coasts crowded with nuclear power plants, there is a growing consensus that we can't simply build our way out of the

West's water crisis. Recognizing the limited amount of water we have now, and understanding the amount we will have in the future, and then learning to live within these constraints through conservation and controlled growth, will prevent the trouble we face from turning into catastrophe. This requires a shift in our values, away from a dream of abundance and a belief in unfettered consumption, toward a realistic embrace of limits, a humble acceptance of scarcity. Floyd Dominy, that self-styled messiah of the parched frontier, left the Bureau long ago. The American West is not the home of Isaiah. The heavens will not pour water on the thirsty land. We established cities where no cities should be, and now we must use science to guide us through the consequences.

A Brief History of Water's Future

William Mulholland, before ascending to the position of Los Angeles's most important hydraulic engineer, lived in a cabin beside one of the ditches he tended. He spent his spare time strolling along the banks of the Los Angeles River, and he wrote that upon first seeing this free-flowing watercourse, "it at once became something about which my whole scheme of life was woven, I loved it so much." He described the river, as it appeared to him in 1877, as a "beautiful, limpid little stream with willows on its banks."

From one of the viewpoints along Mulholland Drive as it curves along the spine of the Santa Monica Mountains and the Hollywood Hills, look out at the sprawling suburbs and the towers stabbing the sky. Gaze at the gridlock and the smog. All this was made possible with water, and that water was brought here by William Mulholland. He controlled a fortune of the West's most precious resource, and his power was enormous. A newspaper headline proclaimed, "Bill" Mulholland, Genius, Superman.

And then, on March 12, 1928, Mulholland came tumbling down as the St. Francis Dam cracked apart and collapsed. One of the worst civil disasters in US history, the flood set loose by the failed structure swelled to a wave that carried thousand-ton chunks of concrete. Detritus left in the flood's wake lay two miles wide and seventy miles long in a muddy path of destruction studded with homes and cars and corpses. Searchers combed through mangled debris, but there were few survivors—more than 450 people died. Bodies that had swept out to sea washed up pale and bloated on beaches weeks later in places as far away as San Diego. Mulholland had enlarged the dam and rushed its construction because of a deadlock with his old crony Fred Eaton. Los Angeles needed a reservoir to store Owens Valley water; Eaton had purchased the only piece of land in the valley suited for the project and kept it for himself when buying up property for the Los Angeles Aqueduct. He set a price of $1 million and wouldn't budge. Mulholland, who had dismissed talk of himself running for elected office by saying, "I would rather give birth to a porcupine backwards than be Mayor of Los Angeles," was motivated less by lust for personal profit and political gain than by a sincere desire to serve the city by bringing it water. He was outraged by Eaton's intransigence and greed. The two men stopped talking, and their stalemate ruined them both. While holding out for $1 million, Eaton eventually went bankrupt. Meanwhile, Mulholland, by stubbornly refusing to pay Eaton's price, was forced to find a less desirable site where he could, against the advice of his engineers, hastily assemble a water storage structure to meet the city's needs.

After the St. Francis Dam collapsed, Mulholland was found by a board of inquiry to have filled the reservoir too quickly. And he had ignored a telltale sign of imminent collapse: As the weight of the full reservoir pressed against the dam, leakage had seeped from spreading cracks. A man who'd risen on a plume of water to great heights had fallen just as far. Initially Mulholland pointed toward Owens Valley saboteurs as the reason for the dam's demise, but when it became obvious he was at fault, he took responsibility for the disaster that unmade him. He resigned his position as head of the Department of Water and Power in disgrace. "I envy the dead," he said.

Putting an end to twenty years of hostility, Mulholland and Eaton met, and the two men wept. People, for all the power they gain, are fragile constructions, and the same is true of the walls they raise to hold back rivers.

Regardless of the dam failure that killed his career, Mulholland had managed to bring water to the desert, allowing Los Angeles to grow into a metropolis fast and bright and spilling across sunny ground like a city summoned in a dream. And Mulholland's achievement went far beyond the corner of California that he built. By snatching water rights from the farmers and ranchers for whom the Bureau of Reclamation planned an irrigation project, and then using those rights to benefit a syndicate of the rich and well connected, Mulholland helped usher in a new era of devious water management in the West. Dead was the dream of little landholdings flowering in the desert due to irrigation projects. Small farmers and independent ranchers didn't stand a chance against the economic and political titans birthed by dams and aqueducts, mighty structures that concentrated scarce water, and with it wealth and power.

An arcadian valley died so that a city pulsing with ambition could spasm into a metropolis. Americans from every corner of the country raced toward this fantasy in the desert. They built an Eden of imported palm trees and azure swimming pools, while Owens Lake, once deep enough to float a steamship, drained to an alkaline pan that clogged the sky with dust. Western farmers and ranchers who scratched out livings in hard lands are celebrated in myth and legend, but these pioneers were pushed to the margins of an empire that rose like a mirage from dry wastes shimmering with heat. Men like Mulholland built the real West. They built it not with gold or cattle or horses, not with barbed wire fences or Winchester rifles. They built it with the only thing that really matters in a thirsty land. They built it with water.

William Mulholland had brought liquid relief to Los Angeles, but the imperial megalopolis wanted more. Los Angeles dusted off a plan Mulholland had drawn up, and in 1941 the city extended its Owens Valley aqueduct 105 miles to the north, where it could slurp up streams that fed Mono Lake, a body of water similar to the lake in Owens Valley that the city had already dried up.

By 1970, driven by insatiable thirst, Los Angeles was reaching 242 miles east to the Colorado River on the California-Arizona border, 338 miles northeast through the Owens Valley to Mono Basin near Yosemite National Park, and 444 miles northwest to the Feather River in the Sacramento Valley of Northern California. But still the city wanted more.

Los Angeles built a second aqueduct to run alongside the one that drains the Owens Valley and Mono Basin, allowing the city to suck groundwater from Owens Valley and divert more flow from the streams that feed Mono Lake. A dynamite blast at the new aqueduct site briefly stopped water from draining out of the Owens Valley. This attack left no lasting damage, however, and water continued to flow to the city. Rebels with explosives were no match for the Los Angeles Department of Water and Power. But a few determined scientists were. David Gaines, a soft-spoken, shaggy-bearded graduate student, led a group of biologists who rode bikes to fieldwork sites in a battle against the goliath of Los Angeles. And the bomb blasts that shattered the wild silence surrounding Mono Lake were detonated not to blow up an aqueduct but to save birds.

Lying at the foot of the Sierra Nevada in a basin that doesn't drain to the sea, Mono Lake is an ancient body of alkaline water that holds a plentitude of life in a simple but fantastically productive food chain. A species of brine shrimp no larger than a thumbnail evolved in the strange chemistry of Mono Lake and is found nowhere else on earth. The shrimp graze on microscopic algae that photosynthesize their energy from the sun. Also feeding on the algae are alkali flies. They cluster together in buzzing black carpets along the lakeshore, and they walk underwater, encased in tiny air bubbles shaped like teardrops, to feed and lay their eggs.

As the alkali fly moves through the stages of its life cycle underwater, its head bursts open and a small sac fills with air, popping the top off the pupae case. The sac deflates, the head is reassembled, and the fly squeezes out of its casing and rises to the surface of the lake to dry its wings. The Wilson's Phalarope, a species of slender-necked shorebird the size of a fist, swims in circles to form a small whirlpool and reaches its bill into the center to gobble flies caught in the vortex. The shrimp and flies in their teeming trillions feed migratory birds by the millions that arrive from as far away as the Arctic and the Equator. Native Americans in the region who harvested fly pupae to make stews rich with fat and protein were displaced by Gold Rush boomtowns. Mark Twain made a go of gold mining in the area but went bust, and he wrote in *Roughing It*, published in 1872, that Mono Lake "lies in a lifeless, treeless, hideous desert . . . this lonely tenant of the loneliest place on earth." Volcanic cinder cones leak steam from their dark vents, and rock formations known as tufa stagger upward in strange towers encrusted with lumps and protuberances, rising from a lake that gleams like liquid steel. Birds lift off the water to fly toward far places. In their shining multitudes they move in white swirls, blending with snows cradled in mountaintops, merging with clouds in distant reaches of the sky. We could probe the outer edges of the universe and not find worlds as strange and wonderful as the ones we routinely destroy.

After Los Angeles began diverting water from four of the five snow-fed streams that pour into Mono Lake, evaporation exceeded inflow. The lake's volume was halved, and its salinity soared. Biologists concerned about the fate of the lake raced to catalog the richness of its life and rushed to spread word across the state that if the diversions continued unabated, the body of water would drain and become a dead chemical sump like Owens Lake. As concern over the plight of this rare and fragile ecosystem spread among the public, SAVE MONO LAKE bumper stickers became all the rage. Whereas the resistance in Owens Valley to Los Angeles's water diversions had been the work of disgruntled locals, efforts to thwart the city's plan to dry up Mono Lake were led by concerned citizens across California.

As the lake level dropped, a landbridge emerged, connecting the mainland to a volcanic cone that held a rookery for California gulls. Coyotes trotted across the new bridge to the island and filled their bellies with gull chicks. The California National Guard twice tried to blast the bridge apart with explosives but both times failed to sever the pathway for predators, and breeding gulls abandoned the island in a cacophony of squawks and ripping of the air with wings.

In 1979 the National Audubon Society joined with the grassroots Mono Lake Committee to file a lawsuit against Los Angeles. The suit centered on the "public trust doctrine." First expressed in the laws of the Roman emperor Justinian, and then incorporated into England's legal system and United States common law, the public trust doctrine protected seashores and navigable rivers for the use and benefit of everyone. These resources belong to all citizens, and the government, which acts as a guardian, is obligated to protect the public's rights of access. American legal scholar Joseph Sax wrote a seminal article in 1970 applying the public trust doctrine to natural resource management. Audubon Society lawyers jumped on the public trust bandwagon and argued that Los Angeles, by dewatering Mono Lake's feeder streams, was harming its ecology in violation of the public trust. The lawsuit pitted the public trust doctrine against appropriative water rights—venerable Roman law versus Gold Rush justice, a storied showdown in the New West.

In 1983, the Supreme Court of California extended the public trust doctrine to apply to Mono Lake. The Court decided that the state had an obligation to protect this scenic gem and ecological treasure—even though Los Angeles owned the right to divert the source streams that supply it with snowmelt, and even though those streams are non-navigable. In effect, the Court had determined that maintaining the aesthetic and recreational values of a natural body of water was as important as vested water rights established through prior appropriation. The implications for western water law were far reaching, and they are still playing out across the region as states grapple with changing values and tackle the question of whether water should be treated as private property, or part of the public trust that must be managed for the benefit of all people—or an uneasy blend of both. In some cases, states broadened the public trust doctrine beyond simply ensuring access to navigable bodies of water to protecting the recreational values, aesthetics, and ecology of all lakes and streams, and the ancient doctrine became a powerful new implement in the toolkit of environmentalists. In other cases, states chose not to extend the public trust to disputes over water rights, fearing the force of the doctrine would pose too profound a challenge to traditional western water law and result in a chaos of competing interests.

Following the 1983 decision to extend the public trust doctrine to Mono Lake's scenic values and ecology, lawsuits brought under the California Fish and Game Code aimed to force California's Water Board to limit the diversions of Los Angeles from the lake's feeder streams. The streams harbored populations of trout—which were part of the public trust, the lawsuit asserted. The Court agreed, and its rulings finally forced Los Angeles to accept a plan to protect Mono Lake and the streams that feed it, ending the city's water binge in the basin. In 1994 Los Angeles agreed to divert only a small portion of the allotment of water it owned the right to use, leaving the bulk of streamflow to nourish the body of water brimming with bizarre life in the desert. Mono Lake's grotesque garden of tufa towers stood farther above the surface than before Los Angeles had begun its diversions; but the lake would not be allowed to drop below a level at which the brine shrimp would crash and the birds disappear. When the city finally curtailed its diversions, the lake level rose, submerging the bomb-blasted landbridge that connected to the island gull rookery, and hungry coyotes paced along the shore.

To make up the shortfall of water to its taps, Los Angeles, instead of going after new water supplies and diverting a distant river as it had always done in the past, enacted an aggressive conservation program that encompassed everything from giving out free low-flow showerheads, to discouraging consumption by raising water prices in summer when use is highest, to recycling effluent. Prompted by public shame and forced by court decisions, the water whore of the West had finally begun to change its ways.

✤

While the Mono Lake saga was unfolding, from the dry bed of Owens Lake clouds of dust spread across the sky. The lake level had started to drop after local ranchers and farmers strangled its supply by diverting the flow of the Owens River to their fields. When the Los Angeles Department of Water and Power began diversions in 1913, the process accelerated until the river was a trickle in a dry trench and all that remained of once blue Owens Lake—which had covered more than a hundred square miles, had provided vast marshlands for waterfowl, and had served as the centerpiece of a scenic region called "the Switzerland of America"—were a few salty pools surrounded by endless acres of desiccated crust spattered with bright red bacteria. The bacteria, which thrive in the brine and blistering heat, cast a pinkish glow across the playa: an alien landscape as hostile and strange as any conjured in science fiction. Gone were the great flocks of shorebirds and waterfowl that had once blocked the sun for hours on end as they passed overhead wheeling and turning. In their stead stretched a void of sky as blue as the vanished lake. The valley's winds, squeezed to turbulent gales when they funneled between mountains, lifted millions of tons of alkali powder each year as they swept across the lakebed—the source of the worst particulate air pollution in the United States. The wind in the dead reeds was a dry whisper that carried arsenic, selenium, and cadmium. In violation of the Clean Air Act, poisonous dust covered the sky in chalky billows, and particles as fine as sifted flour burrowed deep into the lungs of valley residents. Along with hacking coughs and clogged sinuses, they got asthma, bronchitis, and cancer.

Following the completion of its second aqueduct in 1970, Los Angeles began pumping groundwater in the Owens Valley, squeezing the last drops from a drying sponge. Springs and seeps disappeared. Supple wands of tule turned stiff and brittle in the sun. For miles around, trees bare of leaf and bud in summer stood skeletal against the sky, as if some chemical defoliant had been sprayed in this place.

A tangle of court battles ensued, eventually resulting in Los Angeles agreeing to let some water flow into the empty bed of the sixty-two-mile-long Lower Owens River to help mitigate damage caused by groundwater pumping. In 2007, in what the *Los Angeles Times* called "the largest river restoration effort ever attempted in the West," automated gates redirected flow diverted to Los Angeles back into the riverbed. And water began spilling between the banks of the Lower Owens River for the first time in almost half a century. Bass are again cruising the cattails for crayfish and frogs. The smell of new leaves mixes with the scent of dusty sage.

Willows have returned to the riverbanks, providing shelter from the consuming fire of the sun. Canoes drift among herons and kingfishers down the gently flowing stream, and in the spring of each year a pulse of water is released to simulate a flood.

The Los Angeles Department of Water and Power, in addition to launching the river restoration project, has begun wetting portions of the dry bed of Owens Lake. It is using a complicated system of pipelines and pump stations—the fruit of a half-billion-dollar public works project. Water spreads thinly atop desert crust, moistening dust, keeping clouds of it from rising. Not enough of the treasured liquid will be released to restore the lake to its original depth: Just enough is let out by irrigation bubblers to keep the deadly powder down and protect Los Angeles from air quality lawsuits. As soggy pockets form in the basin, geese and ducks find a home. And flies, too—plagues of them are breeding in the spreading wetness. Above the resurrected lakebed, clouds of insects writhe with life.

Two hundred miles to the south, the emerald fields of the San Fernando Valley give way to a sprawling mallscape. The city lies wrapped in roads beneath its lid of smog. Commuters are sealed inside their cars, and the sun strikes with fierce heat against their shells of glass and steel.

━━━

The majority of people in California live in the south. Most of the state's water is in the north. To rectify what former governor Pat Brown called an "accident of people and geography," the most extensively engineered water system in the world transformed California into a plumbed paradise. Every major river of snowmelt that debouched from the Sierra Nevada was dammed, and millions of acres of cropland were irrigated. From dry but fertile plains came heavy harvests of tomatoes, pomegranates, prunes, olives, nectarines, figs, asparagus, melons, peaches, persimmons, plums, pears, walnuts, almonds—the land erupted with food. The state's farms soon produced half the nation's fruits, vegetables, and nuts, turning people across the country into consumers of California water.

As seekers of sunshine and new opportunities flooded into the Golden State, its economy swelled into the eighth largest on earth. But the snow-pack in the Sierra Nevada continues to contract. From 2007 to 2009, as the state's reservoirs fell to their lowest levels in decades, Southern California was forced to enact strict conservation measures. Responding to the crisis, former governor Arnold Schwarzenegger announced that "with California's booming population, and with the impact that global warming will cause our snowpacks, we need more infrastructure."

Much of California's existing water distribution system is designed to tap a delta where two great rivers that drain the High Sierra converge—the Sacramento and the San Joaquin. The bulk of the flow from these watercourses is routed south through the Central Valley Project and the California Aqueduct, two titanic assemblages of pumps, pipelines, and canals that supply water to about twenty-five million Californians. The delta where the rivers join, the West Coast's largest estuary, is threatened by climate change and subsidence. Once a tidal freshwater marsh covered by slabs of peat and forests of reeds, the delta more than a century ago was drained and diked by settlers to reclaim farmland. Now the sea is poised to reclaim the delta, which could be inundated by the waters of San Francisco Bay. The sea is rising, and the peaty soil is sinking as it rots. Egrets white as a winter's moon stand amid dark pools, and black-crowned night herons roost in the trees. The air tastes of salt. Earthen walls stretch away into fog, and water slaps their sides.

Seawater, besides potentially toppling levees and swamping fields and towns beneath a salty bog, could contaminate the pumps that supply water to two-thirds of the state's population. And as if this weren't trouble enough, the crumbly dikes that protect the delta and the pumping stations that supply a region stretching from the Bay Area to the Mexican border lie near an earthquake fault. Geologists warn that a major quake, long overdue in the area, is likely to rattle the region soon.

Aside from the potential disasters of rising seas and shaking ground, the Sacramento–San Joaquin Delta has another problem. The delta smelt, a translucent fish the length of a finger, is in decline. To protect the diminutive creature during a drought, a federal court invoked the Endangered Species Act and ordered a drastic decrease in the amount of water sent south from the delta, clobbering farmers in the San Joaquin Valley. They watched their fields turn brown and dusty, and crops from cantaloupes to onions went to rot as the water supply dwindled. Outraged, the farmers are now bombarding courts with lawsuits demanding that their water rights be given priority over those of a fish that swims in clean water teeming with creatures from plankton to salmon. Scientists see the delta smelt as an indicator species that reflects the overall health of the estuary ecosystem. A congressman called the delta smelt "a worthless little worm that needs to go the way of the dinosaur." Farmers in the San Joaquin Valley are pumping the overburdened aquifer into oblivion, and the ground is sinking toward the hollow darkness inside the world as they try to save their fields.

Schwarzenegger won praise from environmental groups for including ambitious conservation measures in his water legislation (the laws call for cities to reduce their water use 20 percent by 2020). But he raised the hackles of anti-dam advocates by proposing the construction of new water storage systems intended to capture the last drips of moisture as the West dries out. Even more controversial was his revival of the Peripheral Canal, a $10 billion megaproject first proposed more than three decades ago to bail Los Angeles out of water bankruptcy. Because the canal would bypass the delta, the giant project would put less pressure on the embattled smelt—as long as adequate water is left in the rivers that feed the delta. Some environmentalists support the plan, arguing that the Peripheral Canal, by not pumping water directly from the delta, will allow its fragile ecosystem to be restored. Local residents worry that if the threat to the state's water supply is removed by building the canal, interest in preserving the dikes that separate the delta from the sea will disappear and the earthen works will crumble, letting in a flood.

For the economy of the wealthiest and most populous state in the Union to function smoothly, a reliable water system is essential. Many

Southern Californians, as they watch their cities swell and the state's aging water infrastructure grow increasingly creaky, see the Peripheral Canal as a viable solution. Northern Californians tend to view the project as a water grab on par with Los Angeles's heist of the Owens River. They roundly rejected a Peripheral Canal referendum at the polls in 1982, and many have vowed to defeat it again. The *San Francisco Chronicle*, responding to the revived Peripheral Canal plan, editorialized, "Brace yourselves, Northern California voters—there's another civil war at hand."

According to an article in a 2010 issue of *National Geographic*, a whopping 70 percent of residential water in Southern California is used outdoors to fill pools and to spread across lawns, creating a suburban landscape of lush greenery in the desert. New laws in California mandate conservation measures to cut consumption, but water experts such as Peter Gleick point out that there is still tremendous room to reduce use. Matching water quality to water needs is crucial: Storm runoff, reclaimed wastewater, and greywater can be used for landscape irrigation, saving potable water for uses that demand it, such as drinking and cooking. Pouring potable water on lawns along California's semiarid southern coast while the state runs short of water supply is something we do now with hardly a second thought. But it is easy to imagine future historians looking back on our water use in the American West, as we squandered the stuff of life to see the color green, and conclude that we were more than a little daft.

From the proposed Peripheral Canal has flowed fractious debate, and whether the project can help solve California's water crisis remains to be seen. It could be many years before ground is broken for the canal or the plan is abandoned—years that promise to be hotter and drier than in decades past, and years in which the population of California will continue to soar. While the state's water shortage grows worse and its delivery system becomes increasingly precarious, more than 200,000 people move into Southern California each year. Water is a commons, and tragedy, it seems, is near.

❧

Oregon's Elk Creek Dam was authorized by Congress in 1982 to tame a tributary of the Rogue River. Elk Creek wanders in serpentine loops through meadows spangled with wildflowers, and it crashes through lava tubes and ravines of black volcanic rock. When the dam that blocked the stream's flow was about a third finished in 1987, lawsuits to protect salmon and steelhead led to a court injunction that forced construction stoppage. The Corps of Engineers walked away from the project, leaving the worksite an industrial zone strewn with mounds of crushed rock and stacked with twisted rebar. Fish trying to swim past the dam to spawn upstream swirled in a confusion of water at the base of the concrete wall. They were trapped, dumped in trucks, and hauled around the dam so they could continue their journey upriver, through translucent pools tucked between pines to the place where they'd been born.

Litigation and political battles that spanned some twenty years finally resulted in a compromise. The Corps of Engineers "notched" the dam, using explosives to destroy about 15 percent of the structure, and it restored the creek to its original channel, allowing fish to migrate back upstream without the aid of trucks. The rest of the dam remained intact so that someday it could be completed to provide irrigation water to local farmers. Breached and no longer blocking the stream as it tumbles from the mountains to the valleys below, but ready to impound the region's most important resource, the notched dam stands as a monument to the West's ongoing water wars.

When the level of Lake Powell lowered during a long drought, the Cathedral in the Desert emerged, dripping in the sun. People lured by a legendary treasure that had been buried when Glen Canyon Dam was built journeyed to this place to see for themselves what most of them had known only through photographs and prose.

Sandstone slabs arched upward, forming a dome split open at its top by a narrow slot. Streams unrolled like ribbons down a cliff of rainbow-colored rock. Sunlight sheared through the gap in the vaulted roof above, and across the shadowed walls danced little flames of light reflected from the water. You could hear the water talk, its voice echoing through hidden halls of stone.

Then the drought loosened its grip. Swollen with snowmelt, the Colorado once again backed up behind the dam, and the Cathedral in the Desert disappeared beneath the sapphire waters of the reservoir, strewn with beer cans, streaked with the oil from motors. Lake Powell remains less than half full. A bleached bathtub ring circles the red stone basin, proof of how far the waters once rose, a reminder of where the reservoir will seldom reach again. And just below the surface, waiting to be exhumed by deep drought, lies the Cathedral in the Desert.

—◦—

Follow a trail in the foothills of the Colorado Rockies upward to where the fallen leaves of cottonwoods crunch beneath your feet. Climb higher yet to where the aspen torch with color, and then stand atop a slab of rock cracked by frost and polished by time. Look out at the plains bending along the curve of the earth. The prairie moves in waves as the wind sweeps across the grasses. This was once a sea, all of it buried beneath water. And the young earth buckled and heaved, and from a great violence below lifted peaks of stone to hold the snows of upper atmospheres.

Meltwater from an autumn blizzard drips down toppled beds, tracing the slope of the mountain. The water threads through crevices and winds between crags. It stalls below in a basin ringed by wild blueberries and a riot of ferns. Follow the water down and kneel next to a pool. The prints of a mountain lion are pressed into silt at the water's edge, and the tracks trail into darkness deep between the trees. Blades of sunlight slice the water. At the bottom of the pool, stones are as clear as if viewed through clean glass. Bugs striding atop the tensioned surface cast haloed shadows on the pebbled floor. Dragonflies hover on transparent wings. Touch the pool. Cup the water in your hands and sip. It numbs your fingers and lips. It makes your teeth ache with cold, makes your spine shiver with the shock of it. It tastes of iron and moss. Each of us floats in liquid in the womb, and water fills the cells that build us. Some of the water came from icy comets in the Earth's beginning and has passed through the bodies of trilobites and dinosaurs, mammoths and whales. From the tail of the pool, a trickle spills down the mountain, running in search of the sea. It sloshes and drips, surges and falls. The sound of its movement is a language older than any form of life. The trickle merges with many others, joining together in a stream, and from its waters all things flow.

ACKNOWLEDGMENTS

This book was born from countless conversations with kayakers and ranchers, attorneys and anglers, real estate developers and scientists, politicians and environmental activists, historians and city planners. Their many voices focused my attention on the conflicts surrounding water in the West, and I am deeply grateful to them all.

Librarians at the American Heritage Center of the University of Wyoming, the Western History and Genealogy Department of the Denver Public Library, the Bureau of Reclamation Library, the US Geological Survey Library, and the National Center for Atmospheric Research Library helped me navigate the mazelike complexity of water law and lore.

Among the many authors whose writings I found invaluable while investigating the past, present, and future of water in the West were John Wesley Powell, Wallace Stegner, Marc Reisner, Donald Worster, Norris Hundley Jr., William Kahrl, Sandra Postel, Robert Glennon, Charles Wilkinson, James Lawrence Powell, Matt Jenkins, Fred Pearce, and Peter Gleick.

I am especially indebted to Erin Turner for suggesting I write a book about water in the West and for shepherding it through to publication. I am also grateful to Ellen Urban and Joshua Rosenberg for their careful editing.

Thanks go to my Aunt Catherine for bringing me west when I was a boy. Thanks go to my Uncle Steve for sending me to Uganda, where I had to haul jerry cans from a spring and learned that "where there is no water, there is no life." Cheers to Aron Rosenthal and John-Paul Maxfield of Waste Farmers for putting me to work as wingman on Bertha and mixing soil in the shed—they showed me how to get my hands dirty while addressing water use in my own backyard. Joe Novosad guided me into the wilds of Colorado in search of rivers and lakes, and he generously shared his food and ideas. Graham Johnson, a terrific skiing, snowboarding, hiking, and conversational partner, struggled valiantly to stay awake and engaged while I babbled endlessly about water. My friend Mostafa Salehi, who helped me understand the science of hydrology, died while hiking toward the summit of Quandary Peak just as I was finishing this book. I miss his kindness and his wit.

Without the boundless patience of my wife, Amy, this book would not have been possible.

Sources

Listed below, by chapter, are the works referred to in the text, as well as others that shaped this book.

Introduction: Trouble

In this chapter and throughout the rest of the book, for information about the water cycle and other aspects of hydrology, I turned to E. C. Pielou's *Fresh Water*.

Western Water Assessment (WWA), which is a joint effort between the Cooperative Institute for Research in Environmental Sciences at the University of Colorado and the National Oceanic and Atmospheric Administration's Earth System Research Laboratory, is a terrific source for scientific information related to climate change and water supplies. The WWA website is easy to navigate and contains many links to peer-reviewed scientific papers pertaining to water in the West, as well as a comprehensive archive of news stories related to water and climate change.

The National Research Council's 2007 report on the Colorado River Basin is available in its entirety on the National Academies Press website. The Summary and Introduction sections are accessible to the layperson and provide information about the implications of climate change for the Colorado River and the West.

Garrett Hardin's oft-referenced "The Tragedy of the Commons" is a must-read for anyone interested in natural resource issues.

Aguilar, John, Laura Snider, and Brittany Anas. "Parts of Collapsed Bridge Block Boulder Creek." *Denver Post,* June 8, 2010.
Barnard, Jeff. "Oregon Water War Taking Ugly Turn." *Los Angeles Times,* January 13, 2002.

Berkes, Howard. "The Vision of John Wesley Powell." National Public Radio, August 26, 2003. www.npr.org/programs/atc/features/2003/aug/water/part1.html.

Blevins, Jason. "Ditch Riders Are Guardians of State's Water Traffic." *Denver Post,* August 8, 2010.

Brooks, David. "I Dream of Denver." *New York Times,* February 16, 2009.

CEJournal. "The American Dream: to Live (Unsustainably) in the West." February 17, 2009. www.cejournal.net/?p=1018.

DOE/Lawrence Livermore National Laboratory. "Human-Caused Climate Change at Root of Diminishing Water Flow in Western US, Scientists Find." *ScienceDaily,* February 1, 2008. www.sciencedaily.com/releases/2008/01/080131161810.htm.

Franklin, Benjamin. *Poor Richard's Almanac.* As quoted in Bartlett's Familiar Quotations. Boston: Little, Brown and Co., 2002.

Gleick, Peter H., et al. "Water: The Potential Consequences of Climate Variability and Change for the Water Resources of the United States." Pacific Institute and US Geological Survey, September 2000. www.gcrio.org/NationalAssessment/water/water.pdf.

Gouras, Matt. "Resources Take Lead at Western Governors Meeting." *Seattle Times,* June 27, 2010.

Hardin, Garrett. "The Tragedy of the Commons." *Science,* vol. 162, no. 3859, December 13, 1968.

Human, Katy. "Colo. River Basin Forecast Not Good, New Report Asserts." *Denver Post,* February 22, 2007.

Intergovernmental Panel on Climate Change. www.ipcc.ch.

Johnson, Kirk, and Dean E. Murphy. "Drought Settles In, Lake Shrinks and West's Worries Grow." *New York Times,* May 2, 2004.

Knowles, Noah, et al. "Trends in Snowfall Versus Rainfall in the Western United States." *Journal of Climate,* September 15, 2006.

Leopold, Luna B., and Walter B. Langbein. *A Primer on Water.* Washington, D.C.: US Government Printing Office, 1960.

McGuire, Kim. "Rooting Out Defiant Farmers." *Denver Post,* October 24, 2006.

"Melting Snow Is Swelling Colorado Rivers, Creeks." *Denver Post,* June 7, 2010.

Mote, Philip W. "Trends in Snow Water Equivalent in the Pacific Northwest and Their Climatic Causes." *Geophysical Research Letters,* vol. 30, no. 12, 2003.

———, et al. "Declining Mountain Snowpack in Western North America." *Bulletin of the American Meteorological Society,* January 2005.

MSNBC.com. "Scientists Predict Southwest Mega-Drought." April 5, 2007. www.msnbc.msn.com/id/17967097/ns/us_news-environment.

National Research Council, Committee on the Scientific Bases of Colorado River Basin Water Management. "Colorado River Basin Water Management: Evaluating and Adjusting to Hydroclimatic Variability." The National Academies Press, 2007. http://books.nap.edu/catalog.php?record_id=11857#toc.

Paulson, Steven K. "AP: Colo. Water Wars Include Spy Campaign." *Washington Post,* October 19, 2006.

————. "Spies Hired in Colorado's Cold War Over Water." MSNBC.com, October 20, 2006. www.msnbc.msn.com/id/15329885/ns/us_news-environment.

Pielou, E. C. *Fresh Water*. Chicago: University of Chicago Press, 1998.

Quinlan, Paul. "Lake Mead's Water Level Plunges as 11-Year Drought Lingers." *New York Times*, August 13, 2010.

Saunders, Stephen, et al. "Hotter and Drier: The West's Changed Climate." National Resources Defense Council and the Rocky Mountain Climate Organization, March 2008. www.nrdc.org/globalwarming/west/west.pdf.

Saunders, Stephen, and Maureen Maxwell. "Less Snow, Less Water: Climate Disruption in the West." The Rocky Mountain Climate Organization, 2005. www.rockymountainclimate.org/website%20pictures/Less%20Snow%20Less%20 Water.pdf.

Seager, Richard, et al. "Model Projections of an Imminent Transition to a More Arid Climate in Southwestern North America." *Science*, vol. 316, no. 5828, May 25, 2007.

Service, Robert F. "As the West Goes Dry." *Science*, vol. 303, no. 5661, February 20, 2004.

US Global Change Research Program. "Regional Climate Change Impacts." www .globalchange.gov/publications/reports/scientific-assessments/us-impacts/ regional-climate-change-impacts.

Wadhwa, Vivek. "Why Boulder Is America's Best Town for Startups." *Bloomberg Businessweek*, April 22, 2010.

Western Water Assessment. http://wwa.colorado.edu.

Zarembo, Alan. "Shrinking Snowpack a Threat for West." *Seattle Times*, February 1, 2008.

Zumbrun, Joshua. "America's Best- and Worst-Educated Cities." *Forbes Magazine*, November 24, 2008.

CHAPTER 1: INTO THE PARCHED FRONTIER

This chapter and the next one were strongly influenced by the chapter "A Country of Illusion" in Marc Reisner's *Cadillac Desert*—one of the most influential environmental books ever written by an American and widely accepted as the most important book about water in the West. It is, however, the *Ulysses* of environmental books: Everyone agrees that it's groundbreaking, and while many say they've read it, few have persevered from cover to cover. It can be a bit of a slog, but persistent readers are rewarded with acorns of fine writing and humor squirreled away in the dense thickets of text.

When researching Jedediah Smith, I began with Win Blevins's wonderful *Give Your Heart to the Hawks*. Blevins bases his stories of the mountain men in historical fact and uses fictional license to create compelling tales about their adventurous lives. Dale L. Morgan's *Jedediah Smith and the Opening of the West* provides a thorough and scholarly account of Smith's exploits, yet it is a fast and fun read. Harrison Dale's *The Ashley-Smith Explorations and the Discovery of a Central Route to the Pacific, 1822–1829* and Maurice S. Sullivan's *The Travels of Jedediah Smith* are invaluable resources for following the trails of this seemingly superhuman adventurer across the deserts and mountains of the West.

John Wesley Powell's *The Exploration of the Colorado River and Its Canyons* is a gripping adventure narrative that remains in print to this day. Edward Dolnick's *Down the Great Unknown* provides an exhilarating account of Powell and party's descent of the Green and Colorado Rivers. Dolnick uses contemporary river-running terminology and techniques to put into perspective the accomplishment of men who, when they launched their boats into The Great Unknown, didn't wear life jackets and didn't know a haystack from a hydraulic.

For inspiration about descriptions of the West's parched terrain, I turned to Cormac McCarthy, the best prose stylist to ever write about the landscape of the American West.

In this chapter and throughout the rest of the book, for information about water law, I referred to *Water Law in a Nutshell* by David Getches and *Colorado Water Law for Non-Lawyers* by P. Andrew Jones and Tom Cech. The chapter "Harvesting the April Rivers" in Charles Wilkinson's *Crossing the Next Meridian* has a cogent explanation of how prior appropriation became established in California gold camps and evolved into the basis for western water law. The chapter "The Worth of Water in the United States" in Robert Glennon's *Water Follies* points out the environmental consequences of traditional water law in the West.

Barbour, Barton H. *Jedediah Smith: No Ordinary Mountain Man.* Norman: University of Oklahoma Press, 2009.

Blevins, Win. *Give Your Heart to the Hawks: A Tribute to the Mountain Men.* New York: Tom Doherty Associates, 2005.

Bolton, Herbert Eugene. *Coronado: Knight of Pueblos and Plains.* Albuquerque: University of New Mexico Press, 1990.

Dale, Harrison. *The Ashley-Smith Explorations and the Discovery of a Central Route to the Pacific, 1822–1829*. Cleveland, Ohio: The Arthur H. Clark Company, 1918.

DeVoto, Bernard. *Across the Wide Missouri*. Boston: Houghton Mifflin, 1947.

———. *The Course of Empire*. Boston: Houghton Mifflin, 1952.

Dolnick, Edward. *Down the Great Unknown: John Wesley Powell's 1869 Journey of Discovery and Tragedy Through the Grand Canyon*. New York: Harper Collins, 2001.

Getches, David H. *Water Law in a Nutshell*. St. Paul, Minn.: Thompson West, 2009.

Gilbert, Bil, et al. *The Old West Trailblazers*. New York: Time-Life Books, 1973.

Glennon, Robert. *Water Follies: Groundwater Pumping and the Fate of America's Fresh Waters*. Washington, D.C.: Island Press, 2002.

Goodman, George J., and Cheryl A. Lawson. *Retracing Major Stephen H. Long's 1820 Expedition: The Itinerary and Botany*. Norman: University of Oklahoma Press, 1995.

Heapes, Robert. *The Stephen Long Expedition: Through the Great Desert to the Alpine Tundra*. Denver: Colorado Endowment for the Humanities, 1995.

Hollon, W. Eugene. *The Great American Desert Then and Now*. Lincoln: University of Nebraska Press, 1975.

Ives, Joseph C. *Report Upon the Colorado River of the West, Explored in 1857 and 1858 by Lieutenant Joseph C. Ives . . . Under the Direction of the Office of Explorations and Surveys*. Washington, D.C.: Government Printing Office, 1861.

Jones, P. Andrew, and Tom Cech. David H. Getches, fore. *Colorado Water Law for Non-Lawyers*. Boulder: University Press of Colorado, 2009.

Krakauer, Jon. *Under the Banner of Heaven: A Story of Violent Faith*. New York: Doubleday, 2003.

Lewis, Meriwether, William Clark, and members of the Corps of Discovery; Gary E. Moulton, ed. *The Lewis and Clark Journals: An American Epic of Discovery: The Abridgment of the Definitive Nebraska Edition*. Lincoln: University of Nebraska Press, 2003.

McCarthy, Cormac. *Blood Meridian: Or the Evening Redness in the West*. New York: Vintage Books, 1992.

———. *The Crossing*. New York: Random House, 1994.

Meinig, D. W. *The Shaping of America: A Geographical Perspective on 500 Years of History, Volume 2: Continental America, 1800–1867*. New Haven, Conn.: Yale University Press, 1986.

Morgan, Dale L. *Jedediah Smith and the Opening of the West*. Lincoln: University of Nebraska Press, 1964.

O'Dea, Thomas F. *The Mormons*. Chicago: University of Chicago Press, 1957.

Pike, Zebulon Montgomery; Stephen Harding Hart and Archer Butler Hulbert, eds. *The Southwestern Journals of Zebulon Pike, 1806–1807*. Albuquerque: University of New Mexico Press, 2006.

Powell, John Wesley; intro. by Wallace Stegner. *The Exploration of the Colorado River and Its Canyons*. New York: Penguin Books, 1987 (first published in 1895).

Powledge, Fred. *Water: The Nature, Uses, and Future of Our Most Precious and Abused Resource.* New York: Farrar, Straus and Giroux, 1982.

Public Broadcasting Service. *New Perspectives on the West,* "Francisco Vázquez de Coronado." www.pbs.org/weta/thewest/people/a_c/coronado.htm.

Reisner, Marc. *Cadillac Desert: The American West and Its Disappearing Water.* New York: Penguin, 1993.

Smith, Alson Jesse. *Men against the Mountains: Jedediah Smith and the Great South West Expedition.* New York: The John Day Company, 1965.

Stegner, Wallace. *Beyond the Hundredth Meridian.* New York: Penguin, 1992.

Sullivan, Maurice S. *The Travels of Jedediah Smith.* Santa Ana, Calif.: The Fine Arts Press, 1934.

Vélez de Escalante, Silvestre, and Francisco Domínguez; Fray Angelico Chavez, trans.; Ted J. Warner, ed. *The Domínguez-Escalante Journal: Their Expedition through Colorado, Utah, Arizona, and New Mexico in 1776.* Salt Lake City: University of Utah Press, 1995.

Wilkinson, Charles F. *Crossing the Next Meridian: Land, Water, and the Future of the West.* Washington, D.C.: Island Press, 1992.

Winship, George Parker. *The Coronado Expedition.* Chicago: Rio Grande Press, 1964.

Worster, Donald. *A River Running West: The Life of John Wesley Powell.* New York: Oxford University Press, 2001.

———. *Rivers of Empire: Water, Aridity and the Growth of the American West.* New York: Pantheon, 1985.

CHAPTER 2: SETTLING THE GREAT AMERICAN DESERT

Marcia Thomas's *John Wesley Powell: An Annotated Bibliography* helps Powell neophytes and scholars alike navigate the branching rivers of his written work, which touch everything from ethnographic studies of indigenous people to cartographic surveys of arid lands. *Seeing Things Whole,* edited by William deBuys, is a great starting point to get acquainted with Powell's writings and to understand his thinking, which, as deBuys convincingly argues, is relevant not just to the West but to all issues related to how human beings interact with their environment. Long before bioregionalism became sexy, Powell saw land, water, and society as parts of an interconnected whole.

For Powell biographies, Wallace Stegner's *Beyond the Hundredth Meridian* at times veers close to hagiography, but no other book puts Powell into the context of his times as skillfully as Stegner's highly acclaimed account—and the book's introduction by Bernard DeVoto makes a succinct and compelling case for why Powell is important and his ideas about the West worthy of study. Donald Worster is the rare historian who also happens to be a consummate prose stylist—he can turn a phrase and craft a description as deftly as any novelist. Worster's powerful Powell biography, *A River Running West*, examines more sources than Stegner's and is more objective. Worster's article "A River Running West: Reflections on John Wesley Powell" gives a compelling explanation and analysis of Powell's "watershed democracy," wildly controversial at the time he proposed it, strikingly prescient now. Daniel Kemmis's *This Sovereign Land* weaves Powell's ideas into a contemporary plan to govern the Interior West.

Walter Prescott Webb's *The Great Plains* is the touchstone text of the history of Great Plains settlement. Henry Nash Smith's *Virgin Land* is a brilliant dissection of the mythology of the American frontier. It explains the prominent role the West played in the development of Americans' consciousness, and it illuminates the process by which the Great American Desert came to be seen as a paradisiacal garden.

Owen Wister's novel *The Virginian* is a classic work of Wild West lore with contested water rights at the center of the tale.

Mary Austin's book of essays *The Land of Little Rain* provides interesting glimpses of the dry Southwest before large-scale irrigation projects reinvented the region.

Stanley Crawford's *Mayordomo*, a wonderfully told account of his tenure as a "ditch boss" in New Mexico, paints a vivid portrait of an acequia as the vital, flowing heart of a community.

Austin, Mary. *The Land of Little Rain*. Albuquerque: University of New Mexico Press, 1974 (originally published in 1903).

Barr, Zachary. "Two Feet of Rain in One Day." Colorado Public Radio, June 4, 2010.

Belgrad, Daniel. "Power's Larger Meaning: The Johnson County War as Political Violence in an Environmental Context." *The Western Historical Quarterly*, vol. 33, no. 2, Summer 2002.

Berkes, Howard. "The True Legacy of John Wesley Powell." National Public Radio. September 22, 2002. www.npr.org/programs/atc/features/2002/sept/powell.

Blevins, Win. *Give Your Heart to the Hawks: A Tribute to the Mountain Men*. New York: Tom Doherty Associates, 2005.

Colorado Historical Society. Historic Marker Program, Panel 3, Title: Acequias. http://research.databases.historycolorado.org/RIPsigns/show_markertext.asp?id=818.

Crawford, Stanley G. *Mayordomo: Chronicle of an Acequia in Northern New Mexico.* Albuquerque: University of New Mexico Press, 1993.

Davis, John W. *Wyoming Range War: The Infamous Invasion of Johnson County.* Norman: University of Oklahoma Press, 2010.

Garland, Hamlin. *A Son of the Middle Border.* New York: The Macmillan Company, 1917.

Getches, David H. *Water Law in a Nutshell.* St. Paul, Minn.: Thompson West, 2009.

Gilpin, William. *Mission of the North American People, Geographical, Social, and Political.* Philadelphia: J. B. Lippincott & Co., 1873.

Glennon, Robert. *Water Follies: Groundwater Pumping and the Fate of America's Fresh Waters.* Washington, D.C.: Island Press, 2002.

Hobbs, Greg. *The Public's Water Resource: Articles on Water Law, History, and Culture.* Denver, Colo.: Continuing Legal Education in Colorado, 2007.

Jones, P. Andrew, and Tom Cech. David H. Getches, fore. *Colorado Water Law for Non-Lawyers.* Boulder: University Press of Colorado, 2009.

Kemmis, Daniel. *This Sovereign Land.* Washington, D.C.: Island Press, 2001.

Mead, Elwood. *Irrigation Institutions: A Discussion of the Economic and Legal Questions Created by the Growth of Irrigated Agriculture in the West.* New York: Macmillan, 1903.

National Weather Service Forecast Office, Goodland, Kans. "Republican River Flood of May 30, 1935." www.crh.noaa.gov/gld/?n=1935flood.

O'Sullivan, John L. "The Great Nation of Futurity." *The United States Magazine and Democratic Review,* vol. 6, iss. 23, November, 1839.

Powell, John Wesley. *Report on the Lands of the Arid Region of the United States, With a More Detailed Account of the Lands of Utah.* Cambridge, Mass.: Harvard University Press, 1962 (originally published in 1879).

Powell, John Wesley. William deBuys, ed. *Seeing Things Whole: The Essential John Wesley Powell.* Washington, D.C.: Island Press, 2001.

Public Broadcasting Service. *New Perspectives on the West,* "William Gilpin." www.pbs.org/weta/thewest/people/d_h/gilpin.htm.

Reisner, Marc. *Cadillac Desert: The American West and Its Disappearing Water.* New York: Penguin, 1993.

Rivera, José A. *Acequia Culture: Water, Land and Community in the Southwest.* Albuquerque: University of New Mexico Press, 1998.

Roosevelt, Theodore. "First Annual Message, December 3, 1901." The American Presidency Project. www.presidency.ucsb.edu/ws/index.php?pid=29542.

Smith, Henry Nash. *The American West as Symbol and Myth.* New York: Vintage Books, 1950.

Stegner, Wallace. *Beyond the Hundredth Meridian.* New York: Penguin, 1992.

———. "A Geography of Hope." In *A Society to Match the Scenery: Personal Visions of the Future of the American West,* Gary Holthaus, et al., eds. Boulder: University Press of Colorado, 1991.

Stephanson, Anders. *Manifest Destiny: American Expansionism and the Empire of Right.* New York: Hill and Wang, 1995.

Stradling, David, ed. *Conservation in the Progressive Era: Classic Texts.* Seattle: University of Washington Press, 2004.

Thomas, Marcia L. *John Wesley Powell: An Annotated Bibliography.* Westport, Conn.: Praeger, 2004.

Turner, Frederick Jackson. *The Frontier in American History.* New York: Henry Holt and Company, 1920.

Webb, Walter Prescott. *The Great Plains.* New York: Grosset & Dunlap, 1931.

Wilkinson, Charles F. *Crossing the Next Meridian: Land, Water, and the Future of the West.* Washington, D.C.: Island Press, 1992.

Wister, Owen. *The Virginian.* New York: Macmillan, 1928 (originally published in 1902).

Worster, Donald. *Dust Bowl: The Southern Plains in the 1930s.* New York: Oxford University Press, 1979.

———. *A River Running West: The Life of John Wesley Powell.* New York: Oxford University Press, 2001.

———. "A River Running West: Reflections on John Wesley Powell." *Journal of Cultural Geography,* vol. 26, iss. 2, June 2009.

———. *Rivers of Empire: Water, Aridity, and the Growth of the American West.* New York: Pantheon, 1985.

———. "Theodore Roosevelt & the American Conservation Ethic." Theodore Roosevelt Center, April 1, 2009. www.theodorerooseveltcenter.org/Essay.asp?ID=11.

———. "Watershed Democracy: Recovering the Lost Vision of John Wesley Powell." *Journal of Land, Resources & Environmental Law,* vol. 23, no. 1, 2003.

CHAPTER 3: RECLAMATION

The writings of William Smythe give insight into the messianic movement of irrigation in its early years, and Smythe's hyperbole and overblown prose provide great fun. "Civilization will bloom where barbarism has blighted the land," etc. etc.

Despite being written in a style so dry it makes the Mojave Desert seem a swamp, Michael Robinson's *Water for the West* sheds light on the origins of the reclamation movement. From the pages of Marc Reisner's *Cadillac Desert,* Donald Worster's *Rivers of Empire,* Donald Pisani's *Water and American Government,* Dorothy Lampen's *Economic and Social Aspects of Federal Reclamation,* Charles Wilkinson's *Crossing the Next Meridian,* and James Lawrence Powell's *Dead Pool* tumble avalanches of damning details about America's reclamation efforts.

William Kahrl's *Water and Power* stands out among the many accounts of the Los Angeles–Owens Valley conflict. It is thoroughly researched and convincingly told, and it meticulously maintains objectivity while examining a history that has a tendency to induce in people bitterness and rage. Mary Austin's classic novel *The Ford* fictionalizes the fierce battle over water in the Owens Valley. Roman Polanski's *Chinatown* is a fine film but should not be confused with a factual account of the Owens Valley water war. For a quick introduction to the chicanery used by Los Angeles when it set out to invent itself with water, I know of no better resource than the public television documentary *Cadillac Desert: Water and the Transformation of Nature—Mulholland's Dream*.

Austin, Mary. *The Ford*. Boston: Houghton Mifflin, 1917.

Berkes, Howard. "The Vision of John Wesley Powell." National Public Radio. August 26, 2003. www.npr.org/programs/atc/features/2003/aug/water/part1.html.

Berkman, Richard L., and W. Kip Viscusi. *Damming the West: Ralph Nader's Study Group Report on the Bureau of Reclamation*. New York: Grossman Publishers, 1973.

Bible (New International Version). Isaiah 41:18; 43:19–20; 44:3–4: 51:3; 55:13.

Bible (New International Version). Revelation 21:6.

Bourne, Joel K. Jr. "California's Pipe Dream." *National Geographic*, April 2010.

Bureau of Reclamation. "Brief History of the Bureau of Reclamation." www.usbr.gov/history/2011NEWBRIEFHISTORYV1.pdf.

Cadillac Desert: Water and the Transformation of Nature—Mulholland's Dream. Jon Else and Linda Harrar, dirs. and prods. Jon Else, Sandra Postel, and Marc Reisner, writs. Columbia-TriStar Television PBS Home Video, 1997.

Chinatown. Roman Polanski, dir. Robert Towne, writ. Paramount, 1974.

Dawdy, Doris Ostrander. *Congress in Its Wisdom: The Bureau of Reclamation and the Public Interest*. Boulder, Colo.: Westview Press, 1989.

Fogelson, Robert M. *The Fragmented Metropolis: Los Angeles, 1850–1930*. Berkeley: University of California Press, 1993.

Getches, David H. *Water Law in a Nutshell*. St. Paul, Minn.: Thompson West, 2009.

Gressley, Gene M. "Arthur Powell Davis, Reclamation, and the West." *Agricultural History* 42, July, 1968.

Hays, Samuel. *Conservation and the Gospel of Efficiency: The Progressive Conservation Movement, 1890–1920*. Cambridge, Mass.: Harvard University Press, 1959.

Hendricks, William O. "Developing San Diego's Desert Empire." *Journal of San Diego History*, vol. 17, no. 3, Summer 1971.

Hiltzik, Michael. *Colossus: Hoover Dam and the Making of the American Century*. New York: Free Press, 2010.

Hundley, Norris, Jr. *The Great Thirst*. Berkeley: University of California Press, 2001.

———. "The Politics of Reclamation: California, the Federal Government, and the Origin of the Boulder Canyon Act—A Second Look." *California Historical Quarterly*, vol. 52, no. 4, Winter 1973.

———. *Water and the West: The Colorado River Compact and the Politics of Water in the American West*. Berkeley: University of California Press, 2009.

———. "The West against Itself: The Colorado River—An Institutional History." In *New Courses for the Colorado River*, Gary Weatherford and Lee Brown, eds. Albuquerque: University of New Mexico Press, 1986.

Kahrl, William L. *Water and Power: The Conflict over Los Angeles' Water Supply in the Owens Valley*. Berkeley: University of California Press, 1982.

Lampen, Dorothy. *Economic and Social Aspects of Federal Reclamation*. Manchester, N.H.: Ayer Publishing, 1979.

Los Angeles Department of Water and Power. "The Story of the Los Angeles Aqueduct." http://wsoweb.ladwp.com/Aqueduct/historyoflaa/index.htm.

Mulholland, Catherine. *William Mulholland and the Rise of Los Angeles*. Berkeley: University of California Press, 2002.

Nadeau, Remi A. *The Water Seekers*. Santa Barbara, Calif.: Peregrine Smith, 1974.

Pisani, Donald J. *Water and American Government: The Reclamation Bureau, National Water Policy, and the West, 1902–1935*. Berkeley: University of California Press, 2002.

Powell, James Lawrence. *Dead Pool: Lake Powell, Global Warming and the Future of Water in the West*. Berkeley: University of California Press, 2008.

Public Broadcasting Service. *New Perspectives on the West*, "Fred Eaton." www.pbs.org/weta/thewest/people/d_h/eaton.htm.

Public Broadcasting Service. *New Perspectives on the West*, "William Mulholland." www.pbs.org/weta/thewest/people/i_r/mulholland.htm.

Reisner, Marc. *Cadillac Desert: The American West and Its Disappearing Water*. New York: Penguin, 1993.

Robinson, Michael C. *Water for the West: The Bureau of Reclamation 1902–1977*. Chicago: Public Works Historical Society, 1979.

Roosevelt, Theodore. "First Annual Message, December 3, 1901." The American Presidency Project. www.presidency.ucsb.edu/ws/index.php?pid=29542.

Smythe, William E. *The Conquest of Arid America*. New York: Macmillan, 1905.

———. "An International Wedding." *Sunset*, October 1900.

Sperry, Robert. "When the Imperial Valley Fought for Its Life." *The Journal of San Diego History*, vol. 21, no. 1, Winter 1975.

Ward, Diane Raines. *Water Wars: Drought, Flood, Folly and the Politics of Thirst*. New York: Riverhead, 2002.

Warne, William. *The Bureau of Reclamation*. New York: Praeger, 1973.

Widtsoe, John A. *Success on Irrigation Projects*. New York: John Wiley, 1928.

Wilkinson, Charles F. *Crossing the Next Meridian: Land, Water, and the Future of the West.* Washington, D.C.: Island Press, 1992.

Worster, Donald. *Rivers of Empire: Water, Aridity and the Growth of the American West.* New York: Pantheon, 1985.

CHAPTER 4: THE LAW OF THE RIVER

In this chapter and throughout the rest of the book, for information on the Law of the River, I relied on the impressive body of scholarly work produced by Norris Hundley Jr., who calls the Colorado "one of the most litigated, regulated, and argued-about rivers in the world."

Phillip Fradkin's *A River No More* is a highly readable account of the political and legal issues surrounding the Colorado River.

Adler, Robert W. "Revisiting the Colorado River Compact: Time for a Change?" *Journal of Land, Resources, and Environmental Law,* vol. 28, no. 1, 2008.

———. *Restoring Colorado River Ecosystems: A Troubled Sense of Immensity.* Washington, D.C.: Island Press, 2007.

Arnold, Elizabeth. "Divvying Up the Mighty Colorado." National Public Radio, August 27, 2003. www.npr.org/programs/atc/features/2003/aug/water/part2.html.

Bureau of Reclamation, Lower Colorado Region. "The Law of the River." www.usbr.gov/lc/region/g1000/lawofrvr.html.

Cadillac Desert: Water and the Transformation of Nature—An American Nile. Jon Else and Linda Harrar, dirs. and prods. Jon Else, Sandra Postel, and Marc Reisner, writs. Columbia-TriStar Television PBS Home Video, 1997.

Fradkin, Phillip L. *A River No More: The Colorado River and the West.* New York: Knopf, 1981.

Hundley, Norris, Jr. *The Great Thirst.* Berkeley: University of California Press, 2001.

———. "The Politics of Reclamation: California, the Federal Government, and the Origin of the Boulder Canyon Act—A Second Look." *California Historical Quarterly,* vol. 52, no. 4, Winter 1973.

———. *Water and the West: The Colorado River Compact and the Politics of Water in the American West.* Berkeley: University of California Press, 2009.

———. "The West against Itself: The Colorado River—An Institutional History." In *New Courses for the Colorado River,* Gary Weatherford and Lee Brown, eds. Albuquerque: University of New Mexico Press, 1986.

Udall, Morris K. "Selected Speeches: Countdown on the Colorado, Town Hall, Los Angeles, California, December 19, 1967." Reprint of speech in *Congressman's Report,* January 15, 1968. vol. VII, no. 1.

CHAPTER 5: DAM NATION

Michael Hiltzik's *Colossus: Hoover Dam and the Making of the American Century* is thoroughly researched and skillfully told. Joseph Stevens's *Hoover Dam: An American Adventure* contains a compelling account of how and why the monumental public-service project was built. David Macauley's *Building Big* is a wonderfully fun book for children and adults; its fantastic illustrations give a sense of the stunning scale of megadams and reveal important details, such as spillway gates. In *The White Album*, Joan Didion offers a clever postmodern take on America's obsession with mighty waterworks and its dream of controlling nature.

FDR's energetic expansion of the reclamation program during the Great Depression is expertly explained in the "Go-Go Years" chapter in Marc Reisner's *Cadillac Desert* and in Donald Worster's *Rivers of Empire*.

For information about water development in California's Central Valley (and for all things related to California water until 1979), *The California Water Atlas* is a great resource. I am a lifelong aficionado of atlases, and this is one of the finest I have ever had the pleasure to peruse.

The rivalry between the Bureau of Reclamation and the Army Corps of Engineers is meticulously chronicled in the "Rivals in Crime" chapter in *Cadillac Desert*. Arthur Maass's *Muddy Waters*, a classic analysis of public policy by a consummate political scientist, is well researched, well reasoned, and deeply critical of the Army Corps of Engineers. Its account of the battle over the Tulare Basin, with all the waste of money and wanton destruction of natural resources because two bureaucracies were at odds with each other, is enough to make one wonder if American water policy could possibly have been more flawed. The book's foreword, written by former secretary of the interior Harold Ickes, is an absolutely scathing critique of the Corps.

Deserts on the March, Paul Sears's classic analysis of the Dust Bowl, was a groundbreaking work of ecology that persuaded Americans to take soil conservation and land management seriously. Long before "deforestation," "desertification," and "sustainability" were catchwords, Paul Sears was writing passionately about the destruction of the natural world and what might be done to prevent it.

The Mightiest of Them All by L. Vaughn Downs is chockfull of fascinating historical photos and blueprints related to the building of Grand Coulee Dam, but its exhaustive mass of technical details is best avoided by those not in possession of a civil engineering degree. Paul Pitzer's *Grand Coulee* takes a close look at the backgrounds and motivations of the people who brought the monumental project into being.

"A Great Loneliness of Spirit" by Charles Wilkinson and Daniel Conner in *Western Water Made Simple* is an excellent overview of the decimated Columbia River salmon and steelhead runs.

Best, Allen. "Colorado's Thirsty Suburbs Get the State into Trouble." *High Country News*, October 13, 2003.

Burke, Adam. "River of Dreams." *High Country News*, September 24, 2001.

Cadillac Desert: Water and the Transformation of Nature—The Mercy of Nature. Jon Else and Linda Harrar, dirs. and prods. Jon Else, Sandra Postel, and Marc Reisner, writs. Columbia-TriStar Television PBS Home Video, 1997.

Cannon, Brian Q. *Remaking the Agrarian Dream: New Deal Rural Resettlement in the Mountain West.* Albuquerque: University of New Mexico Press, 1996.

Didion, Joan. *The White Album.* New York: Simon and Schuster, 1979.

Downs, L. Vaughn. *The Mightiest of Them All: Memories of Grand Coulee Dam.* New York: ASCE Press, 1993.

Dunar, Andrew J., and Dennis McBride. *Building Hoover Dam: An Oral History of the Great Depression.* New York: Twayne Publishers, 1993.

Eliot, T. S. *Four Quartets.* New York: Harcourt, Brace and World, 1971.

Elwha Watershed Information Resource. "History of Elwha and Glines Canyon Dams." www.elwhainfo.org/elwha-river-watershed/dam-removal/history-elwha-and-glines-canyon-dams.

Fradkin, Phillip L. *A River No More: The Colorado River and the West.* New York: Knopf, 1981.

Freeland, Kathleen B. "Examining the Politics of Reclamation: The 1944 Acreage Limitation Debate in Congress." *The Historian*, vol. 67, iss. 2, June 22, 2005.

Grossman, Elizabeth. *Watershed: The Undamming of America.* Washington, D.C.: Counterpoint, 2002.

Guthrie, Woody. "Ballad of the Great Grand Coulee." In *Roll on Columbia: The Columbia River Songs.* Bill Murlin, ed. Portland, Ore.: Bonneville Power Administration, 1987.

Hiltzik, Michael. *Colossus: Hoover Dam and the Making of the American Century.* New York: Free Press, 2010.

Hundley, Norris, Jr. *Dividing the Waters: A Century of Controversy between the United States and Mexico.* Berkeley: University of California Press, 1966.

———. "The West against Itself: The Colorado River—An Institutional History." In *New Courses for the Colorado River.* Gary Weatherford and Lee Brown, eds. Albuquerque: University of New Mexico Press, 1986.

Jackson, Donald C. *Great American Bridges and Dams.* New York: Wiley 1988.

Kahrl, William L., project dir. and ed., et al. *The California Water Atlas.* Los Altos, Calif.: William Kaufman, 1979.

"Labor: Hoover Dam Strike." *Time*, August 24, 1931.

Maass, Arthur. *Muddy Waters: The Army Engineers and the Nation's Rivers.* New York: Da Capo Press, 1974.

Maass, Arthur, and Raymond L. Anderson. *. . . and the Desert Shall Rejoice: Conflict, Growth, and Justice in Arid Environments.* Cambridge, Mass.: MIT Press, 1978.

Macauley, David. *Building Big.* Boston: Houghton Mifflin, 2000.

"Man-Made River Pierces the Great Divide." *Popular Science*, September 1947.

Mann, Dean E. *The Politics of Water in Arizona.* Tucson: University of Arizona Press, 1963.

Miller, Char, ed. *Water in the 21st-Century West: A* High Country News *Reader.* Corvallis: Oregon State University Press, 2009.

Miller, Joaquin. *Unwritten History: Life among the Modocs.* A. H. Rosenus, ed. and intro. Eugene, Ore.: Orion Press, 1972 (originally published in 1873).

Miller, Leslie A. "The Battle That Squanders Billions." *Saturday Evening Post,* May 14, 1949.

Morgan, Arthur E. *Dams and Other Disasters: A Century of the Army Corps of Engineers in Civil Works.* Boston: Porter Sargent, 1971.

Pisani, Donald J. *From the Family Farm to Agribusiness: The Irrigation Crusade in California and the West, 1850–1931.* Berkeley: University of California Press, 1984.

Pitzer, Paul C. *Grand Coulee: Harnessing a Dream.* Pullman: Washington State University Press, 1994.

Reisner, Marc. *Cadillac Desert: The American West and Its Disappearing Water.* New York: Penguin, 1993.

Sears, Paul. *Deserts on the March.* Washington, D.C.: Island Press, 1988 (originally published in 1935).

Steinbeck, John. *The Grapes of Wrath.* New York: Viking Press, 1958 (originally published in 1939).

Stevens, Joseph E. *Hoover Dam: An American Adventure.* Norman: University of Oklahoma Press, 1990.

Taylor, Paul S. "Central Valley Project: Water and Land." *Western Political Quarterly* 2, 1949.

———. "Excess Land Law on the Kern? A Study of Law and Administration of Public Principle vs. Private Interest." *California Law Review*, vol. 46, no. 2, 1958.

"This Century's Top Ten Construction Projects." *Seattle Daily Journal of Commerce*, December 9, 1999.

Tyler, Daniel. *The Last Water Hole in the West: The Colorado–Big Thompson Project and the Northern Colorado Water Conservancy District.* Niwot: University Press of Colorado, 1992.

US Department of the Interior, Bureau of Reclamation. "Colorado–Big Thompson Project." www.usbr.gov/projects/Project.jsp?proj_Name=Colorado-Big+Thompson+ Project.

US Department of the Interior, Bureau of Reclamation, Lower Colorado Region. "The Colorado River and Hoover Dam: Facts and Figures." www.usbr.gov/lc/region/pao/ brochures/faq.html.

US Department of the Interior, Bureau of Reclamation, Lower Colorado Region. "Hoover Dam." www.usbr.gov/lc/hooverdam/History/storymain.html.

Wilkinson, Charles F., and Daniel Keith Conner. "A Great Loneliness of Spirit." In *Western Water Made Simple,* Ed Marston, ed. Washington, D.C.: Island Press, 1987.

Williams, Albert Nathaniel. *The Water and the Power: Development of the Five Great Rivers of the West.* New York: Duell, Sloan and Pearce, 1951.

Wolf, Donald E. *Big Dams and Other Dreams: The Six Companies Story.* Norman: University of Oklahoma Press, 1996.

Worster, Donald. *Dust Bowl: The Southern Plains in the 1930s.* New York: Oxford University Press, 1979.

———. *Rivers of Empire: Water, Aridity and the Growth of the American West.* New York: Pantheon, 1985.

———. *Under Western Skies.* New York: Oxford University Press, 1992.

CHAPTER 6: WHAT WE HAVE LOST

Russell Martin's *A Story That Stands Like a Dam* tells what can be an emotionally charged story with total objectivity. This is an admirable achievement, and the book is a great starting point for anyone curious to explore Glen Canyon's labyrinthine world of politics and controversy. *Glen Canyon: A Dam, Water and the West,* a PBS documentary produced and directed by Ken Verdoia, is also an excellent resource that provides an unbiased explanation of how the controversial dam came to be.

Wallace Stegner's essay "Glen Canyon Submersus," in which he reminisces about camping "under cliffs that whispered with the sound of flowing water" in the days before the canyon drowned, is a poignant reminder of what was lost when the reservoir filled.

John McPhee's *Encounters with the Archdruid* is my favorite book related to the Glen Canyon Dam controversy. The chapter about Floyd

Dominy and David Brower is one of the best things McPhee has ever written—and that's saying something. The landmark 1963 *Arizona v. California* Supreme Court decision is thoroughly explained in *Water and the West* by Norris Hundley Jr. Hundley contends that the Court committed a grave historical error in its decision; he makes a fascinating argument that, unfortunately, stretches beyond the scope of this book.

Matt Jenkins's *High Country News* article "Seeking the Water Jackpot" is an excellent exploration of how reserved tribal rights affect the Navajo Nation and could alter established water rights throughout the West. Over the years, Jenkins and other *High Country News* reporters have written many dozens of well-researched articles on water in the West, all of them insightful and of great value both to general readers and to western water specialists.

Adler, Robert W. *Restoring Colorado River Ecosystems: A Troubled Sense of Immensity.* Washington, D.C.: Island Press, 2007.

Arnold, Craig Anthony, and Leigh A. Jewell, eds. *Beyond Litigation: Case Studies in Water Rights Disputes.* Washington, D.C.: Environmental Law Institute, 2002.

"Bananas on Pikes Peak?" *New York Times*, April 24, 1955.

Brooks, Nathan. "Indian Reserved Water Rights: An Overview." Congressional Research Service, Library of Congress, 2005. www.policyarchive.org/handle/10207/bitstreams/1917.pdf.

Cadillac Desert: Water and the Transformation of Nature—An American Nile. Jon Else and Linda Harrar, dirs. and prods. Jon Else, Sandra Postel, and Marc Reisner, writs. Columbia-TriStar Television PBS Home Video, 1997.

Central Arizona Project. www.cap-az.com.

Cosco, John M. David R. Brower, fore. *Echo Park: Struggle for Preservation.* Boulder, Colo.: Johnson Books, 1995.

Dean, Robert. "'Dam Building Still Had Some Magic Then': Stewart Udall, the Central Arizona Project, and the Evolution of the Pacific Southwest Water Plan, 1963–1968." *Pacific Historical Review*, vol. 66, no. 1, February, 1997.

DeVoto, Bernard. "Shall We Let Them Ruin Our National Parks?" *Saturday Evening Post*, July 22, 1950.

Fonseca, Felicia. "Navajo Lawmakers Approve Water Rights Settlement." *Albuquerque Journal*, November 4, 2010.

Fradkin, Phillip L. *A River No More: The Colorado River and the West.* New York: Knopf, 1981.

Glen Canyon: A Dam, Water and the West. Ken Verdoia, prod. and dir. KUED, 1999. www.kued.org/productions/glencanyon.

Glen Canyon Institute. "David R. Brower." www.glencanyon.org/about/david-brower.

Harvey, Mark W. T. *A Symbol of Wilderness: Echo Park and the American Conservation Movement.* Albuquerque: University of New Mexico Press, 1994.

Hiltzik, Michael. *Colossus: Hoover Dam and the Making of the American Century.* New York: Free Press, 2010.

Hundley, Norris, Jr. *Dividing the Waters: A Century of Controversy between the United States and Mexico.* Berkeley: University of California Press, 1966.

———. *Water and the West: The Colorado River Compact and the Politics of Water in the American West.* Berkeley: University of California Press, 2009.

———. "The West against Itself: The Colorado River—An Institutional History." In *New Courses for the Colorado River,* Gary Weatherford and Lee Brown, eds. Albuquerque: University of New Mexico Press, 1986.

Inskip, Eleanor. *The Colorado River through Glen Canyon before Lake Powell: A Historic Photo Journal, 1872 to 1964.* Moab, Utah: Inskip Ink, 1995.

Jenkins, Matt. "The Colorado River's Sleeping Giant Stirs." *High Country News,* April 28, 2003.

———. "Seeking the Water Jackpot." *High Country News,* March 17, 2008.

Jennings, Jesse D. Donald Fowler, fore. *Glen Canyon: An Archeological Summary.* Salt Lake City: University of Utah Press, 1998.

Kraker, Daniel. "The New Water Czars." *High Country News,* March 15, 2004.

Leydet, Francois. *Time and the River Flowing: Grand Canyon.* San Francisco: Sierra Club, 1964.

Logan, Michael F. *Desert Cities: The Environmental History of Phoenix and Tucson.* Pittsburgh, Pa.: University of Pittsburgh Press, 2006.

Martin, Russell. *A Story That Stands Like a Dam: Glen Canyon and the Struggle for the Soul of the West.* New York: Henry Holt & Co., 1989.

McKinney, Matthew J. "Instream Flow Policy in Montana: A History and Blueprint for the Future." *Public Land Law Review,* vol. 11, 1990.

McPhee, John. *Encounters with the Archdruid.* New York: Farrar, Straus and Giroux, 1971.

Miller, Leslie A. "Dollars into Dust." *Reader's Digest,* May 1955.

Pielou, E. C. *Fresh Water.* Chicago: University of Chicago Press, 1998.

Porter, Eliot. David Brower, ed. and fore. *The Place No One Knew: Glen Canyon on the Colorado.* San Francisco: The Sierra Club, 1966.

Powell, James Lawrence. *Dead Pool: Lake Powell, Global Warming and the Future of Water in the West.* Berkeley: University of California Press, 2008.

Reisner, Marc. *Cadillac Desert: The American West and Its Disappearing Water.* New York: Penguin, 1993.

Shurts, John. *Indian Reserved Water Rights: The Winters Doctrine in its Social and Legal Context, 1880s—1930s.* Norman: University of Oklahoma Press, 2000.

Silva, Cristina. "Interior Secretary Signs Navajo Water Settlement." *Salt Lake Tribune*, December 17, 2010.

Smart, Christopher. "Glen Canyon Dam: 50 Years of Controversy." *Salt Lake Tribune*, May 31, 2007.

Stegner, Wallace. "Glen Canyon Submersus." In *The Sound of Mountain Water*. Garden City, N.Y.: Doubleday, 1969.

Turner, Tom. *Sierra Club: 100 Years of Protecting Nature*. New York: Harry N. Abrams, 1991.

US Department of the Interior, Bureau of Reclamation. *The Colorado River: A Comprehensive Report on the Development of Water Resources*. Washington, D.C.: US Government Printing Office, 1947.

———. *The Colorado River: A Natural Menace Becomes a National Resource*. Washington, D.C.: US Department of the Interior, Bureau of Reclamation, 1946.

———. "Colorado River Storage Project." www.usbr.gov/projects/Project.jsp?proj_Name=Colorado%20River%20Storage%20Project.

———. *Lake Powell, Jewel of the Colorado*. Washington, D.C.: US Government Printing Office, 1965.

Weatherford, Gary, and Lee Brown, eds. *New Courses for the Colorado River*. Albuquerque: University of New Mexico Press, 1986.

Webb, Walter Prescott. "The American West: Perpetual Mirage." *Harper's*, May 1957.

CHAPTER 7: WHEN DAMS FALL

When researching the Teton Dam collapse, I relied mainly on the chapter "Those Who Refuse to Learn . . ." in Marc Reisner's *Cadillac Desert* and Daniel Jack Chasan's article "Another Teton Dam" on the Crosscut website. The book *That Day in June* contains pulse-quickening eyewitness accounts of the disaster.

I gleaned information about President Carter's ill-fated attempt to overhaul western water policy from the *Cadillac Desert* chapter "The Peanut Farmer and the Pork Barrel" and from Phillip Fradkin's *A River No More*.

The narrative of the near-collapse of Glen Canyon Dam I based on T. J. Wolf's gripping *High Country News* article "How Lake Powell Almost Broke Free of Glen Canyon Dam" and James Lawrence Powell's detailed account in *Dead Pool*.

I relied on George Sibley's *High Country News* article "Glen Canyon: Using a Dam to Heal a River" for information about the history of using managed floods in the Grand Canyon to restore the riparian ecosystem. John Weisheit's "A Legal History of Operations at Glen Canyon Dam," which can be read on the On the Colorado website, lists in chronological order the mind-bogglingly long sequence of legal developments governing the operation of Glen Canyon Dam; it succinctly explains the importance of each one and provides links to relevant legal and scientific documents. Information about restoring Glen Canyon can be found on the Glen Canyon Institute website.

Robert W. Adler's *Restoring Colorado River Ecosystems: A Troubled Sense of Immensity* is passionate without being preachy or partisan, and it examines with great clarity and insight the complicated issues related to the deterioration and potential restoration of Colorado River's natural systems.

An explanation of "instream flow" in Sandra Postel's *Last Oasis* clued me in to the importance of that concept; the book *Instream Flow Protection in the West* satisfied my curiosity about the benefits and limitations of applying the concept to western watercourses.

For an example of a wild stream profoundly influencing a person and resulting in a timeless work of art, read Annie Dillard's *Pilgrim at Tinker Creek*. It contains some of the most muscular sentences ever written in English. Hemingway is a ninety-pound weakling next to Dillard.

Edward Abbey bashes Glen Canyon Dam not only in his iconic *The Monkey Wrench Gang* but in *Desert Solitaire,* a work that contains eloquent pleas to preserve wild places, as well as some of the finest descriptions of the Southwest's landscape, wildlife, and weather ever written. It deserves a place on the bookshelf alongside Henry David Thoreau's *Walden* and Aldo Leopold's *A Sand County Almanac*—though Abbey railed against the notion of being a "nature writer" and eschewed such company.

In *The Milagro Beanfield War,* an exuberant romp of a book and a terrific film, an illegally irrigated beanfield in rural New Mexico becomes a symbol for disenfranchised people wresting control of water—and power—from big business and big government.

The Secret Knowledge of Water by Craig Childs is a beautifully crafted meditation on desert water.

Robert Devine's article "The Trouble with Dams," published in *The Atlantic* in 1995, is an excellent introduction to, well, the trouble with dams—it summarizes their myriad economic and environmental problems. Elizabeth Grossman's *Watershed: The Undamming of America* is essential reading for understanding the monumental task of dismantling America's most undesirable dams. For information about dam removal and restoration on the Elwha River, there are two excellent Internet resources: the "Elwha River Restoration" section of the Olympic National Park website and the Elwha Watershed Information Resource website. The Clark Fork Coalition website has comprehensive information about the complicated Milltown Dam Removal and Cleanup Project.

The chapter "The River Was Crouded with Salmon" in Charles Wilkinson's *Crossing the Next Meridian* is a superb piece of writing that clearly explains the ecology and history of salmon and steelhead in the Pacific Northwest. Wilkinson is an expert on laws pertaining to Native Americans; the "Harvesting the April Rivers" chapter in *Crossing the Next Meridian* makes clear the devastating impact of the San Juan–Chama water project on the Jicarrilla Apache and is especially poignant. Also contained in the chapter is an examination of how government-sponsored water projects in the Southwest caused the collapse of traditional Hispanic farming communities while enriching large farm businesses.

Water War in the Klamath Basin by Holly Doremus and A. Dan Tarlock is an in-depth study of an epic clash over western water that involves law, science, Indian tribes, irrigators, federal marshals, and Dick Cheney.

In the flood of recent books about the worldwide water crisis, *When the Rivers Run Dry* by Fred Pearce floats to the top. Pearce, a consummate science journalist, logs time in more than thirty countries uncovering stories about critical water supplies in peril. His interviews with Dan Beard in the chapter "Wonders of the World" are particularly damning to the Bureau of Reclamation's relentless efforts to not only block every river in the West but to also help other countries dam every river on earth.

Abbey, Edward. *Desert Solitaire*. Tucson: University of Arizona Press, 1988 (first published in 1968).

———. *The Monkey Wrench Gang*. New York: Harper Perennial, 2000 (first published in 1975).

Adler, Robert W. *Restoring Colorado River Ecosystems: A Troubled Sense of Immensity.* Washington, D.C.: Island Press, 2007.

American Rivers. www.americanrivers.org.

Andersen, Matthew E. "Grand Canyon Humpback Chub Population Improving." US Department of the Interior, US Geological Survey Fact Sheet 2007-3113. http://pubs.usgs.gov/fs/2007/3113.

Anderson, Mark T., Julie B. Graf, and G. Richard Marzolf. "Controlled Flooding of the Colorado River in Grand Canyon: the Rationale and Data-Collection Planned." US Department of the Interior, US Geological Survey, Fact Sheet FS-089-96. http://water.usgs.gov/wid/FS_089-96/FS_089-96.html.

Babbitt, Bruce. *Cities in the Wilderness: A New Vision of Land Use in America.* Washington, D.C.: Island Press, 2005.

Bates, Sarah F., et al. *Searching out the Headwaters: Change and Rediscovery in Western Water Policy.* Washington, D.C.: Island Press, 1993.

Becker, Jo, and Barton Gellman. "Leaving No Tracks." *Washington Post,* June 27, 2007.

Brower, David R. "Let the River Run Through It." *Sierra Magazine,* March/April 1997. www.sierraclub.org/sierra/199703/brower.asp.

Burke, Adam. "River of Dreams." *High Country News,* September 24, 2001.

Cadillac Desert: Water and the Transformation of Nature—Last Oasis. Jon Else and Linda Harrar, dirs. and prods. Jon Else, Sandra Postel, and Marc Reisner, writs. Columbia-TriStar Television PBS Home Video, 1997.

Cadillac Desert: Water and the Transformation of Nature—Mercy of Nature. Jon Else and Linda Harrar, dirs. and prods. Jon Else, Sandra Postel, and Marc Reisner, writs. Columbia-TriStar Television PBS Home Video, 1997.

Carson, Rachel. *Silent Spring.* Boston: Houghton Mifflin, 1987 (originally published in 1962).

Chasan, Daniel Jack. "Another Teton Dam." *Crosscut,* May 10, 2008. http://crosscut.com/2008/05/10/real-estate/13606/Another-Teton-Dam.

Childs, Craig. *The Secret Knowledge of Water: Discovering the Essence of the American Desert.* Boston: Little, Brown and Company, 2000.

Clark Fork Coalition. "Milltown Dam Removal and Cleanup Project." www.clarkfork.org/water-watch/milltown-dam-removal-and-cleanup-project.html.

Clifford, Frank. "Controlled Flood to Replenish Grand Canyon." *Los Angeles Times,* March 24, 1996.

Committee on Protection and Management of Pacific Northwest Anadromous Salmonids, National Research Council. *Upstream: Salmon and Society in the Pacific Northwest.* Washington, D.C.: National Academy Press, 1996.

Devine, Robert S. "The Trouble with Dams." *The Atlantic,* August 1995.

Dillard, Annie. *Pilgrim at Tinker Creek.* New York: Harper Perennial, 1998.

Doremus, Holly D., and A. Dan Tarlock. *Water War in the Klamath Basin: Macho Law, Combat Biology, and Dirty Politics.* Washington, D.C.: Island Press, 2008.

Downing, Jim. "Elwha Dam Removal Gets Final Go-Ahead." *Seattle Times,* August 6, 2004.

Duncan, David James. *The River Why*. San Francisco: Sierra Club Books, 1983.

Elwha Watershed Information Resource. www.elwhainfo.org.

Environmental Protection Agency. "Milltown Reservoir Sediments." www.epa.gov/region8/superfund/mt/milltown.

Fradkin, Phillip L. *A River No More: The Colorado River and the West*. New York: Knopf, 1981.

Ghiglieri, Michael Patrick. *Canyon*. Tucson: University of Arizona Press, 1992.

Gillilan, David, and Thomas Brown. *Instream Flow Protection: Seeking a Balance in Western Water Use*. Washington, D.C.: Island Press, 1997.

Glen Canyon Institute. www.glencanyon.org.

Glennon, Robert. *Unquenchable: America's Water Crisis and What to Do about It*. Washington, D.C.: Island Press, 2009.

Gloss, S. P., J. E. Lovich, and T. S. Melis, eds. "The State of the Colorado River Ecosystem in Grand Canyon: US Geological Survey Circular 1282." US Geological Survey, 2005. http://pubs.usgs.gov/circ/1282.

Grand Canyon Monitoring and Research Center. US Department of the Interior, US Geological Survey. www.gcmrc.gov.

Grossman, Elizabeth. *Watershed: The Undamming of America*. Washington, D.C.: Counterpoint, 2002.

Halverson, Anders. *An Entirely Synthetic Fish: How Rainbow Trout Beguiled America and Overran the World*. New Haven, Conn.: Yale University Press, 2010.

Hannon, Steven. "The 1983 Flood at Glen Canyon." Glen Canyon Institute, 2003. www.glencanyon.org/publications/hiddenpassage/hp2stev.php.

Hanscom, Greg. "Reclaiming a Lost Canyon." *High Country News*, November 10, 1997.

Harden, Blaine. "U.S. Orders Modification of Klamath River Dams." *Washington Post*, January 31, 2007.

Henetz, Patty. "Glen Canyon Flush Shows Dam Remains a Sand Trap." *Salt Lake Tribune*, February 2, 2010.

Instream Flow Council. www.instreamflowcouncil.org.

Jenkins, Matt. "Peace on the Klamath." *High Country News*, June 23, 2008.

Knudson, Thomas. "Colorado's 'Shrine of Trout Fishing' Is in Danger." *New York Times*, October 23, 1987.

Latham, Stephen E. "Glen Canyon Dam, Arizona: Dam Failure Inundation Study." Denver: US Department of the Interior, Bureau of Reclamation, July, 1988. www.livingrivers.org/pdfs/LRlibrary/DamFailure.pdf.

Lowry, William R. *Dam Politics: Restoring America's Rivers*. Washington, D.C.: Georgetown University Press, 2003.

MacDonnell, Lawrence J., Teresa A. Rice, and Steven J. Shupe. *Instream Flow Protection in the West*. Boulder: Natural Resources Law Center, University of Colorado School of Law, 1989.

Marston, Ed. "Ripples Grow When a Dam Dies." *High Country News*, October 31, 1994.

———. "Water Pressure." *High Country News*, November 20, 2000.

Martin, Philip. "Imperial Valley: Agriculture and Farm Labor." *Changing Face*, vol. 7, no. 1, January 2001.

Max, Kevin. "Interview: David James Duncan." *1859 Magazine*, Autumn 2009.

Nichols, John. *The Milagro Beanfield War*. New York: Henry Holt & Co., 2000.

Nijhuis, Michelle. "A Downside to Downing Dams?" In *Water in the 21st-Century West: A* High Country News *Reader*. Char Miller, ed. Corvallis: Oregon State University Press, 2009.

Pearce, Fred. *When the Rivers Run Dry: Water—The Defining Crisis of the Twenty-First Century*. Boston: Beacon Press, 2006.

Perry, Tony. "Deepening Woes for the Imperial Valley." *Los Angeles Times*, April 27, 2009.

Postel, Sandra. *Last Oasis: Facing Water Scarcity*. New York: W.W. Norton, 1992.

———. *Pillar of Sand: Can the Irrigation Miracle Last?* New York: W.W. Norton, 1999.

Postel, Sandra, and Brian Richter. *Rivers for Life*. Washington, D.C.: Island Press, 2003.

Powell, James Lawrence. "Calamity on the Colorado." *Orion*, July/August, 2010.

———. *Dead Pool: Lake Powell, Global Warming and the Future of Water in the West*. Berkeley: University of California Press, 2008.

Public Broadcasting Service. Eight, KAET, Arizona Stories, "Glen Canyon & Dam." www.azpbs.org/arizonastories/ppedetail.php?id=80.

Reisner, Marc. *Cadillac Desert: The American West and Its Disappearing Water*. New York: Penguin, 1993.

———. "The Fight for Reclamation." In *Water in the West: A* High Country News *Reader*, Char Miller, ed. Corvallis: Oregon State University Press, 2000.

Robbins, Jim. "Montana Dam Is Breached, Slowly, to Restore a Superfund Site." *New York Times*, May 27, 2008.

Rymer, Russ. "Klamath River: Reuniting a River." *National Geographic*, December, 2008.

Sibley, George. "Glen Canyon: Using a Dam to Heal a River." In *Water in the West: A* High Country News *Reader*, Char Miller, ed. Corvallis: Oregon State University Press, 2000.

Sigler, William F., and John W. Sigler. *Fishes of Utah*. Salt Lake City: University of Utah Press, 1996.

Smalley, Ian. "The Teton Dam: Rhyolite Foundation + Loess Core = Disaster." *Geology Today*, vol. 8, iss. 1, January 1992.

Subcommittee on National Parks and Public Lands and Subcommittee on Water and Power of the Committee on Resources, House of Representatives, September 24, 1997. "Joint Hearing on the Sierra Club's Proposal to Drain Lake Powell or Reduce Its Storage Capability." US Government Printing Office, Washington, D.C., 1998.

"Tearing Down the Elwha River Dam." *Popular Mechanics*, February 10, 2006.

Thomas, Janet, et al., eds. *That Day in June: Reflections on the Teton Dam Disaster*. Rexburg, Idaho: Ricks College Press, 1977.

Upper Colorado Endangered Fish Recovery Program. www.coloradoriverrecovery.org.

US Department of the Interior, Bureau of Reclamation. "Challenge at Glen Canyon." Open Video Project, 1996.

———. *Operation of Glen Canyon Dam: Colorado River Storage Project, Final Environmental Impact Statement.* US Government Printing Office, Washington, D.C., 1995.

US Department of the Interior, Bureau of Reclamation, Upper Colorado Region. "Drought in the Upper Colorado River Basin." www.usbr.gov/uc/feature/drought .html.

US Department of the Interior, National Park Service, Olympic National Park. "Elwha River Restoration." www.nps.gov/olym/naturescience/elwha-ecosystem-restoration .htm.

US Geological Survey. "Endangered Humpback Chub Population Increases 50 Percent from 2001 to 2008." USGS Newsroom, April 27, 2009. www.usgs.gov/newsroom/ article.asp?ID=2206.

US Geological Survey, Grand Canyon Monitoring and Research Center. "Humpback Chub." www.gcmrc.gov/research_areas/humpback_chub/humpback_chub_default .aspx.

Wahl, Richard W. *Markets for Federal Water: Subsidies, Property Rights, and the Bureau of Reclamation.* Washington, D.C.: Resources for the Future, 1989.

Waterman, Jonathan. *Running Dry: A Journey from Source to Sea Down the Colorado River.* Washington, D.C.: National Geographic, 2010.

Weisheit, John. "A Legal History of Operations at Glen Canyon Dam." On the Colorado, October 3, 2008. www.onthecolorado.org/articles.cfm?mode=detail &id=1223044403735.

Wilkinson, Charles F. *Crossing the Next Meridian: Land, Water, and the Future of the West.* Washington, D.C.: Island Press, 1992.

Wolf, T. J. "How Lake Powell Almost Broke Free of Glen Canyon Dam." In *Water in the West: A High Country News Reader*, Char Miller, ed. Corvallis: Oregon State University Press, 2000.

Zaslowsky, Dyan. "Two Forks Journal; Coloradans Anxiously Await Decision over a Proposed Dam." *New York Times*, May 12, 1988.

CHAPTER 8: THE WEALTH BELOW

Much of this chapter is based on the work of Robert Glennon, America's groundwater guru. A professor of law and public policy at the University of Arizona, Glennon has written two fine books about water, including *Water Follies*, which makes painfully obvious the problems with reckless groundwater pumping, especially in Arizona's Santa Cruz and San Pedro River basins.

William Ashworth's *Ogallala Blue* is an excellent study of the past, present, and future of the besieged Ogallala aquifer.

"Another Sign of Long-Term Water Worries." *Lincoln Star Journal*, October 7, 2006.
Ashworth, William. *Ogallala Blue: Water and Life on the High Plains.* New York: W.W. Norton & Co., 2006.
Barker, Rocky. "Idaho Gets Smart about Water." In *Water in the 21st-Century West: A High Country News Reader*, Char Miller, ed. Corvallis: Oregon State University Press, 2009.
Barringer, Felicity. "Rising Calls to Regulate California Groundwater." *New York Times*, May 13, 2009.
Burke, Garance. "California's Groundwater Shrinking Because of Agricultural Use." *Christian Science Monitor*, January 4, 2010.
Friends of the San Pedro River. www.sanpedroriver.org/fsprhome.shtml.
Glennon, Robert. *Unquenchable: America's Water Crisis and What to Do about It.* Washington, D.C.: Island Press, 2009.
———. *Water Follies: Groundwater Pumping and the Fate of America's Fresh Waters.* Washington, D.C.: Island Press, 2002.
Hardin, Garrett. "The Tragedy of the Commons." *Science*, vol. 162, no. 3859, December 13, 1968.
Minard, Anne. "Grand Canyon Oases Face Faraway Threats." In *Water in the 21st-Century West: A High Country News Reader*, Char Miller, ed. Corvallis: Oregon State University Press, 2009.
National Aeronautics and Space Administration, Jet Propulsion Laboratory, California Institute of Technology. "NASA Data Reveal Major Groundwater Loss in California." December 14, 2009. www.jpl.nasa.gov/news/news.cfm?release=2009-194.
The Nature Conservancy. "Arizona, San Pedro River." www.nature.org/ourinitiatives/regions/northamerica/unitedstates/arizona/placesweprotect/san-pedro-river.xml.
Opie, John. *Ogallala: Water for a Dry Land.* Lincoln: University of Nebraska Press, 1993.
Pearce, Fred. *When the Rivers Run Dry: Water—The Defining Crisis of the Twenty-First Century.* Boston: Beacon Press, 2006.
Pellegrino, Evan. "Will San Pedro Become a 'River No More?'" *Tombstone Epitaph*, April 27, 2010.
Popper, Deborah Epstein, and Frank J. Popper. "The Great Plains: From Dust to Dust." *Planning*, 1987.
Reisner, Marc. *Cadillac Desert: The American West and Its Disappearing Water.* New York: Penguin, 1993.
"San Pedro River." Center for Biological Diversity. www.biologicaldiversity.org/programs/public_lands/rivers/san_pedro_river/index.html.

US Department of the Interior, Bureau of Land Management. "San Pedro Riparian National Conservation Area." www.blm.gov/az/st/en/prog/blm_special_areas/ ncarea/sprnca.html.

US Geological Survey. "High Plains Regional Ground-Water Study." http://co.water .usgs.gov/nawqa/hpgw/factsheets/DENNEHYFS1.html.

US Geological Survey, Water Science for Schools. "Artesian Water and Artesian Wells." http://ga.water.usgs.gov/edu/gwartesian.html.

de Villiers, Marq. *Water: The Fate of Our Most Precious Resource.* Boston: Houghton Mifflin, 2000.

Williams, Florence. "Plains Sense." *High Country News,* January 15, 2001.

CHAPTER 9: THE NEW NORMAL

Delving into the world of paleoclimate studies is made less daunting by NOAA's website "North American Drought: A Paleo Perspective." Reconstructions of streamflow based on dendrochronology are clearly explained on the "TreeFlow" website. Climate modeling is made accessible to the layperson on geophysicist Richard Seager's website: "Persistent Drought in North America: A Climate Modeling and Paleoclimate Perspective."

The "Synthesis Report Summary for Policymakers" of the Fourth Assessment Report of the Intergovernmental Panel on Climate Change (IPCC) is succinct and accessible, and becoming familiar with it is essential to understanding the future of the West's water resources. It can be read on the IPCC website.

Barnett, Tim P., et al. "Human-Induced Changes in the Hydrology of the Western United States." *Science,* vol. 319, no. 5866, February 22, 2008.

Barnett, Tim P., and David W. Pierce. "Sustainable Water Deliveries from the Colorado River in a Changing Climate." *Proceedings of the National Academy of Sciences,* April 20, 2009. www.pnas.org/content/early/2009/04/17/0812762106.abstract.

———. "When Will Lake Mead Go Dry?" *Water Resources Research,* vol. 44, 2008. www.agu.org/journals/ABS/2008/2007WR006704.shtml.

Barringer, Felicity. "Water Use in Southwest Heads for a Day of Reckoning." *New York Times,* September 27, 2010.

Brown, Barbara. "Climate Variability and the Colorado River Compact: Implications for Responding to Climate Change." In *Societal Responses to Regional Climatic Change: Forecasting by Analogy,* Michael H. Glantz, ed. Boulder, Colo.: Westview Press, 1988.

Committee on the Scientific Bases of Colorado River Basin Water Management, National Research Council. *Colorado River Basin Water Management: Evaluating and Adjusting to Hydroclimatic Variability.* The National Academies Press, 2007. http://books.nap.edu/catalog.php?record_id=11857#toc.

Cooperative Institute for Research in Environmental Science. "Desert Dust Reduces River Flow, Says New Study." September 20, 2010. http://cires.colorado.edu/news/press/2010/dustonsnow.html.

Davis, Mike. "Denial in the Desert." *The Nation*, April 16, 2007.

Finley, Bruce. "CU Study Warns of Scarce Water." *Denver Post*, July 22, 2009.

Human, Katy. "Droughts Cast on Southwest." *Denver Post*, April 6, 2007.

Intergovernmental Panel on Climate Change. http://www.ipcc.ch.

Miller, Leonard. "Dendrochronology." The Ancient Bristlecone Pine. http://www.sonic.net/bristlecone/dendro.html.

Morello, Lauren. "Scientists See the Southwest as First Major U.S. Climate Change Victim." *New York Times*, December 14, 2010.

National Oceanic and Atmospheric Administration Paleoclimatology Program. "North American Drought: A Paleo Perspective." www.ncdc.noaa.gov/paleo/drought/drght_home.html.

National Science Foundation. "Windborne Desert Dust Falls on High Peaks, Dampens Colorado River Runoff." *ScienceDaily*, September 21, 2010. www.sciencedaily.com/releases/2010/09/100920172746.htm.

Nelson, Barry, et al. "In Hot Water: Water Management Strategies to Weather the Effects of Global Warming." National Resources Defense Council, 2007. www.nrdc.org/globalwarming/hotwater/hotwater.pdf.

Painter, Thomas H., et al. "Response of Colorado River Runoff to Dust Radiative Forcing in Snow." *Proceedings of the National Academy of Sciences*, vol. 107, no. 40, October 5, 2010.

Powell, James Lawrence. *Dead Pool: Lake Powell, Global Warming and the Future of Water in the West.* Berkeley: University of California Press, 2008.

Quinlan, Paul. "Lake Mead's Water Level Plunges as 11-Year Drought Lingers." *New York Times*, August 13, 2010.

Rajagopalan, Balaji, et al. "Water Supply Risk on the Colorado River: Can Management Mitigate?" *Water Resources Research*, vol. 45, 2009.

Riccardi, Nicholas. "Dust Storms Speed Snowmelt in Colorado." *Los Angeles Times*, May 24, 2009.

Saunders, Stephen, et al. "Hotter and Drier: The West's Changed Climate." National Resources Defense Council and the Rocky Mountain Climate Organization, March 2008. www.nrdc.org/globalwarming/west/west.pdf.

Saunders, Stephen, and Maureen Maxwell. "Less Snow, Less Water: Climate Disruption in the West." The Rocky Mountain Climate Organization, 2005. www.rockymountainclimate.org/website%20pictures/Less%20Snow%20Less%20Water.pdf.

Scripps News, Scripps Institution of Oceanography. "Climate Change Means Shortfalls in Colorado River Water Deliveries." April 20, 2009. http://scrippsnews.ucsd.edu/ Releases/?releaseID=977.

———. "Lake Mead Could Be Dry by 2021." February 12, 2008. http://scrippsnews .ucsd.edu/Releases/?releaseID=876.

Seager, Richard. "Persistent Drought in North America: A Climate Modeling and Paleoclimate Perspective." Lamont-Doherty Earth Observatory of Columbia University. http://www.ldeo.columbia.edu/res/div/ocp/drought.

Steinbeck, John. *The Grapes of Wrath*. New York: Viking Press, 1958 (originally published in 1939).

Stevens, William K. "Severe Ancient Droughts: A Warning to California." *New York Times*, July 19, 1994.

Stine, Scott. "Extreme and Persistent Drought in California and Patagonia in Mediaeval Time." *Nature*, vol. 369, 1994.

Streater, Scott. "Climate Change, Water Shortages Conspire to Create 21st Century Dust Bowl." *New York Times*, May 14, 2009.

TreeFlow: Streamflow Reconstructions from Tree Rings. http://treeflow.info.

University of Arizona. "Colorado River Streamflow History Reveals Megadrought Before 1490." *ScienceDaily*, May 18, 2007. www.sciencedaily.com/releases/ 2007/05/070517152428.htm.

Wagner, Frederic H., ed. and principal author. "Preparing for a Changing Climate: The Potential Consequences of Climate Variability and Change." A Report of the Rocky Mountain/Great Basin Regional Assessment Team for the U.S. Global Change Research Program. www.indigodev.com/documents/Rocky_Mtn_Great_ Basin_pcc.pdf.

"Water Worries: The Drying of the West." *The Economist*, January 27, 2011.

Western Water Assessment. "Colorado River Streamflow: A Paleo Perspective." http://wwa.colorado.edu/treeflow/lees/index.html.

———. "WWA's Guide to the IPCC." http://wwa.colorado.edu/climate_change/ipcc .html.

Willoughby, Scott. "Dust, Snow Make for Problematic Mix for Skiers." *Denver Post*, April 20, 2010.

Woodhouse, Connie A., et al. "A 1,200-Year Perspective of 21st Century Drought in Southwestern North America." *Proceedings of the National Academy of Sciences*, vol. 107, no. 50, December 14, 2010.

CHAPTER 10: TAINTED WATERS

E. C. Pielou's *Fresh Water*, Robert Glennon's *Unquenchable*, and Bruce Babbitt's *Cities in the Wilderness* were the sources that most shaped this chapter.

Information about the Red Lady moly mine controversy in Crested Butte, Colorado, can be found on the High Country Citizens' Alliance website. The article "Alaska's Choice: Salmon or Gold" in *National Geographic* provides good background on Alaska's proposed Pebble Mine project. The history of the Atlas uranium mill is explained in detail on the Grand Canyon Trust website.

Reading about bottled water would be about as exciting as reading about western water law, right? Not so. Check out *Bottlemania* by Elizabeth Royte. Her savvy journalism and sparkling prose pop the cap off bottled water.

Alder, Lin. "Cold War Toxin Seeps into Western Water." In *Water in the 21st-Century West: A* High Country News *Reader*, Char Miller, ed. Corvallis: Oregon State University Press, 2009.

Atencio, Ernest. "The Mine That Turned the Red River Blue." *High Country News*, August 28, 2000.

Babbitt, Bruce. *Cities in the Wilderness: A New Vision of Land Use in America.* Washington, D.C.: Island Press, 2005.

Blevins, Jason. "Crested Butte: Coalitions Build to Again Keep Mining Off Beloved Peak." *Denver Post*, December 9, 2007.

Dobb, Edwin. "Alaska's Choice: Salmon or Gold." *National Geographic*, December 2010.

Egan, Dan. "Great Lakes Scourge Infects West." *Milwaukee Journal Sentinel*, February 21, 2009.

Farrell, Patrick. "The Great Salt Lake's Dirty Little Secret." In *Water in the 21st-Century West: A* High Country News *Reader*, Char Miller, ed. Corvallis: Oregon State University Press, 2009.

Finley, Bruce. "Traces of Cosmetics, Medications Create Concerns for Water Supplies." *Denver Post*, September 10, 2010.

Freiderici, Peter. "Facing the Yuck Factor." In *Water in the 21st-Century West: A* High Country News *Reader*, Char Miller, ed. Corvallis: Oregon State University Press, 2009.

Glennon, Robert. *Unquenchable: America's Water Crisis and What to Do about It.* Washington, D.C.: Island Press, 2009.

Grand Canyon Trust. "History of the Atlas Mine Project." www.grandcanyontrust.org/utah/uranium_history.php.

Grunwald, Michael. "Babbitt Pushes Tough Rules On Metal-Mining in Final Days." *Washington Post*, January 18, 2001.

High Country Citizens' Alliance. www.hccaonline.org

Leitzell, Kat. "Smoke Alarm." In *Water in the 21st-Century West: A* High Country News *Reader*, Char Miller, ed. Corvallis: Oregon State University Press, 2009.

McCarthy, Neil, prod. "The Battle of King Salmon—Part Two." www.bbc.co.uk/
worldservice/documentaries/2010/11/101104_doc_salmon_battle_part2.shtml.

Meltzer, Erica. "Increased Flood Risk Follows Wildfires." *Boulder Daily Camera,*
March 2, 2010.

Miller, Char, ed. *River Basins of the American West: A* High Country News *Reader.*
Corvallis: Oregon State University Press, 2009.

———. ed. *Water in the 21st-Century West: A* High Country News *Reader.* Corvallis:
Oregon State University Press, 2009.

Montana Environmental Information Center. "Ban on Cyanide Mining." http://meic
.org/mining/hardrock-mining/cyanide_mining/ban-on-cyanide-mining.

Murphy, Kim. "Alaska Fishermen Circle Their Boats to Fight Mine." *Los Angeles Times,*
August 4, 2010.

———. "Cyanide's Bitter End in Mining for Gold." *Los Angeles Times,* November 17,
1998.

Natural Resources Defense Council. "Bottled Water: Pure Drink or Pure Hype?"
www.nrdc.org/water/drinking/bw/bwinx.asp.

Nijhuis, Michelle. "A Chemical Cocktail Pollutes Western Water." In *Water in the
21st-Century West: A* High Country News *Reader,* Char Miller, ed. Corvallis:
Oregon State University Press, 2009.

Pearce, Fred. *When the Rivers Run Dry: Water—The Defining Crisis of the Twenty-First
Century.* Boston: Beacon Press, 2006.

Penn and Teller. *Bullshit!* "Bottled Water." Season 1, Episode 7. www.sho.com/site/ptbs/
episodes.do?episodeid=118363&ep=107.

Pielou, E. C. *Fresh Water.* Chicago: University of Chicago Press, 1998.

Rappold, R. Scott. "Fight over Red Lady, Mining Continues in Crested Butte." *Colorado
Springs Gazette,* July 5, 2010.

Robbins, Jim. "Bark Beetles Kill Millions of Acres of Trees in the West." *New York
Times,* November 17, 2008.

Roosevelt, Margot. "Alaskan Economy Faces a Fork in the River." *Los Angeles Times,*
September 1, 2007.

Royte, Elizabeth. *Bottlemania: How Water Went on Sale and Why We Bought It.* New York:
Bloomsbury, 2008.

Running, Steven W. "Is Global Warming Causing More, Larger Wildfires?" *Science,*
vol. 313, no. 5789, August 18, 2006.

Schneider, Andrew. "A Wounded Mountain Spewing Poison." *Seattle Post-Intelligencer,*
June 12, 2001. http://oseattlepi.com/specials/mining/27076_lodgepole12.shtml.

Sellers, Kathleen, et al. *Perchlorate: Environmental Problems and Solutions.* Boca Raton,
Fla.: CRC Press, 2007.

Snider, Laura. "Rehab Could Take Years." *Boulder Daily Camera,* September 19, 2010.

"Study: Bottled Water No Better Than Tap Water." *USA Today,* May 2, 2001.

Tavares, Stephanie. "Quagga Mussels a Toxic Threat to Lake Mead." *Las Vegas Sun,*
November 9, 2009.

Underwood, Anne. "Rivers of Doubt." *Newsweek,* June 4, 2007.

University of Colorado at Boulder. "Gender-Bending Fish Problem in Colorado Creek Mitigated by Treatment Plant Upgrade." *ScienceDaily*, June 22, 2010. www.sciencedaily.com/releases/2010/06/100621125139.htm.

Westerling, A. L., et al. "Warming and Earlier Spring Increase Western U.S. Forest Wildfire Activity." *Science*, vol. 313, no. 5789, August 18, 2006.

Williams, A. Park, et al. "Forest Responses of Increasing Aridity and Warmth in the Southwestern United States." *Proceedings of the National Academy of Sciences*, vol. 107, no. 50, December 14, 2010.

Woodbury, Richard, and Frederic Golden. "Environment: Battle over the Red Lady." *Time*, June 29, 1981.

CHAPTER 11: SILT, SALT, AND CIVILIZATION

James Lawrence Powell's *Dead Pool* contains a succinct account of irrigation societies across the span of human history and provides insight into the problems that have plagued them. *Keepers of the Spring* and *When the Rivers Run Dry* by Fred Pearce, *Water* by Marq de Villiers, and *Water* by Steven Solomon offer fascinating background on ancient irrigation societies.

Donald Worster's *Rivers of Empire* is a classic study of America's hydraulic civilization in the West; his lesser-known *Under Western Skies* is every bit as insightful.

Jerry Howard's "Hohokam Legacy: Desert Canals" on the Water History.org website is a fine introduction to Hohokam irrigation achievements. Craig Childs's *High Country News* article "Phoenix Falling?" is a sobering investigation of the similarities between ancient Hohokam civilization and modern-day Phoenix.

Childs, Craig. "Phoenix Falling?" *High Country News*, April 16, 2007.

Glennon, Robert. *Unquenchable: America's Water Crisis and What to Do about It.* Washington, D.C.: Island Press, 2009.

Howard, Jerry B. "Hohokam Legacy: Desert Canals." WaterHistory.org. www.waterhistory.org/histories/hohokam2.

Ingebretsen, Richard J. "Sedimental Journey: A Grim Prospect for Lake Powell." Glen Canyon Institute, August 1998. www.glencanyon.org/publications/hiddenpassage/hp98rich.php.

Jacobsen, Thorkild, and Robert M. Adams. "Salt and Silt in Ancient Mesopotamian Agriculture." *Science*, vol. 128, no. 3334, November 21, 1958.

MacDonald, Glen M. "Water, Climate Change, and Sustainability in the Southwest." *Proceedings of the National Academy of Sciences*, vol. 107, no. 50, December 14, 2010.

Pearce, Fred. *Keepers of the Spring: Reclaiming Our Water in an Age of Globalization.* Washington, D.C.: Island Press, 2004.

———. *When the Rivers Run Dry: Water—The Defining Crisis of the Twenty-First Century.* Boston: Beacon Press, 2006.

Postel, Sandra. *Pillar of Sand: Can the Irrigation Miracle Last?* New York: W.W. Norton, 1999.

Powell, James Lawrence. *Dead Pool: Lake Powell, Global Warming and the Future of Water in the West.* Berkeley: University of California Press, 2008.

Solomon, Steven. *Water: The Epic Struggle for Wealth, Power, and Civilization.* New York: HarperCollins, 2010.

Tennesen, Michael. "A River Runs Through Them." *National Parks*, vol. 80, no. 1, Winter 2006.

Twain, Mark. *Life on the Mississippi.* New York: Harper & Row Publishers, 1917 (originally published in 1883).

de Villiers, Marq. *Water: The Fate of Our Most Precious Resource.* Boston: Houghton Mifflin, 2000.

Worster, Donald. *Rivers of Empire: Water, Aridity and the Growth of the American West.* New York: Pantheon, 1985.

———. *Under Western Skies.* New York: Oxford University Press, 1992.

———. *The Wealth of Nature: Environmental History and the Ecological Imagination.* New York: Oxford University Press, 1993.

CHAPTER 12: WATER IN THE TWENTY-FIRST-CENTURY WEST

Water in the 21st-Century West contains a sampling of stories from *High Country News:* "a nonprofit media organization that covers the important issues and stories that define the American West." The book provides an exemplary overview of the many water issues affecting the contemporary western United States, as does its companion volume, *River Basins of the American West.* The *High Country News* website is also a terrific resource.

Jon Gertner's article "The Future Is Drying Up" in the *New York Times Magazine* is a fine introduction to water issues in the contemporary West and includes an explanation of the Prairie Waters project in Aurora, Colorado.

James Lawrence Powell's *Dead Pool* is a worthy successor to *Cadillac Desert* and is a must-read for all serious students of water in the West.

Aldo Leopold's essay "The Green Lagoons" in *A Sand County Almanac* is a classic piece of writing by a pioneering ecologist and passionate proponent of wilderness conservation. Charles Bergman's *Red Delta* celebrates wetlands reborn in the Colorado River Delta. The book is not so much a dirge for what has been destroyed as it is a loving tribute to what remains, as well as a plan to expand upon the serendipitous restoration of the Cienega. The book's background on paleontology in the delta region is particularly engrossing, and its vivid photographs of landscapes and wildlife illustrate what is at stake in reviving Leopold's land of "a hundred green lagoons."

While learning about the willow flycatcher, I came across the Cornell Lab of Ornithology's All About Birds website. This is an electronic resource certain to make even the most hardened Luddite a believer in the power of technology to inspire passion in people about the natural world.

Searching out the Headwaters, a book published by the Natural Resources Law Center of the University of Colorado School of Law, is a good introduction to, in the words of its authors, "the depth of the chasm between western water policy and what the modern West demands of it." Charles Wilkinson's *Crossing the Next Meridian* is a work elegant and profound that explores the vast distance between modern values and traditional western natural resource law and policies.

Bruce Babbitt's *Cities in the Wilderness* offers a roadmap for revising the land and water policies of a changing West, and Robert Glennon's *Unquenchable* provides a blueprint for overhauling America's water policies to bring them in line with modern science, shifting values, and increasing scarcity.

Jared Diamond's *Guns, Germs and Steel* and *Collapse* contain compelling studies of the limits imposed by nature on humans and how civilizations, if not prepared to live within those limits, fail.

There is no wiser voice on the ethics of how we treat our land and water and each other than Wendell Berry. *The Art of the Commonplace: The Agrarian Essays of Wendell Berry* is a fine introduction to his ideas.

"How to Conserve Water and Use It Effectively" on the Environmental Protection Agency's website has practical tips to help people become part of the solution to the West's water crisis.

General Sources

Environmental Protection Agency. "How to Conserve Water and Use It Effectively." http://water.epa.gov/polwaste/nps/chap3.cfm.

Glennon, Robert. *Unquenchable: America's Water Crisis and What to Do About It.* Washington, D.C.: Island Press, 2009.

High Country News. http://www.hcn.org.

Kingsolver, Barbara. "Water Is Life." *National Geographic,* April 2010.

Miller, Char, ed. *River Basins of the American West: A* High Country News *Reader.* Corvallis: Oregon State University Press, 2009.

———. *Water in the 21st-Century West: A* High Country News *Reader.* Corvallis: Oregon State University Press, 2009.

———. *Water in the West: A* High Country News *Reader.* Corvallis: Oregon State University Press, 2000.

Pearce, Fred. *When the Rivers Run Dry: Water—The Defining Crisis of the Twenty-First Century.* Boston: Beacon Press, 2006.

Postel, Sandra. *Last Oasis: Facing Water Scarcity.* New York: W.W. Norton, 1992.

———. *Pillar of Sand: Can the Irrigation Miracle Last?* New York: W.W. Norton, 1999.

Rogers, Peter, and Susan Leal. *Running Out of Water: The Looming Crisis and Solutions to Conserve Our Most Precious Resource.* New York: Palgrave Macmillan, 2010.

Royte, Elizabeth. "The Last Drop." *National Geographic,* April 2010.

Western Water Assessment. Announcements—Water and Climate in the News. http://wwa.colorado.edu/about_us/announcements/inthenews.html.

Wilkinson, Charles F. *Crossing the Next Meridian: Land, Water, and the Future of the West.* Washington, D.C.: Island Press, 1992.

Agriculture

American Museum of Natural History. "Water Works, Beef: A Thirsty 'Crop.'" www.amnh.org/exhibitions/water/?section=waterworks&page=waterworks_hii.

Bali, Khaled M. "Ag. Water Quality—Frequently Asked Questions." University of California Cooperative Extension, Imperial County. http://ceimperial.ucdavis.edu/Custom_Program275/Water_Quality_FAQs.

Best, Allen. "Colorado's Thirsty Suburbs Get the State into Trouble." In *Water in the 21st-Century West: A* High Country News *Reader,* Char Miller, ed. Corvallis: Oregon State University Press, 2009.

"The Browning of America." *Newsweek,* February 23, 1981.

Donahue, Debra L. *The Western Range Revisited: Removing Livestock from Public Lands to Conserve Native Biodiversity.* Norman: University of Oklahoma Press, 1999.

Erie, Steven P. *Beyond Chinatown: The Metropolitan Water District, Growth, and the Environment in Southern California.* Stanford, Calif.: Stanford University Press, 2006.

Fergusson, Harvey. *Rio Grande.* New York: Tudor, 1933.

Gleick, Peter H. "Making Every Drop Count." *Scientific American*, vol. 284, iss. 2, February 2001.

Goodgame, Dan, James Willwerth, Richard Woodbury, and Dennis Wyss. "Just Enough to Fight Over." *Time*, July 4, 1988.

Horgan, Paul. *Great River: The Rio Grande in North American History.* New York: Rinehart, 1954.

Horsley, Scott. "Water as a Cash Crop." National Public Radio, August 29, 2003. www.npr.org/programs/atc/features/2003/aug/water/part4.html.

Jenkins, Matt. "California Strikes a Water Truce." *High Country News*, October 27, 2003.

———. "California's Water Binge Skids to a Halt." *High Country News*, January 20, 2003.

Lifsher, Marc. "Why Shipping Water to San Diego Has Been Harder Than It Looked." *Wall Street Journal*, July 1, 1998.

Murphy, Dean E. "Agreement in West Will Send Farms' Water to Urban Areas." *New York Times*, October 17, 2003.

Pacific Institute. "Restoration Project Critical to Salton Sea's Future." www.pacinst.org/reports/saltonsea.

Perry, Tony. "Feud over River Water Simmering." *Los Angeles Times*, November 7, 2005.

———. "2 Lawsuits Fault New Water Deal." *Los Angeles Times*, November 12, 2003.

Pimentel, David, Laura Westra, and Reed F. Noss, eds. *Ecological Integrity: Integrating Environment, Conservation and Health.* Washington, D.C.: Island Press, 2000.

Roller, William. "IDD Tasked with Crafting Realistic Salton Sea Plan." *Imperial Valley Press*, January 19, 2011.

Rothman, Hal. *Neon Metropolis: How Las Vegas Started the Twenty-First Century.* New York: Routledge, 2002.

———. "Water and the Future of Las Vegas." In *Water in the West: A High Country News Reader*, Char Miller, ed. Corvallis: Oregon State University Press, 2000.

Steffen, David. "Imperial County, Air Pollution Control District's Federal Lawsuit Challenges Imperial Irrigation District Water Transfer." *Imperial Valley Press*, October 17, 2009.

Water Education Foundation. "California Water Facts." (This fascinating brochure can be ordered from the Water Education Foundation website.) www.watereducation.org.

"Water: Sin Aqua Non." *The Economist*, April 8, 2009.

Woodka, Chris. "Ag Water Transfer Solutions Begin to Surface." *The Pueblo Chieftain*, February 3, 2009.

Wuerthner, George, and Mollie Matteson, eds. *Welfare Ranching: The Subsidized Destruction of the American West*. Washington, D.C.: Island Press, 2002.

Growth, Markets, and Money

Anderson, Terry L., and Pamela S. Snyder. "Priming the Invisible Pump." PERC Policy Series, Property & Environment Research Center, February 1997. www.perc.org/articles/article746.php.

Barlow, Maude. *Blue Covenant: The Global Water Crisis and the Coming Battle for the Right to Water*. New York: New Press, 2007.

McCoy, Charles, and G. Pascal Zachary. "A Bass Play in Water May Presage Big Shift in Distribution." *Wall Street Journal*, July 11, 1997.

Plantico, Cailyn. "The Blue Line Amendment and Enchanted Mesa Purchase: Setting the Stage for Boulder's Open Space Program." City of Boulder, Colorado, Open Space & Mountain Parks Program, September 2008. www.bouldercolorado.gov/files/openspace/pdf_education/e_mesa_purchase.pdf.

Workman, James G. *Heart of Dryness: How the Last Bushmen Can Help Us Endure the Coming Age of Permanent Drought*. New York: Walker & Company, 2009.

Energy

Barrick. Kenneth A. "Protecting the Geyser Basins of Yellowstone National Park: Toward a New National Policy for a Vulnerable Environmental Resource." *Environmental Management*, vol. 45, no. 1, September, 2009.

Biello, David. "What the Frack? Natural Gas from Subterranean Shale Promises U.S. Energy Independence—With Environmental Costs." *Scientific American*, March 30, 2010.

Clutter, Ted J. "Absolute Commitment: Geothermal Operations at The Geysers." *Renewable Energy World North America*, April 27, 2010.

Environmental Protection Agency, Water Sense. "Water Efficiency." www.epa.gov/WaterSense/our_water/why_water_efficiency.html.

"GAO: More Research Needed on Oil Shale, Water." *Salt Lake Tribune*, November 29, 2010.

GasLand. Josh Fox, dir. and writ. HBO Documentary Films, 2010. www.gaslandthemovie.com

Giles, Jim. "Methane Quashes Green Credentials of Hydropower." *Nature* 444, November 30, 2006.

Graham-Rowe, Duncan. "Hydroelectric Power's Dirty Secret Revealed." *New Scientist*, February 24, 2005.

Harmon, Gary. "Water There to Start Oil Shale Work, GAO Says." *Grand Junction Daily Sentinel*, November 30, 2010.

Jaffe, Mark. "Oil-Shale Plans Create Ripple." *Denver Post*, March 19, 2009.

Jalloh, Abubakar. "The Scientist: David Pimentel." *Cornell Daily Sun*, February 11, 2009.

Lewis, Judith. "Watts of Power." *High Country News*, October 26, 2009.

Lustgarten, Abrahm. "The FRAC Act Under Attack." *Salon*, July 14, 2009. www.salon
.com/news/environment/feature/2009/07/14/gas.

MacDonnell, Lawrence J., et al. "Water on the Rocks: Oil Shale Water Rights in
Colorado." Western Resource Advocates, 2009. www.westernresourceadvocates.org/
land/wotrreport/index.php.

Northern Plains Resource Council. "Judge Rules Coal Bed Methane
Wastewater Ponds Unconstitutional." http://northernplains.onenw.org/
judge-rules-coal-bed-methane-wastewater-ponds-unconstitutional.

Powder River Basin Resource Council. "Coalbed Methane." www.powderriverbasin.org/
coalbed-methane.

Simon, Stephanie. "Oil, Water Are Volatile Mix in West." *Wall Street Journal*, March 19,
2009.

Sutor, Julie. "Report: Climate Change to Have Major Impacts on Western Water." *Aspen
Times*, July 14, 2010.

Tellinghuisen, Stacy, and Jana Milford. "Protecting the Lifeline of the West." Western
Resource Advocates and Environmental Defense Fund, 2010. www.western
resourceadvocates.org/water/lifeline.php.

Urbina, Ian. "Drilling Down: Regulation Lax as Gas Wells' Tainted Water Hits Rivers."
New York Times, February 26, 2011.

US Geological Survey, Water Science for Schools. "Challenge Question #1 How Much
Water Does It Take to Grow a Hamburger?" http://ga.water.usgs.gov/edu/sc1.html.

US Geological Surveys Program, Energy Resource Surveys Program, USGS Fact
Sheet FS-019-97. "Coalbed Methane—An Untapped Energy Resource and
Environmental Concern." http://energy.usgs.gov/factsheets/Coalbed/coalmeth.html.

Runoff, Rain Harvesting, and Reclaimed Wastewater

Archibold, Randal C. "From Sewage, Added Water for Drinking." *New York Times*,
November 27, 2007.

Brady, Jeff. "Water Wars Out West: Keep What You Catch!" National Public Radio,
June 1, 2009. www.npr.org/templates/story/story.php?storyId=104643521.

California Environmental Protection Agency, Colorado River Basin Regional Water
Quality Control Board. "Introduction to the New River/Mexicali Sanitation
Program." http://web.archive.org/web/20060930122802/http://www.swrcb.ca.gov/
rwqcb7/newriver/nr-intro.html.

California State Water Resources Control Board. "New River Pollution in Mexico, a
Historical Overview." www.swrcb.ca.gov/rwqcb7/water_issues/programs/new_
river/historical/introduction.pdf.

City of Santa Monica, Office of Sustainability and the Environment. "Urban Runoff."
www.smgov.net/departments/ose/categories/urbanRunoff.aspx.

Freiderici, Peter. "Facing the Yuck Factor." In *Water in the 21st-Century West: A* High
Country News *Reader*, Char Miller, ed. Corvallis: Oregon State University Press,
2009.

Johnson, Kirk. "It's Now Legal to Catch a Raindrop in Colorado." *New York Times*, June 28, 2009.

Riccardi, Nicholas. "Who Owns Colorado's Rainwater?" *Los Angeles Times*, March 18, 2009.

Seattle Department of Planning and Development. "Seattle Promotes Rainwater Harvesting for Beneficial Use." April 1, 2008. www.seattle.gov/dpd/news/20080401a.asp.

"Toxic River Becomes Path to USA." *USA Today*, May 11, 2000.

Walsh, Bryan. "Sewage That's Clean Enough to Drink." *Time*, December 16, 2008.

WaterWorld. "Pioneering Water Reuse in the Old West." www.waterworld.com/index/display/article-display/361962/articles/water-wastewater-international/volume-24/issue-2/editorial-focus/pioneering-water-reuse-in-the-old-west.html.

Water Projects

Aurora Water, Prairie Waters Project. http://prairiewaters.org/whatsnew.asp.

Best, Allen. "Can Big Straw Quench Colorado's Thirst?" *Vail Daily*, July 16, 2007.

———. "Drought of 2002 Was the Worst Since 1685 . . . Or So." *Colorado Central Magazine*, February 2004.

———. "Drought Unearths a Water Dinosaur." In *Water in the 21st-Century West: A High Country News Reader*. Char Miller, ed. Corvallis: Oregon State University Press, 2009.

Burkhart, Michelle. "This 'Big Straw' Takes the Cake." *Gunnison Country Times*, February 12, 2009.

Denver Water. "Moffat Collection System Project." www.denverwater.org/Supply Planning/WaterSupplyProjects/Moffat.

Evans, Clay. "Saving South Boulder Creek." *Boulder Daily Camera*, August 11, 2009.

General Accounting Office. *Animas–La Plata Project*. Washington, D.C.: US Government Printing Office, 1995.

Illescas, Carlos. "Aurora Water Project Ahead of Schedule, Below Budget." *Denver Post*, March 15, 2010.

Ingold, John. "Ship the Mississippi to Colorado?" *Denver Post*, March 19, 2009.

Neary, Ben. "Wyoming Worried about Green River Water Grab." *Salt Lake City Tribune*, May 17, 2010.

Satchell, Michael. "The Last Water Fight: A Dam That Won't Die Shows Power of Pork." *U.S. News & World Report*, October 23, 1995.

Snider, Laura. "Gross Reservoir Expansion Could Restore Stream Flows." *Boulder Daily Camera*, August 9, 2009.

———. "Public Expresses Concern over Gross Reservoir Expansion." *Boulder Daily Camera*, January 20, 2011.

———. "Public Input Sought on Gross Reservoir Expansion." *Boulder Daily Camera*, November 30, 2009.

————. "Rep. Jared Polis Expresses Concern over Gross Reservoir Expansion." *Boulder Daily Camera*, February 23, 2010.

Sturgeon, Stephen C. *The Politics of Western Water: The Congressional Career of Wayne Aspinall.* Tucson: University of Arizona Press, 2002.

Zaffos, Joshua. "The Terrifying Saga of the West's Last Big Dam." In *Water in the 21st-Century West: A* High Country News *Reader.* Char Miller, ed. Corvallis: Oregon State University Press, 2009.

Rainmakers

Bergman, Charles. *Red Delta: Fighting for Life at the End of the Colorado River.* Golden, Colo.: Fulcrum Publishing, 2002.

Bohrer, Becky. "Growing Rain." *Missoulian*, May 27, 2002.

Bookwalter, Genevieve. "Desalination Plant Deemed a Success in Santa Cruz." *Santa Cruz Sentinel*, April 13, 2009.

Coleridge, Samuel Taylor. *Rime of the Ancient Mariner.* New York: Dover Publications, 1970 (originally published in *Lyrical Ballads* in 1798).

Cooley, Heather, Peter H Gleick, and Gary Wolff. *Desalination, with a Grain of Salt: A California Perspective.* Oakland, Calif.: Pacific Institute, 2006.

The Cornell Lab of Ornithology, All About Birds. Willow Flycatcher. www. allaboutbirds.org/guide/Willow_Flycatcher/id.

Davis, Tony. "Yuma Desalination Plant to Start Flowing." *Arizona Daily Star*, May 1, 2010.

George, Jayme. "Are Wyoming's Frozen Reservoirs Slipping Away?" *UWyo*, vol. 8, no.1.

Howe, Jeff. "The Great Southwest Salt Saga." *Wired*, iss. 12.11, November 2004.

Johnson, Kirk. "In Battle of Bug vs. Shrub, Score One for the Bird." *New York Times*, June 22, 2010.

————. "War with Riverbank Invader, Waged by Muscle and Munching." *New York Times*, December 26, 2008.

Leopold, Aldo. "The Green Lagoons" in *A Sand County Almanac: With Essays on Conservation from Round River.* New York: Ballantine Books, 1970 (originally published in 1949).

Longinotti, Rick. "Desalination and the Alternatives: It's Up to the Community." Santa Cruz IMC, March 1, 2010. www.indybay.org/newsitems/2010/03/01/18639136 .php.

Luecke, Daniel F., et al. "A Delta Once More: Restoring Riparian and Wetland Habitat in the Colorado River Delta." Environmental Defense Fund, June 1999. www.edf .org/documents/425_Delta.pdf.

Lyons, Jessica. "Why Fish Biologists Are Plugging for Desal." *Santa Cruz Weekly*, December 8, 2010.

Mahr, Krista. "Making Rain." *Time*, August 2, 2007.

Moseman, Andrew. "Does Cloud Seeding Work?" *Scientific American*, February 19, 2009.

O'Driscoll, Patrick. "West Seeks Help in Cloud Seeding." *USA Today*, December 2, 2003.

Rodebaugh, Dale. "Tamarisk's Bad Rap May Not Be Earned." *Durango Herald*, May 31, 2010.

Sammon, John. "Santa Cruz County Needs Desalination, Officials Say." *Santa Cruz Sentinel*, March 19, 2009.

Smalling, Wes. "In Its Fourth Year, Wyoming's $8.8 Million Cloud-Seeding Experiment Is Drawing Big-Time Attention." *Casper Star-Tribune*, February 15, 2009.

Southwestern Willow Flycatcher Site, US Geological Survey Southwest Biological Center—Colorado Plateau Research Station at Northern Arizona University. http://sbsc.wr.usgs.gov/cprs/research/projects/swwf/cprsmain.asp.

"Tapping the Oceans," *The Economist*, June 5, 2008.

Zurer, Rachel. "The Birds and the Bee(tle)s." *High Country News*, October 1, 2010.

Conservation

BoulderSavesWater.net. "20 Ways to Save Water." www.bouldercolorado.gov/index. php?option=com_content&task=view&id=4771&Itemid=1949.

Cadillac Desert: Water and the Transformation of Nature—Mulholland's Dream. Jon Else and Linda Harrar, dirs. and prods. Jon Else, Sandra Postel, and Marc Reisner, writs. Columbia-TriStar Television PBS Home Video, 1997.

City of Albuquerque. "Per Capita Water Use." www.cabq.gov/progress/ environmental-protection-enhancement/dcc-31/indicator-31-2.

Jackson Hole Land Trust. www.jhlandtrust.org.

Maclean, Norman. "A River Runs Through It" In *A River Runs Through It and Other Stories.* Chicago: University of Chicago Press, 2001 (originally published in 1976).

The Nature Conservancy. "The Blackfoot Valley." www.nature.org/ourinitiatives/regions/ northamerica/unitedstates/montana/placesweprotect/blackfoot-valley.xml.

Selcraig, Bruce. "Albuquerque Learns It Really Is a Desert Town." In *Water in the West: A High Country News Reader*, Char Miller, ed. Corvallis: Oregon State University Press, 2000.

Urie, Heath. "Boulder Residents Saving Water at 1981 Levels; City Council Is Asked to Make Up Revenue Gap with Rate Increase." *Boulder Daily Camera*, August 10, 2010.

Crisis

Adler, Robert W. "Revisiting the Colorado River Compact: Time for a Change?" *Journal of Land, Resources, and Environmental Law*, vol. 28, no. 1, 2008.

Ashby, Charles. "McCain: Renegotiate 1922 Western Water Compact." *Pueblo Chieftain*, August 15, 2008.

Babbitt, Bruce. *Cities in the Wilderness: A New Vision of Land Use in America.* Washington, D.C.: Island Press, 2005.

Bates, Sarah F., et al. *Searching out the Headwaters: Change and Rediscovery in Western Water Policy.* Washington, D.C.: Island Press, 1993.

Beach, William, and Patrick Tyrrell. "The 2010 Index of Dependence on Government." Center for Data Analysis Report #10-08, The Heritage Foundation, October 14, 2010. www.heritage.org/research/reports/2010/10/the-2010-index-of-dependence-on-government.

Berry, Wendell. Norman Wirzba, ed. *The Art of the Commonplace: The Agrarian Essays of Wendell Berry.* Washington, D.C.: Counterpoint, 2002.

Brean, Henry. "Water Authority Digs Deep for Third Intake Pipe at Lake Mead." *Las Vegas Review-Journal,* December 13, 2009.

Cato Institute. "With All Due Respect Mr. President, We're Still Waiting." www.cato.org/files/DownsizingAd.pdf.

Diamond, Jared. *Collapse: How Societies Choose to Fail or Succeed.* New York: Viking, 2005.

———. *Guns, Germs and Steel.* New York: W.W. Norton & Company, 1997.

Environmental Working Group. "Throwing Good Money at Bad Land." September 28, 2010. www.ewg.org/Throwing-Good-Money-at-Bad-Land.

Geran, Nicholas K. "Is Glacier National Park Past Its Peak?" *Los Angeles Times,* June 5, 2010.

Gertner, Jon. "The Future Is Drying Up." *New York Times Magazine,* October 21, 2007.

Gleick, Peter H. "Roadmap for Sustainable Water Resources in Southwestern North America." *Proceedings of the National Academy of Sciences,* vol. 107, no. 50, December 14, 2010.

Gleick, Peter H., with Heather Cooley, et al. *The World's Water, 2008–2009: The Biennial Report on Freshwater Resources.* Washington, D.C.: Island Press, 2009.

Gober, Patricia, and Craig W. Kirkwood. "Vulnerability Assessment of Climate-Induced Water Shortage in Phoenix." *Proceedings of the National Academy of Sciences,* vol. 107, no. 50, December 14, 2010.

Gunther, John. *Inside U.S.A.* New York: Harper & Brothers, 1947.

Jenkins, Mark. "Pipe Dreams." In *Water in the 21st-Century West: A High Country News Reader,* Char Miller, ed. Corvallis: Oregon State University Press, 2009.

———. "Squeezing Water from a Stone." In *Water in the 21st-Century West: A High Country News Reader,* Char Miller, ed. Corvallis: Oregon State University Press, 2009.

Johnson, Kirk, and Dean E. Murphy. "Drought Settles In, Lake Shrinks and West's Worries Grow." *New York Times,* May 2, 2004.

Klinkenborg, Verlyn. "Trying Times Ahead: The Prospect of 60 Million Californians." *New York Times,* July 18, 2007.

MacDonald, Glen M. "Water, Climate Change, and Sustainability in the Southwest." *Proceedings of the National Academy of Sciences,* vol. 107, no. 50, December 14, 2010.

McCool, Dan. "Warning: Water Policy Faces an Age of Limits." *High Country News.* April 22, 2010.

National Oceanic and Atmospheric Association. "NOAA: Past Decade Warmest on Record According to Scientists in 48 Countries." NOAA News, July 28, 2010. www.noaanews.noaa.gov/stories2010/20100728_stateoftheclimate.html.

Pacific Institute. "Water and Sustainability." www.pacinst.org/topics/water_and_
sustainability.

Pollan, Michael. "The Food Movement, Rising." *New York Review of Books*, June 10,
2010.

———. *Omnivore's Dilemma*. New York: Dial Books, 2009.

———. "Wendell Berry's Wisdom." *The Nation*, September 2, 2009.

Rocky Mountain Climate Organization and Natural Resources Defense Council. "New
Study: Climate Change Threatening Glacier National Park Could Harm Montana's
Future Tourism and Economy." www.nrdc.org/media/2010/100407.asp.

Smart, Christopher. "Glen Canyon Dam: 50 Years of Controversy." *Salt Lake Tribune*,
May 31, 2007.

"The Truth about Global Warming." *Washington Post*, August 2, 2010.

Weissenstein, Michael. "The Water Empress of Vegas." In *Water in the 21st-Century West:
A* High Country News *Reader*, Char Miller, ed. Corvallis: Oregon State University
Press, 2009.

Worster, Donald. "Theodore Roosevelt & the American Conservation Ethic."
Theodore Roosevelt Center, April 1, 2009. www.theodorerooseveltcenter.org/
Essay.asp?ID=11

EPILOGUE: A BRIEF HISTORY OF WATER'S FUTURE

Blake Gumprecht's *The Los Angeles River* chronicles the transformation
of a trout-filled stream into a concrete gutter that drains a manufactured
wasteland. *The Great Thirst*, written by the dean of western water historians, Norris Hundley Jr., is an exhaustively researched (799 pages!)
account of California's water development. *Beyond Chinatown* by Steven
Erie is a balanced study of Southern California's often maligned and mis-
understood Metropolitan Water District.

Joel Bourne's *National Geographic* article "California's Pipe Dream" is a
fine introduction to the water dilemmas of the richest and most populous
state in the nation. The article is illustrated by the stirring photographs
of Edward Burtynsky, who pioneered the photography of landscapes that
have been altered by humans on a monumental scale. Matt Jenkins's *High
Country News* article "California's Tangled Water Politics" is a skillful
unraveling of the knotty mess of laws and policies wrapped around the
Sacramento–San Joaquin Delta. The battles over the delta are so complicated they almost make Colorado River controversy seem straightforward
by comparison.

Aquafornia, a website affiliated with the nonpartisan, nonprofit Water Education Foundation, has a comprehensive archive of news stories related to water in California. It is an excellent resource for California's citizens who want to dive into their state's staggeringly complex and contentious water issues. The Water Education Foundation also publishes *Western Water Magazine*, required reading for all water wonks.

Information about Mono Lake and efforts to protect it is available on the Mono Lake Committee website, which provided most of the Mono Lake background for this chapter. The public trust doctrine is explained on the Mono Basin Clearinghouse website, which aspires "to have the most comprehensive listing of scientific information on the Mono Basin, California."

Anderson, Jeffrey. "The Eternal Dustbowl." *LA Weekly*, March 22, 2006.

Aquafornia. http://aquafornia.com.

Archibold, Randal C. "A Century Later Los Angeles Atones for Water Sins." *New York Times*, January 1, 2007.

Arnold, Craig Anthony. "Working Out an Environmental Ethic: Anniversary Lessons from Mono Lake." *Wyoming Law Review*, vol. 4, no. 1, 2004.

Barringer, Felicity. "Effort Falters on San Francisco Bay Delta." *New York Times*, December 14, 2010.

Bourne, Joel K., Jr. "California's Pipe Dream." *National Geographic*, April 2010.

Burke, Garance. "California's Groundwater Shrinking Because of Agricultural Use." *Christian Science Monitor*, January 4, 2010.

"California's Water Wars: Of Farms, Folks and Fish," *The Economist*, October 22, 2009.

Donahue, John M., and Barbra Rose Johnston, eds. *Water, Culture, & Power: Local Struggles in a Global Context*. Washington, D.C.: Island Press, 1998.

Erie, Steven P. *Beyond Chinatown: The Metropolitan Water District, Growth, and the Environment in Southern California*. Stanford, Calif.: Stanford University Press, 2006.

"Fishy Stuff at Elk Creek." *The Economist*, October 17, 2002.

Gumprecht, Blake. *The Los Angeles River: Its Life, Death, and Possible Rebirth*. Baltimore, Md.: Johns Hopkins University Press, 1999.

Hart, John. *Storm over Mono: The Mono Lake Battle and the California Water Future*. Berkeley: University of California Press, 1996.

Hundley, Norris, Jr. *The Great Thirst*. Berkeley: University of California Press, 2001.

Jenkins, Matt. "Breakdown." *High Country News*, April 21, 2010.

———. "California's Tangled Water Politics." *High Country News*, December 20, 2010.

———. "A Dusty Lake Is Plumbed Halfway Back to Life." In *Water in the 21st-Century West: A* High Country News *Reader*, Char Miller, ed. Corvallis: Oregon State University Press, 2009.

Kahrl, William L. *Water and Power: The Conflict over Los Angeles' Water Supply in the Owens Valley.* Berkeley: University of California Press, 1982.

Little, Jane Braxton. "Dust Settles in Owens Valley." In *Water in the 21st-Century West: A High Country News Reader,* Char Miller, ed. Corvallis: Oregon State University Press, 2009.

McCool, Daniel. "As Dams Fall, a Chance for Redemption." In *Water in the 21st-Century West: A High Country News Reader.* Char Miller, ed. Corvallis: Oregon State University Press, 2009.

McKechnie, Ralph. "Corps Complete Notching of Elk Creek Dam." *Upper Rogue Independent,* October 20, 2008.

Mono Lake Committee. www.monolake.org.

"A New Water War." *San Francisco Chronicle,* July 13, 2007.

Postel, Sandra, and Brian Richter. *Rivers for Life.* Washington, D.C.: Island Press, 2003.

Public Broadcasting Service. *New Perspectives on the West,* "Fred Eaton." www.pbs.org/weta/thewest/people/d_h/eaton.htm.

———. *New Perspectives on the West,* "William Mulholland." www.pbs.org/weta/thewest/people/i_r/mulholland.htm.

Sahagun, Louis. "In Owens Valley, Water Again Flows." *Los Angeles Times,* December 7, 2006.

———. "River Is Resurrected." *Los Angeles Times,* July 8, 2007.

Stiles, Jim. "The Brief But Wonderful Return of Cathedral in the Desert." *High Country News,* June 13, 2005.

Twain, Mark. *Roughing It.* New York: Dover Publications, 2003 (originally published in 1872).

US Department of the Interior, US Geological Survey. "Delta Subsidence in California: The Sinking Heart of the State." Fact Sheet 005-00, April 2000. http://ca.water.usgs.gov/archive/reports/fs00500/fs00500.pdf.

Zakin, Susan. "BAY AREA: Delta Blues." In *Water in the 21st-Century West: A High Country News Reader.* Char Miller, ed. Corvallis: Oregon State University Press, 2009.

INDEX

ABOUT THE AUTHOR

Stephen Grace lives in Colorado in the South Boulder Creek watershed, which drains the Rocky Mountains and the Great Plains around his home and forms part of the Boulder Creek watershed, which is part of the St. Vrain Creek watershed, which is part of the South Platte River watershed, which is part of the Platte River watershed, which is part of the Missouri River watershed, which is part of the Mississippi River watershed, which empties into the Gulf of Mexico. *Dam Nation* is his sixth book.